THE CANON OF THE
NEW TESTAMENT

THE CANON OF THE
NEW TESTAMENT

Its Origin, Development, and
Significance

BRUCE M. METZGER

CLARENDON PRESS · OXFORD

Oxford University Press, Great Clarendon Street, Oxford OX2 6DP

Oxford New York

Athens Auckland Bangkok Bogota Bombay
Buenos Aires Calcutta Cape Town Dar es Salaam
Delhi Florence Hong Kong Istanbul Karachi
Kuala Lumpur Madras Madrid Melbourne
Mexico City Nairobi Paris Singapore
Taipei Tokyo Toronto
and associated companies in
Berlin Ibadan

Oxford is a trade mark of Oxford University Press

Published in the United States
by Oxford University Press Inc., New York

British Library Cataloguing in Publication Data
Data available

Library of Congress Cataloging in Publication Data
Metzger, Bruce Manning.
The Canon of the New Testament.
Includes index.
1. Bible. N.T. 2. Canon. I. Title.
BS2320.M47 1987 225.1'2 86–21833
ISBN 0–19–826954–4

3 5 7 9 10 8 6 4 2

Printed in Great Britain on acid-free paper by
Bookcraft (Bath) Ltd., Midsomer Norton, Somerset

Preface

THIS book is designed as an introduction to a topic of theology which, despite its importance and intrinsic interest, receives comparatively little attention. In fact, few works in English consider both the historical development of the New Testament canon and the persistent problems that pertain to its significance.

The word 'canon' is Greek; its use in connection with the Bible belongs to Christian times; the idea of a canon of Scripture originates in Judaism. Each of these statements will be considered in the following pages, the early patristic period receiving the greatest amount of attention.

The development of the canon was inextricably bound up with the history of the ancient Church, both in its literary and institutional aspects. For this reason it seemed necessary to provide, particularly for readers who may have only a limited acquaintance with the Church Fathers, something more than mere lists of the names of those who in the early centuries made use of the several documents that eventually came to be regarded as canonical Scripture. Such biographical information gains in precision when placed in the chronological and geographical framework within which the development took place. Although, as E. R. Dodds once observed, 'There are no periods in history, only in historians', one can detect stages in the clarity with which, in various regions of the early Church, a distinction came to be made between canonical and apocryphal literature.

I wish to thank a number of persons and institutions that have been involved, in one way or another, with the development of the contents of this book. Over the years a succession of students at Princeton Theological Seminary participated in my doctoral seminar on the canon, where we read and discussed the chief Greek and Latin texts that bear on the history of the New Testament canon. I am grateful to those universities and seminaries in North America, Great Britain, Australia, and South Africa that invited me to present lectures involving material now contained in the following pages. Robert W.

Bernard and Loren T. Stuckenbruck produced typescript copy from my handwritten draft; the former also drew up the index. For reading the completed manuscript and making helpful comments, I am indebted to my colleague Professor Raymond E. Brown of Union Theological Seminary. Once again I must express appreciation to the Delegates of the Oxford University Press for their acceptance of this volume that completes a trilogy dealing with the text, the early versions, and the canon of the New Testament. My deepest gratitude, however, extends to my wife, Isobel, whose supportive role over the years cannot be fully expressed in words.

BRUCE M. METZGER

Princeton, New Jersey

Contents

Introduction

THE recognition of the canonical status of the several books of the New Testament was the result of a long and gradual process, in the course of which certain writings, regarded as authoritative, were separated from a much larger body of early Christian literature. Although this was one of the most important developments in the thought and practice of the early Church, history is virtually silent as to how, when, and by whom it was brought about. Nothing is more amazing in the annals of the Christian Church than the absence of detailed accounts of so significant a process.

In view of the lack of specific information, it is not surprising that many questions and problems confront the investigation of the canonization of the New Testament. Some problems are specifically historical, such as those that concern the sequence in which the several parts of the New Testament attained canonical status; the criteria for determining the canonicity of a given book; and the significance of the part played by Marcion and other heretics in stimulating the process of canonization. Other problems bear on textual matters, such as the question of whether the so-called Western type of New Testament text was created in order to be the vehicle of the emerging canonical text; and which forms of text, amid a multitude of textual variations among the manuscripts, should be regarded today as the canonical text. Still other problems involve theological considerations, some of which have far-ranging implications. Central among such problems are questions whether, on the one hand, the canon is to be regarded as open or closed, and, on the other, whether it is profitable to look for a canon within the canon. Still more basic are the questions whether the canon is a collection of authoritative books or an authoritative collection of books—and in either case whether the collection can be held to reflect the divine intention within the history of salvation. Obviously it is easier to raise such questions than to answer them. In fact, it is possible that some of the questions have no answers—or at least no answers that can be regarded as convincing.

Despite the silence of patristic writers as far as explicit accounts of the canonization process are concerned, there is general unanimity among modern scholars as to what must have been some of the factors that brought about the recognition of the New Testament canon. It will be helpful, before giving attention to a multitude of literary testimonies and historical problems, to sketch briefly some of the more firmly established landmarks in what otherwise might well appear to be a wilderness of disparate and disjointed details.

The starting-point of our enquiry is the attempt to identify the authorities that were recognized in primitive Christianity, and to see how they exerted their influence.

(1) From the first day of its existence the Christian Church possessed a canon of sacred writings—the Jewish Scriptures, written originally in Hebrew and widely used in a Greek translation called the Septuagint. The precise boundaries of the Jewish canon may not yet have been finally fixed,[1] but there was already sufficient definition for its books to be referred to collectively as 'Scripture' ($\dot{\eta}$ $\gamma\rho\alpha\phi\dot{\eta}$) or 'the Scriptures' ($\alpha\dot{\iota}$ $\gamma\rho\alpha\phi\alpha\dot{\iota}$), and citations from it were introduced by the formula 'it stands written' ($\gamma\dot{\epsilon}\gamma\rho\alpha\pi\tau\alpha\iota$).

Like every pious Jew, Jesus accepted the Hebrew Scriptures as the word of God and frequently argued from them in his teaching and controversies. And in this respect he was followed by the first Christian preachers and teachers, who appealed to them to prove the correctness of the Christian faith. The high regard of the primitive Church for the Old Testament (to use the traditional Christian designation for the Hebrew Scriptures) was fundamentally due to the conviction that its contents had been inspired by God (2 Tim. iii. 16; 2 Pet. i. 20 f.).

(2) In the oldest Christian communities there was also another authority which had taken its place alongside the Jewish Scriptures, and that was the words of Jesus, as they were handed down in oral tradition. During his public ministry Jesus had claimed to speak with an authority in no way inferior to that of the ancient Law, and had placed his utterances side by side with its precepts by way of fulfilling or even correcting

---

[1] For information about the so-called Synod of Jamnia (*c*. A.D. 90), at which discussions were held concerning the Hebrew Scriptures, see pp. 109–10 below.

and repealing them. This is clearly shown, for example, by his position on the question of divorce (Mark x. 2 f. and parallels) and on unclean foods (Mark vii. 14–19), pronouncements that are reinforced by the implications of the so-called antitheses reported by Matthew in the Sermon on the Mount (Matt. v. 21–48: 'of old it was said... but I say to you').

It is not surprising, therefore, that in the early Church the remembered words of Jesus were treasured and quoted, taking their place beside the Law and the Prophets and being regarded as of equal or superior authority to them. It is to such 'words of the Lord', for example, that the apostle Paul appeals so confidently on various occasions to enforce some lesson (1 Cor. ix. 14; cf. Luke x. 7), or to settle some difficulty (1 Thess. iv. 15; 1 Cor. vii. 10), or to confirm some rite (1 Cor. xi. 23).[2]

At first Jesus' teachings circulated orally from hearer to hearer, becoming, so to speak, the nucleus of the new Christian canon. Then narratives were compiled recording the remembered words, along with recollections of his deeds of mercy and healing. Some documents of this kind underlie our Gospels, and are referred to in the preface to the Third Gospel (Luke i. 1–4).

(3) Parallel with the oral circulation of Jesus' teachings were apostolic interpretations of the significance of his person and work for the lives of believers. These interpretations, along with exhortations, were communicated directly to newly established congregations during the earliest missionary activity. By means of epistles, moreover, it was possible to continue, in some measure, the oversight of congregations after the missionaries had moved on to other areas, or even to communicate directives to believers in cities not previously visited (as, for example, in the Epistles to the Romans and to the Colossians). Such Epistles, as even Paul's critics in the Corinthian church had conceded, were 'weighty and powerful' (2 Cor. x. 10).

---

[2] In addition to such explicit references to the 'words of the Lord', we also find in Paul's Epistles (especially in Rom. xii–xiv and 1 Thess. iv–v) numerous echoes of the ethical teaching of Jesus; cf. A. M. Hunter, *Paul and his Predecessors*, 2nd ed. (Philadelphia, 1961), pp. 47–51, and David L. Dungan, *The Sayings of Jesus in the Churches of Paul; The Use of the Synoptic Tradition in the Regulation of Early Church Life* (Philadelphia, 1971). Note also the phrase, 'Remember the words of the Lord Jesus', in Acts xx. 35 and *1 Clem.* xiii. 1.

On occasions when Paul had to decide a matter on which there was no dominical word, he appealed to his claim that he was one 'commissioned by the Lord', and had the Spirit of God (1 Cor. vii. 25, 40). He regarded his instructions or commands (1 Cor. xiv. 37) to be 'of the Lord'—in other words, that the Lord himself was speaking through him (cf. 1 Thess. ii. 13).

There is no need here to discuss how and when Paul obtained such a profound sense of authority attached to his office as apostle (Rom xi. 13); it is sufficient to recall the supreme crisis of his life, to which he invariably traces back his divinely given apostleship (Gal. i. 11–16). In virtue of his authoritative commission, Paul even claims that he can place under a curse any other gospel as not coming from God (Gal. i. 7–9; cf. 2 Thess. iii. 17). In a similar way, other teachers of the apostolic age also claim authority in issuing precepts and directives (Heb. x. 26–7; xiii. 18–19; 3 John 5–10).

The circulation of Paul's Epistles began already during his lifetime.[3] This is evident from the apostle's command that there should be an exchange of (copies of) epistles between the Colossians and the Laodiceans (Col. iv. 16). He also addresses the Galatian Epistle 'to the churches of Galatia' (Gal. i. 2), and urges that 1 Thessalonians be read 'to all the brethren' (1 Thess. v. 27), which seems to imply the existence of several 'house churches'.

The writers of these apostolic Epistles, though confident that they speak with authority, reveal no consciousness that their words would come to be regarded as a permanent standard of doctrine and life in the Christian Church. They write for an immediate purpose, and just as they would have wanted to speak, had they been able to be present with those whom they address. It is natural that such Epistles were cherished and read again and again by the congregations that had first received them, and by others who came to appreciate copies of such valued testimonies from the apostolic age.[4]

---

[3] On the early, pre-corpus circulation of the Epistles, see Lucetta Mowry, 'The Early Circulation of Paul's Letters', *Journal of Biblical Literature*, lxiii (1944), pp. 73–86, and literature mentioned in chap. XI. v below.

[4] Here and there in patristic writers we find assertions concerning the preservation of the autograph of this or that book of the New Testament. Tertullian (*De praesc. haer.* 36) mentions Thessalonica among the cities to which apostolic Epistles had been addressed and were still read there from the autographs (*apud quas* [sc. *ecclesias*] *ipsae*

(4) As time went on, a Christian literature grew in volume and was circulated throughout different congregations. Toward the close of the first Christian century Clement of Rome wrote an epistle to the church at Corinth, and early in the second century Ignatius, bishop of Antioch, while *en route* to his martyrdom at Rome, dispatched six short epistles to various churches and one to Polycarp of Smyrna. In these and still more in later Christian literature of the second century[5] the writers incorporated ideas and familiar phrases of the apostolic writers, and in a few cases expressly quoted them. Whatever may have been their conscious attitude toward such apostolic documents, it is clear that their thinking was moulded by them from the very first.

At the same time allusions to the superior standing of apostolic writers, living so close to the time of the earthly ministry of Jesus, more and more set the earlier documents apart from contemporary writings and helped to consolidate them as a distinct body of literature. The epistle of Clement and the epistles of Ignatius, for example, clearly breathe the spirit of the sub-apostolic era. Although both display a certain air of authority, there is no longer any consciousness of apostolic authority. They look back at the venerable figures of the apostles as leaders in an age now past (*I Clem.* v. 3–7; xlii. 1 ff.; xlvii. 1 ff.; Ign. *Trall.* ii. 2; *Magn.* vi. 1; vii. 2; xiii. 1). It is not surprising, therefore, that readers could and did distinguish between the 'tone' of certain documents, which subsequently

---

[5] Besides the Christian literature produced by the Apostolic Fathers and the Apologists (considered in the following chapters), one should not overlook the presence of echoes from several New Testament books in such works as 2 Esdras and the *Testaments of the Twelve Patriarchs*.

---

authenticae litterae eorum recitantur, where *ipsae* prevents one from interpreting *authenticae* to mean 'unmutilated' or 'not falsified by heretics'). In a fragment attributed to Petrus I Alexandrinus (d. A.D. 311) we find a reference concerning the reading τρίτη instead of ἕκτη in John xix. 14 and the statement that 'the autograph (ἰδιόχειρος) itself of the Evangelist has been, until now, kept by the grace of God in the most hallowed church in Ephesus and is venerated there by the faithful' (Migne, *Patrologia Graeca*, xviii. 517D; see also Juan Leal, 'El autógrafo del IV Evangelio y la arqueología', *Estudios eclesiásticos*, xxxiv [1960], pp. 895–905, esp. 903–5). For other claims concerning autographs of New Testament books, see Eberhard Nestle, *Introduction to the Textual Criticism of the Greek New Testament*, 2nd ed. (London, 1901), pp. 29–31, and the fragment of a letter attributed to Clement of Alexandria (see pp. 132–3 below).

were identified as canonical, and that of the ever-growing body of patristic literature.

(5) In the age that followed that of the apostles, the expression 'the Lord and the apostles' represented the standard of appeal to which reference was made in all matters of faith and practice. At first a local church would have copies of only a few apostolic Epistles, and perhaps one or two Gospels. In the collections that were gradually formed, a place was found beside the Gospels and the Epistles for two other kinds of books—the Acts of the Apostles and the Apocalypse of John. The credentials of the former rested upon its being the continuation of the earlier book by Luke (Acts i. 1 f.), and the sacredness of the latter was vouched for by the blessing pronounced on the one who would read and on those who listened to its prophetic words (Rev. i. 3).

It was this kind of public reading of Christian documents to which Justin Martyr refers about A.D. 150. He tells us that on Sundays at services of divine worship it was customary to read 'the memoirs of the Apostles [i.e. the Gospels] or the writings of the Prophets' (*I Apol.* lxvii. 3). Thus it came about that Christian congregations grew accustomed to regard the apostolic writings as, in some sense, on a par with the older Jewish Scriptures, and such liturgical custom, though doubtless varying in different congregations, set its seal on certain Gospels and Epistles as worthy of special reverence and obedience.[6]

(6) In the second and third centuries translations were made of apostolic writings into Latin and into Syriac, and eventually also into the Coptic dialects of Egypt.[7] The beginnings of such versions were doubtless in the context of services of public worship, when the reading of short sections of the Greek text was followed by a translation into the vernacular. At first the rendering would have been oral, but soon written copies would have been made available. The range of books so translated

---

[6] See Paul Glaue, *Die Vorlesung heiliger Schriften im Gottesdienste*; 1 Teil, *Bis zur Entstehung der altkatholischen Kirche* (Berlin, 1907), and C. R. Gregory's critical comments, 'The Reading of Scripture in the Church in the Second Century', *American Journal of Theology*, xiii (1908), pp. 86–91. (Adolf von Harnack's *Bible Reading in the Early Church* [London, 1912] deals chiefly with the private use of the Scriptures.)

[7] For an account of the making of such translations, see the present writer's *The Early Versions of the New Testament, their Origin, Transmission, and Limitations* (Oxford, 1977).

formed a collection of Scripture in these districts, though in some cases this collection included books not generally recognized elsewhere; for example, the Syrian and Armenian churches included Paul's Third Epistle to the Corinthians (see chap. IX. II below).

Thus, side by side with the old Jewish canon, and without in any way displacing it, there had sprung up a new, Christian canon.[8] This history of its formation is the history, not of a series of sporadic events, but of a long, continuous process. It was a task, not only of collecting, but also of sifting and rejecting. Instead of being the result of a deliberate decree by an individual or a council near the beginning of the Christian era, the collection of New Testament books took place gradually over many years by the pressure of various kinds of circumstances and influences, some external (see chap. IV below) and others internal to the life of congregations (see chap. XI. I below). Different factors operated at different times and in different places. Some of the influences were constant, others were periodic; some were local, others were operative wherever the Church had been planted.

In order to provide the data from which the preceding synthesis has been constructed, the chapters of Part Two below set forth evidence derived from the writings of Church Fathers that bears on the several stages through which the process of canonization moved. In the earliest period, that of the so-called Apostolic Fathers, not much more is disclosed than testimony as to the bare existence here and there of one or another Gospel or Epistle of the New Testament. In subsequent generations we can gradually perceive the outlines of a collection of four Gospels and of a number of Epistles attributed to Paul and to other early leaders in the apostolic Church. Finally, after many years, during which books of local and temporary canonicity came and went (see chap. VII below), the limits of the New Testament canon as we know it were set forth for the first time in a Festal Letter written A.D. 367 by Athanasius, bishop of Alexandria. But, as evidence from subsequent writers reveals, not all in the Church were ready to

---

[8] As von Harnack has pointed out (*The Origin of the New Testament* [New York, 1925], p. 5), there were four possibilities open to the Church: the Old Testament alone, an enlarged Old Testament, no Old Testament, and a second authoritative collection.

accept precisely the canon as identified by Athanasius, and throughout the following centuries there were minor fluctuations in the East as well as in the West. Such, in brief, is the long and fascinating story concerning the growth and recognition of the canon of the New Testament.

PART ONE

Survey of Literature
on the Canon

I

Literature on the Canon Published Prior to the Twentieth Century

THROUGHOUT the Middle Ages questions were seldom raised as to the number and identity of the books comprising the canon of the New Testament. Even during the period of the Renaissance and Reformation, despite occasional discussions (such as those by Erasmus and Cajetan) concerning the authorship of the Epistle to the Hebrews, several of the Catholic Epistles, and the Book of Revelation, no one dared seriously to dispute their canonicity. Although Luther considered four of the New Testament books (Hebrews, James, Jude, and Revelation) to be inferior to others, neither he nor his followers ventured to omit them from his translation.

By the close of the seventeenth century, however, doubts concerning the canon of the New Testament were awakened by the rise of the Deistic movement. Among prominent leaders of this movement in Great Britain was John Toland (1670–1722), an Irish Roman Catholic who became a Protestant at the age of sixteen.[1] After a period of study successively at Glasgow, Leiden, and Oxford, Toland was catapulted into public notice by the publication of a book entitled *Christianity not Mysterious* (Oxford, 1696; 2nd, enlarged ed., London, 1696). Toland had a knack of raising questions in a manner that the general reading public could understand. Hand-in-hand with advocating the cult of Reason went a repudiation of the leaders of the Church, past and present, whose scholastic jargon Toland dismissed as nothing more than a smoke-screen raised by 'the numerous partisans of error', who, he intimated, were motivated by a love of gain. The book was condemned as a nuisance by the grand jury of Middlesex, and was ordered by the Irish Parliament to be burnt publicly in Dublin by the hangman.

It was in such a climate of charges and counter-charges,

---

[1] In addition to literature on the rise of Deism, see Robert E. Sullivan, *John Toland and the Deist Controversy, A Study in Adaptations* (Cambridge, Mass., 1982).

during which Toland fled to England to avoid imprisonment, that the question of the authenticity of certain books of the New Testament was brought into public debate. The occasion was a passage in another of Toland's books, *The Life of John Milton* (London, 1698), in which he disputed the royal authorship of the *Eikon Basilike*, a volume of spiritual meditations allegedly written by King Charles I shortly before his execution.[2] In that connection Toland took occasion to insinuate that, as people were mistaken on this point, so they might be also about the authenticity of many of the early writings of Christianity, including presumably books of the New Testament.

A reply was made during the course of a sermon preached 30 January 1699 before the House of Commons by the Reverend Offspring Blackall, then one of King William's chaplains and subsequently bishop of Exeter, who charged Toland with creating a scandal by what he had written. The preacher hinted that his hearers' pious intentions to suppress vice and immorality would not be of much effect if the foundations of all revealed religion were thus openly 'pecked at, and undermined, and so weakened'.[3]

Thereupon Toland defended himself in a book entitled *Amyntor; or, a Defence of Milton's Life.*[4] Here he claimed that his earlier statements had to do only with apocryphal writings and that he had no intention of insinuating that any of the books of the New Testament might justly be questioned. In the next breath, however, Toland raised questions that must, on the face of it, cast doubt on the validity of accepting as canonical several books of the New Testament. Thus he admitted that several spurious pieces are quoted by the Fathers as of equal authority with those that are generally received in the New Testament. He urged also that he could not understand why the writings of Mark and Luke should be accepted as canonical whereas those attributed to Clement of Rome and Barnabas are refused, since all four authors were equally companions

---

[2] This book, which, 'if judged by its positive effect, might rank as one of the greatest books ever written in English' (Douglas Bush, *English Literature in the Earlier Seventeenth Century* [Oxford, 1945], p. 216), is still the subject of scholarly controversy as to its true authorship; see Francis F. Madan, *A New Bibliography of the Eikon Basilike of King Charles the First, with a Note on the Authorship* (London, 1950).

[3] Blackall's *Works*, ii (London, 1723), pp. 1076f.

[4] (London, 1699). *Amyntor* is a Homeric word meaning 'defender'.

and fellow-labourers with the apostles. In fact, Toland went so far as to declare, in so many words, that there is not one single book of the New Testament which was not refused by some of the ancient writers as being unjustly attributed to the apostles and as actually forged by their adversaries.

Toland's arguments and innuendoes at once drew forth replies from defenders of the faith, including Samuel Clarke,[5] rector of St James, Westminster, Stephen Nye,[6] rector of Little Hormead, Herts., and John Richardson,[7] formerly Fellow of Emmanuel College, Cambridge. The argument of Richardson was based on the reasonable premiss that 'what the Apostles Wrote, and what they Authoriz'd, can be known in no other way, then by the Testimonies of those who liv'd at the same time with them, and the Tradition of those who succeeded them'. It should not, therefore, be thought surprising, Richardson continued, 'if some Books were sooner and some later receiv'd as Canonical, by the Universal Body of Christians in all Places, because either the Books themselves, or the Testimonials to prove them Apostolical, might, nay Naturally would, be transmitted to some Churches later than others, as they were Situated nearer to, or remov'd farther from, those Cities or Countrys where they were first Publish'd, or enjoy'd a greater or less intercourse with them'.[8]

In the several publications just mentioned the focus is upon one or another of the patristic witnesses to the New Testament canon, and the discussions are frequently conducted in a setting of hostility and acrimony.[9] Much more extensive, and

---

[5] 'Some Reflections on that Part of a Book called Amyntor, or The Defense of Milton's Life, which relates to the Writings of the Primitive Fathers and the Canon of the New Testament', *Works*, iii, pp. 917–26.

[6] *An Historical Account and Defense of the Canon of the New Testament; In answer to Amyntor* (London, 1700).

[7] *The Canon of the New Testament Vindicated; In Answer to the Objections of J.T. in his Amyntor* (London, 1700; 2nd ed., 1701; 3rd ed., corrected, 1719).

[8] Ibid., pp. 8–9.

[9] Much of the literature of this debate is now so tiresome as to be almost unreadable. The solemn parade of authorities, the meticulous care with which every sentence, almost every clause of an adversary's work is refuted, reflect a temper wholly different from that of the modern age. In Toland, however, as G. R. Cragg comments, 'both the method and the outlook are such as "distinguish modernity from near antiquity" (F. R. Tennant). You may agree with him or not, but at least you can read him with relative ease' (*From Puritanism to the Age of Reason, a Study of Changes in Religious Thought within the Church of England 1660 to 1700* [Cambridge, 1966], p. 143).

with proportionately fewer aspersions against those who took a different point of view, is the scholarly work of a Welsh Nonconformist minister, Jeremiah Jones (1693–1724). Entitled *A New and Full Method of Settling the Canonical Authority of the New Testament*, the manuscript, which was left ready for the press at the author's untimely death in his thirty-first year, was published posthumously in two volumes (London, 1726); a third volume (1727) contains the special application of his method to the Gospels and Acts (the volumes were reprinted by the Clarendon Press at Oxford in 1798, and again in 1827). The 'New and Full Method' which Jones employed in his treatise is a detailed historical and philological examination 'to determine the canonical authority of any book, or books, by searching into the most ancient and authentic records of Christianity, and finding out the testimony or traditions of those, who lived nearest the time in which the books were written, concerning them' (vol. i, 1798, p. 47).

The bulk of the more than one thousand pages of the three volumes is taken up with the examination of the contents of the apocryphal gospels, acts, and epistles that had survived. In this connection Jones made available for the first time an English translation of the text of dozens of apocryphal writings,[10] and his treatise remained for many years unique and, for its time, exhaustive in its survey of New Testament apocrypha.

One of the curiosities in the history of the canon was the opinion urged by William Whiston (1667–1752), that eccentric and polymathic scholar who, in 1703, succeeded Sir Isaac Newton in the Lucasian Chair of Mathematics at Cambridge, namely that the Apostolic Constitutions should be regarded as part of the canon of the New Testament. In volume ii of his *Primitive Christianity Reviv'd* (London, 1711) he sets forth the Greek and English text of these eight books of ecclesiastical laws (now generally regarded as originating in the latter half of the fourth century), and in volume iii he attempts to prove (in some 700 pages) that they 'are the most sacred of the canonical Books of the New Testament'; for 'these sacred Christian laws or constitutions were Deliver'd at Jerusalem, and in Mount Sion, by our Saviour to the Eleven Apostles there assembled

---

[10] Jones translated the texts collected by Johann Albert Fabricius in his *Codex Apocryphus Novi Testamenti* (2 vols., Hamburg, 1703; enlarged with a 3rd vol., 1719).

after his Resurrection'. Whiston also became convinced that Paul's Third Epistle to the Corinthians was genuine.[11]

On a more sober basis the Nonconformist apologist, Nathaniel Lardner (1684–1768), promoted the study of the canon by publishing a series of fourteen volumes or fascicles on the subject, *The Credibility of the Gospel History* (London, 1727–57), parts of which were translated into Dutch (1730), Latin (1733), and German (1750–1). In this work the author sought, with disarming candour and immense learning, to reconcile the discrepancies in the New Testament narratives and thus to defend them against Deistical critics. The work is divided into two parts, with a supplement as a third. The first division contains those facts mentioned in the New Testament that are confirmed by contemporary writers, while in the second portion, which is much the longer, the testimonies of the Church Fathers of the first four centuries are collected and carefully weighed, besides being subjected to a thorough criticism that investigates their authority and seeks to determine their date. The supplement discusses the canon of the New Testament, which Lardner believed to have been settled long before the Synod of Laodicea in the fourth century. As might be surmised, Lardner's valuable collection of materials, together with a large apparatus of footnotes, became a mine of information for scholars, to whom it was of greater service than to the ordinary reader for whom it was originally intended. Making good use of the information collected by Lardner, during the next century Christopher Wordsworth delivered the Hulsean Lectures at Cambridge entitled *On the Canon of the Scriptures of the Old and New Testament* (London, 1848).

Meanwhile, on the Continent several French scholars had begun to give attention to questions concerning the canon of Scripture. In addition to his epoch-making studies of the Pentateuch, for which he was deposed from his order, Richard Simon (1638–1712), the 'father of Biblical criticism', dealt with the New Testament canon in his 'Critical History of the Text of the New Testament, wherein is established the

[11] *A Collection of Authentick Records Belonging to the Old and New Testament*, Part II (London, 1728), pp. 585–638.

Truth of the Deeds on which the Christian Religion is based'.[12]

Shortly after the publication of Simon's investigation, the prominent Protestant historiographer, Jacques Basnage de Beauval (1653–1723), devoted a chapter to the canon in his 'History of the Church from Jesus Christ to the Present'.[13] He finds that during the first three centuries there was no decision concerning the limits of the New Testament canon, but each local church had the liberty to choose or reject individual books; this freedom was most noticeable among Eastern Churches in rejecting the Apocalypse.

The celebrated Gallican theologian, Louis Ellies Du Pin (1657–1719), published a *Dissertation préliminaire, ou prolégomènes sur la Bible* (2 vols., Paris, 1699), which was translated into English under the title *A Compleat History of the Canon and Writers of the Books of the Old and New Testament, by way of Dissertation* (2 vols., London, 1699, 1700). Although the title suggests a comprehensive treatment of the subject of the canon, the New Testament volume is disappointing in that most of the author's attention is devoted to literary criticism of the books of the New Testament and to aspects of general introduction bearing on the language, text, and versions of the New Testament.

In Germany during the Enlightenment the pioneer of Biblical criticism, Johann Salomo Semler (1725–91), gave critical attention to questions about the New Testament canon in four rambling volumes entitled 'Treatise on the Free Investigation of the Canon'.[14] The two basic theses that Semler formulates, opening the way for the 'free investigation' of the New Testament, rest on dogmatic and historical presuppositions. On the one hand, Semler declares that the Word of God and holy Scripture are not identical, for holy Scripture contains such books as Ruth, Esther, the Song of Songs, and the Apocalypse, which had importance only for their own times but which, he says, cannot contribute to the 'moral

---

[12] *Histoire critique du texte du Nouveau Testament, où l'on établit la verité des Actes sur lesquels la religion chrétienne est fondée* (Rotterdam, 1689; reprinted, Frankfurt, 1689; English trans., 2 parts, London, 1689).

[13] *Historie de l'église depuis Jésus Christ jusqu'à présent* (Rotterdam, 1699), pp. 419–40.

[14] *Abhandlung von der freien Untersuchung des Kanons* . . . (Halle, 1771–5; 2nd ed., 1776); reprinted and edited by H. Sheible in *Texte zur Kirchen- und Theologiegeschichte*, v (Gütersloh, 1967).

improvement' of persons today. Consequently, by no means all parts of the canon can be inspired, nor can they be accepted by Christians as authoritative.

Semler's second thesis is that the question of whether a book belongs to the canon is a purely historical one, for the canon, as Semler viewed it, represents only the agreement of the clergy in the several regions of the early Church as to which books could be used in the public lections and for instruction. In the earliest stages there was no uniformity in these matters; indeed, with regard to certain books tradition was not merely wavering but is actually unfavourable to their canonicity, or even to any presumption of their apostolic origin. Christians belonging to the diocese of Palestine accepted the writings of those apostles who carried on their ministry among the uncircumcised, and who were unacquainted with Paul's Epistles. On the other hand, the party of Christians that belonged to Paul's diocese, being quite aware that James, Peter, and Jude had not sent it any Epistles, was not able to introduce those writings among its congregations.

The publication of Semler's broadside attack stimulated other scholars of the latter part of the eighteenth century to give attention to the canon. Schmid's learned and detailed treatise[15] sought to vindicate the traditional understanding; Corrodi,[16] on the other hand, carried Semler's ideas still further, while Weber[17] followed a middle course. After the dogmatic controversies aroused by Semler's treatise had subsided, a sober, critical analysis of Eusebius' testimony to the New Testament canon, based on *Hist. eccl.* iii. 25, was published by Friedrich Lücke of Berlin.[18]

During the early part of the nineteenth century Eichhorn included in his 'Introduction to the New Testament'[19] a

---

[15] Christoph Fred. Schmid, *Historia antiqua et vindicatio canonis sacri Veteris Novique Testamenti* (Leipzig, 1775), pp. 279–736.

[16] (H. Corrodi), *Versuch einer Beleuchtung des Geschichte des jüdischen und christlichen Bibel-Kanons*, 2 vols. (Halle, 1792). Neither this book nor the next to be mentioned was available to the present writer; information concerning their titles and contents was obtained from Paul W. Schmiedel's article on 'Kanon' in the celebrated multi-volume work of J. S. Ersch and J. G. Gruber, *Allgemeine Encyklopädie der Wissenschaften und Künste*, ii Section, xxxii (Leipzig, 1882; reprinted, Graz, 1983), pp. 309–37.

[17] Christian Fr. Weber, *Beiträge zur Geschichte des neutestamentlichen Kanons* (1798).

[18] *Ueber den neutestamentlichen Kanon des Eusebius von Cäsarea* (Berlin, 1816).

[19] J. G. Eichhorn, *Einleitung in das Neue Testament*, 2 vols. (Leipzig, 1804–12).

discussion of the New Testament canon. He was the first to
attribute to Marcion the stimulus to collect New Testament
writings, and argued that the core of the future canon was
established by about A.D. 175. De Wette extended the history of
the gradual development of the canon up to the year 400,[20]
while Schleiermacher, beginning from the finished product
about 400, carried the investigation back to the 'chaotic
darkness of the second century'.[21] Kirchhofer, making use of
Lardner's extensive collection of patristic testimonies concerning the use of New Testament books, drew up an extensive
collection of documents for the history of the canon from its
origins to the time of Jerome. Subsequently this collection,
considerably enlarged and enriched with a detailed introduction, was issued in Great Britain by A. H. Charteris.[22]

In the United States of America the first book to deal solely
with the canon of the Bible was written by Archibald
Alexander (1772–1851), the founder (1812) and first professor
at Princeton Theological Seminary.[23] Basing his work on the
historical methodology of Jones and on the patristic testimonies
gathered by Lardner, Alexander argued that the criterion of
New Testament canonicity is apostolic authorship, whether
direct or indirect (the latter in the case of Mark and Luke).
Apostolicity is to be established by historically verified testimonies of patristic writers of the early Christian centuries.

[20] W. M. L. De Wette, *Lehrbuch der historisch-kritischen Einleitung in die kanonischen
Bücher des Neuen Testaments* (Berlin, 1826; 6th ed., 1860; English trans., 1858).

[21] F. D. E. Schleiermacher, *Einleitung ins Neue Testament*, ed. by G. Wolde
(*Sämmtliche Werke*, 1. Abteilung, viii; Berlin, 1845), pp. 32–75.

[22] J. Kirchhofer, *Quellensammlung zur Geschichte des neutestamentlichen Kanons bis auf
Hieronymus* (Zurich, 1844); translated and augmented by A. H. Charteris, *Canonicity. A
Collection of Early Testimonies to the Canonical Books of the New Testament* (Edinburgh and
London, 1880).

[23] *The Canon of the Old and New Testaments Ascertained; or, the Bible Complete without the
Apocrypha and Unwritten Tradition* (Philadelphia, 1826; London, 1831; revised ed.,
Philadelphia, 1851; Edinburgh, 1855). Prior to Alexander's book, the first theologian
in America to give attention to the canon of the Scriptures seems to have been
Jonathan Edwards (d. 1758). His comments, which depend in part on the work of
Jones, are concerned to show that there are no 'lost' books of the Bible; see his
Miscellaneous Observations on Important Theological Subjects (Edinburgh and London,
1793), pp. 185–223). In a series of sermons (still unedited) preached in May 1748 on
1 Cor. xiii. 8–13, a passage Edwards took as bearing on the canon ('the perfect',
ver. 10), he devoted 'no less than 26 pages and nine arguments to show that the canon
is closed' (John H. Gerstner, 'Jonathan Edwards and the Bible', in *Inerrancy and the
Church*, ed. by John D. Hannah [Chicago, 1984], p. 273).

An important work bearing indirectly on the question of the canonicity of the Gospels was Andrews Norton's three volumes entitled *The Evidences of the Genuineness of the Gospels*.[24] Here the author, who had previously held the chair of Biblical Literature at the newly established (1819) Harvard Divinity School, carefully examines the testimonies of the Fathers concerning the writing, the transmission, and the historicity of the four Gospels.

After Alexander's death his son, Joseph Addison Alexander (1809–60), became professor of New Testament at Princeton Seminary and continued to give attention to the canon of the New Testament. In his posthumously published lecture notes,[25] he concentrated on the seven New Testament books the canonicity of which had been disputed in the early Church—Hebrews, James, 2 Peter, 2 and 3 John, Jude, and Revelation. In his examination of patristic testimonies bearing on the use of these books, Alexander was more careful than his father had been not to gloss over the paucity of early testimony concerning several of the Epistles. This paucity was attributed by him to (1) the limited number of writings now extant from that period; (2) the slow communication of that day, preventing the rapid dissemination of some of the New Testament books; and (3) the authority which still belonged to oral tradition.

Toward the close of the nineteenth century two other Princeton-trained scholars (both graduates of the Seminary class of 1876), who later became professors at their Alma Mater, gave further attention to aspects of the canon.

[24] (Cambridge, Mass., 1837; 2nd ed., 1848).

[25] *Notes on New Testament Literature and Ecclesiastical History* (New York, 1860; reprinted, 1888). For the criteria of New Testament canonicity formulated by J. A. Alexander, see Earl W. Kennedy, 'The Criteria of New Testament Canonicity as Formulated by Princeton Theologians', Th.M. thesis, Princeton Theological Seminary, 1958. Besides those mentioned above, Kennedy provides information, chiefly from records of their lectures, on the views of Charles Hodge, Archibald Alexander Hodge, Casper Wistar Hodge, Sr. and Jr., and William Park Armstrong. Perhaps the most unexpected comment on the canon as being open was made by A. A. Hodge (1823–86). Being asked the question, 'If a manuscript were found which could be proved by internal and external evidence to be by an Apostle, would you have it engrossed in the Canon?' he replied, 'Yes, if it were written in the capacity of an Apostle, and not, for instance, a letter from Peter to his wife's mother, however excellent the advices to the old lady might be' (quoted by C. A. Salmond in *Princetoniana* [Edinburgh, 1888], p. 131).

Benjamin B. Warfield sought to defend the authenticity and canonicity of 2 Peter,[26] and in 1888 George T. Purves delivered the L. P. Stone lectures at Princeton Seminary, which were published under the title *The Testimony of Justin Martyr to Early Christianity*.[27] Warfield also published a pamphlet that was frequently reprinted, entitled *The Canon of the New Testament: How and When Formed*.[28]

Among mid-nineteenth-century monographs on the canon one of the most influential on the Continent was the work of Karl August Credner of Giessen. His 'History of the New Testament Canon',[29] edited after his death in 1857 by G. Volkmar and published in Berlin in 1860, is characterized by richness of information as well as by clarity and objectivity in presentation. After a general account of the growth of the concept of a canon of New Testament writings, as differentiated from apocryphal documents, Credner analyses at length the evidence of the Muratorian Fragment and other Western and Eastern witnesses. In 1863 Adolf Hilgenfeld likewise gave attention to the information provided by the Muratorian Fragment (which he translated into Greek) in tracing the development of the New Testament canon.[30] Against the generally accepted point of view of his fellow-countrymen was the small booklet published by the Leipzig palaeographer and text-critic, Constantin von Tischendorf,[31] in which he contended that already by the beginning of the second century the canon of the New Testament was fully established.

One of the most important of the nineteenth-century British contributions to the study of the canon was Brooke Foss Westcott's *A General Survey of the History of the Canon of the New*

---

[26] 'The Canonicity of Second Peter', *Southern Presbyterian Review*, xxxiii (1882), pp. 45–75.

[27] (New York, 1889). The testimony of Justin to the New Testament is considered on pp. 170–250.

[28] Published by the American Sunday School Union (Philadelphia, 1892), and reprinted (posthumously) in Warfield's *Revelation and Inspiration* (New York, 1927), pp. 451–6; in his *Studies in Theology* (New York, 1932), pp. 639–45; and in his *Theology and Authority of the Bible* (Philadelphia, 1948; London, 1951), pp. 411–16.

[29] *Geschichte des neutestamentlichen Kanons* (Berlin, 1860); this is a complete recasting of Credner's earlier book, *Zur Geschichte des Kanons* (Halle, 1847).

[30] *Der Kanon und ihre Kritik des Neuen Testaments in ihrer geschichtlichen Ausbildung und Gestaltung . . .* (Halle, 1863).

[31] *Wann wurden unsere Evangelien verfasst?* (Leipzig, 1865); the 4th ed., greatly enlarged (1866), was translated under the title, *Origin of the Four Gospels* (Boston, 1867).

Testament.[32] In this comprehensive work the author methodically traces the history of the acknowledgment of the authority of New Testament books from the age of the Apostolic Fathers, through the age of the Apologists, the age of Diocletian, and the age of Councils, including also a short discussion of the views of the Reformers. According to Westcott, the formation of the canon was among the first instinctive acts of the Christian society, resting upon the general confession of the Churches and not upon independent opinions of its members. The canon was not the result of a series of contests; rather, canonical books were separated from others by the intuitive insight of the Church.

A much more compact treatise, yet dealing with both Testaments, is Samuel Davidson's *The Canon of the Bible: Its Formation, History, and Fluctuations* (London, 1877). It was also published, somewhat condensed, in vol. v of *Encyclopaedia Britannica*, 9th ed. (1878). At greater length, John James Given, professor in Magee College, Londonderry, gave consideration to the principal theories of canonicity as applied to both Old and New Testament, as well as tracing the history of the formation of the canon.[33]

On the Continent two quite different approaches to the canon were published in French in the early 1860s. Louis Gaussen, a vigorous proponent of Reformed orthodoxy, whose earlier book, *Théopneustie* (Geneva, 1840; English trans., *Theopneustia; the Plenary Inspiration of the Holy Scriptures*, London, 1841) had been attacked by members of his own theological school at Geneva where he served as Professor of Dogmatics, responded with *The Canon of the Holy Scriptures from the Double Point of View of Science and of Faith.*[34] The 'double point of view' embraces arguments addressed, in the first part, 'to unbelievers', and, in the second part, 'to believers only'. A totally different approach was that of Eduard Reuss of the University of Strassburg in his *History of the Canon of the Holy Scriptures in the Christian*

---

[32] (London, 1855; 6th ed., 1889; reprinted, Grand Rapids, 1980). A popular account that considers also the Old Testament was issued under the title, *The Bible in the Church* (London and Cambridge, 1864; reprinted, Grand Rapids, 1980).

[33] *The Truth of Scripture in Connection with Revelation, Inspiration, and the Canon* (Edinburgh, 1881).

[34] *Le Canon des saintes écritures au double point de vue de la science et de la foi* (Lausanne, 1860; English trans., London, 1862).

Church.[35] Here attention is drawn to the continuing disputes and lack of unanimity in the Church concerning the boundaries of the canon. Different from both Gaussen and Reuss is Alfred Loisy's more matter-of-fact survey, in historical sequence, of the literary evidence bearing on the development of the canon from the patristic period to the Council of Trent.[36]

Elsewhere on the Continent several scholars (Scholten,[37] Hofstede de Groot,[38] and Cramer[39]) considered aspects of the history of the canon. In connection with his radical reinterpretation of ecclesiastical history, Franz Overbeck concentrated on patristic debate over acceptance of Hebrews and also on the evidence provided by the Muratorian Canon.[40]

About this time in England an anonymous work in three volumes (written, as was widely known, by Walter R. Cassels, a retired India merchant) revived some of the arguments of eighteenth-century Deism. Entitled *Supernatural Religion* (London, 1874–7), the author's purpose was to show from patristic testimony that the canonical Gospels are so far removed in time from the events they record that they lose all competence as witnesses to the reality of the miraculous. Among the rejoinders called forth by this work, those by William Sanday[41] and J. B. Lightfoot[42] are generally regarded as the most competent in tracing the use of the New Testament books by the early Fathers.

[35] *Histoire du canon des saintes écritures dans l'église chrétienne* (Paris, 1863; English trans., Edinburgh, 1887). Differently organized, and supplied with extensive bibliographic details, is Reuss's *Die Geschichte der heiligen Schriften Neuen Testaments* (Brunswick, 1842), translated into English from the fifth German edition, *History of the Sacred Scriptures of the New Testament* (Boston, 1884).

[36] Alfred Loisy, *Histoire du canon du Nouveau Testament* (Paris, 1891).

[37] J. H. Scholten, *De oudste getuigenissen aangande de Schriften des Nieuwen Testaments, historisch onderzoekt* (Leiden, 1866); German trans. by Carl Manchot (Bremen, 1867).

[38] Petrus Hofstede de Groot, *Basilides am Ausgange des apostolischen Zeitalters als ersten Zeuge für Alter und Autorität der neutestamentlichen Schriften inbesondere des Johannesevangeliums* (Leipzig, 1868).

[39] Jacob Cramer, *De kanon der Heilige Schrift in de eerste vier eeuwen der christlijke kerk, geschiedkundig onderzoek* (Amsterdam, 1883).

[40] *Zur Geschichte des Kanons: Die Tradition der alten Kirche über den Hebräerbrief*; 2. *Der neutestamentliche Kanon und das Muratorische Fragment* (Chemnitz, 1880).

[41] *The Gospels in the Second Century; An Examination of the Critical Part of a Work entitled 'Supernatural Religion'* (London, 1876). Sanday's later essay, 'The Canon of the New Testament' (*Oxford House Papers*, 3rd Ser. [London, 1897], pp. 105–45), can be characterised as *multum in parvo*.

[42] *Essays on the Work entitled Supernatural Religion* (London, 1889).

Stimulated no doubt by the ferment[43] caused by the publication of *Supernatural Religion*, the Oxford Society of Historical Theology appointed a small committee to prepare a volume exhibiting those passages of early Christian writers which indicate, or have been thought to indicate, acquaintance with any of the books of the New Testament. The outcome several years later was the publication of a volume entitled *The New Testament in the Apostolic Fathers* (Oxford, 1905). The members of the committee that produced the volume were J. V. Bartlet, P. V. M. Benecke, A. J. Carlyle, J. Drummond, W. R. Inge, and K. Lake.

Among introductions to the New Testament that devote extensive consideration to questions pertaining to the canon are those by Heinrich J. Holtzmann,[44] Bernhard Weiss,[45] and Adolf Jülicher.[46] According to Jülicher it was the public reading (*anagnosis*) of Christian books and epistles in a liturgical setting, along with Old Testament books already regarded as authoritative, that was chiefly responsible for their being recognized eventually as canonical Scripture.

Still an indispensable mine of information are Theodor Zahn's two volumes on the history of the New Testament canon,[47] as well as the nine volumes of 'Investigations'[48] that he edited on various problems bearing on the canon. A concise summary of Zahn's mature views on the canon, namely, that it came into existence by the end of the first century, is provided in his *Grundriss der Geschichte*

[43] The stir which the book made in Britain was even greater than that caused by the publication in 1860 by the notorious—or celebrated—*Essays and Reviews*; see H. S. Nash in the *New Schaff-Herzog Encyclopedia of Religious Knowledge*, xi (New York and London, 1911), pp. 166–7. Even Matthew Arnold, for example, in his chapter on 'The Bible-Canon' (in *God and the Bible* [London, 1884], pp. 96–134) makes repeated reference, usually adversely, to *Supernatural Religion*.

[44] *Lehrbuch der historisch-kritischen Einleitung in das Neue Testament* (Freiburg i. B., 1885; 3rd ed., 1892), pp. 75–204.

[45] *Einleitung in das Neue Testament* (Berlin, 1886; 3rd ed., 1897); English trans., *A Manual of Introduction to the New Testament*, i (London, 1887), pp. 28–148.

[46] *Die Einleitung in das Neue Testament* (Tübingen, 1894; 2nd ed., 1900); English trans., *An Introduction to the New Testament* (London, 1904), pp. 459–566; revised German ed. by Erich Fascher (1931), pp. 450–558.

[47] *Geschichte des neutestamentlichen Kanons: Das Neue Testament vor Origenes* (Leipzig, 1888–9); 2. *Urkunden und Belege zum ersten und dritten Band* (Erlangen and Leipzig, 1890–2). (Vol. 3 was never published.)

[48] *Forschungen zur Geschichte des neutestamentlichen Kanons und der altkirchlichen Literatur* (Erlangen, 1881–1929).

des neutestamentlichen Kanons.[49] Zahn's chief rival was Adolf Harnack, whose first publication on the canon, *Das Neue Testament um das Jahr 200*,[50] criticized Zahn's reconstruction of the development of the canon. According to Harnack, the canon constituted one of the three barriers (the other two were the creed and the bishopric) which the Church erected in its struggle with heresy, particularly Gnosticism. The process involved essentially the competition of many books and the survival of those most useful to the Church. Harnack described the role of the Church in canonization as one of selection; Zahn, on the other hand, emphasized the idea of growth.

The debate between Zahn and Harnack over the date at which the New Testament canon was formed involved, to a great extent, a difference of definition rather than of facts. Harnack understood the New Testament canon as a collection of books that possessed authority because they were regarded as holy Scripture. Accordingly he placed the rise of the New Testament canon at the close of the second century. Zahn, on the other hand, equally understood it as a collection of books possessing authority, but he did not insist that this authority should be based on the thesis that 'the New Testament is holy Scripture'. He was satisfied if, for instance, the four Gospels are an authority because of the authority of the Lord's sayings which they contain. He could, therefore, speak of the existence of a New Testament 'canon' a hundred years earlier than Harnack could. The actual facts were hardly touched by the controversy, for it is altogether possible that small collections of gospel materials and apostolic epistles were made here and there before the end of the first century, but that only in later generations did such collections obtain exclusive canonical authority on the level of inspired Scripture. In short, 'canonical' means authoritative books, but 'the canon' means the only authoritative books. Use does not equal canonicity; though a certain kind of use does, namely, use that excludes any other.

---

[49] (Leipzig, 1901; 2nd ed., 1904; 3rd enlarged ed., Wuppertal, 1985). The book reproduces Zahn's article on the canon in Herzog–Hauck's *Realencyclopedie*, 2nd ed., ix (1901), pp. 768–98, to which an appendix has been added. A much abbreviated account is Zahn's article on 'The Canon of the New Testament' in the *New Schaff-Herzog Encyclopedia of Religious Knowledge*, ii (New York and London, 1908), pp. 393–400.

[50] (Freiburg i. B, 1889). Harnack's ideas on the canon were expressed also in his *Lehrbuch der Dogmengeschichte*, 3rd ed., 1894; English trans., *History of Dogma* (London, 1900; reprinted, New York, 1961), pp. 38–60.

II

Literature on the Canon Published
During the Twentieth Century

IN recounting the principal books and monographs of the present century on the New Testament canon it will be useful, in addition to maintaining as far as possible a chronological sequence, to group some publications according to topic or national background. Thus, literature of Dutch, South African, Scandinavian, and Japanese scholars is sufficient in quantity for each national group to be identified separately, while the rise of interest at mid-century in hermeneutical problems makes it appropriate to trace the development of discussion of the 'canon within the canon' as part of the wider question of unity and diversity within the Scriptures. An evaluation of contributions to this and to other contemporary problems of the canon will be reserved for consideration in the final chapter.

The first major contributions of the twentieth century to the study of the canon was made by the Egyptologist, Johannes Leipoldt, who in 1907 and 1908 published a two-volume history of the New Testament canon[1] that traces its development from the beginnings to the present day. He proceeds from the premiss that it was the early Christian apocalypses, in view of the high honour paid to prophets and their messages, that constituted the basis of the New Testament canon.

Another noteworthy contribution was that of the American-born scholar, Caspar René Gregory, who earlier had been student assistant to Charles Hodge, the venerable theologian at Princeton Theological Seminary. In 1907, as Professor of New Testament in the University of Leipzig, he published in the International Theological Library a volume entitled *Canon and Text of the New Testament*.[2] Written in a somewhat colloquial

[1] *Geschichte des neutestamentlichen Kanons*, 2 vols. (Leipzig, 1907, 1908; reprinted, 1974).
[2] It also appeared, slightly expanded, in German under the title *Einleitung in das Neue Testament* (Leipzig, 1909).

style that was not, in the opinion of some reviewers, altogether in keeping with other contributions in the series, the book is scholarly in substance and generally judicious in evaluating disputed points. A few years later Alexander Souter, Regius Professor of Humanity (i.e. Latin) at Aberdeen, dealt with the same two subjects, but in reverse order.[3] Although the size of Souter's book did not permit lengthy discussions, most of the leading questions were discussed, and room was found at the close of the book for more than twenty 'Selected Documents' in Greek and Latin illustrating the development of the canon. More extensive collections of texts bearing on the history of the early Church and of the canon were published by Erwin Preuschen[4] and Daniel J. Theron.[5]

During the first half of the present century a number of short and less technical studies of the subject appeared in English and in German. Among these were *The Rise of the New Testament* by David S. Muzzey[6] and *The Formation of the New Testament*[7] by George H. Ferris; the latter questioned the validity of the idea of a written canon. Of greater depth are two books, one written by Edward C. Moore,[8] Professor of Theology at Harvard, who dealt with the canon in terms of the interaction between its development and the evolution of the organization of Church government as interpreted by Rudolf Sohm; and the other by Henry C. Vedder,[9] Professor of Church History at Crozer Theological Seminary, who vigorously opposed the views of Harnack and Ferris.

A lecture on 'The Formation of the New Testament' by the leading *Neutestamentlicher* of his generation, Heinrich J. Holtzmann,[10] delivered in the Nicolai Church at Strassburg,

---

[3] *The Text and Canon of the New Testament* (London, 1913). A revised ed. prepared by C. S. C. Williams was published in 1954. Williams also contributed the chapter on 'The History of the Text and Canon of the New Testament to Jerome' to vol. ii of *The Cambridge History of the Bible*, ed. by G. W. H. Lampe (Cambridge, 1969), pp. 27–53.

[4] *Analecta; Kürzere Texte zur Geschichte der alten Kirche und des Kanons;* ii. Teil, *Zur Kanonsgeschichte*, 2nd ed. (Tübingen, 1910).

[5] *Evidence of Tradition; Selected Source Material for the Study of the History of the Early Church, Introduction, and Canon of the New Testament* (London, 1967; Grand Rapids, 1968).   [6] (New York, 1900).   [7] (Philadelphia, 1907).

[8] *The New Testament in the Christian Church* (New York, 1904).   [9] *Our New Testament: How Did We Get It?* (Philadelphia, 1957).

[10] *Die Entstehung des Neuen Testaments* (Strassburg, 1904). A slightly enlarged edition appeared in the series of *Religionsgeschichtliche Volksbücher* (Tübingen, 1911).

and a series of five lectures given at Bonn by the rising scholar from Jena, Hans Lietzmann, to a group of teachers from Rheinland and Westfalen on 'How Did the Books of the New Testament Become Holy Scripture?'[11] present authoritative accounts of scholarly material in an agreeable style.

More unconventional is the approach of Johannes Bestmann, who focused attention on the production of the later books of the New Testament and their relation to the Odes of Solomon, 4 Ezra, and the Testaments of the XII Patriarchs.[12] A more traditional approach characterizes the publications of Paul Ewald,[13] Paul Dausch,[14] and Nathan Bonwetsch.[15]

Harnack continued to give attention to problems of the canon (see the close of the previous chapter), one of the more influential of his publications being *Die Entstehung des Neue Testament und die wichtigsten Folgen der neuen Schöpfung* (Leipzig, 1914).[16] Among the theories advocated is the view that the origin of the New Testament is to be found in prophetic-apocalyptic literature; that Marcion was 'the creator of the Christian Bible'; and that the Muratorian Canon was an official document of the Church at Rome.

Among books in English written for the non-specialist reader are *The Formation of the New Testament*,[17] by Edgar J. Goodspeed; *Which Books Belong in the Bible? A Study of the Canon*,[18] by Floyd V. Filson; and *The Making of the Bible*,[19] by William Barclay. Robert M. Grant's *The Formation of the New Testament*[20] is marked by pungent clarity and independent critical

[11] *Wie wurden die Bücher des Neuen Testaments heilige Schrift?* (*Lebensfragen*, 21; Tübingen, 1907); reprinted in Lietzmann's *Kleine Schriften*, ed. by K. Aland (*Texte und Untersuchungen*, lxviii; Leipzig, 1958), pp. 15–98.

[12] *Zur Geschichte des Neutestamentlichen Kanons* (Gütersloh, 1922).

[13] *Der Kanon des Neuen Testaments* (*Biblische Zeit- und Streitfragen*, II Ser., 7; Berlin, 1907).

[14] *Der Kanon des Neuen Testaments* (*Biblische Zeitfragen*, I, 5; Münster i. W., 1910; 4th ed., 1921).

[15] *Die Entstehung des Neuen Testaments* (*Für Gottes Wert und Luthers Lehr!*, III, 2; Gütersloh, 1910).

[16] English trans., *The Origin of the New Testament Canon and the Most Important Consequences of the New Creation* (New York, 1925).

[17] (Chicago, 1926).   [18] (Philadelphia, 1957).

[19] In the series *Bible Guides*, of which it is no. 1 (London and New York, 1961).

[20] (New York, 1965). In Britain it appeared in Hutchinson's University Library series (London, 1965); it was translated into French (Paris, 1969) and into Italian (Brecia, 1973). Grant also contributed the chapter on 'The New Testament Canon' to vol. i of *The Cambridge History of the Bible*, ed. by P. R. Ackroyd and C. F. Evans (Cambridge, 1970), pp. 284–308.

judgement. A conservative, dogmatic point of view governs the work of R. Laird Harris.[21] C. F. D. Moule's introductory volume to Black's New Testament Commentaries examines the process by which the New Testament came to be, a process that involved the effect of worship on the early Church, the Church's growing self-awareness, and the impact of theological attacks on the Church.[22] In a fresh and suggestive manner, Moule also deals with the demand for 'authority' that underlay the impulse to form a canon of Scripture—an authority that rested upon the testimony of eye-witnesses.

The Netherlands for the past century has produced a variety of studies on the canon, some from a historical and some from a theological point of view. Among the former is a doctoral dissertation on the canonicity of the Book of Revelation written by Ned B. Stonehouse[23] under the supervision of F. W. Grosheide at the Free University of Amsterdam. In his Introduction to the New Testament, de Zwaan of Leiden concludes a discussion of the canon by observing that 'among the various documents of early Christian literature, the New Testament has a unity with its own character'.[24] More than once prior to his untimely death, van Unnik of Utrecht dealt with individual problems pertaining to the canon, following a philological approach. In his analysis of a passage from Eusebius (*Hist. eccl.* v. xvi. 3) he discusses with typical thoroughness the question whether the phrase 'neither to add nor to take away', which is used by a second-century anonymous writer, can refer to a fixed corpus of writings comprising the New Testament; he concludes that it does.[25] In another, shorter study he argues that it was the same anonymous writer who first linked the

---

[21] *Inspiration and Canonicity of the Bible, An Historical and Exegetical Study* (Grand Rapids, 1957).

[22] *The Birth of the New Testament* (London, 1962; 3rd ed., completely revised, 1982).

[23] *The Apocalypse in the Ancient Church; a Study in the History of the New Testament Canon* (Goes, 1929). Stonehouse deals in more general terms with the canon in 'The Authority of the New Testament' in *The Infallible Word; a Symposium by Members of the Faculty of Westminster Theological Seminary* (Philadelphia, 1946), pp. 88–136.

[24] J. de Zwaan, *Inleiding tot het Nieuwe Testament*, 2nd ed., iii (Haarlem, 1948), pp. 156–91; the quotation is from p. xi.

[25] W. C. van Unnik, 'De la règle μήτε προσθεῖναι μήτε ἀφελεῖν dans l'histoire du canon', *Vigiliae Christianae*, iii (1949), pp. 1–36; reprinted in *Sparsa Collecta, The Collected Essays of W. C. van Unnik*, i (Leiden, 1980), pp. 123–56.

name 'the New Testament' to a collection of books.[26] As Pro-rector of the University of Utrecht, van Unnik delivered a learned address on the status of an eye-witness and an ear-witness in vouching for trustworthiness of what was included in early collections of New Testament books.[27]

From a theological point of view Grosheide expanded the first part of his pamphlet on 'Canon and Text of the New Testament'[28] into a full-scale discussion of the proposition that 'the concept of the canon is bound up with the concept of God, [for] God is ὁ κανών'.[29] Several writers deal with the canon in connection with the authority of the Scripture, including Greidanus,[30] Ridderbos,[31] Arntzen,[32] and Kam-phuis—the last under the title, 'Signals from Church History concerning the Future and the Canon'.[33] In a suggestive study of how and why certain books became canonical and are now

---

[26] "Ἡ καινὴ διαθήκη—A Problem in the Early History of the Canon', *Studia Patristica*, iv (*Texte und Untersuchungen*, lxxix; Berlin, 1961), pp. 212–27; reprinted in *Sparsa Collecta*, ii (Leiden, 1980), pp. 157–71. In this article van Unnik makes a retraction with regard to the previously mentioned study; he now thinks that the anonymous writer had in mind the total message, to which nothing is to be added and nothing is to be taken away.

[27] *Oog en oor; criteria voor de eerste samenstelling van het Nieuwe Testament* (Rede ter gelegenheid van de 337ᵉ dies natalis der Rijksuniversiteit te Utrecht, op 30 Maart 1973).

[28] F. W. Grosheide, *Kanon en tekst van het Nieuwe Testament* ('Levensvragen', Ser. viii, no. 9; Baarn, 1916).

[29] *Algemeene Canoniek van het Nieuwe Testament* (Amsterdam, 1936), p. 9. Grosheide also edited a brief collection of Greek and Latin texts for use in studying the canon, entitled *Some Early Lists of the Books of the New Testament* (Leiden, 1948).

[30] Seakle Greidanus, *Schriftgeloof en canoniek* (Kampen, 1927).

[31] Herman Ridderbos, *Heilsgeschiedenis en heilige Schrift van het Nieuwe Testament. Het gezag van het Nieuwe Testament* (Kampen, 1955); English trans., *The Authority of the New Testament Scriptures* (Philadelphia, 1963). Some of the same ideas are also expressed in Ridderbos' article, 'De Canon van het Nieuwe Testament', *Kerk en theologie*, ix (1958), pp. 81–95; translated into English, 'The Canon of the New Testament', *Revelation and the Bible, Contemporary Evangelical Thought*, ed. by Carl F. H. Henry (Grand Rapids, 1958), pp. 189–203. According to Ridderbos, there are basically three distinctive views of the canon, namely those of the Roman Catholic, the Lutheran, and the Reformed Churches.

[32] M. J. Arntzen, 'De Omvang van de Canon', *Gereformeerde Weekblad*, 20 Sept. 1968, pp. 53 f., later embodied in his chapter 'Inspiration and Trustworthiness of Scripture', in *Interpreting God's Word Today*, ed. by Simon Kistemaker (Grand Rapids, 1970), pp. 179–212 (the norm of apostolicity is 'contestable because letters of Paul, which should have been part of the canon, are lost', p. 208).

[33] J. Kamphuis, *Signalen uit de kerkgeschiedenis over de toekomst en de canon* (Groningen, 1975).

considered to be holy Scripture, F. J. Theunis, SJ,[34] traces the
patristic use of the phrases 'faith as *kanōn*' and 'truth as *kanōn*',
referring not only to doctrines but also to 'the concrete existing
Christian reality (a living *kanōn*)' as prototypical of the written
canon. The volume, 'Canon or Creed' by Dr Jan Verburg,[35] a
scholarly pastor in The Hague, is a remarkably wide-ranging
yet concise discussion of the interaction of oral tradition with
the developing canon (which in principle is open) and the
consequences for exegesis, ethics, and ecclesiastical practices.

Among South African scholars who have dealt briefly with
the canon are Groenewald,[36] Joubert,[37] Duvenage,[38] Botha,[39]
whose inaugural lecture as professor of New Testament at the
University of South Africa touches on all the expected facets of
the subject of the canon, and Riekert,[40] who, opposing Sundberg, argues that the distinction between Scripture and canon
is untenable. A. B. du Toit of Pretoria, in a comprehensive
text-book on the canon, argues that the internal witness of the
Holy Spirit does not create the authority of Scripture, but is
the means by which believers acknowledge its *autopistia*, while
'the specific distinguishing criterion for canonicity [is] the
witness to Christ'.[41] He thus brings together the characteristic
emphases of Calvin and of Luther.

Among Scandinavian studies on the canon are those of

[34] 'Omtrent Kanon en Schrift' (with a short English summary, 'The Canon
in Relation to Scripture'), *Bijdragen; tijdschrift voor filosophie en theologie*, xl (1980),
pp. 64–87.
[35] *Canon of credo; een kritisch onderzoek naar de Bijbel op grond van zijn ontstaansgeschiedenis*
(Kampen, 1983).
[36] E. P. Groenewald, *Die Nuwe Testament deur die Eeue bewaar* (Pretoria, 1939),
pp. 18–27.
[37] H. L. N. Joubert's 'Hoe en waarom word 'n Sewe-en-twentigtal Boeke as die
Nuwe-Testamentiese Kanon aanvaar?' *Koers*, ix (1941), pp. 58–66, is wide-ranging yet
pithy and compendious.
[38] S. C. W. Duvenage, 'Die gesag van die Heilige Skrif', *Koers*, xxxv (1967),
pp. 5–53, esp. pp. 40–4.
[39] F. J. Botha, *Die Kanon van die Nuwe Testament*, with a summary in English
(*Mededelings van die Universiteit van Suid-Afrika*, A, 43; Pretoria, 1967).
[40] S. J. P. K. Riekert, 'Critical Research and the One Christian Canon Comprising
Two Testaments', *Neotestamentica*, xiv (1981), pp. 21–41.
[41] In *Handleiding by die Nuwe Testament*, vol. i, by J. H. Roberts and A. B. du Toit;
Afdeling B: *Kanoniek van die Nuwe Testament* (Pretoria, 1978; 2nd corrected ed., 1984);
English trans., *Guide to the New Testament*, vol. i, Section B: *The Canon of the New
Testament* (Pretoria, 1979), p. 155.

Fridrichsen,[42] Odland,[43] Torm, [44] Hartman,[45] and Lindblom[46] many of which appeared in connection with volumes of introduction to the New Testament as a whole. The question of the extent of the canon of the Nestorian Syrian Church in China is examined in a valuable article written by Sten Bugge.[47]

Among Japanese scholars who have given attention to aspects of the New Testament canon and early apocryphal writings are Watanabe, Sekine, Arai, and Takemori. The last named has provided an account in English of the contributions of his colleagues.[48]

Significant modern Roman Catholic investigations of the canon include the following. The Abbé Jacquier's attractively written volume[49] provides a broad canvas with detailed information arranged according to geographical divisions of the early Church. Somewhat more individualistic in treatment, but no less careful to remain within the dogmatically prescribed limits,[50] is Lagrange's spirited treatment of the early history of the canon.[51] More massive are Zarb's volumes that deal with the canon of both Testaments.[52] The question of the relation of 'Canon and Church' is discussed in Nikolaas Appel's dissertation at the University of Paderborn.[53] After

[42] Anton Fridrichsen, *Den nytestamentlige skriftsamlings historie* (Christiana, 1918); supplemented by Krister Stendahl in Gösta Lindeskog, Anton Fridricksen, and Harald Riesenfeld, *Inledning till Nya Testamentet* (Stockholm, 1950), pp. 235–90; slightly revised (1958), pp. 235–91.

[43] Sigurd V. Odland, *Det nytestamentlige kanon* (Christiana, 1922).

[44] Friedrich Torm, *Inledning til det Ny Testamente*, 4th ed. (Copenhagen, 1964).

[45] Lars Hartman *et al.*, *En bok om Nya Testamentet* (Lund, 1970), pp. 93–105.

[46] Joh. Lindblom, *Kanon och Apokryfer. Studier till den Bibliska Kanons historie* (Stockholm, 1920).

[47] 'Den syriske kirkes nytestamentlige kanon i China', *Norsk teologisk tidsskrift*, xli (1940), pp. 97–118.

[48] Masaichi Takemori, 'Canon and Worship', in *Saved by Hope; Essays in Honor of Richard C. Oudersluys*, ed. by James I. Cook (Grand Rapids, 1978), pp. 150–63.

[49] Ernst Jacquier, *Le Nouveau Testament dans l'église chrétienne;* i, *Préparation, formation et définition du Canon du Nouveau Testament*, 3rd ed. (Paris, 1911).

[50] On Lagrange's concern to remain obedient to the Church, see his autobiography, *Père Lagrange, Personal Reflections and Memoirs*, English trans. (New York, 1985).

[51] M.-J. Lagrange, *Introduction à l'étude du Nouveau Testament;* i, *Histoire ancienne du Canon du Nouveau Testament*, 2nd ed. (Paris, 1933).

[52] Serafino Zarb, *De historia canonis utriusque Testamenti*, 2nd ed. (Rome, 1934), and *Il canone biblico* (Rome, 1937).

[53] *Kanon und Kirche; Die Kanonkrise im heutigen Protestantismus als kontroverstheologisches Problem* (Paderborn, 1964).

asking 'Whence does the Bible get its Authority?'[54] Ohlig gives systematic consideration to 'The Theological Foundation of the New Testament Canon in the Ancient Church'.[55] J.-M. Charensol's slender volume on 'The Birth of the New Testament'[56] carries the history of the development of the canon up to the close of the second century. Returning to an aspect of his earlier dissertation, Appel discusses 'The New Testament Canon: Historical Process and Spirit's Witness'.[57] Somewhat similar in orientation is the article by Robert Murray, SJ, 'How did the Church determine the Canon of the New Testament?'[58] Readers will appreciate R. J. Dillon's wide-ranging address to the Catholic Theological Society, entitled 'The Unity of the Gospel in the Variety of the Canon'.[59] A concise yet comprehensive treatment of the history of the canon from the beginnings up to the Muratorian Fragment has been contributed by Alexander Sand to the comprehensive *Handbuch der Dogmengeschichte*.[60] Johannes Beumer[61] interacts with Helmut Koester and others in a careful examination of the earliest testimonies (prior to 200) to New Testament writings; J.-N. Aletti, SJ,[62] considers the history of the formation of the canon up to the late fourth century, and discusses the canon's normative function within the Church; Anton Ziegenaus[63] argues that, though the concept of the unity of the New Testament is foreign to the New Testament writers, their books emphasize the unity of the Church and do not actively promote pluralism.

By the second half of the twentieth century a fresh interest in

[54] Karl-Heinz Ohlig, *Woher nimmt die Bibel ihre Autorität?* (Düsseldorf, 1970).

[55] *Die theologische Begründung des neutestamentlichen Kanons in der alten Kirche* (Düsseldorf, 1972).

[56] *La naissance du Nouveau Testament* (*Alethina*, v; Lausanne, 1971).

[57] *Theological Studies*, xxxii (1971), pp. 627–46.

[58] *Heythrop Journal*, xi (1970), pp. 115–26.

[59] *Proceedings of the Catholic Theological Society of America*, xxvii (1972 [1973]), pp. 85–115.

[60] *Kanon; von den Anfängen bis zum Fragmentum Muratorianum* (*Handbuch der Dogmengeschichte*, i, 3a(1); Freiburg, 1974).

[61] 'Zur Vorgeschichte des neutestamentlichen Schriftkanons nach den Zeugnissen des frühen Christentums', *Königsteiner Studien*, xviii (1972), pp. 145–66.

[62] 'Le Canon des Ecritures, Le Nouveau Testament', *Études*, cccxl, i (1973), pp. 109–24.

[63] 'Die Bildung des Schriftkanons als Formprinzip der Theologie', *Münchener theologische Zeitschrift*, xxix (1978), pp. 264–83.

certain theological aspects of the canon emerged and gained momentum in Europe. At first it began with a new look at the relation of tradition and Scripture in the early Church. Dr Ellen Flesseman-van Leer surveyed what can be learned on this subject from the Apostolic Fathers, the Apologists, and from Irenaeus and Tertullian.[64] The investigation was carried further by R. P. C. Hanson, who concentrated on Origen.[65] Besides the monographs by Appel and Ohlig, mentioned in the preceding paragraph, important theological contributions were made by Diem, who dealt with the problem of how the canon is authenticated,[66] and by Frank, who considered 'The Meaning of the Formation of the Canon'. According to Frank, 'The foundation of a New Testament holy Scripture is present in the Didache (about A.D. 100)'.[67]

The diversity of emphases among the several books of the New Testament, and even within the same book, attracted the attention of Ernst Käsemann,[68] Kurt Aland,[69] Wolfgang Trilling,[70] Willi Marxsen,[71] John Charlot,[72] and others. The presence in the later books of the New Testament of what was designated (but with what justification is another matter[73])

[64] *Tradition and Scripture in the Early Church* (Assen, 1954).

[65] *Origen's Doctrine of Tradition* (London, 1954), and *Tradition in the Early Church* (London and Philadelphia, 1962).

[66] Hermann Diem, *Das Problem des Schriftkanons* (Zollikon—Zurich, 1952); cf. also Diem's *Dogmatics* (Philadelphia, 1959), pp. 204–23. For an appreciative evaluation, see the article entitled 'Ernst Käsemann, Hermann Diem, and the New Testament Canon', by G. Clarke Chapman, Jr., in *Journal of the American Academy of Religion*, xxxvi (1968), pp. 3–12.

[67] Isidor Frank, *Der Sinn der Kanonbildung. Eine hist.-theol. Untersuchung der Zeit vom 1 Clemensbrief bis Irenäus (Freiburger theologische Studien*, xc; Freiburg, 1971), p. 203.

[68] 'The Canon of the New Testament and the Unity of the Church', *Essays on New Testament Themes* (London, 1964), pp. 95–107. For an evaluation, see Chapman's article mentioned above.

[69] *The Problem of the New Testament* (London, 1962).

[70] *Vielfalt und Einheit im Neuen Testament. Zur Exegese und Verkündigung des Neuen Testaments* (Einsiedeln, 1965).

[71] *Das Neue Testament als Buch der Kirche* (Gütersloh, 1966), English trans., *The New Testament as the Church's Book* (Philadelphia, 1972).

[72] Charlot finds extensive textual, historical, and theological disunity throughout the New Testament; see his *New Testament Disunity; its Significance for Christianity Today* (New York, 1970).

[73] Martin Hengel rightly reminds us, 'If we want to, we can find "early catholic traits" even in Jesus and Paul: the phenomena thus denoted are almost entirely a legacy of Judaism' (*Acts and the History of Early Christianity* [London, 1979], p. 122).

'Early Catholicism' (i.e. emergent Catholicism)[74] prompted theologians—chiefly Lutheran—to look for a 'canon within the canon'.[75] An extremely radical application of the Pauline principle of justification by faith is expressed by Schulz,[76] who, while not asking that the deutero-Pauline writings, Acts, and the Catholic Epistles be removed from the New Testament, urges that when these books are used in preaching, a stand be taken against them!

By way of concluding the present chapter, attention is drawn to half a dozen recently published books on the canon that take quite different approaches to their subject-matter. The most important is von Campenhausen's magisterial work[77] on the development of the Christian Bible up to the time of Origen. Within this important but limited span of time he concentrates on the history of the concept of Scripture and of the canon and provides rich documentation on the significant part played by key figures in the Church of the period.

Second in importance is Ernst Käsemann's compilation of fifteen essays written between 1941 and 1970 by different authors who deal mainly with the question of a canon within

---

[74] Cf. Willi Marxsen, *Der 'Frühkatholizismus' im Neuen Testament* (*Biblische Studien*, xxi; Neukirchen, 1958); John H. Elliott, 'A Catholic Gospel: Reflections on "Early Catholicism" in the New Testament', *Catholic Biblical Quarterly*, xxxi (1969), pp. 213–3; D. J. Harrington, 'The "Early Catholic" Writings of the New Testament: The Church Adjusting to World History', *The Word in the World*, ed. by R. J. Clifford and G. W. MacRae (Cambridge, Mass., 1973); A. Sand, 'Überlegungen zur gegenwärtigen Diskussion über den "Frühkatholizismus,"' *Catholica*, xxx (1979), pp. 49–62; and Reginald H. Fuller, 'Early Catholicism, An Anglican Reaction to a German Debate', *Die Mitte des Neuen Testaments . . . Festschrift für Eduard Schweizer*, ed. by Ulrich Luz and Hans Weder (Göttingen, 1983), pp. 34–41.

[75] Cf. Inge Lønning, *'Kanon im Kanon,' Zum dogmatischen Grundlagenproblem des neutestamentlichen Kanons* (*Forschungen zur Geschichte und Lehre des Protestantismus*, x Reihe, vol. xliii; Oslo and Munich, 1972); W. Schragge, 'Die Frage nach der Mitte und dem Kanon im Kanon des Neuen Testaments in der neueren Diskussion', *Rechtfertigung; Festschrift für Ernst Käsemann*, ed. by Johannes Friedrich, Wolfgang Pohlmann, und Peter Stuhlmacher (Tübingen and Göttingen, 1976), pp. 415–42; and Ludovík Fazekás, 'Kanon im Kanon', *Theologische Zeitschrift*, xxxvii (1981), pp. 19–34.

[76] Sigfried Schulz, *Die Mitte der Schrift; der Frühkatholizismus im Neuen Testament als Herausforderung an den Protestantismus* (Stuttgart, 1976).

[77] Hans Freiherr von Campenhausen, *Die Entstehung der christlichen Bibel* (Tübingen, 1968, 2nd ed., 1977); English trans., *The Formation of the Christian Bible* (Philadelphia, 1972). On von Campenhausen's opinion (pp. 230ff.), that it was Montanism that finally forced the Church to delimit the canon, see the present writer's comments in *Gnomon*, xlii (1970), pp. 729 f.

the canon.[78] Two of the contributors[79] are Roman Catholic scholars; among the Protestants, exegetes outnumber theologians and church historians together. The editor provides a spirited analysis and critique of each essay, probing the exegetes concerning their systematic assumptions and central themes, and confronting the others with exegetical challenges.

In a book subtitled *An Ecumenical Approach*,[80] a Protestant New Testament historian and a Roman Catholic patristic scholar collaborate in an attempt to understand the complex problems of the growth of the canon. William R. Farmer over emphasizes persecution and martyrdom as major factors that influenced the development of the canon, and Denis M. Farkasfalvy, O.Cist., focuses on Irenaeus' understanding of 'apostolicity', as the key to the development of the canon.

Altogether different from all other books thus far mentioned is Anton Mayer's attempt to show, from a sociological vantage point, how Jesus' original teachings were 'censored' and 'deproletarianized' by Paul, Luke, and other New Testament authors, and how their writings, through political stratagems, were canonized, resulting in the triumph of sexism, anti-Semitism, and capitalism![81]

In Brevard S. Childs' *The New Testament as Canon: An Introduction*,[82] as was true also with regard to his earlier book on the Old Testament,[83] the author's concern is to raise literary and theological questions that are involved when the New Testament is interpreted, book by book, in its present

---

[78] *Das Neue Testament als Kanon; Dokumentation und kritische Analyse zur gegenwärtige Diskussion* (Göttingen, 1970). Among evaluations of the contributions to the volume, the most severe (not to say immoderate) criticism levelled at both the editor and the contributors is Gerhard Maier's *Das Ende der historisch-kritischen Methode* (Wuppertal, 1974), English trans. *The End of the Historical-Critical Method* (St Louis, 1977).

[79] All the contributors are of Teutonic background; for a discussion from a different point of view, see Geoffrey Wainwright, 'The New Testament as Canon', *Scottish Journal of Theology*, xxviii (1975), pp. 551–71.

[80] *The Formation of the New Testament Canon: An Ecumenical Approach* (New York, 1983). Each author had given earlier attention to aspects of his subject; Farmer in *Jesus and the Gospel; Tradition, Scripture, and the Canon* (Philadelphia, 1982), and Farkasfalvy in 'Theology of Scripture in St. Irenaeus', *Revue bénédictine*, lxxviii (1968), pp. 319–33.

[81] *Der zensierte Jesus; Soziologie des Neuen Testaments* (Olten and Freiburg i. B., 1983).

[82] (London, 1984; Philadelphia, 1985).

[83] *Introduction to the Old Testament as Scripture* (Philadelphia and London, 1979). For a critique of what Childs calls 'canonical criticism' of the Old Testament, see James Barr, *Holy Scripture; Canon, Authority, Criticism* (Philadelphia, 1983), pp. 130–71.

canonical form as the authoritative Scripture of the Christian Church. He argues that the process of canonization began within the New Testament period, shaping the literature throughout its development, and was not a post-apostolic stage in the formation of the canon—to which stage he devotes next to no attention. Since his use of the word 'canon' has three distinct meanings (as a fixed collection of books, as the final form of a book or group of books, and as a principle of finality and authority), the reader is struck by the seemingly indiscriminate way in which the word 'canonical' is attached to a vast range of words, creating a kind of mystique.[84]

Multum in parvo describes Harry Y. Gamble's *The New Testament Canon, its Making and Meaning* (Philadelphia, 1985), a slender volume that deals concisely with historical factors in the formation of the canon, as well as with theological implications of the Church's decision to have a canon.

In *Pseudonymity and Canon*[85] David G. Meade addresses the tension between historical concerns of literary criticism and theological concerns of canonicity. As in the case of Jewish religious literature, where attribution of authorship is primarily an assertion of authoritative tradition, not of literary origins, so too, Meade argues, in the case of the deutero-Paulines and the Petrine literature in the New Testament, 'the discovery of pseudonymous origins or of anonymous redaction in no way prejudices either the inspiration or the canonicity of the work. Attribution, in the context of canon, must be primarily regarded as a statement (or assertion) of authoritative tradition'.[86]

Joseph F. Kelly's book, *Why is There a New Testament?* (Wilmington, 1986), written, he says, for 'a non-specialist audience', deals with the composition, transmission, and canonization of the books of the New Testament.

[84] The word 'canonical' qualifies nearly thirty different words, including addressee, approach, collection, concern, context, corpus, editors, fashion, function, harmony, intention, interpretation, issue, model, perspective, problem, process, reading, referentiality, rendering, role, setting, significance, shape, shaping, stage, stance, and unity.

[85] (Tübingen, 1986); see p. 284 n. 35 below.

[86] Pp. 215–6.

PART TWO

Formation of the Canon

III

Period of Preparation:
The Apostolic Fathers

THE title 'Apostolic Fathers' refers to a circle of authors who
are supposed to have had personal knowledge of some of the
apostles, but did not actually belong to their number. Originally the title 'Fathers of the Apostolic Age' was given to five
authors whose works the patrologist J. B. Cotelier first
gathered together in 1672. The edition included the writings
of Barnabas, Clement of Rome, Hermas, Ignatius, and Polycarp.[1] In 1693 William Wake issued an English translation of
the several documents under the title, *The Genuine Epistles of
the Apostolical Fathers*.[2] Later it became customary to add to
the corpus the anonymous *Epistle to Diognetus*,[3] the fragmentary remains of Papias, and (after 1883 when its complete text
was first published) the *Didache*, entitled in the manuscript
'The Teaching of the Lord to the Gentiles through the
Twelve Apostles'.

As a title 'Apostolic Fathers' does not represent any ancient
tradition; there are no traces of any early collection of the
writings of Apostolic Fathers, and each of them has a separate
literary history. They span the period from about A.D. 95 to about
150, and are witnesses to the development of different emphases and styles of Christianity—for this was an epoch of

[1] *Sanctorum Patrum qui temporibus apostolicus floruerunt, Barnabae, Clementis, Hermae,
Ignatii, Polycarpi, opera edita et inedita, vera et suppositicia...*, 2 vols. (Paris, 1672). For an
account of the early editions of the Apostolic Fathers, see J. A. Fischer, 'Die ältesten
Ausgaben der Patres Apostolici. Ein Beitrag zu Begriff und Begrenzung der Apostolischen Väter', *Historisches Jahrbuch*, xciv (1974), pp. 157–90; xvc (1975), pp. 88–119.
[2] (London, 1693; 4th ed., 1737). See also H. J. de Jonge, 'On the Origin of the
Term "Apostolic Fathers"', *Journal of Theological Studies*, NS xxix (1978), pp. 503–5.
[3] Actually the *Epistle to Diognetus*, a highly rhetorical apology for Christianity which
is now usually dated to the late second or early third century, has no reason to be
included in the corpus of Apostolic Fathers. Furthermore, since the anonymous author
makes only one passing allusion (in xii. 5) to a New Testament text (1 Cor. viii. 1), the
epistle has nothing of significance to contribute to the history of the canon of the New
Testament, and will not be considered in the present chapter.

transition and of consolidation. Christianity was beginning, little by little, to become an institution, and church leaders began placing emphasis on ecclesiastical organization. In addition to coming from widely spread geographical backgrounds, the Apostolic Fathers also represent a certain amount of doctrinal diversity in terms of developments within Jewish Christianity, on the one hand, and within Hellenistic Christianity, on the other.

The Apostolic Fathers seldom make express citations from New Testament writings. On the contrary (and particularly as regards the Gospels and the words of Jesus) we have allusions and reminiscences that are often difficult to identify and delicate to interpret. At most, the Apostolic Fathers disclose for this or that geographical area a certain (or rather, an uncertain) amount of knowledge and use of several first-century documents that later came to be gathered into what we know as the New Testament.[4]

I. CLEMENT OF ROME

The writing that goes under the title of *I Clement* is an epistle written about A.D. 95–6[5] in the name of the church in Rome and traditionally ascribed to Clement, one of the prominent Christian leaders in Rome. At Corinth several younger members, it seems, had risen against certain presbyters and ousted them from their position. When this became known to the Roman church, Clement drew up a rather lengthy communication calling the factions to repentance—for God, he declares, requires due order in all things. The deposed presbyters must be reinstated, he insists, and legitimate superiors appointed by the apostles or their successors must be obeyed. At the conclusion Clement expresses hope that the bearer of the

---

[4] In addition to the several monographs bearing on specific Apostolic Fathers (mentioned below), the two most comprehensive general works are *The New Testament in the Apostolic Fathers*, by a Committee of the Oxford Society of Historical Theology (Oxford, 1905), and Helmut Koester, *Synoptische Überlieferung bei den Apostolischen Vätern* (*Texte und Untersuchungen*, lxv; Berlin, 1957).

[5] The traditional dating of *1 Clement* is disputed by A. E. Wilhelm-Hooijbergh ('A Different View of Clemens Romanus', *Heythrop Journal*, xvi [1975], pp. 266–88), and by John A. T. Robinson (*Redating the New Testament* [London, 1976], pp. 327–35), who date it, respectively, to A.D. 69 and early 70.

epistle will return soon with good news that peace has been restored.

Throughout his epistle Clement weaves together a great number of quotations from the Old Testament, as well as a few from several New Testament books.[6] Those from the Old Testament are frequently introduced by such well-known formulas[7] as 'the Scripture says' (ἡ γραφὴ λέγει), 'it is written' (γέγραπται), 'that which is written' (τὸ γεγραμμένον), and are for the most part made with great exactness from the Greek text of the Septuagint.

On the other hand, the few New Testament quotations are made in a different way. Instead of introducing gospel material with formulas of citation that imply a written record, Clement twice urges his readers to 'remember the words of the Lord Jesus'. In xiii. 2 Clement puts together a cento of phrases, some of which are found in Matthew and Luke, others of which have no exact parallels in the four Gospels. He writes:

> Especially remember the words of the Lord Jesus which he spoke when teaching gentleness and long-suffering. For he spoke thus: 'Be merciful, that you may obtain mercy; forgive, that you may be forgiven; as you do [to others], so shall it be done to you; as you give, so shall it be given to you; as you judge, so shall you be judged; as you show kindness, so shall kindness be shown to you; with what measure you measure, it shall be measured to you.

These phrases appear to come from Matt. v. 7; vi. 14–15; vii. 1–2, 12; Luke vi. 31, 36–8, but there is no very explicit parallel in our gospels. It may be that Clement is either quoting by memory from Matthew or Luke, or is making use of some written or unwritten form of the catechesis of Jesus' teaching current in the Roman church.[8] The question is complicated by

---

[6] Cf. Donald A. Hagner, *The Use of the Old and New Testaments in Clement of Rome* (Supplements to *Novum Testamentum*, xxxiv; Leiden, 1973).

[7] On formulas used by Jews and Christians in quoting from and referring to the Scriptures of the Old Testament, see the chapter on 'The Formulas Introducing Quotations of Scripture in the New Testament and in the Mishnah', in the present writer's *Historical and Literary Studies, Pagan, Jewish, and Christian* (Leiden, 1968), pp. 52–63.

[8] Cf. M. Mees, 'Schema und Dispositio in ihrer Bedeutung für die Formung der Herrenwörte aus dem I Clemensbrief, Kap. 13.2', *Vigiliae Christianae*, viii (1971), pp. 257–72.

the fact that an analogous combination is found in Clement of Alexandria (*Strom.* II. xviii. 91); Polycarp (*Phil.* xi. 3) also reproduces some of the same elements of the series.

The other reference to Jesus' teaching occurs in xlvi. 7–8, where Clement writes:

> Remember the words of the Lord Jesus; for he said, 'Woe to that man. It would be better for him if he had not been born, rather than that he should offend (σκανδαλίσαι) one of my elect. It would be better for him that a millstone were hung on him, and he be cast into the sea, than that he should pervert (διαστρέψαι) one of my elect.

Here one recalls the words of Jesus found in Mark ix. 42; Matt. xviii. 6–7; and Luke xvii. 1–2, but there is no parallel to the clauses about offending and perverting the elect. Obviously Clement has knowledge of a tradition that preserves the words of Jesus; it is not certain, however, that he has before him written copies of any of the Synoptic Gospels, or, if he had written copies, that he felt impelled to quote exactly.

In addition to these two direct references to Jesus' words, Clement's epistle contains one or two other instances of possible allusions to Synoptic tradition. Perhaps the most noteworthy of these is the use he makes in xxiv. 5 of imagery from the parable of the sower (Matt. xiii. 3; Mark iv. 3; Luke viii. 5) in his homily on 1 Cor. xv. 36 ff. But whether he is depending on a written gospel or on oral tradition is difficult to decide. In any case, it is remarkable that Clement invokes the absolute authority of the words of Jesus only twice, whereas he refers to passages in books of the Old Testament more than one hundred times.

Clement's testimony concerning several of the Pauline Epistles is more definite. In chap. xlvii he invites his readers in Corinth to consult the epistle which 'the blessed apostle Paul' had sent them. He does this in a manner which suggests that a copy of Paul's Epistle was as accessible in Rome as in Corinth. Elsewhere Clement appears to make definite allusions to several other Epistles of Paul, including Romans, Galatians, Philippians, and Ephesians. This may presuppose the existence of a collection of Pauline Epistles. It is to be noted that when Clement refers to these Epistles as writings filled with good counsel given by one to whom the Corinthian believers should pay attention, he does not present them as invested with divine authority. In fact, after giving in xxxv. 5–6 a paraphrase of Rom. i. 29–32, Clement continues, 'For the Scripture says...', and then presents a quotation from Psalm l. 16–23. This leads us to conclude that for Clement the Pauline Epistles were not Scripture, though he obviously regards them as possessing a certain kind of authority.

Besides referring to several Epistles of Paul, Clement makes repeated allusions to the Epistle to the Hebrews. These reminiscences are scattered throughout the first half of his epistle (xvii. 1, 5; xix. 2; xxi. 9; xxvii. 2) and reaches a climax in xxxvi. 2–5, a passage that consists almost entirely of echoes from Hebrews i. 1–3. Elsewhere Clement incorporates occasional phrases that have led some to think he may have also known Acts, James, and 1 Peter.

By way of summary, we see that Clement's Bible is the Old Testament, to which he refers repeatedly as Scripture (γραφή), quoting it with more or less exactness. Clement also makes occasional reference to certain words of Jesus; though they are authoritative for him, he does not appear to enquire how their authenticity is ensured. In two of the three instances that he speaks of remembering 'the words' of Christ or of the Lord Jesus, it seems that he has a written record in mind, but he does not call it a 'gospel'. He knows several of Paul's epistles, and values them highly for their content; the same can be said of the Epistle to the Hebrews, with which he is well acquainted. Although these writings obviously possess for Clement considerable significance, he never refers to them as authoritative 'Scripture'.

II. IGNATIUS OF ANTIOCH

According to Origen, Ignatius was the second bishop of Antioch, the successor of the apostle Peter; according to Eusebius, he was the third, following Peter's successor, Euodius. Nothing is known of his life except his journey under armed guard from Antioch to Rome, where his martyrdom took place under the Emperor Trajan about A.D. 110.

En route Ignatius wrote seven epistles, four from Smyrna and three from Troas.[9] At Smyrna he wrote epistles of encouragement to the churches of Ephesus, Magnesia, and Tralles in Asia Minor; in the fourth epistle, addressed to the church in Rome, he asks them not to deprive him of martyrdom by intervening on his behalf with the pagan authorities. At Troas, having received news that the persecution at Antioch had ceased, he wrote to the churches of Philadelphia and Smyrna as well as to Polycarp, the bishop of Smyrna, asking them to send legates to congratulate the Christians at Antioch on the restoration of peace.

The style of these epistles is of inimitable originality. Written in an abrupt and incoherent style, overloaded with metaphors and elaborate rhetoric, they none the less manifest such strong faith and overwhelming love of Christ as to make them one of the finest literary expressions of Christianity during the second century. It agrees with the style of Ignatius, and particularly with the circumstances under which the epistles were composed, that quotations are few in number, brief in extent, and made evidently from memory.

Throughout his epistles Ignatius frequently uses language that echoes characteristic phrases found in the Pauline writings.[10] Apparently struck by Paul's depreciating reference to himself as 'the offscouring ($\pi\epsilon\rho\iota\psi\eta\mu\alpha$) of all things' (1 Cor. iv.

---

[9] The Epistles of Ignatius are extant in three recensions: (*a*) The short or original recension exists in Greek only and comprises the seven epistles mentioned in the text above. (*b*) The long recension includes the seven authentic epistles along with six spurious epistles, dating from the fourth century. This longer recension is extant in numerous Greek and Latin manuscripts. (*c*) The Syriac abridgement came to light in 1845 when W. Cureton published a Syriac MS containing a recension of only the three genuine epistles to the Ephesians, to the Romans, and to Polycarp. As would be expected, there have been extensive and heated discussions as to which recension, or combination of recensions, represents Ignatius' own work. Among more recently published monographs the following may be mentioned: M. P. Brown, *The Authentic Writings of Ignatius. A Study of Linguistic Criteria* (Durham [NC], 1963; R. Weijenborg, *Les Lettres d'Ignace d'Antioche* (Leiden, 1969); J. Rius-Camps, *The Four Authentic Letters of Ignatius, the Martyr* (Rome, 1979); R. Joly, *Le Dossier d'Ignace d'Antioche* (Brussels, 1979); W. R. Schoedel, 'Are the Letters of Ignatius of Antioch Authentic?', *Religious Studies Review*, vi (1980), pp. 196–201; C. P. H. Bammel, 'Ignatian Problems', *Journal of Theological Studies*, N.S. xxxiii (1982), pp. 62–97; Jack Hannah, 'The Long Recension of the Ignatian Epistles by the Redactors of Paul and John', *Proceedings of the Eastern Great Lakes Biblical Society*, iii (1983), pp. 108–121; and William R. Schoedel, *Ignatius of Antioch* (*Hermeneia*; Philadelphia, 1984), pp. 3–7.

[10] Cf. Heinrich Rathke, *Ignatius von Antiochien und die Paulusbriefe* (*Texte und Untersuchungen*, xcix; Leipzig, 1967), pp. 57–65.

13), Ignatius twice employs it with reference to himself in his *Epistle to the Ephesians* (viii. 1; xviii. 1). He uses Paul's expression 'lest I be found a castaway' (1 Cor. ix. 27) in *Trall.* xii. 3, and in *Rom.* v. 1 he incorporates almost verbatim Paul's phrase from 1 Cor. iv. 4, 'but not by this am I justified'. Again and again he makes use of phrases drawn from Paul's vivid description of himself when writing to the Corinthians: 'Last of all, as to one untimely born, he [Christ] appeared to me. For I am the least of the apostles, unfit to be called an apostle because I persecuted the church of God. But by the grace of God I am what I am' (1 Cor. xv. 8–10). These words obviously made such an impression on Ignatius that he includes echoes from the passage in five of his letters:

I am unworthy, being the very least of them and an untimely birth; but I have obtained mercy to be someone (*Rom.* ix. 1).

I who am the very least of the faithful (*Eph.* xxi. 2).

I am not worthy to be called a member [of the church in Syria], being the very least of them (*Trall.* xiii. 1).

I am not worthy to be called a member (*Magn.* iv. 1).

I am not worthy to belong to it [the church], being the very least of them. But by God's will I have been judged worthy, not because of the witness of my own conscience, but by the grace of God (*Smyrn.* xi. 1).

In addition to 1 Corinthians, parallels in phraseology make it probable that Ignatius was acquainted also with several other Pauline Epistles, including Romans, Ephesians, and Philippians. It is possible that he had knowledge of Hebrews and 1 Peter, though echoes from these are rather faint.

We turn now to enquire how far Ignatius knew about Jesus and his ministry, and whether this knowledge rested on his use of written gospels or only on oral tradition. The evidence, as we shall see, is very scanty.

As for the Synoptic Gospels, there are much closer parallels in Ignatius with Matthew than with Mark or Luke. In an elaborate statement of Christian doctrine at the opening of his *Epistle to the Smyrnaeans*, Ignatius states that Jesus was 'baptized by John so that all righteousness might be fulfilled by him' (i. 1). It is significant that of the Evangelists it is Matthew

alone who states that, in order to persuade John to baptize
him, Jesus urged that 'thus it is fitting for us to fulfill all
righteousness' (Matt. iii. 15). Later in the same epistle, when
speaking of a difficult and mysterious subject (the judgement of
angels who do not believe in Christ's blood), Ignatius states
bluntly, 'He who receives this, let him receive it' (ὁ χωρῶν
χωρείτω, vi. 1). One is reminded of Jesus' words reported by
Matthew in another context, 'He who is able to receive this, let
him receive it' (ὁ δυνάμενος χωρεῖν χωρείτω, Matt. xix. 12).

These reminiscences, as well as several instances of what
seem to be echoes of Matthew in Ignatius (e.g. *Polyc.* ii. 2 and
Matt. x. 16; *Eph.* v. 2 and Matt. xviii. 19, 20), have led most
scholars to conclude that Ignatius was acquainted either with
Matthew or a document very closely akin to it.[11]

The question whether Ignatius knew the Gospel according
to Luke depends largely upon what one thinks of the similarities between the following passages.

Smyrn. iii. 1–2	Luke xxiv. 39
For myself, I know and believe that he was in the flesh even after the resurrection. And when he came to those with Peter, he said to them, 'Lay hold and handle me, and see that I am not a phantom (δαιμόνιον) without a body.	See my hands and my feet, that it is I myself; handle me, and see, for a spirit (πνεῦμα) does not have flesh and bones as you see that I have.

Whether this shows that Ignatius is dependent upon Luke or is
quoting from some other source, oral or written, it is difficult to
decide with certainty.

In contrast to the paucity of allusions to the Synoptic
Gospels, Ignatius' epistles not infrequently present echoes of
the fourth Gospel.[12] The following are several of the more
significant instances.

[11] According to J. Smit Sibinga, Ignatius was acquainted with the so-called
M-material (or part of it) in its pre-Matthean form ('Ignatius and Matthew', *Novum
Testamentum*, viii [1966], pp. 263–83).

[12] Among many discussions of the question, see W. von Loewenich, *Das Johannes-
Verständnis im zweiten Jahrhundert* (Giessen, 1932), pp. 25–38; W. J. Burghardt, 'Did
Saint Ignatius of Antioch know the Fourth Gospel?' *Theological Studies*, i (1940),
pp. 1–26 and 130–56; and Christian Maurer, *Ignatius von Antiochen und das Johannes-
evangelium* (Zurich, 1949).

(1) To the Magnesians (vii. 2) Ignatius speaks concerning God: '[He] manifested himself through Jesus Christ his Son, who is his word that proceeded from silence,[13] who in all respects was well-pleasing to him that sent him'. Here we have two rather obvious allusions to the Johannine Gospel (i. 1 and viii. 28–9).

(2) To the Philadelphians (vii. 1) he writes: 'Even though certain persons desired to deceive me after the flesh, yet the spirit [i.e. Ignatius' own spirit] is not deceived, for it is from God. For it knows whence it comes and whither it goes' (πόθεν ἔρχεται καὶ ποῦ ὑπάγει). The same five Greek words occur in John iii. 8 with regard to the divine Spirit.

(3) Ignatius writes to the Romans (vii. 2) that 'the prince of this age (ὁ ἄρχων τοῦ αἰῶνος) desires to take me captive, and to corrupt my mind which is toward God'. This reminds one of repeated references in the Fourth Gospel (xii. 31; xiv. 30; xvi. 11) to 'the prince of this world' (ὁ ἄρχων τοῦ κόσμου). A few sentences later Ignatius refers to the 'living water' that speaks within him, saying, 'Come to the Father' (cf. John iv. 10; vii. 38). In the next line he declares: 'I have no desire for corruptible food or for the delights of this life. I desire the "bread of God", which is the flesh of Christ, "who was of the seed of David", and for my drink I desire his blood, which is love incorruptible.' Here we find phrases like those in John vi. 33 and vii. 42, as well as other echoes of Johannine theology.

(4) To the Philadelphians (ix. 1) he makes use of the metaphor of Christ as the door, emphasizing the Johannine doctrine of the pre-incarnate activity of the Logos: 'He [the high priest] is the door of the Father, through which enter Abraham and Isaac and Jacob and the Prophets and the Apostles and the Church. All these things combine in the unity of God'. Here it is remarkable how many themes that occur in the Fourth Gospel seem to be amalgamated in Ignatius' thinking (cf. John x. 7, 9; xiv. 6; viii. 30–59; xvii. 20–3).

Such instances of parallels, sometimes of words and sometimes of ideas, show that Ignatius was well acquainted with Johannine theology and suggest that he may have gained this

---

[13] Although this 'procession from silence', in harmony with various Gnostic systems, may refer to the divine generation of the Word in eternity, the context seems rather to refer to the Incarnation (cf. Wis. xviii. 14–15 according to patristic exegesis).

familiarity from having read the Fourth Gospel. The absence
of any explicit quotation from this Gospel is quite in harmony
with what was mentioned earlier regarding Ignatius' literary
style and the circumstances under which he was writing.

Ignatius uses the introductory formula 'It is written'
(γέγραπται) only three times, all of them referring to the Old
Testament—two from the book of Proverbs (*Magn.* xii. 1 and
Eph. v. 3; the latter may be based upon 1 Peter v. 5), and the
other in connection with a highly condensed and curiously
ambiguous report of a debate that he had, apparently with
Judaizing Christians at Philadelphia (*Philad.* viii. 2–ix. 1). In
that debate his opponents declared (according to the interpretation adopted by most commentators[14] on the passage) that if
they did not find it in the 'archives' (ἀρχείοις, here referring to
the Old Testament), they did not believe it in the Gospel
(εὐαγγέλιον). When he retorted that Scripture in fact supported
him ('But it is written', γέγραπται), they answered, 'That is just
the question'—in other words, they questioned the messianic
interpretation that he placed on proof-texts drawn from the
Old Testament 'archives'.

The passage concludes with Ignatius' passionate affirmation
that may represent not so much what he said then as what he
now regards as an appropriate way of ending such debates: 'As
for me, the archives are Jesus Christ; the unadulterated archives
are his cross and his death and his resurrection, and the faith
which is through him;—in these I wish to be justified through
your prayers. The priests [representing the Old Testament]
likewise were good, but the High Priest [Jesus Christ] is greater'.
Here the archives (ἀρχεῖα) and the Gospel (τὸ εὐαγγέλιον)
are opposed as the Old Testament and the New, and to
those who wanted proof from the former Ignatius replies

---

[14] The literature on the interpretation of Ignatius' cryptic statement is extensive; in
addition to the standard commentaries on his epistles by J. B. Lightfoot, Walter Bauer,
J. A. Kleist, R. M. Grant, and W. R. Schoedel, see E. Flesseman-van Leer, *Tradition and
Scripture in the Early Church* (Assen, 1954), pp. 34 f.; Einar Molland, 'The Heretics
Combatted by Ignatius of Antioch', *Journal of Ecclesiastical History*, v (1954), pp. 1–6,
esp. pp. 4–6; and W. R. Schoedel, 'Ignatius and the Archives', *Harvard Theological
Review*, lxxi (1978), pp. 97–106. The supposition of Salomon Reinach that the archives
were in Caesarea where 'critical' Gnostics would have investigated the records of the
life of Jesus deserves no refutation ('Ignatius, Bishop of Antioch, and the ἀρχεῖα',
Anatolian Studies, presented to Sir W. M. Ramsay, ed. by W. H. Buchler and W. M. Calder
[Manchester, 1923], pp. 339–40).

that the foundation of Christian faith is not the Old Testament but Jesus Christ, who is greater than Old Testament worthies.

The upshot of all this is that the primary authority for Ignatius was the apostolic preaching about the life, death, and resurrection of Jesus Christ, though it made little difference to him whether it was oral or written. He certainly knew a collection of Paul's Epistles, including (in the order of frequency of his use of them) 1 Corinthians, Ephesians, Romans, Galatians, Philippians, Colossians, and 1 Thessalonians. It is probable that he knew the Gospels according to Matthew and John, and perhaps also Luke. There is no evidence that he regarded any of these Gospels or Epistles as 'Scripture'.

III. THE DIDACHE

The *Didache* is a short manual of moral instruction and church practice. Although referred to by more than one patristic author (Eusebius and Athanasius even considered it to be on the fringe of the New Testament canon), no copy was known until 1875 when a manuscript (written A.D. 1056) was discovered by Philotheos Bryennios, the Metropolitan of Nicomedia, in the library of the Jerusalem Monastery of the Holy Sepulchre at Constantinople.[15]

Questions concerning author, date, and place of origin of the *Didache* are notoriously difficult. Although several scholars have assigned the *Didache* to the first century,[16] and others have dated it to the third or even fourth century,[17] most prefer

---

[15] Διδαχὴ τῶν δώδεκα ἀποστόλων ἐκ τοῦ Ἱεροσολομιτικοῦ χειρογράφου νῦν πρῶτον ἐκδιδομένη μετὰ προλεγομένων καὶ σημειωσείων (Constantinople, 1883). The publication of the *editio princeps* stimulated a very great number of studies and investigations, among which one of the more influential was F. E. Vokes's *The Riddle of the Didache* (London, 1938). Vokes reviews subsequent literature in his two articles, 'The Didache Re-Examined', *Theology*, lxiii (1955), pp. 12–16, and 'The *Didache*—Still Debated', *Church Quarterly*, iii (1970), pp. 57–62.

[16] Notably J.-P. Audet, who argues in his magisterial edition, *La Didachè; Instructions des Apôtres* (Paris, 1958), that the first half (through xi. 2) comes from about A.D. 70, while the rest was added not long afterwards. Grant dates the completed work about A.D. 90 (in E. J. Goodspeed, *A History of Early Christian Literature*, revised and enlarged by R. M. Grant [Chicago, 1966], p. 13), while J. A. T. Robinson thinks that it should be dated before A.D. 60 (*Redating the New Testament* [Philadelphia, 1976], p. 327). Willy Rordorf and André Tuilier in *La Doctrine des douze apôtres* (*Didachè*) (Paris, 1978) date the completed work to the latter part of the first century.

[17] Charles Bigg, for example, was convinced that the *Didache* belongs to the fourth century; see his *Doctrine of the Twelve Apostles* (London, 1898).

a date in the first half of the second century. Certainly it seems to reflect the life of an early, and perhaps isolated, Christian community. Whether it originated in Syria or Egypt is disputed, but the former is more likely.

Of the sixteen brief chapters, chaps. i–vi describe the 'Way of Life' and the 'Way of Death', while chaps. vii–xv contain instructions on baptism, fasting, prayer, the Eucharist, and how to treat prophets, bishops, and deacons. Chap. xvi is a prophecy of the Antichrist and the Second Coming of Christ. The authority for these teachings, as suggested by the subtitle, is none other than Jesus through the mediation of the apostles. The word 'apostles', however, does not occur in the book itself, except at xi. 3–6 where it refers, not to the Twelve or Paul, but to itinerant evangelists. The title, therefore, seems to have been added sometime after the document was drawn up.

Among written sources used by the author, we find two quotations from the Old Testament (xiv. 13 from Mal. i. 11, 14, and xvi. 7 from Zech. xiv. 5), two from the New Testament (both from Matthew), and one probably from some unknown apocryphal book (i. 6, 'It has been said, "Let your alms sweat into your hands until you know to whom you are giving"'). The two quotations from Matthew are, 'Do not pray as the hypocrites, but as the Lord commanded in his gospel, pray thus: "Our Father who art in heaven . . . for thine is the power and the glory forever"' (viii. 2, from Matt. vi. 5 ff.), and 'Let no one eat or drink of your eucharist except those who have been baptised in the name of the Lord; for to this also the saying of the Lord is applicable, "Do not give that which is holy to the dogs"' (ix. 5, from Matt. vii. 6).

Apart from such explicit quotations, the *Didache* also contains three separate references to what the Lord commanded in the Gospel (xi. 3; xv. 3 and 4), as well as echoes from several other New Testament books. An analysis of these reminiscences shows that the Gospel according to Matthew was the chief source for the author's knowledge of the teaching of Jesus, but alongside this written gospel he was familiar also with phrases from oral tradition.

In the eucharistic prayers (chaps. ix–x) there seem to be faint echoes of the eucharistic passages of the Fourth Gospel (vi. 25–58) and of Jesus' prayer in John xvii, but they are not sufficiently precise to assure us that the author had read a copy of the Gospel according to John. At most they reflect a tradition common to him and the Fourth Evangelist.

On the question of the use of the Pauline Epistles, almost every intermediate position has been held between that of Harnack, who could find no single clear trace of their use, and that of J. Armitage Robinson, who thought that the Didachist was thoroughly acquainted with 1 Corinthians: 'He has imitated its subdivision, borrowed its words and phrases, and modified its thoughts to suit his own purposes.'[18] Most investigators, however, find little influence from Paul.

By way of summary, we can see from the *Didache* that itinerant apostles and prophets still find an important place in the life of the Church, but this authority is declining. Their activity is surrounded with all sorts of precautions and rests ultimately on the authority of the traditional teaching deriving from the Lord, whose manner they must exhibit: 'Not everyone who speaks in a spirit is a prophet, except he have the ways of the Lord. By their ways, then, the false prophet and the true prophet shall be distinguished' (xi. 8). The author refers to the gospel, but he cites only words of Jesus. This 'gospel', which is without doubt the Gospel according to Matthew, is not regarded as a necessary source from which the words of the Lord, with indispensable warrants, come to the faithful, but quite simply as a convenient collection of these words.

IV. PAPIAS OF HIERAPOLIS

Among the first of those who show some interest in early Christian writings as well as in oral traditions was Papias, bishop of Hierapolis in Phrygia, a city in which a Christian church had been established through the efforts of Epaphras, one of the apostle Paul's fellow workers (Col. iv. 12–13). Next to nothing is known of Papias' life beyond the comment of Irenaeus (*Ad. Haer.* v. xxxiii. 3–4) that he was 'a man of long ago' (ἀρχαῖος ἀνήρ) who had heard the apostle John preach and was also a friend of Polycarp, bishop of Smyrna. From this

---

[18] *Barnabas, Hermas and the Didache* (London, 1920), p. 97. Cf. J. R. McRay, 'The Use of 1 Corinthians in the Early Church', Ph.D. diss., University of Chicago, 1968, who concludes that the author probably knew 1 Corinthians (pp. 31–3).

it appears that Papias must have lived from about A.D. 70 to about 140.[19]

Papias is best remembered as the author of a treatise in five books entitled *Expositions of the Sayings of the Lord* (Λογίων κυριακῶν ἐξηγήσεις), of which, unfortunately, only small fragments survive today. From the preface of this work it seems that Papias was eager to learn details of the life of Christ from living tradition, transmitted by disciples of the Lord. After stating that he was not so much concerned with the quantity of the tradition he could obtain but with its quality as corresponding to the truth, he continues:

If ever anyone came who had been a follower of the presbyters[20] I inquired into the words of the presbyters, what Andrew or Peter or Philip or Thomas or James or John or Matthew or any other of the Lord's disciples had said, and what Aristion and the presbyter John, the Lord's disciples, were saying. For I did not think that information from books would help me so much as the utterances of a living and surviving voice.[21]

From this quotation it is clear that the sayings of the Lord which Papias undertook to explain were drawn not only from written documents but also from oral tradition. His informants of what Andrew, Peter, Philip, Thomas, James, John, and Matthew had said, or what Aristion and the presbyter John were saying, must have been Palestinian Christians who had emigrated to Asia Minor after the fall of Jerusalem in 70. They obviously enjoyed considerable prestige from the fact that they had lived in the same country with Jesus, and so were considered to be bearers of a tradition that was particularly authentic and precious. Papias thus recognized two sources of Christian tradition: one was conveyed by word of mouth, the other was embodied in written gospels. That he preferred the

---

[19] For a discussion of various opinions as to the date of Papias, see Ulrich H. J. Körtner, *Papias von Hierapolis; Ein Beitrag zur Geschichte des frühen Christentums* (Göttingen, 1983). An earlier dating of Papias' literary work (A.D. 95–110) is proposed by Robert W. Yarborough, 'The Date of Papias; A Reassessment', *Journal of the Evangelical Theological Society*, xxvi (1983), pp. 181–91.

[20] In the New Testament and in early Christian literature the term 'presbyter' is somewhat vague in its connotations. By itself it means 'an elderly person'; later it came to designate one who, by reason of age, possessed rank and influence in the community. Another connotation was 'a person of the older generation'.

[21] Quoted by Eusebius, *Hist. eccl.* III. xxxix. 4.

former was due more to psychological than dogmatic reasons; later in the second century tastes would begin to shift from oral to written sources.[22]

Some of these oral traditions are dramatic enough.[23] According to Eusebius (*Hist. eccl.* III. xxxix. 9), Papias had learned from the daughters of Philip (cf. Acts xxi. 8) about the resurrection of a dead man in his [Philip's] own time. He also tells a tale about Justus Barsabbas' drinking a deadly poison without suffering any harm.

Besides such oral traditions, which Papias delighted to collect, he also included in his *Expositions* two brief accounts

[22] On the change from an oral to a written culture in the Mediterranean world, particularly during the early patristic period when literacy had not yet been deeply interiorized, see Walter J. Ong, *Interfaces of the World; Studies in the Evolution of Consciousness and Culture* (Ithaca, NY, 1977), pp. 260–71, and Charles Talbert's response to Albert Lord, 'Oral Literature and the Gospels', *The Relationships among the Gospels: An Interdisciplinary Dialogue*, ed. by William O. Walker, Jr. (San Antonio, 1978), pp. 93–102. Ong also discusses features of the consciousness of self and the world as held by people in the second and third centuries in his article, 'World as View and World as Event', *American Anthropologist*, lxxi (1969), pp. 634–47, and in his book, *Orality and Literacy: The Technologizing of the World* (London, 1982).

For a comparison of early Christianity with other religions in the use of sacred books, see Allen Menzies, 'The Natural History of Sacred Books; Some Suggestions for a Preface to the History of the Canon of Scripture', *American Journal of Theology*, i (1897), pp. 71–94; Raymond T. Stamm, 'The Function of Sacred Books in Early Christianity and the Graeco-Roman Religions', Ph.D. diss., University of Chicago, 1926; *Holy Book and Holy Tradition*, International Colloquium held in the Faculty of Theology, University of Manchester, ed. by F. F. Bruce and E. G. Rupp (Manchester and Grand Rapids, 1968); Christopher Evans, *Is 'Holy Scripture' Christian?* (London, 1971), pp. 21–36; and the discussions on 'Oral and Written Documentation of Religious Tradition', *Science of Religion; Studies in Methodology* (= *Procedings of the Study Conference of the International Association for the History of Religions*, held in Turku, Finland, 27–31 August 1973), ed. by Lauri Honko (The Hague, 1979), pp. 3–139. In W. H. Kelber's *The Oral and the Written Gospel* (Philadelphia, 1983), 'the antithesis between orality and textuality seems to be very much overdrawn and indeed melodramatized' (J. D. G. Dunn, *Interpretation*, xxxix [1985], p. 74).

[23] From Apollinaris of Laodicea we learn that Papias included in the fourth book of his *Expositions* grotesque legends concerning the end of Judas Iscariot: 'His body bloated to such an extent that, even where a wagon passes with ease, he was not able to pass; no, not even his bloated head by itself could do so. His eyelids, for example, swelled to such dimensions, they say (φησίν), that neither could he himself see the light at all, nor could his eyes be detected even by a physician's optical instrument... After suffering an agony of pain and punishment, he finally went, as they say (φησίν), to his own place; and owing to the stench the ground has been deserted and uninhabited till now; in fact, even to the present day no one can pass that place without holding one's nose so abundant was the discharge from his body and so far over the ground did it spread'. (Apollinaris's text is reconstructed from various sources by A. Hilgenfeld, 'Papias von Hierapolis', *Zeitschrift für wissenschaftliche Theologie*, xviii [1875], pp. 262–5.)

about the composition of the Gospels of Mark and Matthew.
The notice he gives to the second is very brief, merely one
sentence: 'Matthew composed the sayings (or, oracles, τὰ
λόγια) in a Hebrew dialect, and each one interpreted (or,
translated) them as best he could'.[24]

This enigmatic account refers, it is generally supposed, to
one of the sources of the present Gospel according to Matthew,
and may imply that the collecting of the sayings of Christ was
attributed to Matthew because, in view of his earlier profession
as tax collector, one could be sure that he knew how to write.[25]
The reference to Matthew's composition in 'a (or, the) Hebrew
dialect' (Ἑβραΐδι διαλέκτῳ) is ordinarily taken to mean a
Semitic language, either Hebrew itself or an Aramaic dialect.
The suggestion that the expression should be understood
merely as an account in Greek written in a Hebraic literary
style[26] does not take seriously the concluding reference to the
difficulty one experienced in translating or interpreting the
document.

The idea of improvised translations made from a Semitic
original may have arisen when it became necessary to explain
the divergences that would become apparent when one compared the Gospel according to Matthew, the Gospel according
to the Hebrews, and other Aramaic or Greek gospels that were
related. We can detect here an apologetic intention in Papias'
comment concerning Matthew's work.

Such apologetic interest is still more prominent in his
comments on Mark—showing that criticisms directed against
Mark were more pointed than those directed against Matthew.
According to Papias, again as quoted by Eusebius (*Hist. eccl.* III.
xxxix. 15),

The presbyter used to say this: Mark, having become Peter's
interpreter (ἑρμηνευτής, perhaps 'spokesman' or 'secretary') wrote
down accurately all that he remembered [of Peter's preaching]

---

[24] Quoted by Eusebius, *Hist. eccl.* III. xxxix. 16.

[25] It is also possible to understand Papias' reference to λόγια ('oracles') as the
utterances of Old Testament prophets (see Lampe, ed., *Patristic Greek Lexicon*, p. 806a);
in that case Matthew would have gathered Old Testament proof-texts predicting the
Messiah.

[26] So Joseph Kürzinger, 'Das Papiaszeugnis und die Erstgestalt des Matthäusevan-
geliums', *Biblische Zeitschrift*, N.F. iv (1960), pp. 19–38; and Robert Gundry, *Matthew;
A Commentary on his Literary and Theological Art* (Grand Rapids, 1982), pp. 609–22.

without, however, recording in order (τάξει) the things said or done by the Lord. For he neither heard the Lord nor followed him, but afterwards, as I have said, [heard and followed] Peter, who adapted his discourse to the needs (πρὸς τὰς χρείας)[27] [of his hearers], but not making, as it were, an arrangement (σύνταξιν) of the Lord's sayings, so that Mark did nothing wrong in thus writing down single points as he remembered them. For he was careful of one thing—to omit nothing of what he had heard or to falsify anything in them.

From this account we can detect that three criticisms had been raised against Mark's Gospel: (a) Mark had not heard Jesus, nor had he followed him. (b) What he wrote lacked order, either rhetorical or chronological.[28] (c) His Gospel is incomplete.

In reply to these criticisms, Papias states that the guaranty of the Gospel is furnished by Peter, and that the conditions under which it was written explain why it is without perfect order and presents some gaps—which are a kind of testimony to Mark's honesty in taking down all that Peter was accustomed to preach.

Other scattered evidence preserved by Eusebius, Jerome, Philip of Side, as well as several later Fathers, indicates that Papias knew the Fourth Gospel, 1 Peter, 1 John, and the Apocalypse. As for the Gospel according to Luke and the Epistles of Paul, we hear nothing in the extracts that have happened to survive.[29]

By way of summary, Papias stands as a kind of bridge

[27] For an alternative interpretation of χρεία, i.e. brief biographical apophthegms or gnomic sayings for instructional purposes, cf. R. O. P. Taylor, *The Groundwork of the Gospels* (Oxford, 1946), pp. 29 f., 75–90, and Josef Kürzinger, 'Die Aussage des Papias von Hierapolis zur literarischen Form des Markusevangeliums', *Biblische Zeitschrift*, N.F. xxi (1977), pp. 245–64, reprinted in his *Papias von Hierapolis und die Evangelien des Neuen Testaments* (Regensburg, 1983), pp. 43–67.

[28] Grant (*The Formation of the New Testament*, p. 71) thinks that the criticism of Mark's order was in comparison with that of the Gospel of John (since the arrangement of Mark is close to that of Matthew and Luke). The word τάξις, however, has other meanings beside 'order'. Thus, Kleist urges the consideration that in Koine and Modern Greek τάξις can mean 'verbatim, with full detail, without any gaps in the narrative' (see J. A. Kleist, 'Rereading the Papias Fragment on St. Mark', *St. Louis University Studies*, Ser. A: *Humanities*, i [1945], pp. 1–17), and Kürzinger (op. cit.) maintains that Papias is using τάξις as a Greek rhetorical term, signifying 'literary composition', and by it defends Mark's uncouth style as literature.

[29] Although one might have expected to find some reference made by Papias to the Gospel according to Luke, it would have been altogether unusual for him to refer to Paul's Epistles in his *Expositions of the Sayings of the Lord*.

between the oral and the written stages in the transmission of the gospel tradition. Although he professes to have a marked preference for the oral tradition, one nevertheless sees at work the causes that, more and more, would lead to the rejection of that form of tradition in favour of written gospels. On the whole, therefore, the testimony of Papias concerning the development of the canon of the New Testament is significant chiefly in reflecting the usage of a community in which devotion to oral tradition hindered the development of a clear idea of canonicity.

V. THE EPISTLE OF BARNABAS

The *Epistle of Barnabas* is a theological tract and an epistle only in appearance. Both Clement of Alexandria and Origen valued the work highly and attributed its composition to Barnabas, the companion and co-worker of the apostle Paul. But such attribution of authority is certainly mistaken, if only because the epistle implies that the fall of Jerusalem (A.D. 70) took place some little time earlier (xvi. 3f.). The unknown author was probably a Christian teacher of Gentile origin who is concerned to prove that the death of Christ on the cross is a sacrifice that fulfills a plan set forth in the Old Testament (ix. 7–9). Throughout his interpretation of the Old Testament he takes a radically anti-Jewish attitude that was unique in primitive Christian literature. In a sustained attack upon Judaism, the writer declares that the distinctive enactments of the Mosaic Law, including animal sacrifices and the material temple, are mistakes arising from Jewish blindness and reliance upon an evil angel (ix. 4). By means of allegorical interpretation Barnabas imposes upon the Old Testament, including even the dietary laws in Leviticus, a meaning totally foreign to the intention of the original authors. In view of his fondness for such symbolic and typological interpretation, it is generally thought that the author was a resident in or near Alexandria. Most scholars think that the general tenor of the contents of the epistle suggests a date in the first half of the second century.

In his frequent quotations from the Old Testament, Barnabas is fairly exact in citing well-known contexts belonging to the Psalter and to the book of Isaiah, but elsewhere he appears to trust to memory, and not to concern himself greatly about the precise words of his author. There are nearly one hundred instances that involve formulas of quotation, most of which are general and vague; for example, 'Scripture says', 'it is written', 'the prophet says', 'the Lord (or God) says (or said)', 'it (or he) says'. Occasionally he refers to the book or speaker by name (Jacob, Moses, David, Isaiah, Daniel).

Besides quoting Old Testament prophets, Barnabas also cites as prophets the authors of the Wisdom of Solomon (ii. 12), 2 Esdras (xii. 1), and 2 Baruch (xi. 9f.), the last two of whom wrote during the early Christian era. He not only refers to Enoch in support for a prediction of the last times, but also quotes a statement from 1 Enoch with the formula 'For the Scripture says' (xvi. 5–6). It is clear that, unlike other Apostolic Fathers, such as Hermas, Barnabas is a 'scholarly' author who has read widely and quotes frequently from a variety of books. The question arises, did his sources include any books of the New Testament?

As regards the gospels, the following three passages are taken by some as showing that Barnabas was acquainted with the Gospel according to Matthew.

(1) In vii. 3 he states that when Jesus was crucified 'he was given vinegar ($ \ddot{o}\xi o s $) and gall ($ \chi o\lambda\acute{\eta} $) to drink'. All four Gospels mention that vinegar was offered to Jesus, but only Matthew (xxvii. 34) refers to 'wine mixed with gall' being also given. But it is also possible that Barnabas, looking for Old Testament types and prophecies, was influenced by Ps. lxix. 21 ('They gave me gall for food, and for my thirst they gave me vinegar to drink') rather than by Matthew's account.

(2) In iv. 14 Barnabas exhorts his readers to take heed 'lest haply we be found, as it is written ($ \dot{\omega}s\ \gamma\acute{\epsilon}\gamma\rho\alpha\pi\tau\alpha\iota $), "many are called, but few are chosen"' ($ \pi o\lambda\lambda o\grave{\iota}\ \kappa\lambda\eta\tau o\acute{\iota},\ \dot{o}\lambda\acute{\iota}\gamma o\iota\ \delta\grave{\epsilon}\ \dot{\epsilon}\kappa\lambda\epsilon\kappa\tau o\acute{\iota} $). While this looks very much like a quotation from Matthew (xxii. 14), it is also just possible, as some think, that Barnabas and Matthew are drawing upon a common source for the saying, whose proverbial character seems proved by its having been added to Matt. xx. 16 in many manuscripts (C D N W $ \Theta $ Fam.1 Fam.13 *et al.*).

(3) Barnabas knows also that Jesus 'came not to call the righteous but sinners' (v. 9), a statement that occurs verbatim in Matthew (ix. 13) and in Mark (ii. 17).

Whether Barnabas knew the Fourth Gospel is much less certain. In the context of discussing the bronze serpent that Moses was told to put on a pole (Num. xxi. 7f.), Barnabas declares (xii. 7) that here we have again 'the glory of Jesus'—an apparent allusion to John iii. 14.

As for Barnabas' knowledge of other New Testament books, some have found what may be echoes of passages from 1 and 2 Timothy. His reference to Jesus as calling sinners, including the apostles, who were 'lawless beyond all sin' (v. 9), reminds one of the saying in 1 Tim. i. 15, 'Christ Jesus came into the world to save sinners—of whom I am the chief'. Again, the statement that according to Old Testament prophets it was ordained that the Lord was to 'be made manifest in the flesh' (v. 6) may echo the first line of what is often taken as an early creedal statement preserved in 1 Tim. iii. 16, 'He was manifested in the flesh, vindicated in the Spirit, etc.' It is just possible that Barnabas also knew 2 Timothy, for his mention of 'grace', 'manifested', and 'the destruction of death' (v. 6) recalls a similar combination of words in 2 Tim. i. 9–10. The same epistle seems to be echoed in the reference to the Son of God as the Lord and 'Judge of the living and the dead' (2 Tim. iv. 1; *Barn.* vii. 2), unless in both cases a common formula of Christian faith is cited independently.

Among several other reminiscences that could be mentioned, reference may be made to the word ποδήρη in Barnabas' description of Jesus when he will come on the day of judgement wearing a scarlet robe 'down to the feet' (vii. 9). The substantival use of this word, found in the New Testament only in Rev. i. 13 in the description of the heavenly Christ, suggests that Barnabas may have been influenced by the Apocalypse.

By way of summary, one can see that for Barnabas the Scriptures are what we call the Old Testament, including several books outside the Hebrew canon. Most of his contacts with Synoptic traditions involve simple sentences that might well have been known to a Christian of that time from oral tradition. As against the single instance of his using the formula, 'it is written', in introducing the statement, 'Many are called, but few are chosen', must be placed his virtual neglect of the New Testament. If, on the other hand, he wrote shortly before or after 130, the focus of his subject-matter would not make it necessary to do much quoting from New Testament books—if indeed he knew many of them. In either case he provides little or no evidence for the development of the New Testament canon.

VI. POLYCARP OF SMYRNA

The epistle that Polycarp, bishop of Smyrna, wrote to the Christians at Philippi is intimately connected with the epistles and martyrdom of Ignatius. About A.D. 110 while *en route* to Rome where he suffered martyrdom, Ignatius passed through Smyrna and was warmly greeted by the church and its bishop. Subsequently he was taken by his guards to Philippi, where local Christian leaders visited him. After his departure they wrote to Polycarp requesting him to send them copies of the epistles that Ignatius had written to him and to several churches in Asia Minor. This he did, adding a kind of covering letter of his own (see xiii. 2). In this Polycarp urges his readers to stand fast in the faith (chaps. iv–vi), to avoid heretical teachings (chap. vii), to look to the examples of martyrdom suffered by Ignatius and others (chap. ix), and to persevere in philanthropy and good works (chap. x). He concludes by saying that he is sending them copies of the epistles of Ignatius, as they requested, and asks them to send him the latest news about Ignatius and his companions (xiii. 2).

A problem arises when one compares this last request—which implies that Ignatius 'and those who are with him' (*qui cum eo sunt*) have not yet suffered martyrdom—with Polycarp's earlier statement (ix. 1f.) concerning the faithfulness and fortitude of Ignatius and other Christian martyrs, who are now with the Lord (εἰσὶ παρὰ τῷ κυρίῳ). In 1936 P. N. Harrison[30] attempted to reconcile the two passages by the theory that the present epistle really consists of two epistles: one, a short note (chaps. xiii—xiv), written not long after Ignatius had been taken to Rome for martyrdom, and the other (chaps. i–xii), written at a time of crisis in the Philippian

---

[30] P. N. Harrison, *Polycarp's Two Epistles to the Philippians* (Oxford, 1936). For what can be said against Harrison's theory, see especially H.-C. Puech in *Revue de l'histoire des religions*, cxix (1939), pp. 96–102; in support of the theory (though not for the late date that Harrison suggests for the second letter), see L. W. Barnard, *Studies in the Apostolic Fathers and their Background* (Oxford, 1966), pp. 31–40.

church, perhaps about A.D. 135. These two epistles, Harrison argued, were later combined into one. While this theory has gained approval from a number of scholars, there is, however, no compelling reason for dating the second epistle as late as 135; a year or so after the first epistle would satisfy the internal evidence of the text. In fact, it is altogether possible that Polycarp treats Ignatius' zeal for martyrdom as so certain to reach its goal that he can speak of death as already accomplished; in this case there was one epistle, written early rather than late.[31] In any case, however, the difference between 110 and 135 is not very great.

Despite the proximity in time between Ignatius and Polycarp, as well as the obvious affinity of their spirits in Christian fortitude, one recognizes in Polycarp a temperament much less oriented to ecclesiastical polity and possessing a much wider acquaintance with the New Testament. Proportionate to the length of what they wrote, Polycarp has two or three times more quotations and reminiscences from the New Testament than does Ignatius; of 112 Biblical reminiscences, about one hundred are from the New Testament with only a dozen from the Old Testament. Quotations that enable us to gain a rather precise idea of the authority that Polycarp recognized in them include the following.

The primary authorities which he identifies as spiritual norms for the Christian life are three in number:

So then 'let us serve him [Christ] with fear and all reverence', as he himself commanded us, as did the apostles, who preached the gospel to us, and the prophets, who proclaimed beforehand the coming of our Lord (vi. 3).

Here we can see a change of perspective; the centre of gravity is displaced. In place of the authority of the prophets stands the authority of the gospel, and it is from the authority of the gospel and because they announced it that the authority of the prophets is derived. As for the apostles, they appear as intermediaries between the gospel of the Lord and the believers.

From another passage in his epistle we see that Polycarp

---

[31] This is now the view taken by Henning Paulsen in his revision of Bauer's *Die Apostolischen Väter*, 2nd ed. (*Handbuch zum Neuen Testament*, xviii; Tübingen, 1985), pp. 112-3.

assumes that a body of teaching, oral or written and similar to the Sermon on the Mount, was familiar to the Philippian church:

Remember what the Lord taught when he said, 'Do not judge, that you may not be judged; forgive and you will be forgiven; be merciful, that you may obtain mercy; the measure you give will be the measure you get'; and 'Blessed are the poor, and those who are persecuted for righteousness' sake, for theirs is the kingdom of God' (ii. 3).

Here one finds a combination of Matt. vii. 1–2 and Luke vi. 36–8, but there are also some elements that are not present in the canonical Gospels. The second part of the passage is a combination of two of Jesus' beatitudes (Matt. v. 3 and 10). In both cases the words are cited as the words of Jesus and not as Scripture. Polycarp feels no need to guarantee the words he cites by the authority of the evangelists who report them.

In another case the citation is textual:

Let us persevere in fasting, and beseech the all-seeing God 'not to lead us into temptation', even as the Lord said, 'The spirit is willing, but the flesh is weak' (vii. 2).

This last statement is drawn from Matt. xxvi. 41 and is expressly presented as a word of the Lord. It is significant also that, in the preceding phrase, Polycarp reproduces a petition from the Lord's Prayer without mentioning its origin. The 'word of the Lord' supplies authority by its own content and because it comes from the Lord.

Among other New Testament writings to which Polycarp alludes, we find that he is acquainted with Romans, 1 Corinthians, Galatians, Ephesians, Philippians, 2 Thessalonians, 1 Timothy, and 2 Timothy. The absence of reminiscences from 2 Corinthians, Colossians, 1 Thessalonians, Titus, and Philemon can perhaps be considered fortuitous.

As for the other New Testament epistles, Polycarp almost certainly knows the Epistle to the Hebrews; he calls Christ 'the eternal high priest' (xii. 2; cf. Heb. vi. 20; vii. 3) and seems to echo Heb. xii. 28 ('let us serve him with fear and all reverence', vi. 3). In his warning against heresy (vii. 1) the ringing declaration, 'Everyone who does not confess that Jesus Christ

has come in the flesh is an antichrist', is obviously derived from
1 John iv. 2–3. Many allusions to 1 Peter—which he must have
known practically by heart—occur throughout his epistle.

How far did Polycarp consider these and other similar
statements made by the apostles to be 'Scripture'? It is possible
that he does so on one occasion when he remarks, 'As it is said
in these Scriptures, "Be ye angry and sin not" and "Let not the
sun go down upon your wrath"' (xii. 1). The former of these
two quotations comes from Ps. iv. 5, and both occur together in
Eph. iv. 26—an epistle which he knows and alludes to several
times elsewhere. The words 'these Scriptures' and the linking
word 'and' seem to imply that Polycarp regards himself as
making two separate quotations, but it is also possible that the
collocation of the two passages is due to his quoting both from
Ephesians. In either case he calls Ephesians 'Scripture'. Since,
however, this is the only place where he designates as 'Scripture' a quotation from the New Testament, some have argued
that Polycarp, quoting from memory, mistakenly attributes
both passages to the Old Testament.[32] It is difficult to decide
firmly among these several ways of understanding Polycarp's
words, but the first mentioned has the advantage of taking his
statement in its natural sense.[33]

By way of summary, the short *Epistle of Polycarp* contains
proportionately far more allusions to the writings of the New
Testament than are present in any other of the Apostolic
Fathers. He certainly had a collection of at least eight Pauline
Epistles (including two of the Pastorals),[34] and was acquainted
as well with Hebrews, 1 Peter, and 1 John. As for the Gospels,
he cites as sayings of the Lord phrases that we find in Matthew
and Luke. With one exception, none of Polycarp's many

[32] E.g. W. Bauer, *Der Polycarpbrief* (Tübingen, 1920), pp. 296 f., and H. Koester,
Synoptische Überlieferung bei den Apostolischen Vätern (*Texte und Untersuchungen*, lxv; Berlin,
1957), p. 113.

[33] See C. M. Nielsen, 'Polycarp, Paul and the Scriptures', *Anglican Theological
Review*, xlvii (1965), pp. 199–216.

[34] Polycarp supplies the earliest clear reminiscences we have of the Pastoral Epistles.
Against the hypothesis that the author of the Pastorals was Polycarp himself (so H. von
Campenhausen, 'Polykarp und die Pastoralen', *Sitzungsberichte der Heidelberger Akademie
der Wissenschaften*, philos.-hist. Kl., 1951, 2; reprinted in his *Aus der Frühzeit des
Christentums* [Tübingen, 1963], pp. 197–252), is the striking literary difference between
the Pastorals and Polycarp's epistle, to say nothing of placing the Pastorals after the
time of Marcion.

allusions is cited as Scripture—and that exception, as we have seen, is held by some to have been mistakenly attributed to the Old Testament. At the same time Polycarp's mind is not only saturated with ideas and phrases derived from a considerable number of writings that later came to be regarded as New Testament Scriptures, but he also displays latent respect for these apostolic documents as possessing an authority lacking in other writings. Polycarp, as Grant remarks,[35] 'clearly differentiates the apostolic age from his own time and, presumably for this reason, does not use the letters of Ignatius as authorities—even though they "contain faith, endurance, and all the edification which pertains to our Lord" (xiii. 2)'.

VII. HERMAS OF ROME

One of the most popular books produced in the early Church was the *Shepherd* of Hermas. Not only was it frequently quoted and for a time regarded as inspired, but more than twenty separate parchment or papyrus fragments, dating from the second to the sixth centuries, have survived of the Greek text,[36] as well as portions of it in two Latin versions (of the second and the fourth/fifth century respectively) and in two Coptic versions (Sahidic and Achmimic). There is also a paraphrastic Ethiopic translation, and scraps in Middle Persian were found among the Manichaean texts from Turfan.

The book is a picturesque religious allegory, in most of which a rugged figure dressed like a shepherd is Hermas' guide.

[35] R. M. Grant, *The Formation of the New Testament* (New York, 1965), p. 106.

[36] To the list of seventeen items given by G. H. R. Horsley, *New Documents Illustrating Early Christianity*, ii (North Ryde, 1982), pp. 16 f., must be added the recently published P.Oxy. 3526, 3527, and 3528, as well as P. Bodmer XXXIX (as yet unpublished, but see A. Carlini, 'Un nuovo testimone delle visioni de Erma', *Atene e Roma*, NS xxx [1985], pp. 107–202) and two Papyri Graecae Wessely Pragenses (for an announcement of their forthcoming publication, see *Studi classici e orientali*, xxxiii [1983], p. 117).

It is remarkable that two of the Greek fragments that preserve 'Mandates' date, as it seems, from the second century: P. Mich. 130, late 2nd cent., and P. Iand. 4. Concerning the latter, previously dated to the 3rd/4th cent., P. J. Parsons (in a letter dated 28 Oct. 1985) reports that, in a discussion concerning the fragment at an international conference of classical scholars held at Dublin in 1984, there was general agreement that it 'should be dated earlier (with all the usual reservations about palaeographic dating): I thought ii A.D., and other palaeographers present agreed on earlier ii rather than later ii'. The implication of the latter opinion, if sustained, for the date of the origin of the *Shepherd* is obvious.

From this the book took its name, 'The Shepherd' (ὁ Ποιμήν). Comprising a rambling *mélange* of five 'Visions', twelve 'Mandates', and ten 'Similitudes', the book is characterized by strong moral earnestness. It is primarily a call to repentance and adherence to a life of strict morality, addressed to Christians among whom the memory of persecution is still fresh (*Vis.* iii. 2. 5; *Sim.* ix. 28), and over whom now hangs the shadow of another great tribulation (*Vis.* ii. 2; iv. 2).

Although Origen and Jerome thought the author of the *Shepherd* to be the Hermas mentioned by Paul in the Epistle to the Romans (xvi. 14), internal and external evidence alike points to an author who lived at a somewhat later date. The writer indicates that he is contemporary with a certain Clement who has had the function of communicating with believers in other cities (*Vis.* ii. 4). If, as would seem probable, we are to identify this Clement with the bishop of Rome who wrote to the church at Corinth about A.D. 96, then the *Shepherd* would have to be placed at the end of the first century or the beginning of the second. On the other hand, according to a statement in the Muratorian Canon (see Appendix IV. I below; the point recurs in the *Liberian Catalogue*, also known as 'The Chronographer of 354'), our author was a brother of Pius, bishop of Rome, who died about 154. The presence of certain literary and theological differences within the book has long puzzled commentators, several of whom have suggested multiple authorship.[37] Perhaps the least unsatisfactory resolution of the conflicting evidence is to suppose that Hermas was a younger contemporary of Clement and wrote (and perhaps published) sections of his rambling treatise at intervals over a considerable period of time, finally gathering them together in one volume toward the middle of the second

---

[37] S. Giet, for example, has argued that the book was produced by three different writers; cf. his *Hermas et les pasteurs: les trois auteurs du Pasteur d'Hermas* (Paris, 1963). The evidence, however, may just as well point not to several authors but to one not very competent author who wrote his work in three stages; see R. M. Grant in *Gnomon*, xxxvi (1964), pp. 357–9; R. Joly, 'Hermas et le Pasteur', *Vigiliae Christianae*, xxi (1967), pp. 201–18; and L. W. Barnard, 'The Shepherd of Hermas in Recent Study', *Heythrop Journal*, ix (1968), pp. 29–36. On the 'textual fluidity' of the text of the *Shepherd*, see 'La tradizione testuale del Pastore di Erma e i nuovi papiri', by Antonio Carlini in *Le strade del testo*, ed. by G. Cavallo (Bari, 1987), pp. 23–47.

century.[38] It must be acknowledged, however, that in view of the lack of conclusive evidence and amid conflicting interpretations among scholars who have given attention to the *Shepherd*, the problem of its date continues to be unresolved.

The personality of Hermas is clearly revealed in the book. With garrulous *naïveté* he relates all manner of intimate details concerning himself and his family. We learn that, as a Christian slave, he had been sold in Rome to a woman called Rhoda, who set him free. As a freedman he married, acquired a fortune (though not always by lawful transaction), and through ill luck had again been reduced to poverty. He tells us that during the persecution his children apostatized, that they betrayed their own parents, and that they led a disorderly life. Hermas depicts himself as slow of understanding, but insatiable in curiosity (*Mand.* xii. 4, *Sim.* v. 5), and at the same time as 'patient and good tempered, and always smiling', 'full of all simplicity and of great guilelessness' (*Vis.* i. 2). We may conclude that he was a simple man of limited outlook, but genuinely pious and conscientious. At any rate, his book was highly esteemed in the early Church for its moral value, and, according to Athanasius, served as a textbook for catechumens. In fact, in parts of the Church during the second and third centuries it was sometimes regarded as inspired Scripture—so, for example, by Irenaeus and Clement of Alexandria. In codex Sinaiticus, a fourth-century copy of the Greek Bible, the *Shepherd* (with the *Epistle of Barnabas*) stands after the close of the New Testament.

Hermas makes no definite quotation from either Old or New Testament. At the same time, however, here and there one detects echoes of Scriptural words and ideas, which the author handles with a light touch, working them into new combinations. He seems to have known the Gospel according to John

---

[38] On the basis of codicological computations, it appears that the Michigan codex of Hermas (second half of 3rd cent.) and P. Oxy. 3527 (early 3rd cent.) originally excluded the first four 'Visions', in which the figure of the Shepherd does not appear. Did the two parts of the *Shepherd* have a separate textual history at any stage? Variations among the manuscript witnesses as to the titles of the several 'Visions' suggested to Kirsopp Lake that two books by Hermas 'have been combined into one, the first book having been "The Visions of Hermas" and the second "The Shepherd" ' (*Harvard Theological Review*, xviii [1925], p. 279).

and at last one of the Synoptic Gospels,[39] as well as the Epistle to the Ephesians and the Epistle of James, as the following citations will show. In *Sim.* ix. 12, the declaration that one enters the kingdom of God only by receiving the Name of the Son of God seems to be a reminiscence of John iii. 18. In *Sim.* ix. 20, Hermas, thinking of the Parable of the Wheat and the Tares, declares that those involved in much business are like thorns, and are choked by their business transactions. 'Such persons', he concludes, 'will have difficulty in entering into the kingdom of God.' But though the rich have difficulty entering the kingdom (cf. Matt. xix. 23ff.), the childlike will live free from wickedness in a state of innocence and will, 'without doubt, dwell in the kingdom of God' (*Sim.* ix. 29ff.).

It is likely that Eph. iv. 3–6, which enjoins peace and unity in one body and one Spirit, supplied Hermas with ideas concerning the ideal state for the members of the Church. In *Sim.* ix. 13 he twice alludes to believers as those who become or possess 'one spirit and one body'. In *Sim.* ix. 17 Hermas declares that those who have been baptized 'have one understanding and one mind, and their faith became one and their love one', and in ix. 18 he looks forward to the time when the Church, having been purified, will become 'one body, of one mind, of one understanding, of one faith, of one love'.

The coincidence of Hermas with expressions in the Epistle of James are exceedingly numerous, and whole sections of the *Shepherd* seem to have been framed with evident recollection of that Epistle (for example, *Vis.* iii. 9; *Mand.* ii. 9; *Sim.* v. 4).[40] The word δίψυχος ('double-minded'), which in the New Testa-

---

[39] It has been thought that Hermas alludes to the four Gospels in *Vis.* iii. 13, where he makes a cryptic reference to a couch that has 'four feet and stands firmly; for the world also is upheld by means of four elements'. Charles Taylor argued that this statement was the source of the famous saying of Irenaeus that there can be neither more nor fewer than four Gospels, because there are four regions of the world, and four catholic winds, etc.; see Taylor's *The Witness of Hermas to the Four Gospels* (Cambridge, 1892), pp. 13 ff. The weakness of the argument is that we do not know definitely that Hermas had four and only four Gospels (for further considerations against Taylor's interpretation, see Koester, op. cit., pp. 253 ff.).

[40] The parallels have been set forth by Theodor Zahn (*Der Hirt des Hermas* [Gotha, 1868], pp. 396–409), J. B. Mayor (*The Epistle of St. James* [Cambridge, 1910], pp. lxxiv–lxxviii), and E. Masseux (*Influence de l'Évangile de saint Matthieu sur la littérature chrétienne avant saint Irénée* [Louvain, 1950], pp. 310–21).

ment occurs only in James (i. 8 and iv. 8) and not in the Septuagint or anywhere in secular Greek, seems to have caught Hermas' fancy; he uses it 19 times, as well as the cognate verb δυψυχεῖν 20 times, and the substantive δυψυχία 16 times.[41]

By way of summary, it is obvious that Hermas was not given to making quotations from literature; in fact, the only actual book anywhere named and quoted in the *Shepherd* (*Vis.* ii. 3) is an obscure Jewish apocalypse known as the book of *Eldad and Modat*.[42] Despite reminiscences from Matthew, Ephesians, and James, Hermas makes no comment that would lead us to think that he regarded them as canonical Scripture. From the testimony contained in the *Shepherd*, it can in any case be observed how uneven during the course of the second century was the development of the idea of the canon.

VIII. THE SO-CALLED SECOND EPISTLE OF CLEMENT

The writing that goes by the name of the 'Second Epistle of Clement' is neither an epistle nor a genuine work of Clement of Rome. The writer distinctly states (chap. xix) that he is reading aloud and that he is doing so in a religious meeting. Clearly we have here an early Christian sermon. The style is different from that of *1 Clement*; it is less elegant, and the preacher does not refer to himself in the first person plural (as is the habit of the author of *1 Clement*), but employs the singular form. Furthermore, the writer contrasts himself and his hearers with the Jewish nation in a manner quite unlike the genuine Clement, and his quotations are not, like Clement's, almost exclusively from the Old Testament, but frequently include references to gospel history.

Both the date and place of composition are difficult to determine. In the absence of any direct references to contemporary events, the most that one can do is to consider its place in the general development of Christian doctrine. On this basis it has been generally assigned to the half century between

---

[41] According to O. J. F. Seitz, 'Relationship of the Shepherd of Hermas to the Epistle of James', *Journal of Biblical Literature*, lxiii (1944), pp. 131–40 (cf. idem, lxvi [1947], pp. 211–19), both James and Hermas drew the word δίψυχος from an earlier document now lost. The numerous echoes in Hermas from James, however, make this hypothesis unnecessary.

[42] The title is derived from an incident in the history of Moses (Num. xi. 26).

A.D. 120 and 170, and within these limits ±150 is usually accepted.[43] Still more uncertain is its place of origin. Its traditional association with *1 Clement* suggests a Roman origin, and Harnack attributed it to Pope Soter (A.D. 166–70). Others (as F. X. Funk, G. Krüger) have supposed that it had been a favourite sermon with the Corinthians, who kept reading it in church along with *1 Clement*, and so the two came to be associated together. Still others (J. R. Harris, J. V. Bartlet, B. H. Streeter) have assigned it to Alexandria, for the unknown author includes quotations that remind one of the *Gospel of the Egyptians* and the Greek *Gospel of Thomas*, both of which were of Egyptian provenance. As can be appreciated, none of these proposals rests on sufficiently compelling evidence to warrant drawing a firm conclusion, and so the question of the historical context of *2 Clement* must be left unresolved.

The main object of the author of *2 Clement* is to inculcate personal holiness of life, and in support of his teaching he frequently appeals to the Old Testament and to the words of the Lord. In the case of the Old Testament he sometimes identifies the passages he cites by mentioning the name of the author, as, for example, Isaiah (iii. 5) or Ezekiel (vi. 8). In the case of the New Testament, however, though he is obviously acquainted with the Gospels of Matthew and of Luke, he never cites them as the narratives of the Evangelists. In such cases his favourite formula of introduction is 'the Lord says'. Thus, in support of his exhortation to practise good works, he quotes as a saying of the Lord, 'Not everyone who says to me, "Lord, Lord," shall be saved, but the one who does righteousness' (iv. 2), which is obviosly an echo of the tradition incorporated at the close of the Matthean form of the Sermon on the Mount (Matt. vii. 21).

A little more remote from what is preserved in the canonical Gospels is the statement, 'The Lord said, "My brethren are those who do the will of my Father"' (ix. 11). Here we seem to have a fusion of the structure of Luke viii. 21 ('My mother and my brethren are those who hear the word of God and do it') with the phrasing of Matt. xii. 49f. ('Behold my mother and

---

[43] Instead of the usual dating of *2 Clement*, however, Karl P. Donfried prefers a date about A.D. 98–100; see his *The Setting of Second Clement in Early Christianity* (*Supplements to Novum Testamentum*, xxxviii; Leiden, 1974), pp. 1–19.

my brethren! For whoever does the will of my Father in heaven is my brother, and sister, and mother').

Similarly 2 *Clement* makes a composite quotation of Matt. vi. 24 (or Luke xvi. 13) with Luke ix. 25: 'The Lord says, "No servant can serve two masters." If we desire to serve both God and mammon, it is unprofitable to us. "For what is the advantage if someone gains the whole world but loses one's soul?"' (vi. 1–2)

In other cases 2 *Clement* cites as words of the Lord clauses and whole sentences that are not preserved in our canonical Gospels. In vii. 5 we read:

> The Lord says in the gospel, 'If you did not guard that which is small, who shall give you that which is great? For I tell you that the one who is faithful in that which is least, is faithful also in that which is much.'

Although the last clause occurs verbally in Luke xvi. 10, the first part is not found in the present text of the Gospels.

Still more expanded is the following quotation preserved in v. 2–4:

For the Lord says, 'You shall be as lambs in the midst of wolves'. And Peter answering says to him, 'If then the wolves tear the lambs?' Jesus said to Peter, 'Let the lambs have no fear of the wolves after they [the lambs] die; and you, do not fear those who kill you and can do nothing more to you, but fear him who, after you die, has power over soul and body to cast them into the Gehenna of fire' (v. 2–4).	Behold, I send you forth like lambs in the midst of wolves (Luke x. 3).

Do not fear those who kill the body and after that have nothing more that they can do. But... fear him who, after he has killed, has power to cast into the Gehenna (Luke xii. 4–5); ('...fear him who can destroy both soul and body in Gehenna' Matt. x. 28; 'the Gehenna of fire' Matt. v. 22; xviii. 9). |

Here it is obvious that expressions from Luke and Matthew have been fused together and placed in an enlarged setting similar to the dialogue of Jesus and Peter about lambs in John

xxi. 15–17. We have, however, no data for determining the source of these words. Their length and style seem to indicate that they were derived from writings and not from oral tradition, but no other trace of the conversation has been preserved.

Another citation still more remote from the canonical accounts is the following:

For when the Lord himself was asked by someone when his kingdom would come, he said: 'When the two shall be one, and the outside as the inside, and the male with the female [is] neither male nor female' (xii. 2).

This citation reminds one of logion 22 in the *Gospel of Thomas*:

They [the disciples] said to him, 'Shall we, being children, enter the kingdom?' Jesus said to them, 'When you make the two one, and make the inside like the outside, and the outside like the inside, and the upper side like the under side, and when you make the male and the female into a single one, so that the male will not be male and the female will [not] be female.'

Since part of this saying also occurs in the *Gospel of the Egyptians*,[44] where it is expanded and presented as Jesus' reply to a query posed by Salome, it may be concluded that *2 Clement* has drawn upon a piece of oral tradition that also found embodiment in the *Gospel of Thomas* and the *Gospel of the Egyptians*. Of the three developments of the same saying, its precise wording, according to Baarda's detailed analysis,[45] is probably best preserved in *2 Clement*.

There remains one other citation of Jesus' words that, unlike those so far examined, is identified as 'Scripture'. Immediately after quoting a passage from the Old Testament (Isa. liv. 1), the author continues, 'Another Scripture also says (καὶ ἑτέρα δὲ γραφὴ λέγει), "I came not to call the righteous, but sinners"' (ii. 4). Since the parallelism with Matt. ix. 13 and Mark ii. 17 is

---

[44] As quoted by Clement of Alexandria, *Strom.* III. xiii. 92.
[45] Tjitze Baarda, '2 Clement 12 and the Sayings of Jesus', *Logia; Les Paroles de Jésus—The Sayings of Jesus*, ed. by Joël Delobel (Leuven, 1982), pp. 529–56, esp. p. 547.

exact, the citation seems to show that the author of *2 Clement* regarded the Gospel according to Matthew (which was more widely used in the early Church than Mark) as Scripture, on a par with Isaiah.[46]

As for reminiscences from the Epistles, in xi. 7 the author speaks of the promises 'which no ear has heard, nor eye has seen, nor the human heart conceived' (1 Cor. ii. 9). His statement (xiv. 2) that the 'living Church is the body of Christ' seems to echo Eph. i. 22. In xvi. 4 the words 'love covers a multitude of sins' (ἀγάπη καλύπτει πλῆθος ἁμαρτιῶν) are identical with what is said in 1 Pet. iv. 8 (and *1 Clem.* xlix. 5). The statement 'He is faithful who promised' (xi. 6) seems to come from Heb. x. 23.

In xiv. 2 we find an important but somewhat imprecise reference to the authorities from which the author of *2 Clement* derives his teaching. In developing an allegorical understanding of the pre-existence of the Church, he relies upon 'the books and the apostles' (τὰ βιβλία καὶ οἱ ἀπόστολοι). What did our author mean by these two terms taken in tandem? Although it is unlikely that he had given much reflection to the matter, by the term 'the books' he would undoubtedly have meant the Old Testament, for he has just finished quoting Jer. vii. 11 and Gen. i. 27. By the term 'the apostles', though in the context he has Eph. i. 22–3 specifically in mind, he probably would have included other Christian books that are taken as co-ordinate with the Jewish Scriptures. At the same time, however, it is significant that he does not venture to include the apostolic documents under the rubric, 'the books', i.e. his Bible.

By way of recapitulation, the unknown author of *2 Clement* certainly knew and used Matthew and Luke, 1 Corinthians, and Ephesians. There is no trace of the Johannine Gospel or Epistles, or of the Book of Acts. And one cannot say more than that he may have known Hebrews, James, and 1 Peter. Of the

---

[46] Contrary to this common-sense way of understanding the citation, Donfried (op. cit., p. 59) thinks it probable that 'in his use of γραφή our preacher is referring to words of Jesus transmitted orally'—but how γραφή can refer to *oral* transmission is hard to understand. Certainly *2 Clement*'s comment implies, as Bultmann correctly saw, that 'around the middle of the second century words of the Lord transmitted in a written tradition already count as Scripture' (*Theology of the New Testament*, ii, p. 140).

eleven times that he cites words of Jesus, five are not to be found in the canonical Gospels. The presence of these latter, as well as the citation in xi. 2–4 of an apocryphal book of the Old Testament, introduced as 'the prophetic word' (ὁ προφητικὸς λόγος), shows that our homilist's quotations of divinely authoritative words are not controlled by any strict canonical idea, even in relation to Old Testament writings.

IX. SUMMARY

The extant works of the Apostolic Fathers are of relatively small compass, making in all a volume about the same size as the New Testament. Except for the *Shepherd* of Hermas, the *Didache*, and Papias' *Expositions*, all are in the form of epistles after the model of Paul's. They originated, not in scientific study, but in practical religious feeling, and contain not analyses of doctrine so much as simple direct assertions of faith and exhortations to a holy life. In such documents we do not expect to find discussions of canonicity, but, at most, testimony here and there as to the existence of this or that book which later came to be regarded as belonging to the holy Scriptures of the New Testament.

Despite wide differences among the Apostolic Fathers as to geographical milieu and, more importantly, ideological orientation, it is possible to draw several generalized conclusions. It is natural that attitudes toward the Old Testament and toward individual books of the New Testament (so far as they were known) would differ in accord with the background of the several authors. For early Jewish Christians the Bible consisted of the Old Testament and some Jewish apocryphal literature. Along with this written authority went traditions, chiefly oral, of sayings attributed to Jesus. On the other hand, authors who belonged to the 'Hellenistic wing' of the Church refer more frequently to writings that later came to be included in the New Testament. At the same time, however, they very rarely regarded such documents as 'Scripture'.

Furthermore, there was as yet no conception of the duty of exact quotation from books that were not yet in the full sense canonical. Consequently, it is sometimes exceedingly difficult to ascertain which New Testament books were known to early

Christian writers;[47] our evidence does not become clear until the end of the second century.

In short, we find in both the Jewish and the Hellenistic groups a knowledge of the existence of certain books that later will comprise the New Testament, and more than once they express their thoughts through phrases drawn from these writings. These reminiscences tend to show that an implicit authority of such writings was sensed before a theory of their authority had been developed—in fact, before there was even a consciousness of their authority. This authority, moreover, did not have, to any degree, an exclusive character.

On the other hand, we see that the words of Jesus are taken as the supreme authority. Sometimes these quotations are similar to what we find in the four Gospels; at other times they differ. Already at the time of Papias we find the beginning of a movement, unconscious at first, that will tend to subordinate the authority of the words of Jesus to the warranty arising from the fact that these words are preserved in such and such books which deserve the reader's confidence.

---

[47] For this reason it is generally preferable, in estimating doubtful cases, to regard variation from a canonical text as a free quotation from a document known to us than to suppose it to be a quotation from a hitherto unknown document, or the persistence of primitive tradition. On the other hand, repeated citation of a divergent quotation suggests an alternative source; see Richard Glover, 'Patristic Quotations and Gospel Sources', *New Testament Studies*, xxxi (1985), pp. 235–51.

IV

Influences Bearing on the Development of the Canon

THE evidence provided in the preceding chapter from the writings of the Apostolic Fathers does scarcely more than point to the existence and, to some extent, the dissemination of certain early Christian writings in the form of gospels and epistles. Certainly there is little enough recognition of their being regarded as 'holy Scripture'. By the close of the second century, however, we can see the outline of what may be described as the nucleus of the New Testament. Although the fringes of the emerging canon remained unsettled for generations, a high degree of unanimity concerning the greater part of the New Testament was attained among the very diverse and scattered congregations of believers not only throughout the Mediterranean world but also over an area extending from Britain to Mesopotamia. By the end of the third century and the beginning of the fourth century, the great majority of the twenty-seven books that still later came to be widely regarded as the canonical New Testament were almost universally acknowledged to be authoritative. There were, to be sure, a good many competing works that possessed temporary and local canonicity, but during the following generations the limits of the canon became progressively clarified.

Before the fascinating story of this development can be told, however, we must take account of several movements, persons, and other influences that exerted pressure on the early Church to ascertain still more exactly which books were authoritative in matters of faith and life. Some of these external pressures were of a religious nature; others were socio-political or, one may say, broadly cultural.

I. GNOSTICISM

One of the chief opponents of orthodox Christianity was Gnosticism, a syncretistic religion and philosophy that flour-

ished for about four centuries alongside early Christianity.
Most of the several varieties of Gnostic thought were characterized by the assertion that elect souls, being divine sparks
temporarily imprisoned in physical bodies as a result of a
precosmic catastrophe, can obtain salvation by means of a
special *gnosis* (γνῶσις, 'knowledge') of their origin and destiny.
The purpose of the extensive Gnostic literature that developed
was not only to instruct believers about the origin and
structure of the visible world and of the worlds above, but to
supply also—and this was the most important and complicated
task—the means whereby one could be victor over the powers
of darkness and return to the realm of the highest God.

In the New Testament there are several indications that the
invasion of Christianity by Gnosticism was already in progress.
Here and there we find a sharp polemic against errorists
who claim superior knowledge (Col. ii. 8 and 18; Tit. i. 16; 2
Tim. iii. 7) and who have appropriated the term *gnosis* (1 Tim.
vi. 20). The rank errorists denounced in 2 Peter and Jude show
some affinity with the Ophite sect, the Cainites.

But all of this belongs to the earliest period of contact
between Christianity and Gnosticism; it was not until the mid-
second century that the real showdown between the two took
place. By that time several systems of Gnostic thought had
developed that called themselves Christian because they gave
Christ a more or less central position. Such syncretistic Gnosticism, if successful, would have obliterated the distinctive
historical features of Christianity, and it was not surprising that
Irenaeus, Hippolytus, and other Church Fathers vehemently
opposed these tendencies in order to protect Christianity from
internal destruction.

Until 1945 all that we had for the reconstruction of Gnostic
systems of thought were the quotations included by patristic
authors in their warfare against their opponents. But in that
year some peasants discovered at Nag Hammadi on the east
bank of the Nile in Upper Egypt what proved to be a whole
Gnostic library, dating from about A.D. 400 and comprising some
fifty treatises in Coptic, collected into thirteen codices totalling
about a thousand pages. Most of these supply first-hand
information that supplements our knowledge of Gnosticism
derived from patristic writers. In general the newly discovered

documents not only confirm our previous impression of Gnosticism as tedious and verbose, but also provide proof that the Fathers did not, as has sometimes been alleged, fabricate their opponents' views; whatever distortion there was came from selection, not invention.

From such sources as these we can now appreciate still more fully the problems confronted by orthodox writers of the Great Church. It is not the intention here to identify and trace the development of all the various schools of Gnostic theologies; it will be sufficient to mention three features that seem to be characteristic of several Gnostic systems. These are a philosophical dualism that rejected the visible world as being alien to the supreme God; belief in a subordinate deity (the Demiurge) who was responsible for the creation of the world; and, in some systems, a radical distinction between Jesus and Christ, with the corollary that Christ the Redeemer only seemed to be a real human being (Docetism, from δοκεῖν 'to seem').

The purpose of the present Chapter is to ascertain how far Gnostic teachers utilized writings of the New Testament and how far they produced rival gospels, acts, and apocalypses. In opposition to the latter, the Great Church was compelled (*a*) to develop her own creed into a clear system, for the false *gnosis* had to be opposed by the more precise definition of the true; (*b*) to determine which writings she could regard as authoritative, for each of the Gnostic schools had its own special revelation; and (*c*) to seek for a just view of the relation of Judaism to Christianity, and of the permanent value of the Old Testament, which many Gnostics rejected.

The Church countered the claims of Gnostics by stating that nothing of their systems was to be found in the four Gospels, the Acts of the Apostles, and the Epistles of Paul as they were used by the congregations. The Gnostics acknowledged this, but asserted that such teachings had not been communicated by the Lord to the general public, but only to his most trusted disciples. For proof, the Gnostics appealed to a number of 'gospels' which they had written for this express purpose. These Gnostic gospels often deal with the period between the resurrection and the ascension of Christ, about which the canonical Gospels say very little. The Gnostics also produced other texts in which the apostles report what the Lord had secretly communicated to them. Of course the Gnostics asserted that the true teaching of the risen Lord was to be seen more clearly in these writings than in the gospels and epistles used by the Great Church. Alongside such 'secret' traditions the Gnostics would, naturally, also know and even utilize the books received by the Church, while interpreting them in their own special manner.

It was not easy for the Church to defend herself against Gnosticism. Certain elements in the gospel tradition itself seemed to give verisimilitude to the Gnostics' claim. For example, in the account of the Transfiguration it is said that Jesus, having revealed his messianic glory to his three most intimate disciples, commanded them to tell no one what they had seen until the Son of man had risen from the dead (Mark ix. 9). Likewise, at the opening of the Book of Acts (i. 3) mention is made of instructions given by the risen Lord to his disciples but without providing details, so it could appear that this was the time when the secret teachings were communicated. It is in such a setting, in fact, that even a book that is not heretical, the *Epistle of the Apostles* (see pp. 180–2 below), places its special teaching.

One can understand that, in defending itself against Gnosticism, a most important problem for the Church was to determine what really constituted a true gospel and a genuine apostolic writing. In order to prevent the exploitation of secret traditions, which were practically uncontrollable, the Church had to be careful to accept nothing which did not bear the stamp of apostolic guarantee. The indirect consequence of this was a devaluation of oral tradition, which, as we have seen, Papias towards 130 still preferred to books. On the other hand, in order to prevent Gnostics from 'twisting the Scriptures', the Church would insist on the 'rule of faith' as the norm of Biblical interpretation.

1. BASILIDES

One of the earliest of scholarly Gnostics was Basilides, who taught in Alexandria during the reign of the Emperor Hadrian (A.D. 117–38). Different accounts of his teachings are given by Irenaeus[1] and by Hippolytus,[2] but most scholars agree that

---

[1] Irenaeus, *Adv. Haer.* I. xxiv. 3–6.   [2] Hippolytus, *Ref.* vii. 14–27.

Hippolytus more accurately represents Basilides, while Irenaeus gives a popularized form of his system. One can appreciate that, since Gnostic systems were in a state of continual and rapid evolution, polemical writers of the Church naturally had no interest in antiquarian researches but attacked the teaching in the form in which it was influencing the Church in their time.

In the 30s of the second century Basilides wrote a considerable work, comprising twenty-four books, under the title of *Exegetica*, of which only a few fragments have been preserved. According to Hegemonius,[3] the thirteenth book dealt with the account of the Rich Man and Lazarus (Luke xvi. 19–31). Clement of Alexandria quotes several passages from the twenty-third book, where Basilides, in dealing with the problem of sin and suffering, makes unmistakable reference to the Sermon on the Mount, with its pronouncement on adultery and murder (Matt. v. 21–30),[4] as well as to the Pauline statement in the Epistle to the Romans, 'I was once alive apart from the law' (vii. 9).[5] Origen indicates that Basilides discussed the passage in Romans concerning the groaning and travailing of the creation awaiting the revelation of the sons of God (viii. 19).[6]

From Irenaeus we learn (*Adv. Haer.* I. vii. 2; III. xviii. 6) that Basilides denied that Jesus really suffered on the cross. On the *Via Dolorosa* Jesus handed the cross over to Simon of Cyrene, to whom he lent his own form and who was crucified as if he were Jesus, while the true Jesus Christ, standing unseen nearby in the form of Simon, laughed[7] at his enemies, and then ascended to the Father. According to Clement of Alexandria (*Strom.* vii. 17), the followers of Basilides boasted that their master had received special information from a certain Glaucias, who, so it was said, had been an interpreter of the Apostle Peter.

---

[3] Hegemonius, *Acta Archelai* lxvii. 4–11.   [4] Clement, *Strom.* IV. xii. 81.
[5] Ibid. IV. xii. 83.   [6] Origen, *Epist. ad Rom.* v. vi. 36.
[7] This version of Jesus' escape from being crucified was current among other Gnostics as well (and was taken over much later by Islam; cf. the Koran, iv. 156). Among the Nag Hammadi tractates, the *Second Treatise on the Great Seth* (lvi. 10–15) and the *Apocalypse of Peter* (lxxxv. 4–25 and 83.1) speak of the Saviour as laughing at the ignorance or blindness of his executioners. For a discussion of these and other texts, see John Dart, *The Laughing Savior; The Discovery and Significance of the Nag Hammadi Library* (New York, 1976), pp. 107–9.

2. CARPOCRATES

Carpocrates was an Alexandrian Platonist who, according to Irenaeus (*Adv. Haer.* I. xxv), founded a Gnostic sect in the early part of the second century. He regarded Jesus as the son of Joseph, and just like other men, except that he perfectly remembered those things which he had witnessed within the sphere of the unbegotten God. For this reason a power descended on him from the Father, that by means of it he might escape from the angelic creators of the world. The Carpocratians, according to Irenaeus and Hippolytus, practised magical arts and had recourse to familiar spirits and dream-sending demons. They were the first-known sect that used pictures of Christ, deriving them from a pretended original belonging to Pontius Pilate.

Recently there has come to light a fragment of a letter attributed to Clement of Alexandria that refers to a second Gospel of Mark current among the Carpocratians (see pp. 132–3 below). Phrases in the letter have been taken by the editor to imply that the sect practised nocturnal homosexual rites of initiation in imitation of Jesus' secret teachings delivered at night to a young man whom he had raised from the dead.

3. VALENTINUS AND HIS FOLLOWERS

Still more influential in developing Gnostic theology and in attracting followers was Valentinus, the founder of the sect of Valentinians. According to Irenaeus, Valentinus was a native of Egypt who moved to Rome where he established a large school and spread his doctrines in the West (*c.* 140–*c.* 165). He claimed to have derived them from Theodas (or Theudas), a pupil of the apostle Paul.[8] He also claimed to have received revelations from the Logos in a vision. Later, aspiring to be elected bishop 'on account of his intellectual force and eloquence',[9] he was passed over, whereupon he seceded from the Church and moved away from Rome, perhaps going to Cyprus.

Valentinus' system is an elaborate theogonic and cosmogonic epic. It describes in three acts the creation, the fall, and the redemption; first in heaven, then on earth. The spiritual world or 'pleroma' comprises thirty 'aeons' forming a succes-

---

[8] So Clement, *Strom.* vii. 17.   [9] Tertullian, *Adv. Valentinianos*, 4.

sion of pairs (syzygies). The visible world owes its origin to the fall of Sophia ('wisdom'), whose offspring, the Demiurge, is identified with the God of the Old Testament. Human beings belong to one of three classes, the spiritual people (*pneumatikoi*, or true Gnostics), those who merely possesses a soul (*psychikoi*, or ordinary, unenlightened church members), and the rest of humankind, who are made up solely of matter (*hylikoi*) and are given over to eternal perdition.

Valentinus derived his teachings from his own fertile imagination, from Oriental and Greek speculations (including Pythagorean elements), and from Christian ideas. Clement of Alexandria (*Strom.* vi. vi. 52) represents Valentinus as making a distinction between things written in 'common books' and things found 'written in the Church of God'—from which some have concluded that Valentinus had a canon of 'church' books.[10] He made much of the Prologue of John's Gospel and the Epistles to the Colossians and Ephesians. By employing fanciful exegesis he attached his own mythological speculations to apostolic words, such as Logos, Only Begotten, Truth, *Pleroma*, Aeons, Ecclesia. It was with good reason that Irenaeus expressed outrage that Valentinians should make a confession in common with other Christians: 'Such persons are, to outward appearances, sheep, for they appear to be like us, from what they say in public, repeating the same words as we do; but inwardly they are wolves' (*Adv. Haer.* iii. xvi. 8). 'Although they may say things resembling the doctrine of the faithful', they actually 'hold views that are not only different, but are absolutely opposite, and in all points full of blasphemies' (ibid. iii. xvii. 4).[11]

Valentinus produced a variety of writings, and used another gospel besides the canonical ones, called the *Gospel of Truth* (*Evangelium Veritatis*).[12] A treatise in Coptic with this title was recently recovered at Nag Hammadi, and scholars are divided

[10] See Gerald Cowen, 'Gnostic Concepts of a New Testament Canon', Th.D. thesis, New Orleans Baptist Theological Seminary, 1971, p. 23.

[11] Concerning Valentinian hermeneutics, see Carola Barth, *Die Interpretation des Neuen Testaments in der valentinianischen Gnosis* (*Texte und Untersuchungen*, xxxvii, 3; Leipzig, 1911).

[12] According to Irenaeus (*Adv. Haer.* iii. xi. 9) a work with this title was produced by the disciples of Valentinus, which was composed not long before the time of his own writing (*c.* A.D. 180).

as to whether it derives from Valentinus. More like a medita-
tion on the Christian life and salvation than a traditional
gospel, the treatise shows little trace of the elaborate speculations that are usually associated with the Valentinian system.
Some scholars, however, believe that they are presupposed,
though not emphasized, in order to conciliate orthodox opinion; others think that the work has no connection with
Valentinus. In any case, its author not only was acquainted
with several books of the Old Testament, but also made use of
the Gospels of Matthew and John, Romans, 1 Corinthians,
Galatians, Ephesians, Colossians, and the Book of Revelation,
while there are also traces of knowledge of Acts, 1 John, and
1 Peter.[13] Although the range is almost coextensive with the
New Testament, one must beware of concluding that for the
author of the *Gospel of Truth* (whoever it was), these writings
were canonical; the most that can be said is that they obviously
possessed a certain degree of authority and were useful in
developing his thought and exhortation.

The influence of Valentinus is seen in the oldest commentary
written on a New Testament book. This was the work of his
disciple, Heracleon, who, probably after the middle of the
second century, wrote a detailed commentary on John's Gospel, of which Origen has preserved many fragments and which
he criticizes in his own commentary on the Fourth Gospel.[14]
Here the author's allegory is carried out completely in such a
way that, for example, the Demiurge speaks through the
Baptist, and the Samaritan woman appears as a type of the
pneumatic woman who is dissatisfied with the Jacob's well of
the Old Testament and so turns to the living water of *gnosis* and
longs for her future spouse in the *pleroma*.[15] Heracleon's
commentary on John also includes quotations from and allusions to passages in Matthew, as well as allusions to Romans, 1
Corinthians, and possibly Galatians.

---

[13] For a detailed list of echoes and allusions see W. C. van Unnik, 'The "Gospel of
Truth" and the New Testament', in *The Jung Codex*, ed. by F. L. Cross (London,
1955), pp. 115–21, and Jacques-E. Ménard, *L'Évangile de verité* (*Nag Hammadi Studies*, ii;
London, 1972), pp. 3–8.

[14] See Origen's *Commentary on John*, ed. by E. Preuschen, p. cii, and A. E. Brooke,
The Fragments of Heracleon (*Texts and Studies*, i. 4; Cambridge, 1891).

[15] For Heracleon's hermeneutics, see Elaine H. Pagels, *The Johannine Gospel in
Gnostic Exegesis: Heracleon's Commentary on John* (Nashville, 1973).

Another of Valentinus' disciples, Ptolemy, is known as the author of an open letter to a wealthy and eminent Christian lady, Flora by name, whom he tries to convert to the Valentinian system.[16] He deals chiefly with the objection that the creation of the world and the composition of the Old Testament could not have been the work of the highest God. He appeals to apostolic tradition and to the words of Christ, who alone knows the Father of all and first revealed him. More than once Ptolemy refers to what 'our Saviour' has said, quoting in these cases Jesus' words as presented in the Gospel according to Matthew. Once he refers to Paul, and several times, without mentioning the specific Epistles, he quotes from the text of Romans, 1 Corinthians, and Ephesians. He also cites John i. 3, attributing it to 'the apostle' but without naming him.

Other members of the school of Valentinus were Marcus and his followers, the Marcosians. Marcus appears to have been an older contemporary of Irenaeus who speaks of him as though he were still living and teaching in the Rhone valley (*Adv. Haer.* I. xiii. 2). The fragments that remain of Marcus' teachings contain allusions to passages in Matthew, Mark, and Luke. It seems that he accepted one or more of Paul's Epistles, and the Apostle is referred to by name in one place. Irenaeus also records (ibid. I. xx. 1) that the Marcosians used many apocryphal writings:

They [the Marcosians] adduce an unspeakable number of apocryphal and spurious writings, which they themselves have forged, to bewilder the minds of the foolish.... Among other things they bring forth that false and wicked story which relates that our Lord, when he was a boy learning his letters, when the teacher said to him, as is usual, 'Pronounce Alpha', replied, 'Alpha'. But when, again, the teacher bade him to say, 'Beta', the Lord replied, 'First tell me what Alpha is, and then I will tell you what Beta is'.[17]

This sect sought to show by means of the system of gematria that the heavenly Christ came upon the earthly Jesus in the

---

[16] The *Epistola ad Floram* is preserved by Epiphanius (*Haer.* xxxi. 3–7); for analyses, see A. Harnack, 'Der Brief des Ptolemäus an die Flora. Eine religiöse Kritik am Pentateuch in 2. Jahrhundert', *Sitzungsberichte der königlich preussischen Akademie der Wissenschaften* (1902), pp. 507–45, and G. Quispel's edition of the epistle, with commentary, in *Sources chrétiennes*, xxiv (Paris, 1951).

[17] This story is known also through the Greek *Gospel of Thomas* vi. 1.

form of a dove at the time of his baptism in the Jordan. 'Proof' was found in the fact that the numerical value of the letters in the Greek word for dove (περιστερά) comes to 801, and that the same numerical value is found in the statement of Christ in the Apocalypse (Rev. i. 8), 'I am the Alpha and the Omega' (used as numerals, α is 1 and ω is 800).[18]

4. NAG HAMMADI TRACTATES

As was mentioned earlier, the library of Gnostic documents that turned up a few years ago in Egypt has provided us with hitherto unknown treatises used by Gnostic sects in the early Christian centuries.[19] Although the Coptic manuscripts date from about A.D. 400, the Greek originals of Gnostic treatises may have come from as early as the second or third century. There are fifty-two tractates in all, but of these, six are repeated within the various codices. Inasmuch as few of the treatises had been previously known (in Greek, Latin, or Coptic), the Nag Hammadi library adds to the literature surviving from antiquity thirty more or less complete texts and ten fragmentary ones.

In terms of content and theology, the majority of the Nag Hammadi texts are clearly Gnostic in character (39 tractates), and about half of these (20) can be labeled as Christian Gnostic. In addition there are three that can be regarded as Christian but not explicitly Gnostic (*The Acts of Peter and the Twelve Apostles*, *The Act of Peter*, and *The Teaching of Silvanus*). Two are neither Christian nor Gnostic (*The Thunder, Perfect Mind* and *The Sentences of Sextus*). Finally, there is a translation of a fragment of Plato's *Republic* (588b–589b). The translations into Coptic vary greatly in quality, as can be seen by comparison of tractates that survive in duplicate copies or by comparing the inept and inaccurate Coptic rendering with the Greek original of Plato's *Republic*.

As for the use of the Old Testament in the Nag Hammadi documents,[20] it is the opening chapters of Genesis that are most

---

[18] Irenaeus, *Adv. Haer.* I. xiv. 6.

[19] A preliminary English translation, made by several scholars and edited by James M. Robinson, is available in *The Nag Hammadi Library in English* (San Francisco, 1977).

[20] See R. McL. Wilson, 'The Gnostics and the Old Testament', *Proceedings of the International Colloquium on Gnosticism*, Stockholm, 20–5 Aug. 1973 (Stockholm, 1977), pp. 164–8.

frequently referred to, with only occasional references to the Prophets and almost no allusions to the historical books. There is, as would be expected, a tendency to allegorize Old Testament texts.

As for the use made of New Testament books in the Nag Hammadi documents, one finds a wide variation. Some tractates, as would be surmised from what has been said above, have no quotation, allusion, or echo whatsoever. On the other hand, others present not a few parallels to passages in the gospels and epistles that are in our New Testament. The document that shows the greatest number of points of contact with the canonical Gospels is the *Gospel of Thomas*,[21] which begins: 'These are the secret words which the living Jesus spoke and (which) Didymus Judas Thomas wrote down'. The treatise which follows consists of 114 items (logia), almost all of which are introduced by the words 'Jesus said'. Among these sayings we find a good many that show similarities with sayings of Jesus recorded in Matthew, particularly in the Sermon on the Mount and the collection of parables in Matthew xiii. Similarly, when compared with Luke the *Gospel of Thomas* is closest to the collections of sayings found in chapters vi, xi, and xii. There seem to be no parallels to material that is peculiar to Mark. The parallels to John are few in number, chiefly relating to Jesus' conversation with the woman of Samaria (chap. iv) and the Farewell Discourses in chaps. xii–xvii.[22] Only those passages are selected which proclaim the presence of divine wisdom as the true destiny of human existence. Nothing is presented from the sayings of Jesus that involves a futuristic eschatological component.

Many are the problems that arise from a critical evaluation of these parallels. Where the parallels are close, in most cases there can be little doubt that the form presented by *Thomas* is secondary. In other cases, however, comparison suggests that logia in *Thomas* derive from a source common to it and the canonical Gospels. It would appear that the compiler of the

[21] This work must be distinguished from the Syriac *Gospel of Thomas* (which has survived in two recensions), as well as from the lost Naassene *Gospel of Thomas* mentioned by Hippolytus (*Philos.* v. 7).

[22] For a detailed list of parallels between Thomas and Matthew, Luke, and John, see R. M. Grant (with D. N. Freedman), *The Secret Sayings of Jesus according to the Gospel of Thomas* (London, 1960), pp. 103 f.

Gospel of Thomas, who seems to have written in Syria about A.D. 140, also made use of the *Gospel of the Egyptians* and the *Gospel according to the Hebrews* (see chap. VII.II and III below). Although the *Gospel of Thomas* is based largely on a selection of material from the Church's gospels, more than once its author gives a Gnostic twist to canonical sayings of Jesus, as well as incorporating sayings from other sources. Three typical examples are the following:

LOGION 37

His disciples said:
   On what day will you be revealed to us and on what day will we see you?
Jesus said:
   When you undress without being ashamed, and take your garments and lay them under your feet like little children and tread on them; then [you will see] the Son of the Living One and you will have no fear.

LOGION 77

Jesus said:
   I am the light that is over everything. I am the All; the All has gone forth from me, and to me the All has returned. Split (a piece of) wood; I am there. Lift up a stone, and you will find me there.

LOGION 114

Simon Peter said to them:
   Let Mary go away from us, because women are not worthy of life.
Jesus said:
   Lo, I shall lead her in order to make her a male, so that she too may become a living spirit, resembling you males. For every woman who makes herself male will enter into the kingdom of Heaven.

In the codex that contains the *Gospel of Thomas*, the treatise that follows is the *Gospel of Philip*. This document (the original of which is considered to date from the second century) provides striking confirmation of some aspects of Irenaeus' account of Valentinianism and to this extent confirms the substantial reliability of his report. A collection of disjointed excerpts, the *Gospel of Philip* emphasizes Gnostic sacramental theology and practice: 'The Lord did everything in a mystery, a baptism and a chrism and a eucharist and a redemption and a bridal chamber' (§ 67 [= 68 Wilson]).

New Testament echoes and allusions in *Philip* range from clear and unmistakable quotations to insignificant reminiscences. According to a tally made by Wilson,

> Of the four Gospels, the author's preference is clearly for Matthew and John, although there is at least one distinct allusion to Luke; there does not appear to be any evidence for knowledge of Mark. With the Fourth Gospel may be linked a couple of allusions to 1 John, and there is at least one clear citation of 1 Peter. Among the Pauline letters he knows and quotes from Romans, 1 and 2 Corinthians, Galatians and Philippians.[23]

The author of the *Gospel of Philip* never identifies any of the sources from which he quotes,[24] nor does he ever employ any formula of citation (such as 'it is written'). Often the allusions are worked into the context, suggesting that their language had become a natural vehicle for the expression of his ideas.[25] All of this implies, of course, that he had given careful attention to some of the New Testament books and saw fit to adopt their ideas and, at times, their phraseology.

The tractate entitled the *Exegesis of the Soul* (or, *Expository Treatise on the Soul*), written perhaps about A.D. 200, dramatically portrays the fall and the deliverance of the soul and exhorts the elect to live a life of asceticism. Three quotations are included from Homer's *Odyssey* as well as several from the Old and New Testaments. Some of the Biblical citations are identified by name: 'the prophet Hosea', introducing a quotation of Hos. ii. 2–7; 'Ezekiel', citing xvi. 23–6; and 'Paul, writing to the Corinthians [1 Cor. v. 9], said, "I write you in the letter, 'Do not associate with prostitutes,' not at all (meaning) the prostitutes of this world or the greedy or the thieves or the idolators,

---

[23] See R. McL. Wilson, *The Gospel of Philip*, translated from the Coptic text, with an Introduction and Commentary (New York, 1962), p. 7. Wilson provides an index to New Testament echoes and allusions (pp. 197 f).

[24] One must, however, keep in mind, as van Unnik points out, that 'in the cultured world of those days, a good style required the employment of reminiscences of well-known authors in their arguments, without express quotation. The practised ear of the educated hearer would recognize these as a matter of course' ('The "Gospel of Truth" and the New Testament', in *The Jung Codex*, p. 107).

[25] See R. McL Wilson, 'The New Testament in the Nag Hammadi Gospel of Philip', *New Testament Studies*, ix (1963), pp. 291–4, and Eric Segelberg, 'The Gospel of Philip and the New Testament', in *The New Testament and Gnosis; Essays in honour of Robert McL. Wilson*, ed. by A. H. B. Logan and A. J. M. Wedderburn (Edinburgh, 1983), pp. 204–12.

since then you would have to go out from the world"—here he is speaking spiritually—"For our struggle is not against flesh and blood"—as he said [Eph. vi. 12]—"but against the world rulers of this darkness and the spirits of wickedness"' (131.2–13).

Near the close of his treatise the author uses a quotation from John vi. 44 in order to illustrate how the rejuvenation of the soul 'is due not to rote phrases or to professional skills or to book learning', but is a gift of grace; 'therefore the Saviour cries out, "No one can come to me unless my Father draws him and brings him to me, and I myself will raise him up on the last day."' The author follows this with three other quotations from the New Testament:

'The Saviour said, "Blessed are those who mourn, for it is they who will be pitied; blessed those who are hungry, for it is they who will be filled"' (135. 15–19, quoting Matt. v. 4 and 6);

'Again he said, "If one does not hate his soul (or, himself), he cannot follow me"' (135. 20, quoting Luke xiv. 26); and

'Therefore, "Before Christ's appearance John came preaching the baptism of repentance"' (135. 23–5, quoting Acts xiii. 24).

Unlike the Nag Hammadi treatises already considered, other tractates included in the library present fewer and fainter reminiscences and echoes from New Testament books. The *Apocryphon of James*, originating in the second or third century, perhaps in Egypt, comprises various sayings of the resurrected Christ in response to questions and statements made by several of his disciples. There are allusions to each of the Gospels, and in one passage (8. 5–9) the author mentions six parables of Jesus: those of 'The Shepherds', 'The Seed', 'The Building', 'The Lamps of the Virgins', 'The Wage of the Workmen', and 'The Didrachmae and the Woman'. The first three are found in both Matthew and Luke, the next two are peculiar to Matthew, and the last is peculiar to Luke. There are a good many allusions to the Gospel according to John, which seems to have been the author's favourite New Testament book. There is one possible allusion to Mark: 'For the kingdom of heaven is like an ear of grain after it had sprouted in a field. And when it had ripened, it scattered its fruit and again filled the field with ears for another year' (12. 22–7; cf. Mark iv. 26–30).

The teaching of the *Treatise on Resurrection*, addressed to a certain Rheginos, is permeated with Valentinian symbols and imagery. Written probably in the late second century, its doctrine is strikingly similar to the 'over-realized eschatology' of Hymenaeus and Philetus who taught that 'the resurrection [of believers] has already occurred' (2 Tim. ii. 18). Using Rom. viii. 17 and Eph. ii. 5–6, the author declares that the elect have already participated in Christ's death, resurrection, and ascension (45. 24–8). Immediately following death a spiritual resurrection of the believer takes place, and an allusion to the Transfiguration scene in the Synoptic Gospels[26] is made in order to prove the continuity between the deceased and the resurrected person (48. 3–11).

The tractate *Trimorphic Protennoia*, a Barbeloite treatise that offers theosophical and apocalyptic speculation on the nature of history and the cosmos, is thought to have attained its present form around or shortly after A.D. 200. Although the original form of the tractate is considered by some to have somehow influenced the formulation of the Prologue to the Fourth Gospel, in its present form it appears to have been heavily Christianized.[27] The name 'Christ' occurs several times, and there are numerous allusions to the Fourth Gospel, the Synoptic Apocalypse (Mark xiii), and 1 Corinthians xv.

The *Hypostasis of the Archons*, which may have been composed originally in Egypt sometime during the third century, opens with a reference to 'the great apostle' who 'told us that "our contest is not against flesh and (blood); rather, the authorities and spirits of wickedness"' (Eph. vi. 12). The author goes on to give a thoroughly Gnostic interpretation of Genesis i–vi, partially in the form of a discourse between an angel and a questioner.

Because of limitations of space, only one other treatise from the Nag Hammadi library can be mentioned here, the *Epistle of Peter to Philip*. Although the principal section of the document, a dialogue of the resurrected Saviour with his disciples, contains no reference to the New Testament, both the opening and the closing sections, particularly the narrative materials,

---

[26] Since reference is made to the appearance of Elijah and Moses, rather than to Moses and Elijah, it appears that Mark's account (ix. 2–8) is being referred to, rather than that in Matthew or Luke, which have the sequence of Moses and Elijah.

[27] For a balanced evaluation see Yvonne Janssens, 'The Trimorphic Protennoia and the Fourth Gospel', in *The New Testament and Gnosis; Essays in honour of Robert McL. Wilson*, pp. 229–44.

show unmistakable acquaintance with the conclusion of the Gospel according to Luke and the first chapter of Acts, as well as what is commonly called the Great Commission at the end of Matthew. The author makes free use of these materials, but does not quote them verbatim. It is also possible, according to the opinion of Luttikhuizen,[28] that the author of the epistle has been guided in his thinking by 1 Peter in the New Testament.

By way of summary, it is clear that a variety of second-century Gnostic leaders used New Testament Gospels and Epistles in support of their teaching; there is little or no evidence that they used the Book of Acts. As early as about 130 Basilides refers to passages that are found in Matthew and Luke, and Heracleon is the first person known to consider the interpretation of the Gospel according to John important enough to write a commentary on it. With the possible exception of Valentinus, none of the Gnostics seems to have drawn up a canon list. There was wide divergence of opinion among the various groups as to which books should be regarded as authoritative; on the one hand, Marcion (who, as we shall see, is not to be classified as a full-fledged Gnostic) had a closed, limited canon. On the other hand, Marcus and the Marcosians appealed to a broad spectrum of authoritative books. All in all, the role played by Gnostics in the development of the canon was chiefly that of provoking a reaction among members of the Great Church so as to ascertain still more clearly which books and epistles conveyed the true teaching of the Gospel.

II. MARCION

At the end of July, A.D. 144, a hearing took place before the clergy of the Christian congregations in Rome. Marcion, a wealthy Christian ship-owner who had come from Sinope, a sea-port of Pontus along the Black Sea, stood before the presbyters to expound his teachings in order to win others to his point of view. For some years he had been a member of one of the Roman churches, and had proved the sincerity of his faith by making relatively large contributions. No doubt he was a respected member of the Christian community.

But what he now expounded to the presbyters was so monstrous that they were utterly shocked! The hearing ended

---

[28] G. P. Luttikhuizen, 'The Letter to Peter from Philip and the New Testament', *Nag Hammadi Studies*, xiv (1978), 102.

in a harsh rejection of Marcion's views; he was formally excommunicated and his largesse of money was returned. From this time forward Marcion went his own way, energetically propagating a strange kind of Christianity that quickly took root throughout large sections of the Roman Empire and by the end of the second century had become a serious threat to the mainstream Christian Church.

1. MARCION'S IDEAS

Marcion wrote only a single work, which he called *Antitheses* (Ἀντιθέσεις, 'Contradictions') in which he set forth his ideas. Since it has not been preserved (as can easily be understood about a book so dangerous to the Church), we have to content ourselves with deducing its contents from notices contained in the writings of opponents—particularly in Tertullian's five volumes written against Marcion. This, as Tertullian explains in the opening paragraph, was

a new work which we are undertaking in lieu of the old one. My original tract, which was too hurriedly composed, I had subsequently superseded by a fuller edition. This latter I lost, before it was completely published, by the fraud of a person who was then a Christian (*frater*), but became afterwards an apostate.... The necessity thus arose for an amended work, and the occasion of the new edition induced me to make a considerable addition to the treatise.

The main points of Marcion's teaching[29] were the rejection of the Old Testament and a distinction between the Supreme God of goodness and an inferior God of justice, who was the Creator and the God of the Jews.[30] He regarded Christ as the messenger of the Supreme God. The Old and New Testaments, Marcion argued, cannot be reconciled to each other. The code of conduct advocated by Moses was 'an eye for an eye', but

[29] According to Irenaeus (*Adv. Haer.* i. xxvii. 1–3) Marcion had come under the influence of a Syrian Gnostic named Cerdo.

[30] The classic treatment of Marcion is Adolf von Harnack's *Marcion: Das Evangelium vom fremden Gott* (*Texte und Untersuchungen*, xlv; Leipzig, 1921; 2nd ed., 1924; reprinted, Darmstadt, 1960). For a critique of von Harnack, see Barbara Aland, 'Marcion. Versuch einer neuen Interpretation', *Zeitschrift für Theologie und Kirche*, lxx (1973), pp. 420–47, who argues that Marcion was closer to Gnostic theologies than Harnack would admit, especially in Marcion's concept of the creator deity and his (non-) use of the Old Testament. At the same time, however, Marcion developed a non-Gnostic soteriology, rejected cosmological mythology, and radicalized Paul's view of human inability to transcend the world. See also comments by Balás (p. 99 n. 50 below).

Christ set this precept aside. Elisha had had children eaten by
bears; Christ said, 'Let the little children come to me'. Joshua
had stopped the sun in its path in order to continue the
slaughter of his enemies; Paul quoted Christ as commanding,
'Let not the sun go down on your wrath'. In the Old
Testament divorce was permitted and so was polygamy; in the
New Testament neither is allowed. Moses enforced the Jewish
sabbath and Law; Christ has freed believers from both.

Indeed, even within the Old Testament itself Marcion found
contradictions. God commanded that no work should be done
on the sabbath, yet he told the Israelites to carry the ark
around Jericho seven times on the sabbath. No graven image
was to be made, yet Moses was directed to fashion a bronze
serpent. The deity revealed in the Old Testament could not
have been omniscient, otherwise he would not have asked,
'Adam, where are you?' (Gen. iii. 9).

Marcion, therefore, rejected the entire Old Testament.
Furthermore, in his opinion the twelve apostles misunderstood
the teaching of Christ, and, holding him to be the Messiah of
the Jewish God, falsified his words from that standpoint.
Marcion explained this corruption of the true gospel on the
basis of the Epistle to the Galatians in which Paul emphasizes
that there is only one gospel (namely, that which is proclaimed
by him, Gal. i. 8–10), and states that false brethren are
attempting to turn believers from this gospel (i. 6–9; ii. 11).
Convinced that among the early apostolic leaders only Paul
understood the significance of Jesus Christ as the messenger of
the Supreme God, Marcion accepted as authoritative the nine
Epistles sent by Paul to seven churches as well as the one to
Philemon. These ten Epistles became for him the source, the
guarantee, and the norm of true doctrine.

As for the Gospels that were current among the churches,
the only one that Marcion felt he could trust was the Gospel
according to Luke. We cannot say with certainty why he had
confidence in this Gospel, but perhaps the reason was that he
regarded the author, Luke, as a disciple of Paul and believed
him to be more faithful to tradition than the other evangelists.
In any case, this was for Marcion *the* Gospel, without identification as to its human author—a deficiency for which Tertullian castigates Marcion (*Adv. Marc.* iv. 2).

But even this short, two-part canon, comprising the 'Evangelion' and the 'Apostolikon', needed pruning and editorial adjustment. Passages that Marcion could regard only as Judaizing interpolations that had been smuggled into the text by false apostles—these had to be removed so that the authentic text of Gospel and Apostle could once again be available. With thorough-going heedlessness of the consequences, Marcion undertook to expunge everything from the text of Luke and the epistles which echoed or otherwise implied a point of contact with the Old Testament. Since Jesus, according to Marcion, had only the appearance of being human, he could not have been born of a woman. Therefore Marcion omitted most of the first four chapters of Luke (the birth of John the Baptist, the nativity, Jesus' baptism and temptation, with his genealogy, and all reference to Bethelehem and Nazareth). Marcion's gospel began with Luke iii. 1, 'In the fifteenth year of Tiberius Caesar,' and continued with iv. 31, 'God descended into Capernaum, a city of Galilee'. In the last chapters of Luke the omissions are rather more numerous than in the first; the resurrection of Jesus is passed over in silence.[31]

As for the Epistles, Marcion removed whatever he judged were interpolations—that is, anything that did not agree with his understanding of what Paul should have written. Thus, Gal. iii. 16–iv. 6 was deleted because of its reference to Abraham and his descendants; and 2 Thess. i. 6–8, because God is not concerned with 'flaming-fire' and punishment.

No doubt Marcion had a sincere intention to restore the Gospel according to Luke and the Epistles of Paul to what he thought was their original and authentic form[32] But his criteria

---

[31] For a convenient list of the more significant of Marcion's omissions and alterations in Luke and the Pauline Epistles, see Ernest Evans, *Tertullian Adversus Marcionem*, ii (Oxford, 1972), pp. 643–6.

[32] The oft-quoted quip of Harnack (*History of Dogma*, i, p. 89), 'Marcion was the only Gentile Christian who understood Paul, and even he misunderstood him', was originally made by Franz Overbeck in conversation with Harnack at a dinner party in the 1880s. He coined it in imitation of the saying among Hegel's disciples that the only one who understood him had misunderstood him. That is how Overbeck tells the story in his posthumously published *Christentum und Kultur* (Basle, 1919), pp. 218 f.

On Marcion's thorough-going recasting of Pauline theology, see R. Joseph Hoffmann's monograph, *Marcion; On the Restitution of Christianity. An Essay on the Development of Radical & Paulinist Theology in the Second Century* (Chico, 1984)—though some of the author's supporting arguments are more ingenious than convincing.

were subjective, and he merely conformed the texts to his own ideas. Had he succeeded in his aim, access to the sources of Christianity would have been blocked forever.

In preparing his edition of the *Apostolikon*, Marcion apparently arranged the Epistles in accord with their length—except for Galatians which he placed first as being the most important. It was followed by Corinthians (1 and 2), Romans, Thessalonians (1 and 2), Ephesians (which Marcion called 'Laodiceans'[33]), Colossians with Philemon (who lived at Colossae), and Philippians. All told, seven churches were addressed by Paul in Marcion's *Apostolikon*—a feature that leads us to consider at this point the seven 'Marcionite' Prologues to the Pauline Epistles.[34]

2. THE 'MARCIONITE' PROLOGUES

A considerable number of manuscripts of the Latin Vulgate Bible, including the famous codex Fuldensis of A.D. 546, contain short introductory Prologues to the several Pauline Epistles, giving a brief statement concerning the identity of the recipients of each Epistle and the circumstances that led the apostle to write. The detective work of identifying seven of these Prologues as 'Marcionite' was the result of an observation made earlier this century by the Benedictine scholar, Donatien De Bruyne,[35] who noticed what he took to be tell-tale Marcionite features. One of the leading themes of these Prologues is the opposition of Pauline teaching to Judaizing Christianity. In most of the Prologues it is emphasized that the recipients of

---

[33] This is a reasonable inference from Col. iv. 16, if Marcion's text of Ephesians lacked the phrase 'in Ephesus' (ἐν Ἐφέσῳ) in the opening sentence. These two words are absent from 𝔭⁴⁶ and the principal witnesses to the Alexandrian text (ℵ* B* 1739).

[34] On the other hand, the so-called 'anti-Marcionite' prologues to the Gospels need not detain us. These are prologues appearing in some thirty-eight Latin codices (dated between the fifth and tenth centuries) before the Gospels of Mark, Luke, and John. De Bruyne ('Les plus anciens prologues latins des Évangiles', *Revue bénédictine*, xl [1928], pp. 193–214) thought that they (along with a prologue to Matthew, now lost) had been composed for use in an anti-Marcionite edition of the four Gospels published at Rome between A.D. 160 and 180 in opposition to Marcion's truncated *Evangelion*. Subsequent investigation, however, culminating in Jürgen Regul's monograph, *Die antimarcionitischen Evangelienprologe* (Freiburg, 1969), has led most scholars to conclude that the prologues were independent one of another and did not belong to a single set, and that they date, at the earliest, from the fourth century, after Marcionism no longer posed a serious threat to the Church.

[35] 'Prologues bibliques d'origine marcionite', *Revue bénédictine*, xiv (1907), pp. 1–16.

the Epistles had received from Paul the word of truth (*verbum veritatis*) and had been led astray by false apostles (*falsis apostolis*). This strongly suggested to De Bruyne a Marcionite origin for the Prologues, since, as we have seen, for Marcion Paul was the apostle *par excellence* and the other apostles were false. Furthermore, it appears that the Prologues, to judge by connective words, presuppose an edition in which the Epistles to seven churches were arranged in the same order as in Marcion's *Apostolikon*. Still more significant, only a Marcionite would have described the teaching of the 'false apostles' as this is described in the Prologue to the Epistle to the Romans, namely that their converts 'had been brought in to the Law and the Prophets' (*in legem et prophetas erant inducti*). It was the very essence of second-century catholic theology that the Old Testament prophets spoke God's word about Christ and the Church, whereas it was Marcion alone who rejected their writings.

Finally, as confirmatory negative evidence, De Bruyne pointed out that, though this characteristic language is found in seven of the Prologues, in the case of the Prologues for 2 Corinthians, 2 Thessalonians, Hebrews, and the three Pastoral Epistles and Philemon it is modified or lacking. Since Marcion rejected the Pastorals (and Philemon is a private letter without doctrinal teaching), this difference can be readily explained by the supposition that the Prologues for these were added later to a complete corpus of Pauline Epistles which now included them. Furthermore, after the edition of Paul's Epistles to seven churches (for which one Prologue served to introduce 1 and 2 Corinthians, and so too for 1 and 2 Thessalonians) had been enlarged to thirteen (or fourteen) Epistles, obviously additional Prologues needed to be drawn up. The latest of these (probably not before A.D. 350–80) was the Prologue to Hebrews, the wording of which differs markedly among the manuscripts, at least six different forms being extant.

Immediately after De Bruyne's investigations were published, his theory was adopted by other scholars, such as J. Rendel Harris,[36] Adolf Harnack,[37] and F. C. Burkitt,[38] and

---

[36] 'Marcion and the Canon', *Expository Times*, xviii (1906–7), pp. 392–4.

[37] *Theologische Literaturzeitung*, xxxii (1907), cols. 138–40.

[38] *The Gospel History and Its Transmission*, 2nd ed. (Edinburgh, 1907), pp. 353–7.

further evidence was adduced for believing that the earliest set of seven Prologues had been written originally in Greek. Unaware of De Bruyne's article, Peter Corssen[39] independently arrived at the same conclusion, and more recently Schäfer[40] has restated and strengthened the theory. As a consequence of these studies, the Marcionite origin of the Prologues became common opinion, and they are identified as such in Wordsworth and White's large edition of the New Testament Vulgate.

On the other hand, objections to De Bruyne's views were raised by Mundle,[41] Lagrange,[42] Frede,[43] and, still more recently, by Dahl.[44] The last mentioned scholar states concisely the chief argument for each side, and points to another interpretation of the evidence:

> The most obvious argument for a Marcionite origin is derived from the order of Paul's letters to churches presupposed by the Prologues. It is equally obvious that their attestation in Catholic biblical manuscripts constitutes a difficulty for the hypothesis. Almost all scholars have failed to pay sufficient attention to the possibility that the Prologues presuppose an edition which was very similar to, but not identical with, Marcion's *Apostolikon*.[45]

However one may estimate the strengths and weaknesses of the debate concerning the Marcionite origin of the Prologues, they still deserve to be studied for their own sake. For centuries they have been a regular part of the Latin New Testament, and were taken over in pre-Reformation vernacular versions of

[39] 'Zur Überlieferungsgeschichte des Römerbriefes', *Zeitschrift für die neutestamentliche Wissenschaft*, x (1909), pp. 1–45 and 97–102.

[40] Karl Th. Schäfer, 'Marcion und die ältesten Prologe zu den Paulusbriefen', *Kyriakon: Festschrift für Johannes Questen*, ed. by Patrick Granfield and J. A. Jungmann, i (Münster i. W., 1970), pp. 135–50, and 'Marius Victorinus und die marcionitischen Prologe zu den Paulusbriefen', *Revue bénédictine*, lxxx (1970), pp. 7–16.

[41] Wilhelm Mundle, 'Der Herkunft der "Marcionitischen" Prologe zu den Paulusbriefen', *Zeitschrift für die neutestamentliche Wissenschaft*, xxiv (1925), pp. 56–77.

[42] M.-J. Lagrange, 'Les Prologues prétendus marcionites', *Revue biblique*, xxxv (1926), pp. 161–73.

[43] H. J. Frede, *Altlateinische Paulus-Handschriften* (Freiburg i. B., 1964), pp. 165–78.

[44] N. A. Dahl, 'The Origin of the Earliest Prologues to the Pauline Letters', *The Poetics of Faith; Essays offered to Amos Wilder*, ed. by Wm. A. Beardslee (*Semeia*, xii; Missoula, 1978), pp. 233–77.

[45] Ibid., p. 236. Dahl's ideas are elaborated in the research of John J. Clabeaux, 'The Pauline Corpus which Marcion Used: The Text of the Letters of Paul in the Early Second Century', Ph.D. diss., Harvard University, 1983.

the Bible. They contribute, as a concomitant to the canonizing process of the New Testament, to our understanding of conflicts in early Christianity between Paul and the 'false apostles'. In short, they belong to an early stage in the formation of the second half of the New Testament.

3. MARCION'S INFLUENCE

The basis of Marcion's edition of the Gospel according to Luke and ten of the Pauline Epistles was the so-called 'Western' text, which was, it seems, the most widespread, popular text of the New Testament in the second century. In addition to making the deletions of all that involved approval of the Old Testament and the creator God of the Jews, Marcion modified the text through transpositions and occasional additions in order to restore what he considered must have been the original sense. The subsequent influence of Marcion's text has left its mark here and there on the transmission of (non-Marcionite) copies of Luke and Paul.[46] Although textual critics differ as to how many variant readings in the New Testament manuscripts trace their origin to Marcion's edition, few doubt that, to some extent at least, his shadow must be taken into account in textual evaluation of such passages as the following.

(*a*) Luke v. 39 ('the old wine is better') was omitted by Marcion, probably because it seemed to him to exalt the Old Testament over the New Testament. The same omission occurs in MS D and the Old Latin.

(*b*) In Rom. i. 16 ('to the Jew first and also to the Greek') the omission of 'first' in several witnesses (B G Old Lat Sah) was probably due to the influence of Marcion, to whom the privilege accorded the Jews was unacceptable.

(*c*) In Luke xi. 2 MSS 162 and 700 preserve the Marcionite form of the petition in the Lord's Prayer, 'Let thy holy Spirit

---

[46] For examples of probable Marcionite textual disturbance in New Testament manuscripts, see August Pott, 'Marcions Evangelientext', *Zeitschrift für Kirchengeschichte*, xlii (1923), pp. 202; Robert S. Wilson, *Marcion. A Study of a Second-Century Heretic* (London, 1933), pp. 145–50; E. C. Blackman, *Marcion and His Influence* (London, 1948), pp. 50–2 and 128–71; H. J. Vogels, 'Der Einfluss Marcions und Tatians auf Text und Kanon des NT', in *Synoptische Studien*. Alfred Wikenhauser ... dargebracht (Munich, 1953), pp. 278–89; and idem, *Handbuch der Textkritik des Neuen Testaments*, 2nd ed. (Bonn, 1955), pp. 140–4.

come upon us and cleanse us', replacing the petition concerning the kingdom.

Another significant feature of Marcion's conception of Scripture was the organic way in which the two elements *Gospel* and *Apostle* stood in balanced relation to one another. Neither of the two could be understood alone, but each guaranteed the sense and illustrated the importance of the other. Thus the two parts of the Marcionite canon constituted a genuine unity, the significance of which was still further increased for him by the fact that the Old Testament was no longer regarded as sacred Scripture. Although Marcion's collection of sacred writings had apparently no comprehensive title,[47] yet it must be regarded as a coherent canon; it took the place of the Old Testament and therefore had the character of a canon of Scripture, and it comprised a fixed number of books.

The question whether the Church's canon preceded or followed Marcion's canon continues to be debated. According to the Church Fathers, Marcion rejected certain books, and selected others for his canon out of a more comprehensive Church canon. Harnack, on the other hand, developed the thesis that Marcion was the first to construct a formal canon of Christian Scripture and that the Church followed his lead, eventually adopting four Gospels and thirteen Epistles of Paul, in addition to other books as well.[48] John Knox, following suggestions made by F. C. Baur and others, went still further and maintained that Marcion had a kind of proto-Luke which the Church later enlarged in the interest of anti-Marcionite polemic, producing our present Luke sometime after A.D. 150.[49] Knox was unable, however, to show that after the middle of the second century conditions prevailed in the Church to render possible the immediate general acceptance of a newly redacted gospel.

Such estimations of the degree of influence exerted by

[47] While this may appear surprising, yet, as von Campenhausen remarks, it 'ceases to be strange when we realize that at that time no exact designation for the Old Testament as a whole was current either' (*The Formation of the Christian Bible*, p. 163 n. 67).

[48] Harnack, *Marcion*, pp. 210–15, and *Origin of the New Testament*, pp. 30–5 and 57–60, followed by von Campenhausen, 'Marcion et les origines du canon néotestamentaire', *Revue d'histoire et de philosophie religieuses*, xlvi (1966), pp. 213–26.

[49] John Knox, *Marcion and the New Testament. An Essay in the Early History of the Canon* (Chicago, 1942), pp. 19–38. For several earlier scholars who anticipated Knox's ideas, see Ernst Jacquier, *Le Nouveau Testament dans l'Église chrétienne*, i. 3ᵉ éd. (Paris, 1911), pp. 158 f.

Marcion's canon fail to distinguish the fundamental idea of canonicity from the actual drawing up of a list of canonical books. The canon of the four Gospels was already in the process of development, and the authority of apostolic writings was beginning to be placed alongside the gospel writings. The canon of Marcion may have been the first that was publicly proposed, but it does not at all follow, as Evans has correctly perceived, 'that except for the needs of controversy against him the great church would not at some time have defined its own canon, or that its introduction of Petrine and Johannine elements was designed as a counterweight to the influence of Marcion and St. Paul'.[50] It is nearer to the truth to regard Marcion's canon as accelerating the process of fixing the Church's canon, a process that had already begun in the first half of the second century. It was in opposition to Marcion's criticism that the Church first became fully conscious of its inheritance of apostolic writings. As Grant aptly puts it, 'Marcion forced more orthodox Christians to examine their own presuppositions and to state more clearly what they already believed'.[51]

III. MONTANISM

A significant factor in the 'hardening' of the canon of the New Testament was the influence of Montanism, an enthusiastic and apocalyptic movement that broke out in the second half of the second century. It originated in Phrygia, deep in the hinterland of Asia Minor, and quickly spread through the whole Church, both East and West. It claimed to be a religion of the Holy Spirit and was marked by ecstatic outbursts which it regarded as the only true form of Christianity.[52]

---

[50] Op. cit., p. xvi. Cf. also the measured remarks of David L. Balás in 'Marcion Revisited: A "Post-Harnack" Perspective', in *Texts and Testament; Critical Essays on the Bible and Early Church Fathers*, ed. by W. Eugene March (San Antonio, 1980), pp. 97–108.

[51] R. M. Grant, *The Formation of the New Testament*, p. 126.

[52] Cf. P. de Labriolle, *La Crise montaniste* (Paris, 1913); idem, *Les Sources du l'histoire de Montanisme* (Fribourg-Paris, 1913); Agostino Faggiotto, *L'eresia dei Frigî* (*Scrittori cristiani antichi*, ix; Rome, 1924); F. E. Vokes, 'The Use of Scripture in the Montanist Controversy', *Studia Evangelica*, ed. by F. L. Cross, v (Berlin, 1968), pp. 317–20; Frederick C. Klawiter, 'The New Prophecy in Early Christianity; the Origin, Nature, and Development of Montanism', Ph.D. diss., University of Chicago, 1975; and H. Paulson, 'Die Bedeutung des Montanismus für die Herausbildung des Kanons', *Vigiliae Christianae*, xxxii (1978), pp. 19–52.

Montanism first appeared, according to Epiphanius, in the year 156, or, if we follow Eusebius, in 172.[53] The movement began at Ardoban, a village on the borders of Mysia and Phrygia. Here Montanus, sometimes described as a former priest of Cybele,[54] fell into a trance soon after his conversion and began to speak in tongues. He announced that he was the inspired instrument of a new outpouring of the Holy Spirit, the 'Paraclete' promised in John's Gospel (xiv. 15–17; xvii. 7–15). Associated with Montanus were two women, Prisca (or Priscilla) and Maximilla, who, being struck by the prophetic afflatus, left their husbands and joined themselves to the mission of Montanus.

The fundamental conviction of the New Prophecy in its earliest form was that the Heavenly Jerusalem was shortly to descend upon earth and be located at the little Phrygian town of Pepuza, some twenty miles north-east from Hierapolis.[55] Here the three of them settled and began to utter prophetic oracles. Their pronouncements were written down and gathered together as sacred documents similar to the words of Old Testament prophets or the sayings of Jesus.

About a score of such oracles have survived, plainly showing the ecstatic character of this form of utterance, in that the prophet does not speak in his or her own name as a human

[53] The conflict between Epiphanius (*Panarion*, xlviii. 1.2) and Eusebius (*Hist. eccl.* IV. xxvii. 1) has resulted, as would be expected, in a wide diversity of opinion among scholars; for a summary and discussion (which concludes in favour of Eusebius) see T. D. Barnes, 'The Chronology of Montanism', *Journal of Theological Studies*, n.s. xxi (1970), pp. 403–8, and his monograph entitled *Tertullian, a Historical and Literary Study* (Oxford, 1971), esp. pp. 130–42.

[54] According to Didymus (*De Trin.* iii. 41) Montanus had been 'an idol priest'. The epithets *abscissus* and *semivir* ('mutilated and emasculated') applied to him by Jerome (*Ep. ad Marcellam*, xli. 4) suggest that Jerome may have believed him to have been a priest of Cybele. On the other hand, Wilhelm Schepelern, after a careful examination of literary and epigraphic evidence, concludes: 'In spite of the Phrygian origin of the New Prophecy, neither our Montanist nor our anti-Montanist sources furnish us a valid basis to support the view that Montanism in its original form was an off-shoot of the Phrygian cult' (*Montanismen og de Phrygiske Kulter* [Copenhagen, 1920], German trans., *Der Montanismus und die Phrygischen Kulte; eine religionsgeschichtliche Untersuchung* [Tübingen, 1929], p. 160).

[55] The location of Pepuza has been sought by travellers in Asia Minor for nearly a hundred years. The most recent investigator, August Strobel, is convinced that it lay somewhere in or near the upland plain of Kırbasan south of Uşak, north-west of Kinar, and a little to the north of the upper Mæander (*Das heilige Land der Montanisten. Eine religionsgeographische Untersuchung* [*Religionsgeschtliche Versuche und Vorarbeiten*, xxxvii; Berlin, 1980], pp. 29–34).

being, but the Spirit of God is the speaker. Epiphanius quotes Montanus as saying, 'I am neither an angel nor an envoy, but I the Lord God, the Father, have come'.[56] Didymus reports another saying of Montanus, 'I am the Father and the Son and the Paraclete'.[57] Montanus' view of the divine activity is expressed in another oracle: 'Behold, man is as a lyre and I hover over him as a plectrum. Man sleeps but I watch. Behold, it is the Lord who removes the hearts of men and gives them [other] hearts.'[58] The leaders of the movement thought of their mission as the final phase of revelation: 'After me', declared Maximilla, 'there will be no more prophecy, but the End.'[59]

Such pronouncements were made still more impressive by the manner in which they were presented. According to Epiphanius, a ceremony was held frequently in the churches of Pepuza when seven virgins, dressed in white and carrying torches, entered and proceeded to deliver oracles to the congregation. He comments that 'they manifest a kind of enthusiasm that dupes those who are present, and provokes them to tears, leading to repentance'.[60]

Along with their vivid expectation of the near approach of the end of the world, the Montanists also soon developed ascetic traits and disciplinary rigorism in the face of the growing worldliness of the Great Church. Another feature of the Montanist movement was what may be called a demo-cratic reaction against the clerical aristocracy, which from the time of Ignatius was becoming more and more institutional-ized. A feature offensive to some in the Great Church was the admission of women to positions of leadership.[61]

The movement spread abroad speedily, and was soon to be found in Rome as well as in North Africa. The temperament of the West led to suppression of ecstatic features and an emphasis on ethical requirements. By about the year 206 Montanism won the allegiance of Tertullian, who became an enthusiastic advocate of a strict and rigid penitential discipline.

At first the Church was perplexed as to what stand it should

[56] *Haer.* xlviii. 2.   [57] *De Trin.* III. xli. 1.   [58] Epiphanius, *Haer.* xlviii. 4.
[59] Ibid., xlviii. 11.   [60] Ibid., xliv. 2.
[61] See, e.g., Elaine Pagels, *The Gnostic Gospels* (New York, 1979), pp. 59–69, and F. C. Klawiter, 'The Role of Martyrdom and Persecution in Developing the Priestly Authority of Women in Early Christianity; A Case Study of Montanism', *Church History*, xlix (1980), pp. 251–61.

take toward the new movement. It felt instinctively that Montanus' preaching could not be the work of the Spirit; at the same time, however, it did not have the weapons to fend off this new development. Attempts were made by applying exorcism to cast out the spirit at work in the two prophetesses. When this measure failed, synods began to convene to consider counter-measures. Eventually the bishops and synods of Asia Minor, though not with one voice, declared the new prophecy to be the work of demons, and cut off the Montanists from the fellowship of the Church.

During the following decades the fate of the Montanists was sealed. First, after some vacillation, the bishop of Rome, then the bishop of Carthage and the remaining African bishops, followed the example of their colleagues in Asia Minor and pronounced the 'Cataphrygians' (οἱ κατὰ Φρύγας) to be a heretical sect.

We must now examine the bearing of this movement and its writings upon the development of the New Testament canon. The influence of Montanism in this regard was twofold: the production of new 'sacred' scriptures, and the development within the Great Church of a mistrust of apocalyptic literature, including even the Johannine Apocalypse. Some Catholics also rejected the Epistle to the Hebrews because of the use that Montanists made of vi. 1–6.

The spirit-oracles of the great Montanist prophets were collected and written down at an early stage. Hippolytus, given to hyperbole, speaks of an 'infinite' number of such alleged utterances of the Paraclete.[62] One such collection was drawn up 'according to Asterius Orbanus' (κατὰ Ἀστέριον Ὀρβανόν),[63] a title that reminds one of the manner in which the canonical Gospels are customarily entitled. Except for occasional quotations made by their opponents, however, none of these Montanist 'new scriptures' (καιναὶ γραφαί)[64] have survived—probably because at a later date imperial decrees ordered the destruction of all Montanist codices.[65]

---

[62] Hippolytus, *Ref.* viii. 19.

[63] So Eusebius (*Hist. eccl.* v. xvii. 17) in citing the anonymous anti-Montanist author.

[64] Ibid., VI. xx. 3.

[65] *Cod. Theod.* XVI. v. 34.1. Schneemelcher unwarrantably doubts that such literature ever existed (*New Testament Apocrypha*, ii [Philadelphia, 1964], p. 863 n. 2).

There was also a 'catholic epistle' composed by one Themiso (or Themison), a prominent Montanist who seems to have assumed the leadership of the sect following the death of Montanus and the two prophetesses. We hear of him and his encyclical epistle through fragments of a work by Apollonius of Ephesus, written, so Eusebius tells us, forty years after Montanus began his bogus prophesying. The excerpts quoted by Eusebius are devoted mostly to personal abuse, or, as Apollonius calls it, 'recognizing a tree by its fruits'. Of Themiso he says:

> Themiso, . . . boasting that he was a martyr, dared, in imitation of the apostle, to compose a 'catholic epistle' ($\kappa\alpha\theta o\lambda\iota\kappa\dot{\eta}\nu$ $\dot{\epsilon}\pi\iota\sigma\tau o\lambda\dot{\eta}\nu$), and in it to instruct those whose faith was better than his own, contending with empty-sounding words and uttering blasphemies against the Lord, the apostles, and the holy Church.[66]

Which apostle it was that Themiso dared to imitate we do not know; probably it was Paul, who was often referred to simply as 'the apostle'.[67] Unfortunately for us, Apollonius is more interested in denouncing Themiso than in giving us information as to the contents of the epistle. Since, however, Themiso 'dared . . . to instruct those whose faith was better than his', the epistle was addressed to the Church as a whole, and not simply to Montanist congregations. That he 'uttered blasphemies against the Lord, the apostles, and the holy Church' must mean that the epistle presented as authoritative teaching the emphases that were characteristic of Montanist tenets.

To what extent Themiso may have claimed special inspiration for his epistle we do not know. In any case, the epistle, along with other writings in which Montanists set forth their visions and the stories of their martyrs, had wide circulation within the sect and were read aloud in services of public worship.

How far such documents had positive influence on the New Testament text and canon has been variously estimated. Rendel Harris thought that he could detect nearly a dozen instances of pro-Montanist glosses preserved in the so-called

---

[66] Eusebius, *Hist. eccl.* v. xviii. 5.

[67] According to T. Barns, the 'Catholic Epistle' of Themiso was 2 Peter (*Expositer*, VI Ser., viii [1903], pp. 40–62).

Western text of codex Bezae. Most of these involve the addition
of references to the Holy Spirit in the Book of Acts,[68] but
whether they were inspired by Montanist doctrine is not
known. It is certainly significant, as von Campenhausen
remarks, that

> Nowhere do we hear that these writings were described as a 'New
> Gospel', were cited as 'scripture', or were combined as a third section
> with the old Bible to form a new Montanist canon... The real
> authority to which appeal was made in the Montanist camp was not
> a new canon, but the Spirit and his 'gifts'; and it was recognition of
> these which was demanded from the catholic church.[69]

If it appears that little or no Montanist influence intruded
itself into the New Testament, the same cannot be said concerning the pressure that was exerted negatively, arising from an
anti-Montanist reaction. It is understandable that, in the give-
and-take of disputation between the orthodox and the followers
of Montanus,[70] a kind of backlash would make itself felt. In the
Great Church there developed a certain mistrust of all recent
writings of a prophetical nature. Not only did such a feeling tend
to discredit several apocalypses that may have been, in various
parts of the Church, on their way to establishing themselves, but
also, as was mentioned earlier, even the Apocalypse of John was
sometimes brought under a cloud of suspicion because of its
usefulness in supporting the 'new prophecy'.

One such instance involved a vigorous anti-Montanist
named Gaius (or Caius), said by Eusebius to be 'a very learned
man' (*Hist. eccl.* VI. xx. 3) and evidently a respected Roman
presbyter. Early in the third century Gaius published a notable
disputation against the Montanist Proclus,[71] in which he seems

---

[68] J. Rendel Harris, *Codex Bezae. A Study of the So-called Western Text of the New
Testament* (*Texts and Studies*, ii, no. 1; Cambridge, 1891), pp. 148–53.

[69] *The Formation of the Christian Bible*, pp. 227 f.

[70] For an entertaining example of such a dialogue between a Catholic and a
Montanist, dating from the fourth century, see de Labriolle, *Les Sources de l'histoire de
Montanisme*, pp. 93–108. (It has been announced that an English translation of
Montanist texts and testimonies, with the original Greek texts, will be published by
Ronald E. Heine in the series *Texts and Translations* of Scholars Press.)

[71] Fragments of Gaius' *Dialogue against Proclus* have been preserved by Dionysius bar
Salibi in his commentary *In Apocalypsin, Actus et Epistulas Catholicas*, ed. by I. Sedláček
(Paris, 1909); cf. John Gwynn, 'Hippolytus and his "Heads against Caius"', *Herma-
thena*, vi (1888), pp. 397–418, and R. M. Grant, *Second-Century Christianity, a Collection of
Fragments* (London, 1946), pp. 105–6.

to have been a spokesman for the extreme anti-Montanists. As such he was not content with rejecting the new scriptures of the Montanists, but, in order to undermine and undercut the theology and practices of his opponents, he went to the extent of revising the New Testament. Gaius not only denied the Pauline authorship of the Epistle to the Hebrews—an Epistle which, with its declaration of the hopelessly lost condition of the apostate (vi. 4–6), must have had the effect of justifying Montanism's harsh penitential practice—but he also rejected the Book of Revelation and the Gospel of John, the latter with its reference to the promised Paraclete. The reasons alleged for not receiving the Apocalypse have to do with its garish imagery and millenarianism, while the differences between the Synoptic Gospels and John's Gospel were taken to prove that the latter is wrong and so ought not to be included among books recognized by the Church.

Besides Gaius' debate with Proclus, we hear of an obscure Christian group in Asia Minor that Epiphanius (*Haer.* li. 3) jocosely dubbed the 'Alogi', a *double entendre* for 'irrational' and 'rejecting the Logos'. In their reaction to Montanism they, like Gaius, questioned the authority of those sacred books on which the Montanists were accustomed to base their claims, except that they were not content merely to reject John's Gospel and Apocalypse—they defamed them by attributing them to the arch-heretic Cerinthus.[72]

Yet another who attacked the Montanists was the anonymous author of a refutation of the heresy, written in 192/3 and quoted at some length by Eusebius (*Hist. eccl.* v. xvi. 2–xvii. 4). A point that is most interesting for the history of the development of the canon is a reference at the beginning of the treatise (v. xvi. 3) where the author says that he had long hesitated to draw up such an anti-Montanist treatise.

not through lack of ability to refute the falsehood or bear testimony for the truth, but from fear and apprehension that I might perchance seem to some to be adding a new article or precept to the word of the new covenant of the gospel (τῷ τῆς τοῦ εὐαγγελίου καινῆς διαθήκης

---

[72] Cf. August Bludau, *Die ersten Gegner der Johannesschriften* (*Biblische Studien*, xxii; Freiburg i. B., 1925), pp. 220–30, and J. D. Smith, 'Gaius and the Controversy over the Johannine Literature', Ph.D. diss., Yale University, 1979.

λόγῳ), to which no one who has chosen to live in accordance with the gospel itself can add and from which one can not take away.

The Greek words cited within parentheses can also be translated, 'the word of the New Testament of the gospel', and the expression, irrespective of the English rendering, as van Unnik notes, makes 'the first unequivocal connection between καινὴ διαθήκη and Christian literature'.[73] The anonymous author obviously is speaking about a relatively closed collection of books, but at the same time he implies that his own treatise might conceivably come to be included in it. He does not explicitly specify the contents of this 'word' (λόγος), except that it embodies the terms of the 'new covenant'. Here we see the transition between the message given in ἡ καινὴ διαθήκη τοῦ εὐαγγελίου and the collection of books that will soon be described as 'the New Covenant' or 'the New Testament'.

To sum up, the influence of the Montanist movement on the conception of the canon was the opposite of that exerted by Marcion. Whereas the latter had spurred the Church to recognize the breadth of the written corpus of authoritative writings, the insistence of the former on the continuous gift of inspiration and prophecy influenced the Church to emphasize the final authority of apostolic writings as the rule of faith. By rejecting the extravagances of Montanism, the Church took the first step toward the adoption of a closed canon of Scripture.

IV. PERSECUTIONS AND THE SCRIPTURES

Apart from the pressures exerted by various Gnostic and Montanist groups upon the Great Church to determine which books should be regarded as authoritative, during periods of persecution another set of circumstances confronted believers, forcing them to be certain which books were Scripture and which were not. When the imperial police knocked at the door and demanded of Christians that they surrender their sacred books, it became a matter of conscience in deciding whether one could hand over the Gospel of John as well as, say, the

---

[73] W. C. van Unnik, "Ἡ καινὴ διαθήκη — a Problem in the Early History of the Canon', *Studia Patristica*, i (*Texte und Untersuchungen*, lxxix; Berlin, 1961), p. 217; reprinted in *Sparsa Collecta*, ii (Leiden, 1980), p. 162.

Gospel of Thomas without incurring the guilt of sacrilege.[74] In such an existential moment most Christians would naturally be careful to determine on solid grounds precisely which were the books for adherence to which they were prepared to suffer. The persecution under Diocletian may almost be said to have given the touch by which previously somewhat unsettled elements of the canon were further crystallized and fixed.

The situation in A.D. 303 was serious enough. On February 23rd of that year in Nicomedia there was posted an imperial edict ordering all copies of the Christian Scriptures and liturgical books to be surrendered and burned, all churches to be demolished, and no meetings for Christian worship to be held.[75] The punishment inflicted for resistance was imprisonment, torture, and, in some cases, death.

Several documents—mainly Acts of Martyrs and documents relating to the beginnings of the Donatist controversy—describe with vivid detail the thoroughness of the search for Christian literature. There is, for example, the account of a police raid at Cirta, the capital of Numidia (now part of Algeria), reported in the *Gesta apud Zenophilum*.[76] The curator (mayor) comes to 'the house where the Christians used to meet', and a demand is made for books; the library of the church is found empty, but the police go on to the houses of the church officials. One Catulinus, a subdeacon, brings out a very large codex (*codicum unum pernimium maiorem*). The officer asks, 'Why have you given over only one codex? Bring forth the Scriptures which you have'. Catulinus and Mareuclius reply, 'We don't have any more, because we are subdeacons; the readers (*lectores*) have the codices'. Further interrogation leads

[74] During the Diocletian persecution Mensurius, the bishop of Carthage, hid his copies of the Scriptures in a safe place, and in their stead handed over to the waiting magistrates writings of 'the new heretics'— identified by Frend as probably Manichean documents (see W. H. C. Frend, *Martyrdom and Persecution in the Early Church* [New York, 1967], p. 372).

[75] Diocletian's edict rested on the Roman statute that forbade not only the exercise of magical arts but also the science of magic, and therefore condemned all books of magic to be burned. The Christians were accused of employing magic, and their Scriptures were treated as books of magic.

[76] *Corpus Scriptorum Ecclesiasticorum Latinorum*, xxvi, pp. 186–8. Part of the account is also quoted by Augustine in *Contra Cresconium*, iii. 29. For a translation of the entire account, see *The New Eusebius, Documents Illustrative of the History of the Church to A.D. 337*, ed. by James Stevenson (London, 1963), pp. 287–9.

to a visit to the home of Eugenius, who produces four codices; Felix, five; Victorinus, eight; Projectus, five large and two small codices; Victor the schoolmaster (*grammaticus*) brings out two codices and four 'quinions' (that is, apparently loose sheets, or gatherings, not yet sewn together into a book). Coddeo is not at home, but his wife gives the officer six codices. All this is the product of a single round.

In other instances stiffer resistance is offered when believers were asked to give up their Christian books. In the account of the martyrdom of Agapê, Irenê, and Chionê,[77] at successive hearings the three women were interrogated by the prefect Dulcitius of Thessalonica, who inquired, 'Do you have in your possession any writings, parchments, or books (ὑπομνήματα ἢ διφθέραι ἢ βιβλία) of the impious Christians?' Chionê replied, 'We do not, Sir. Our present emperors have taken these from us'. On the next day when Irenê was once again brought before the court, the prefect asked, 'Who was it that advised you to retain these parchments and writings (τὰς διφθέρας ταύτας καὶ τὰς γραφάς) up to the present time?' 'It was almighty God', Irenê replied, 'who bade us love him unto death. For this reason we did not dare to be traitors, but we chose to be burned alive or suffer anything else that might happen to us rather than betray them' (προδοῦναι αὐτάς, i.e. the writings).

After sentencing the young woman to be placed naked in the public brothel, the prefect gave orders that the writings (τὰ γραμματεῖα) in the cabinets and chests belonging to her were to be burned publicly. The account concludes by describing how, in March and April of the year 304, the three became martyrs for their faith by being burned at the stake.

V. OTHER POSSIBLE INFLUENCES

(1) An aspect of ancient book-making that at an early date may have had some bearing on the eventual gathering together of the four Gospels in one document, or the Epistles of Paul in one document, was the adoption among Christians by the end of the first century or at the beginning of the second century of

[77] For the text and translation see Herbert Musurillo, *The Acts of the Christian Martyrs* (Oxford, 1972), pp. 281–93.

the codex or leaf-book, which replaced the use of the time-
honoured roll. The maximum length of a roll convenient to
handle appears to have been about thirty-five feet in length.[78]
(The Gospel according to Luke or the Book of Acts would
require, it is reckoned, a roll of about thirty to thirty-two feet in
length.) As long as Christians used the roll in the transmission
of their sacred books, the four Gospels or the Pauline Epistles
could be collected only by assembling several rolls in the same
box or chest. When, however, the codex form of book was
adopted, several or even all of the separate documents of what
came to be called the New Testament could be physically
assembled in one volume.[79] Furthermore, such a format
would, in the course of time, promote a degree of fixity in the
sequence of documents included in the collection.[80]

(2) Several significant collections of books and lists of
'canonical' authors were being drawn up by Jews and by
pagans during the early centuries of the Christian era. Although in most cases direct influence on the Church is out of
the question, at the same time one can observe that such developments were taking place more or less contemporaneously
with the emergence of the New Testament canon. Thus, the
precise limits of the Jewish Scriptures seem to have been settled
by about the end of the first Christian century. After the fall of
Jerusalem A.D. 70, both a rabbinical school (Beth ha-Midrash)
and court (Beth Din, or Sanhedrin) were established at Jamnia
(also called Jabneh), a city a dozen miles south of Joppa.
Here among the subjects discussed over the years was the status
of certain Biblical books (e.g. Ecclesiastes, Esther, and the
Song of Songs) whose canonicity may have been still open to

[78] See Metzger, *Manuscripts of the Greek Bible* (New York, 1981), pp. 15–16, and
Menahem Haran, 'Book-Size and the Device of Catch-Lines in the Biblical Canon',
Journal of Jewish Studies, xxxvi (1985), pp. 1–11.

[79] There is, however, as Roberts and Skeat remind us, no evidence whatsoever to
indicate that the codex played any part in the selection of the books that were
assembled (C. H. Roberts and T. C. Skeat, 'The Christian Codex and the Canon of
Scripture', *The Birth of the Codex* [London, 1983], pp. 62–6).

[80] For a discussion of how a (relatively) fixed order was maintained for treatises in
roll-form, see N. M. Sarna, 'The Order of the Books', *Studies in Jewish Bibliography,
History, and Literature in honor of I. Edward Kiev*, ed. by Charles Berlin (New York, 1971),
pp. 407–13.

question.[81] It is widely supposed that a particular Sanhedrin at Jamnia, convened about the year 90, finally settled the limits of the Old Testament canon. The debates, as Bentzen suggests, seem to have been concerned 'not so much ... with acceptance of certain writings into the canon, but rather with their *right to remain there*. ... The synod of the rabbis tried to account for the right of the *books* to be part of the *Book*' (Bentzen's italics).[82]

By about A.D. 200, principally through the work of Rabbi Judah ha-Nasi, various collections of oral Mishnaic material (*mishnayot*) were made, culminating in the authoritative written Mishnah.[83] This, in slightly different recensions, formed the basis of both the Palestinian and Babylonian Talmuds.

The collection of a quite different type of material in the West took place at the beginning of the third century through the efforts of the celebrated Roman jurist, Ulpian. With assiduous industry, Ulpian assembled the very voluminous legal decisions made by earlier emperors on points laid before them, and arranged them in epitomes. Eventually extracts of his work formed about a third of the comprehensive Justinian Code.

[81] The precise status of the rabbinical assembly at Jamnia is disputed; see Jack P. Lewis, 'What Do We Mean by Jabneh?' *Journal of Bible and Religion*, xxxii (1964), pp. 125–32, reprinted in *The Canon and Massorah of the Hebrew Bible*, ed. by S. Z. Leiman (New York, 1974), pp. 254–61; Robert C. Newman, 'The Council of Jamnia and the Old Testament Canon', *Westminster Theological Journal*, xxxviii (1975–6), pp. 319–49; G. Sternberger, 'Die sogenannte "Synod von Jabne" und die frühe Christenheit', *Kairos*, xix (1977), pp. 14–21; Jack N. Lightstone, 'The Formation of the Biblical Canon of Late Antiquity: Prolegomena to a General Reassessment', *Studies in Religion*, viii (1979), pp. 135–42; and Roger T. Beckwith, *The Old Testament Canon of the New Testament Church, and its Background in Early Judaism* (London, 1985; Grand Rapids, 1986), pp. 176–7.

[82] A. Bentzen, *Introduction to the Old Testament*, i (Copenhagen, 1948), p. 31. It may be that the debates over what were termed the Gilyonim and the books of the Minim resulted, as Moore thought, in the repudiation of Christian gospels; see George F. Moore, 'The Definition of the Jewish Canon and the Repudiation of Christian Scriptures', *Essays in Modern Theology and Related Subjects, a Testimonial to Charles Augustus Briggs* (New York, 1911), pp. 99–125. (According to Moore, the purpose of a 'canon' is always to fence out, rather than to fence in; cf. his *Judaism*, i, pp. 86 f., 243 f.; iii, pp. 34 f. and 67–9.) Cf. also K. G. Kuhn, 'Gilyonim und sifre Minim', *Judentum-Urchristentum-Kirche: Festschrift für Joachim Jeremias*, ed. by Walter Eltester (Berlin, 1960), pp. 24–61.

[83] It is possible also, as Hermann L. Strack conjectured, that 'the Jews were led to codify in a definitive form and thus also to commit to writing their oral traditions with a view, in part at least, to the New Testament canon then in process of formation' (*Introduction to the Talmud and Midrash* [Philadelphia, 1931], p. 12); cf. also W. D. Davies, *The Setting of the Sermon on the Mount* (Cambridge, 1964), p. 274.

Perhaps of somewhat greater significance as providing a model of sorts for the canonization of Christian writings was the Alexandrian custom of drawing up lists of authors whose writings in a given literary genre were widely regarded as standard works. These exemplars were called 'canons' (κανό-νες). Scholars attached to the celebrated Alexandrian Library and Museum, including Zenodotus of Ephesus (*fl. c.* 285 B.C.), Aristophanes of Byzantium (*fl. c.* 195 B.C.), and Aristarchus of Samothrace (*fl. c.* 185 B.C.), collected writings of earlier authors, prepared corrected texts, and published what were regarded as standard editions, together with separate treatises on the texts. Eventually there was drawn up the so-called Alexandrian canon, the exact authorship and date of which are uncertain; it contained lists of 'standard' epic poets, iambic poets, lyric poets, elegiac poets, tragic poets, comic poets, historians, orators, and philosophers.[84] In the case of the canon of the ten Attic orators, 'the evidence favors the view that the canon only slowly developed through the activities of the Greek and Roman Atticizing movement, and did not reach a final and fossilized form until the second century of our Era.'[85] Whether and to what extent one thinks that educated Christians were influenced by the example of the Alexandrian canon of classical Greek authors, it is at least significant that for a certain period of time both canons were developing simultaneously.

The collection of Orphic fragments had already begun at an early date, and Clement of Alexandria was well aware of the elaborate discussions concerning the genuineness of Orphic literature current in his day.[86] Practically nothing had been written by Orpheus himself, and almost everything in the Orphic tradition was open to debate.

The collection of authoritative magical texts, completed

---

[84] See O. Kroehnert, *Canonesne poetarum scriptorum artificum per antiquitatem fuerunt?* (Koenigsberg, 1897), and Hugo Rabe, 'Die Listen griechischer Profanschriftsteller', *Rheinisches Museum für Philologie*, lxv (1910), pp. 339–44.

[85] See A. E. Douglas, 'Cicero, Quintilian, and the Canon of Ten Attic Orators', *Mnemosyne*, ix ser., iv (1956), p. 40. Douglas takes a strict view of what constitutes a canon: 'A list that fluctuates as to number and composition through the ages is not a canon..., indeed, it is not even a list, but a series of lists. Therefore the term "canon" has no value unless the list so designated had both authority and permanence'.

[86] *Strom.* I. xxi. 131.

perhaps at the close of the second century and preserved in the great Paris Magical Papyrus (Bibl. Nat., suppl. grec 574), written about A.D. 300, has been thought to show some (superficial) analogies with the emergence of the scriptural canon.[87] However one may estimate such a comparison, certainly the emergence of the Christian canon contributed to the superstitious use of amulets containing Biblical texts.[88]

---

[87] So H. D. Betz, 'The Formation of Authoritative Tradition in the Greek Magical Papyri', *Jewish and Christian Self-Definition*; iii, *Self-Definition in the Greco-Roman World*, ed. by B. F. Meyer and E. P. Sanders (Philadelphia, 1982), pp. 161–70. Betz asks: 'Was there an urge to assemble the tradition because of the competing Christian and Jewish canons of the Bible?' (p. 169).

[88] Cf. H. Mulder, 'De canon en het volksgelof. Een onderzoek van de amuletten der ersten Christenen', *Gereformeerd theologisch tijdschrift*, liv (1954), pp. 97–138; also published separately (Kampen, 1954).

V

Development of the Canon in the East

AFTER the period of the Apostolic Fathers we enter a new era in the history of the books of the New Testament in the Christian Church. Now the canonical Gospels come to be regarded as a closed collection, and are accepted under this form throughout the whole Church. The Epistles of Paul likewise come to be known and accepted as inspired Scripture, and here and there the same is true for the Acts of the Apostles and the Book of Revelation. Several other books are still on the fringe of the canon, not recognized by all, such as the Epistle to the Hebrews and the Epistles of James, of Peter, of John, and of Jude. We must now see how these several writings were regarded in various regions into which the Christian faith had spread.

I. SYRIA

The churches of Eastern Syria in the Kingdom of Osrhoëne seem to have been the first to develop in a country that had not been under the extensive influence of Hellenism. The political fortunes of Edessa, capital of Osrhoëne, present a remarkable contrast to those of other centres of early Christianity. Until A.D. 216 in the reign of the Emperor Caracalla, Edessa lay outside the Roman Empire. Christianity seems to have reached the Euphrates valley about the middle of the second century, that is, while the country was still an independent state. Its people, unlike the Greek-speaking Syrians in the west with their headquarters at Antioch, used Syriac as their mother tongue. It is not surprising that the Christianity of Edessa began to develop independently, without the admixture of Greek philosophy and Roman methods of government that at early date modified primitive Christianity in the West and transformed it into the amalgam known as Catholicism.

According to early traditions and legends embodied in the *Doctrine of Addai* (*c.* A.D. 400), the earliest New Testament of the

Syriac-speaking Church consisted of the Gospel, the Epistles of
Paul, and the Book of Acts. Just prior to his death, Addai
admonishes his hearers in the following words:

> The Law and the Prophets and the Gospel from which you read
> every day before the people, and the Epistles of Paul which Simon
> Cephas sent us from the city of Rome, and the Acts of the Twelve
> Apostles which John the son of Zebedee sent us from Ephesus—from
> these writings you shall read in the Churches of the Messiah, and
> besides them nothing else shall you read.[1]

Here we are struck, among other details, by the term 'the
Gospel', a term that, in this context, refers to Tatian's *Diatessaron*, or harmony of the four Gospels.

I. TATIAN

The figure of Tatian remains enigmatic. The only work of his
preserved in its entirety is his *Oration to the Greeks* (Λόγος πρὸς
Ἕλληνας),[2] a passionate, violently anti-Hellenic writing. From
it we learn that he was born of pagan parents in the land of the
Assyrians (chap. 42) and received an education in Greek
culture and its philosophical systems. Coming to Rome, he
made the acquaintance of Justin Martyr and was converted to
Christianity under his influence. While there, as it seems, he
composed his most important work, the 'Diatessaron',[3] in
which the four Gospels are woven together into a coherent and
continuous account. The term *diatessaron* (τὸ διὰ τεσσάρων),
borrowed from musical terminology and designating a series of
four harmonic tones, is altogether appropriate as the descriptive title of a work that smoothly harmonizes the four accounts.
Tatian gave to his harmony the chronological framework of

[1] The translation of the Syriac text is that of George Phillips in *The Doctrine of
Addai, the Apostle* (London, 1876); Phillips' edition of the Syriac text is reprinted by
George Howard in *The Teaching of Addai* (Chico, 1981), who supplies his own
translation (p. 93).

[2] According to Eusebius, Tatian wrote many books; of these the names of the
following have survived: *On Animals, On Demons, Book of Problems* (an attempt to deal
with contradictions found in the Bible), *Against Those Who have Discussed Divine Things,
On Perfection According to the Saviour*, and a recension of the Pauline Epistles. One
wonders how many of Paul's Epistles were included in Tatian's edition.

[3] For information concerning the sources of our knowledge of Tatian's *Diatessaron*,
as well as discussion of the many problems concerned with its form and content, see
Metzger, *The Early Versions of the New Testament* (Oxford, 1977), pp. 10–36.

the Fourth Gospel (but without following it slavishly), into which the Synoptic accounts are fitted.

In 1933 a parchment fragment of the *Diatessaron*, measuring about four inches (9 cm.) square and containing on one side the greater part of fourteen lines of Greek writing, came to light during excavations on the site of the ancient Roman fortress-town of Dura-Europos on the lower Euphrates.[4] Inasmuch as the town fell to the Persians under King Shapur I in A.D. 256-7, the fragment cannot be more than eighty years removed from the autograph.

The left-hand margin of the parchment has suffered damage, and the first half-dozen or so letters at the beginning of each line have had to be restored. In the following English translation the restorations have been enclosed within square brackets and the modern Scripture references within parentheses.

...the mother of the sons of Zebed]ee (Matt. xxvii. 56) and Salome (Mark xv. 40) and the wives [of those who] had followed him from [Galile]e to see the crucified (Luke xxiii. 49b–c). And [the da]y was Preparation; the sabbath was daw[ning] (Luke xxiii. 54). And when it was evening (Matt. xxvii. 57), on the Prep[aration], that is, the day before the sabbath (Mark xv. 42), [there came] up a man (Matt. xxvii. 57), be[ing] a member of the council (Luke xxiii. 50), from Arimathea (Matt. xxvii. 57), a c[i]ty of [Jude]a (Luke xxiii. 51b), by name Jo[seph] (Matt. xxvii. 57), g[o]od and ri[ghteous] (Luke xxiii. 50), being a disciple of Jesus, but se[cret]ly, for fear of the [Jew]s (John xix. 38). And he (Matt. xxvii. 57) was looking for [the] k[ingdom] of God (Luke xxiii. 51c). This man [had] not [con]sented to [their] p[urpose] (Luke xxiii. 51a)....

The *Diatessaron* supplies proof that all four Gospels were regarded as authoritative, otherwise it is unlikely that Tatian would have dared to combine them into one gospel account. At a time when many gospels were competing for attention, it is certainly significant that Tatian selected just these four—nor does the presence of an occasional extra-canonical phrase or

---

[4] The fragment was edited by Carl H. Kraeling, *A Greek Fragment of Tatian's Diatessaron from Dura* (Studies and Documents, iii; London; 1935), and re-edited, with a few minor corrections, by C. Bradford Welles, *et al.*, in *The Parchments and Papyri* (*The Excavations at Dura-Europos...*, Final Report, ii, part 1; New Haven, 1959), pp. 73–4.

clause[5] in the fabric of the *Diatessaron* neutralize this consideration.

About the year 172 Tatian returned to the East, where he became the founder of the sect of the Encratites (i.e. 'the Self-disciplined'). This group rejected matrimony as adultery, condemned the use of meat in any form, the drinking of wine, and went so far as to substitute water for wine in the Eucharistic service.

While in the East Tatian transferred his Greek harmony into Syriac[6] and introduced it among local churches. It is disputed whether the individual Gospels had been already translated into Syriac; in any case, it was Tatian's private judgement that the format of a fourfold harmony was the most convenient way in which to present the whole Gospel story at once instead of confusing people by offering them four parallel and more or less divergent narratives. Tatian's influence at Edessa must have been considerable, for he succeeded in getting his book read in the churches of that city, and thereafter its use spread throughout the region (see chap. IX. II below).

As for the rest of the New Testament, we learn from Jerome's preface to his commentary on Titus that Tatian rejected some of Paul's Epistles, as Marcion did, but, unlike Marcion, accepted the Epistle to Titus. It is understandable that his own rejection of marriage, meat, and wine compelled him to deny the authority of 1 Timothy, where all three are accepted (iv. 3; v. 14; v. 23). In the case of Titus, it may be, as Grant suggests,[7] that the presence of the word ἐγκρατής in this epistle (i. 8) and the author's opposition to 'Jewish myths' (i. 14) and to 'genealogies' (iii. 9) made it attractive to Tatian.

In Tatian's *Oration*, as also in the fragments of his other works that later writers have quoted, there are allusions to

---

[5] Several of these extra-canonical phrases come, as it seems, either from the *Gospel according to the Hebrews* or from the *Protoevangelium of James*; see Metzger, *The Early Versions*, pp. 29 f. It is not known whether they were present in the *Diatessaron* from the beginning, or whether some were incorporated after Tatian had published his harmony of the four Gospels.

[6] On the much-debated questions concerning the language in which the *Diatessaron* was first composed, and the place at which it was first published, see Metzger, op. cit., pp. 30 f.

[7] R. M. Grant, 'Tatian and the Bible', *Studia Patristica*, i, ed. by K. Aland and F. L. Cross (*Texte und Untersuchungen*, lxiii; Berlin, 1957), pp. 297–306; cf. p. 301.

several Pauline Epistles.[8] He alludes to or quotes passages from Romans, 1 and 2 Corinthians, Galatians, Ephesians, Philippians, and Colossians, as well as the Epistle to the Hebrews.

2. THEOPHILUS OF ANTIOCH

The testimony of Theophilus has reference to Western Syria, a country of Greek culture and one of the most ancient centres of Christianity. It was here, according to Acts xi. 26, that followers of Jesus were first called Christians. According to Eusebius (*Hist. eccl.* IV. xx. 1), Theophilus was the sixth bishop of Antioch (*fl.* A.D. 180). His writings reveal that he was born near the Euphrates, was of pagan parentage, and had received a Hellenistic education. In addition to his three books in defence of the Christian faith addressed to his friend Autolycus, he composed several works that have not survived, perhaps including a Commentary on the Four Gospels[9] and treatises against Marcion and Hermogenes. The purpose of the *Ad Autolycum* was to set before the pagan world the Christian idea of God and the superiority of the doctrine of creation over the immoral myths of the Olympian pantheon. Theophilus is the first theologian to use the word Triad ($\tau\rho\iota\acute{a}s$) of the Godhead (ii. 15).

Theophilus had the greatest reverence for the Jewish Bible—the holy Scriptures, as he often calls it. It was, he says, by reading these 'sacred writings of the holy prophets, who by the Spirit of God had foretold the future', that he had been converted (i. 14). In the second book of his treatise he calls the prophets 'spirit-bearers of the Holy Spirit' (ii. 9), who were inspired and made wise by God.

---

[8] The rumour that Eusebius (*Hist. eccl.* IV. xxix. 6) reports, 'they say ($\phi a\sigma\acute{\iota}$) that he ventured to paraphrase some words of the apostle [Paul], as though correcting their style', may imply (as McGiffert thought) that Tatian wrote a work on Paul's epistles, but more likely it means that Tatian was accustomed to weave Pauline phrases into his own compositions.

[9] In his letter (*Epist.* cxxi. 6.15) to a lady of Gaul named Algasia, Jerome answers her query about the meaning of the parable of the Unjust Steward by quoting from a commentary on the four Gospels that bore the name of Theophilus who was bishop of Antioch. Jerome seems to say that Theophilus had first made a harmony of the four Gospels (*quattuor evangelistarum in unum opus dicta compingens*). But in his notice of Theophilus in the *De viris illustribus* (§ 25), Jerome shows hesitation on grounds of style in accepting Theophilus as the author of the commentary. See W. Sanday, 'A Commentary on the Gospels attributed to Theophilus of Antioch', *Studia Biblica* (Oxford, 1885), pp. 89–101.

In a parallel manner, but not so frequently, he quotes from and alludes to the Gospels of Matthew and John. Once he quotes (ii. 13) a statement that comes from Luke (xviii. 27). To him the Evangelists were not less inspired by the Holy Spirit than the prophets of the Old Testament: 'Confirmatory utterances are found both with the prophets and in the gospels, because they all spoke inspired by one Spirit of God' (iii. 2). The Gospel according to Matthew is to him 'holy word' (ἅγιος λόγος, iii. 13). Theophilus explicitly mentions John by name as one of 'those who were spirit-bearing', and adds words from the Prologue of the Gospel as a specimen of his teaching: 'And hence the holy writings (αἱ ἅγιαι γραφαί) and all the spirit-bearing men (πάντες οἱ πνευματοφόροι), one of whom, John, says, "In the beginning was the Word, and the Word was with God"—showing that originally God was alone and the Word was in him' (ii. 22).

As for the Pauline Epistles, here and there throughout his treatise we find a dozen or more reminiscences from Romans, 1 and 2 Corinthians, Ephesians, Philippians, Colossians, and the three Pastorals. The question arises whether Theophilus regarded any of them as Scripture. Harnack, in an article devoted to this question,[10] argued that he did not, first because Theophilus never cites Paul as Scripture and, secondly, because there is no evidence elsewhere in Syria during the third century that shows that these Epistles were regarded as Scripture. On the other hand, however, Theophilus does refer to a combination of Tit. iii. 1, 1 Tim. ii. 2, and Rom. xiii. 7–8 as 'the divine word' (ὁ θεῖος λόγος, iii. 14). This seems to show, as Grant comments,[11] that he regarded them as inspired, and at least on the way to becoming Scripture.

As for the Book of Acts, Theophilus probably alludes to it when he quotes the negative Golden Rule. This is found in the Western text of the decrees of the Apostolic Council (Acts xv. 20 and 29), to which he seems to be referring in ii. 34.

---

[10] 'Theophilus von Antiochia und das Neue Testament', *Zeitschrift für Kirchengeschichte*, xi (1889–90), pp. 1–21.

[11] R. M. Grant, 'The Bible of Theophilus of Antioch', *Journal of Biblical Literature*, lxvi (1947), pp. 173–96; cf. also Apolinar Aguado Esteban, 'San Teófilo de Antioquía y el Canon del Nuevo Testamento', *Estudios bíblicos*, iii (1931–2), pp. 176–91, 281–9; iv (1933), pp. 3–11, 290–326.

Of Hebrews and the Catholic Epistles we find no clear allusion in what survives of Theophilus' writings. According to Eusebius (*Hist. eccl.* IV. xxvi. 1), in a work now lost Theophilus quoted 'testimonies from the Book of Revelation' in refutation of the heretic Hermogenes.

By way of summary, we may conclude that in Theophilus' time the New Testament at Antioch consisted of at least three of the four Gospels, the Acts of the Apostles, a collection of Pauline Epistles, and possibly the Apocalypse. The holy Scriptures of the Jews are still pre-eminent; but the Gospels and the Epistles of Paul are also inspired, and Theophilus is able to present them in his apology to Autolycus as virtually on a par with the Scriptures of the Jewish canon.

3. SERAPION OF ANTIOCH

About the year 200 Serapion, the successor to Theophilus in the episcopal see of Antioch, dealt with the question whether a disputed book should be read in church services. A short time before, while visiting Rhossus, a village in Cilicia on the Syrian coast of the gulf of Issus, the bishop found that disagreement had arisen among the faithful over a gospel ascribed to Peter (see chap. VII. 1. 4 below). Although he did not himself examine the book closely, he rather hastily gave his permission for them to continue to use it. After returning to Antioch, however, and having obtained a copy of the book, he wrote to the church, saying that he had found it tinged with Docetic heresy: 'most of it is indeed in accordance with the true teaching of the Saviour, but some things are additions to that teaching, which items also we place below for your benefit.' Unfortunately Eusebius, to whom we are indebted for a copy of this part of Serapion's letter, did not see fit to quote the specific points which the bishop found objectionable. The clear implication is that Serapion wished the reading suspended till he would make a second visit (which, he says, they can expect quickly), at which time he would probably give directions to cease using it.

The opening section of Serapion's letter indicates some of the difficulties that such 'fringe' literature occasioned for orthodox believers: 'For our part, brethren, we receive both Peter and the other apostles as Christ; but as men of experience (ἔμπειροι) we reject the writings falsely inscribed with their names, since we know that such were not handed down to us.'[12]

From this we can learn something as to the authority and standard of the New Testament books at the close of the second century. Serapion accepts the writings of Peter and the other apostles as the words of Christ, but he rejects writings falsely ascribed to them, since he knows that they were not supported by acknowledged tradition. Theoretically such criteria may have been satisfactory, but in actuality their application could lead to obvious difficulties.

II. ASIA MINOR

I. THE MARTYRDOM OF POLYCARP

Shortly after Polycarp, the heroic bishop of Smyrna, had suffered martyrdom because of his faith (22 February 155 or 156), the neighbouring church of Philomelium in Pisidia, near Phrygia, requested from the believers at Smyrna a full account of his trial and martyrdom. Although the document that was drawn up is frequently included in the corpus of the Apostolic Fathers, its author, identified at the close (chap. xx) as Marcianus or Marcion,[13] clearly stands outside the group known as the Apostolic Fathers.

Eusebius provides a somewhat more concise account of Polycarp's martyrdom (*Hist. eccl.* IV. xv. 1–45). The difference between the two accounts has usually been explained as the result of condensation on the part of Eusebius, but some have argued that a subsequent editor (or editors) of the *Martyrdom* enlarged the recital of Polycarp's trial and death by introducing features that would parallel the experiences of Jesus during his trial and passion.[14]

This hypothesis has been carefully examined by Barnard[15]

---

[12] Quoted by Eusebius, *Hist. eccl.* VI. xii. 3.

[13] The manuscripts differ; two read Μάρκου, one reads Μαρκίωνος, and the others, along with Eusebius, read Μαρκιανοῦ.

[14] Hans von Campenhausen, 'Bearbeitungen und Interpolationen des Polykarp-martyriums', *Sitzungsberichte der Heidelberger Akademie der Wissenschaften*, philos.-hist. Kl., 2, 1957, reprinted in *Aus der Frühzeit des Christentums* (Tübingen, 1963), pp. 253–301.

[15] L. W. Barnard, 'In Defence of Pseudo-Pionius' Account of Polycarp's Martyrdom', *Kyriakon; Festschrift Johannes Quasten*, ed. by P. Granfield and J. A. Jungmann, i (Münster i. W., 1970), pp. 192–204.

and by Dehandschutter,[16] both of whom conclude that the present text of the *Martyrdom* dates from within a year or two of Polycarp's death and preserves in substance the actual letter sent by the Smyrnaean church to the church at Philomelium. Furthermore, as Conzelmann[17] has pointed out, it is not necessary to assume that the 'Gospel-editor', who is alleged to have expanded the original text, did his rewriting after the time of Eusebius, for a copy of the expanded text, though earlier than Eusebius, may not have come into the historian's hands. Because, however, the text of the *Martyrdom* is not altogether free from critical suspicion, in the following list of reminiscences from the New Testament it will be specified which are preserved also in Eusebius' abbreviated account.

Although the *Martyrdom of Polycarp* contains no explicit quotation from a New Testament book, the careful reader will detect more than one echo of phrases from the gospel narratives and from the apostolic letters.[18]

(1) 'That I may share ... in the cup of thy Christ' (xiv. 2 and Eus. iv. xv. 33) is a reminiscence of Matt. xx. 22 and xxvi. 39.

(2) 'Things which neither ear has heard nor eye seen nor human heart conceived' (ii. 3) comes from 1 Cor. ii. 9.

(3) 'We have been taught to render honour ... to magistrates and authorities appointed by God' (x. 2 and Eus. iv. xv. 22) seems to be a recollection of Rom. xiii. 1 and 7, and Titus iii. 1.

(4) 'That we might follow his example, not with an eye to ourselves but also to our neighbour' (i. 2) reminds one of Paul's admonition in Phil. ii. 4.

(5) The phrase 'Christ ... the blameless One for sinners' (xviii. 2) may be reminiscent of 1 Pet. iii. 18.

(6) The opening sentence of the *Martyrdom*, reported also by Eusebius, concludes with an expansion of the salutation of Jude 2: 'May mercy, peace, and love from God the Father and our Lord Jesus Christ be multiplied.'

[16] Boudewijn Dehandschutter, *Martyrium Polycarpi. Een literairkritische studie* (Louvain, 1979), pp. 140–55.

[17] Hans Conzelmann, 'Bemerkungen zum Martyrdom Polykarps', *Nachrichten der Akademie der Wissenschaften zu Göttingen*, phil.-hist. Kl., 1978, no. 2, pp. 41–58.

[18] Concerning the detection of Biblical reminiscences, see Marie-Louise Guillaumin, 'En marge du "Martyre de Polycarp"; Le Discernment des allusions scripturaires', in *Forma futuri; Studi in onore del Cardinale Michele Pellegrino* (Turin, 1975), pp. 462–9.

By way of summary, the author of the *Martyrdom of Polycarp* appears to have some acquaintance with several of the apostolic Epistles, from which he borrowed phrases (without acknowledgement) and wove them into his narrative. This suggests that his mind was imbued with a knowledge of these texts, but we have no means of determining what authority he attributed to them.

2. MELITO OF SARDIS

One of the most voluminous writers of his time was Melito, bishop of Sardis, the capital of Lydia, who flourished during the reign of Marcus Aurelius (A.D. 161–80). He was the author of a score of works, but unfortunately in most cases only the titles are known from a list that Eusebius (*Hist. eccl.* IV. xxvi. 7) copied probably from a collection in the library of Caesarea. These covered a wide range of interests, from a book on the *Devil and the Apocalypse of John*[19] to others on such varied topics as the Church, Truth, Creation, Baptism, the Birth of Christ, Hospitality, the Lord's Day, and even on the Corporeality of God.

During the twentieth century two papyrus codices have turned up that contain the Greek text of a paschal homily, *On the Passover*,[20] a declamatory address of short, impressive phrases frequently balanced by repetition or antithesis.[21] Interpreting the Passover as symbolic of the redemptive work of Christ, Melito expands on the slaying of the firstborn in Egypt and the preservation of the Hebrews. The Jewish law, he says, was simply a temporary sketch or model for Christianity, which is the true and enduring work of God. The sufferings of Christ were foreshadowed in those of many Old Testament worthies. Throughout the homily one comes upon echoes of New Testament expressions, but there are no direct references to New Testament books themselves.

[19] Jerome understood this to be two distinct treatises, but the form of expression in Greek would rather indicate that both subjects were discussed in a single treatise of more than one book.

[20] The Chester Beatty–Michigan papyrus, edited by C. Bonner (*Studies and Documents*, xii; Philadelphia–London, 1940), and the Bodmer papyrus, edited by M. Testuz, *Méliton de Sardes, Homélie sur la pâque* (*Papyrus Bodmer*, xiii; Cologny–Geneva, 1960).

[21] On Melito's style, see A. Wifstrand in *Vigiliae Christianae*, ii (1948), pp. 201–23, and Thomas Halton, 'Stylistic Device in Melito Περὶ Πάσχα', *Kyriakon; Festschrift Johannes Quasten*, pp. 249–55.

As regards the canon of the Old Testament we learn something of interest from the extract that Eusebius (*Hist. eccl.* IV. xxvi. 13) gives us from the Preface to Melito's work called *Selections*. This treatise, in six books, had been drawn up for a friend named Onesimus, who had asked Melito to make a kind of anthology of extracts from the Law and the Prophets concerning the Saviour, and also to give him information as to the number and order of the Old Testament books. In order to separate the apocryphal books from the canonical books Melito made a pilgrimage to Palestine, 'where these things were preached and done', so as to acquire accurate information, presumably from Greek-speaking Jewish Christians. This list corresponds to the Hebrew canon, with none of the additional books that are in the Greek Septuagint. The expressions that occur in the extract, 'the old books' (τὰ παλαιὰ βιβλία) and 'the books of the Old Covenant' (τὰ τῆς παλαιᾶς διαθήκης βιβλία), have been thought to imply the recognition of 'the books of the New Covenant' as a written antitype to the Old.

By way of summary, the scanty remains of Melito's literary output provides no clear instance of a direct quotation from the New Testament as such. At the same time his interest in developing allegorical exegesis of the Old Testament in accord with the events of the earthly ministry of Jesus, as well as his care to ascertain precisely the canon of the Old Testament, make it probable that he may well have given similar attention to ascertaining authentic New Testament documents.

III. GREECE

1. DIONYSIUS OF CORINTH

Dionysius was bishop of Corinth in the third quarter of the second century, till about A.D. 170. He was a famous person in his day, held in high esteem as a writer of pastoral or catholic epistles (καθολικαὶ ἐπιστολαί), addressed to widely scattered congregations, including those in Athens, Nicomedia, Rome, Lacedaemon, Gortyna in Crete, and other cities. They are all lost, with the exception of a summary of the contents of seven of them given by Eusebius, and four excerpts from his epistle to the church at Rome, addressed to Soter, who was bishop at that time.[22]

Among the items that Eusebius reports (*Hist. eccl.* IV. xxiii. 10–11) we find an interesting passage extracted from Dionysius' epistle to the Romans. This mentions that on that very day, a Sunday, they had been reading the epistle which Soter had recently written to the Corinthians, and that they would not fail to read it from time to time for the instruction of the faithful, just as they continue to read the epistle formerly written to them by Clement. This shows that, in this locality and probably elsewhere, the public reading in divine services included epistolary communications. Dionysius, it is true, says nothing in this passage directly bearing on the writings of the New Testament, but if the *Epistle of Clement* was still being read at Corinth sixty years after his death, it is certainly probable that the apostle Paul's communications to Corinth were similarly treasured and read publicly.

In another place Dionysius speaks of his own epistles, complaining that they had been mutilated by interpolations and abridgements:

When the brethren asked me to write epistles, I did so. And the apostles of the devil have filled them with tares, cutting out some things and adding others. For them the woe is reserved.[23]

Here the reference to 'the woe' seems to reflect a knowledge of the dire penalty threatened in the Book of Revelation for those who add to or take away from its words (xxii. 18 f.). Dionysius then continues:

It is no wonder, therefore, that some have attempted to tamper with the Scriptures of the Lord (τῶν κυριακῶν γραφῶν) as well, since they have plotted against writings that are of less account.

From this it is evident that 'the Scriptures of the Lord'—that is, the gospels, or gospels known and read at the time of Dionysius—(*a*) were distinguished from other books 'that are

---

[22] Cf. Adolf von Harnack, *Die Briefsammlung des Apostels Paulus und die anderen vorkonstantinischen christlichen Briefsammlungen* (Leipzig, 1926), pp. 36–40, and Pièrre Nautin, *Lettres et écrivains chrétiens des II* et III* siècles* (Paris, 1961), pp. 13–32.

[23] Quoted by Eusebius, *Hist. eccl.* IV. xxiii. 12.

of less account', (*b*) that they were jealously guarded, and (*c*) that they had been corrupted for heretical purposes.

Thus, though we have fewer than eighty lines preserved from what had been an extensive correspondence of Dionysius, the sections that are extant provide us with the most ancient testimony (though only by way of inference) to a periodic reading of the Pauline Epistles. Dionysius seems also to know the malediction that stands at the close of the Book of Revelation (xxii. 18, 19).

2. ATHENAGORAS

The ablest of the Christian apologists of the second century was Athenagoras, described in the earliest manuscript of his works as 'the Christian philosopher of Athens'.[24] Lucid in style and weighty in argument, he was the first to elaborate a philosophical defence of the Christian doctrine of God as Three in One.

About A.D. 177 Áthenagoras addressed his *Supplication for the Christians* to the Emperor Marcus Aurelius and his son Commodus. In it he refutes one by one three accusations levelled against the Christians, namely, atheism, Thyestian banquets (meals at which human flesh is eaten),[25] and Oedipal incest. In his discussion and defence Athenagoras makes explicit use of several books of the Old Testament, occasionally quoting passages from Exodus, Proverbs, Isaiah, and Jeremiah. In the case of the New Testament he contents himself with citing words and phrases found in Matthew and/or Luke, but without specifying the name of the Gospel. He declares (xi. 2) that Christians have been brought up on such teachings (λόγοι) as:

I say to you, love your enemies, bless those who curse you, pray for

---

[24] According to a fragment of the fifth-century *Christian History* by Philip of Side (in Pamphilia), Athenagoras was the first director of the school of catechetics at Alexandria and flourished about the time of Hadrian and Antoninus. Since Philip's dating of Athenagoras is an obvious mistake, it is probable that the statement of his connection with the school at Alexandria is also an error, especially since Eusebius tells us that Pantaenus was the founder of the school.

[25] That such meals were actually held by pagans of the time seems to be probable on the basis of evidence analysed by Albert Henrichs, 'Pagan Ritual and Alleged Crimes of the Early Christians: A Reconsideration', *Kyriakon; Festschrift Johannes Quasten*, pp. 18–35.

those who persecute you, that you may be children of your Father in heaven, who makes his sun to shine on the evil and on the good, and sends his rain on the just and on the unjust (Matt. v. 44–5; Luke vi. 27–8).

Other passages from Matthew (v. 28) and from Mark (x. 11), in which words of Jesus concerning divorce are cited, he introduces by the simple formula φησί, which may possibly imply 'the Scripture says', but more probably should be taken simply as 'he says' (xxxii. 2 and 5). There are also several tacit references to the Fourth Gospel, such as 'the Word' (x. 1; cf. John i. 3) and 'to know the true God and his Word, to know the unity of the Son with the Father' (xii. 3; cf. John i. 1 and xvii. 3).

As for the Pauline Epistles, Athenagoras includes phrases from Rom. i. 27 (*Suppl.* xxxiv. 2) and xii. 1 (*Suppl.* xiii. 2), Gal. iv. 9 (*Suppl.* xvi. 3), and 1 Tim. ii. 2 (*Suppl.* xxxvii. 2–3). From these we conclude that he possessed a collection of several of the Pauline Epistles, including at least one of the Pastorals, but we cannot say how he regarded them.

Athenagoras' other treatise,[26] *On the Resurrection from the Dead*, promised at the end of his *Supplication* (xxxvii. 1), is one of the best early Christian discussions of the subject. In this work the author endeavours to refute objections and then to defend the doctrine positively. It is clear that he has read what Paul says in 1 Corinthians xv, for he quotes words from verse 53, 'in the language of the apostle, "this corruptible (and dissoluble) must put on incorruption"'. But beyond this phrase, the numerous texts of the New Testaments on the subject of the resurrection are not quoted and have not even influenced his style.

By way of summary, it appears that, in accord with the purposes which Athenagoras had in mind, he did not see fit to make frequent quotations from either Old or New Testament.

---

[26] The lack of external evidence and the doubts raised by the textual tradition have led some scholars to judge that the treatise on the resurrection is by another author, living in the third or early fourth century. So R. M. Grant, 'Athenagoras or Pseudo-Athenagoras', *Harvard Theological Review*, xlvii (1954), pp. 121–9, and W. R. Schoedel, *Athenagoras* (Oxford, 1972), pp. xxv–xxxii. For what can be said in support of ascribing the treatise to Athenagoras, see L. W. Barnard, *Athenagoras: A Study in Second Century Christian Apologetic* (*Théologie historique*, xviii; Paris, 1972), pp. 28–33, and idem, 'Athenagoras, de Resurrectione', *Studia Theologia* xxx (1976), pp. 1–43, esp. 4–11.

Nevertheless, he makes tacit references to Matthew, Mark, and John, and to several of Paul's Epistles.

3. ARISTIDES

The earliest defence of Christianity that has come down to us is the *Apology* of Aristides, who was a Christian philosopher of Athens. The *Apology* was addressed to the Emperor Antoninus Pius, probably between A.D. 138 and 147, since Marcus Aurelius is not mentioned in the address as co-emperor.

This *Apology* is a relatively recent addition to early Christian literature, for until about a century ago all that we knew of Aristides and his work was derived from brief references in Eusebius and Jerome.[27] The first step towards its recovery was made in 1878, when the Mechitarist Fathers published at Venice a portion of a Christian apology in an Armenian translation (of the tenth century), which they attributed to Aristides. The authenticity of the work was confirmed eleven years later when Rendel Harris discovered in a seventh-century manuscript at the monastery of St Catherine on Mount Sinai an almost complete text of the book in a Syriac version. Then, shortly afterwards, J. A. Robinson, who had seen Harris's work in proof, made the surprising discovery that the greater part of the Greek text, though in free redaction, had already been embedded in chapters xxvi and xxvii of an early medieval romance, *The History of Barlaam and Josaphat*, preserved among the writings of St John of Damascus.[28] More recently, two considerable portions of the original Greek text (chapters v and vi and xv. 6–xvi. 1) have turned up among the Egyptian papyri.[29]

The main subject of the *Apology* is that the Christians alone possess the true knowledge of God. Although Aristides includes no express quotations from Scripture, the emperor is referred

[27] Eusebius, *Hist. eccl.* IV. iii. 3; *Chron.* ad a. 2140; Jerome, *De viris ill.*, 20, and *Epist.* lxx.

[28] J. Rendel Harris, *The Apology of Aristides on Behalf of the Christians, from a Syriac Ms. Preserved on Mount Sinai*, edited with an Introduction and Translation. With an Appendix Containing the Main Portion of the Original Greek Text by J. A. Robinson, 2nd ed. (*Texts and Studies*, I, 1; Cambridge, 1893).

[29] *Oxyrhynchus Papyri*, xv. 1778, and British Museum Inv. no. 2486, edited by H. J. M. Milne in *Journal of Theological Studies*, xxv (1923–4), pp. 73–7; both are dated to the fourth century.

for information to a gospel which is written[30] and which he is invited to read in order to 'perceive the power which belongs to it' (§ 2, Syriac text; cf. § 15, Greek text). In this connection Aristides makes reference to the main events of the life of Jesus, including his birth 'from a Hebrew virgin' (Syriac and Armenian texts; 'pure virgin' Greek text), his twelve disciples, his death, resurrection, and ascension. This last may show that Aristides knew the Acts of the Apostles.

In his discussion of the errors of the pagans (§ 3), Aristides uses phrases that seem to be borrowed from several of the Pauline Epistles, as the following examples will show:

(1) 'And through him [God] all things consist' (δι' αὐτοῦ δὲ τὰ πάντα συνέστηκεν, § 1; cf. Col. i. 17, καὶ τὰ πάντα ἐν αὐτῷ [Christ] συνέστηκεν, and δι' αὐτοῦ in i. 16).

(2) 'The barbarians, as they did not comprehend God, went astray among the elements [cf. Col. ii. 8]; and they began to worship created things instead of the Creator of them' (§ 3).

(3) 'The Greeks, indeed, though they call themselves wise, proved more foolish than the Chaldeans' (σοφοὶ λέγοντες εἶναι ἐμωράνθησαν, § 8; cf. Rom. i. 22, φάσκοντες εἶναι σοφοὶ ἐμωράνθησαν).

(4) Greek philosophers 'err in seeking to liken them [i.e. pagan gods] to God, whom no man has at any time seen, nor is able to see unto what he is like' (§ 13, Syriac text; cf. 1 Tim. vi. 16).

From such examples as these we can see that, though Aristides makes no direct quotation from any New Testament book, here and there his diction shows traces of the language of apostolic writers. At the same time, however, it must be noted that nowhere does he refer to these writings as canonical. Obviously they are useful as providing information, but Christianity, in his view, is worthy of the emperor's attention because it is eminently reasonable, and gives an impulse and power to live a good life.

---

[30] Here the Greek text (§ 15) is somewhat elaborated: 'If you would read, O King, you may judge the glory of his presence (παρουσία) from the holy Gospel writing, as it is called among themselves (ἐκ τῆς παρ' αὐτοῖς καλουμένης εὐαγγελικῆς ἁγίας γραφῆς)'. Instead of saying simply that the Gospels exist (as does the Syriac text), here the author of the *History of Barlaam* explicates and develops the text which he reproduces and describes the Gospel as 'holy' Scripture. It is not difficult to decide which form is original.

IV. EGYPT

Alexandria, founded by Alexander the Great in 331 B.C. on the mouth of the Nile, was the metropolis of Egypt, destined to become one of the chief centres of Christianity, the rival of Antioch and Rome. Since the time of the first Ptolemies it boasted two great libraries of learning, the Museion and the Serapeion.[31]

At Alexandria the religious life of Palestine and the intellectual culture of Greece met and mingled, and prepared the way for what became the first school of Christian theology. Originally designed only for the practical purpose of preparing converts for baptism, the 'catechetical school' (τὸ τῆς κατηχήσεως διδασκαλεῖον) was under the supervision of the bishop. But in the city which was the home of Philonic theology, of Gnostic speculations, and of Neoplatonic philosophy, the school soon assumed a more learned character, and became, at the same time, a kind of theological seminary. It had at first but a single teacher, afterwards two or more, but without fixed salary, or special buildings. The teachers gave their voluntary lectures in their homes, generally after the style of the ancient philosophers. It is not surprising that more than one director of this school has something to tell us about the development of the canon.

1. PANTAENUS

The first head of the catechetical school known to us was Pantaenus, who flourished, according to Eusebius (*Hist. eccl.* v. x. 1), during the reign of the Emperor Commodus (A.D. 180–92). Probably a native of Sicily, he was converted from Stoicism to Christianity and subsequently undertook missionary work in foreign parts. His journeys took him as far as 'India'[32] where he found a copy of the Gospel according to Matthew in Hebrew letters, left there by the apostle Batholomew. Whatever one may think of this story—and Eusebius reports it as tradition

[31] See Edward A. Parsons, *The Alexandrian Library, Glory of the Hellenic World* (Amsterdam and New York, 1952); Richard Pfeiffer, *A History of Classical Scholarship* (Oxford, 1968), pp. 95–102; and Peter M. Fraser, *Ptolemaic Alexandria* (Oxford, 1972), esp. chap. 6, 'Ptolemaic Patronage: the Museion and Library'.

[32] Whether this was the sub-continent of India, or southern Arabia, or Ethiopia, need not be decided here.

(λέγεται)—'after many good deeds Pantaenus finally became head of the school at Alexandria, and expounded the treasures of divine doctrine both orally and in writing' (*Hist. eccl.* v. x. 4).

Although none of his writings have survived, we know the opinion of Pantaenus on a question concerning the New Testament that was greatly disputed in the early Church: the authorship of the Epistle to the Hebrews. According to Eusebius, who reports the view of 'the blessed presbyter', that is, Pantaenus, it was the work of the apostle Paul, but in composing it he had preferred to preserve anonymity:

> Since the Lord, being the apostle of the Almighty, was sent to the Hebrews, Paul, having been sent to the gentiles, through modesty did not inscribe himself as an apostle of the Hebrews, both because of respect for the Lord and because he wrote to the Hebrews also out of his abundance, being a preacher and apostle for the gentiles (*Hist. eccl.* vi. xiv. 4).

This opinion of Pantaenus, which was later to be adopted by both Clement of Alexandria and Origen, appears to be an attempt at conciliation, made necessary by the existence of two types of the *corpus Paulinum*, one with and the other without the Epistle to the Hebrews.

2. CLEMENT OF ALEXANDRIA

Titus Flavius Clement, the successor to Pantaenus, was probably an Athenian by birth and of pagan parentage. Although well versed in all branches of Greek literature and in all the existing systems of philosophy, in these he found nothing of permanent satisfaction. In his adult years he embraced the Christian religion, and by extensive travels East and West sought the most distinguished teachers. Coming to Alexandria about A.D. 180 he became a pupil of Pantaenus. Captivated by his teacher, whom he was accustomed to call 'the blessed presbyter', Clement became, successively, a presbyter in the church at Alexandria, an assistant to Pantaenus, and, about 190, his successor as head of the catechetical school.

Clement continued to work in Alexandria for the conversion of pagans and the education of Christians until, as it appears, the persecution under the Emperor Septimus Severus in 202 compelled him to flee, never to return. In the year 211 we meet again with Clement carrying an episcopal communication from Cappadocian Caesarea to Antioch. About five years later, he was mourned as deceased.[33]

During his tenure as its head, Clement stamped his personality upon the catechetical school, uniting thorough Biblical and Hellenic learning with genius and speculative thought. It was the age of Gnosticism, and Clement agreed with the Gnostics in holding 'gnosis'—that is, religious knowledge or illumination—to be the chief element in Christian perfection; but for him the only 'gnosis' was that which presupposed the faith of the Church (παράδοσις).

The writings of Clement disclose the amazingly broad scope of his knowledge of both classical and Biblical literature. On page after page of his treatises we find copious citations of all kinds of literature. According to Stählin's tabulation, Clement cites some 359 classical and other non-Christian writers, 70 Biblical writings (including Old Testament apocrypha), and 36 patristic and New Testament apocryphal writings, including those of heretics.[34] The total number of citations amounts to about 8,000, more than a third of which come from pagan writers. Furthermore, the statistics reveal that he quotes from New Testament writings almost twice as often as from the Old Testament.

Clement uses the word 'canon' some twenty-one times in several different connections ('canon of truth', 'canon of faith', and 'ecclesiastical canon'), but he does not apply it to a collection of books. At the same time, he makes a marked difference between those books that he accepts as authoritative and those he does not, with a small, somewhat fluctuating group between the two.

One finds in Clement's work citations of all the books of the New Testament with the exception of Philemon, James, 2 Peter, and 2 and 3 John.[35] As might have been expected, the type of New Testament text with which he is acquainted

---

[33] Eusebius, *Hist. eccl.* vi. xiv. 18–19.

[34] See the lists in Otto Stählin, *Clemens Alexandrinus*, iv (*Die griechischen christlichen Schriftsteller der ersten drei Jahrhunderte*, xxxix; Leipzig, 1936), pp. 1–66.

[35] Nevertheless, the fact that Clement (*Strom.* ii. xv. 66) makes reference, in quoting 1 John v. 16–17, to John's 'longer epistle' (ἐν τῇ μείζονι ἐπιστολῇ) implies that he knew of one other Johannine letter, and possibly only one other.

belongs to the early Egyptian group.[36] That he accepted the fourfold canon of the Gospels is shown by a passage from his lost *Hypotyposes*,[37] in which he states that the Gospels containing the genealogies of Jesus (Matthew and Luke) were written first, then Mark, and, last of all, John, which he characterizes as a 'spiritual Gospel'. He insists upon the accord of the teaching of the Synoptics and John, which may imply that the fourfold canon was not yet unanimously recognized.

Clement knows other gospels besides the four that he accepts as primary. According to Stählin's index he refers to the *Gospel of the Egyptians* eight times, the *Gospel of the Hebrews* three times, and the *Traditions of Matthias* three times. If on one occasion he cites the *Gospel according to the Hebrews* with the formula, 'It is written' ($\gamma \acute{\epsilon} \gamma \rho \alpha \pi \tau \alpha \iota$), he also remarks another time, by way of diminishing its authority, that this gospel is invoked by the Gnostics. On another occasion he says, 'We do not have this saying [of Jesus to Salome] in the four traditional Gospels, but in the *Gospel according to the Egyptians*'.[38]

In 1958 a portion of a letter purporting to be by Clement to a certain Theodore was found by Morton Smith at the Mar Saba Monastery in Judea.[39] It is written in an eighteenth-

[36] For a thorough analysis of the New Testament text-type used by Clement, see M. Mees, *Die Zitate aus dem Neuen Testament bei Clemens von Alexandrien*, 2 vols. (Bari, 1970), whose research extends the earlier studies by R. J. Swanson, 'The Gospel Text of Clement of Alexandria', Ph.D. diss., Yale University, 1956), and James A. Brooks, 'The Text of the Pauline Epistles in the *Stromata* of Clement of Alexandria', Ph.D. diss., Princeton Theological Seminary, 1966.

[37] Quoted by Eusebius, *Hist. eccl.* VI. xiv. 5‑7.

[38] *Strom.* III. xiii. 93. The saying is quoted on p. 171 below.

[39] For an account of its discovery, see Morton Smith, *Clement of Alexandria and a Secret Gospel of Mark* (Cambridge, Mass., 1973), and his briefer and more journalistic book, *The Secret Gospel; The Discovery and Interpretation of the Secret Gospel According to Mark* (New York, 1973). The quotations given in the text are from Smith's translation.

Reactions to the two volumes were diverse. The attribution of the letter to Clement has been widely accepted, but Clement's attribution of the Gospel to 'Mark' has been almost universally rejected. Instead, the gospel fragments have been explained as (1) an apocryphal gospel of the common second-century variety, (2) a pastiche composed from the canonical Gospels, or (3) an expansion of Mark that imitated Markan style and used earlier material. On several occasions Smith replied to those who differed from his interpretation of the document, writing, on one occasion, that the names of two scholars who had written unfavourable reviews of his work (P. J. Achtemeier, in *Journal of Biblical Literature*, xciii [1974], pp. 625‑8, and J. A. Fitzmyer, in *America*, [23 June 1973], pp. 570‑2) rhyme with 'liar'! More sober is his survey subtitled 'The Score at the End of the First Decade' [following the publication of Clement's letter], in *Harvard Theological Review*, lxxv (1982), pp. 449‑61.

century hand on some blank pages at the back of a book printed in 1646; from this letter it would appear that Clement knew three versions of Mark. (*a*) The first of these was the one in general use, which Mark had written in Rome on the basis of Peter's preaching. (*b*) Later, after Peter's martyrdom, 'Mark came over to Alexandria, bringing both his own notes and those of Peter, from which he transferred to his former book the things suitable to whatever makes for progress toward knowledge. Thus he composed a more spiritual Gospel[40] for the use of those who were being perfected.' Still later, when dying, 'he left his composition to the church in Alexandria, where it even yet is most carefully guarded, being read only to those who are being initiated into the great mysteries'. Nothing more is known of this 'secret Gospel of Mark' except a few quotations from it included in the copy of Clement's letter.[41] (*c*) Sometime later, the heretic Carpocrates 'so enslaved a certain presbyter of the church in Alexandria that he got from him a copy of the secret Gospel, which he both interpreted according to his blasphemous and carnal doctrine and, moreover, polluted, mixing with the spotless and holy words utterly shameless lies. From this mixture is drawn off the teaching of the Carpocratians' (see chap. IV. I. 2 above).

As would be expected, Clement's quotations from the Pauline Epistles are fewer in number than those that he makes from the Gospels, but not very much fewer (about 1,575

---

[40] Cf. Clement's comment on John's Gospel quoted at n. 37 above.

[41] It is perhaps to be expected that the quotations from 'Secret Mark', though limited in extent, have stimulated elaborate and complicated theories. Helmut Koester, for example, finds reasons to postulate the successive development of (1a) Proto-Mark (which was used by Luke), (1b) a revision of Proto-Mark (used by Matthew), (2) a thorough revision of Proto-Mark (known to us as the Gospel of Matthew), (3) another revision of Proto-Mark (known as the Gospel of Luke), (4a) a further development of Proto-Mark resulting in 'Secret Mark', (4b) a different edition of 'Secret Mark', used by the Carpocratians, (5a) canonical Mark, developed from 'Secret Mark', and (5b) canonical Mark with the subsequently acquired long ending, xvi. 9–20. ('History and Development of Mark's Gospel', *Colloquy on New Testament Studies...*, ed. by Bruce Corley [Macon, 1983], pp. 35–47.) One is reminded of Harnack's comment about a scholar who had elaborated extremely subtle analyses of literary relationships: 'He can hear grass grow!' Neither Koester nor his student, J. D. Crossan, who adopts this theory (*Four Other Gospels; Shadows on the Contours of the Canon*, 1985), pays any attention to the implications of the theory for dating. Credibility is altogether strained by the proposal that the canonical Gospel of Mark, later used by both Matthew and Luke, is the orthodox revision of 'Secret Mark' made in reaction to perverse Gnostic use of it.

quotations compared with about 1,375). As for the Epistle to the Hebrews, he adopts the theory of Pantaenus (see above, p. 130), while elaborating it by the idea that the one who translated it into Greek, was Luke.

Since Clement is conscious that all knowledge of truth is based on inspiration, so all writings, that is all parts, paragraphs, or sentences of writings that contain moral and religious truth, are in his view inspired. He refers to Orpheus as 'the theologian', and speaks of Plato as being 'under the inspiration of God'. Even the Epicurean Metrodorus uttered certain words 'divinely inspired' (ἐνθέως).[42] It is not surprising, then, that he can quote passages as inspired from the epistles of Clement of Rome and of Barnabas, the *Shepherd* of Hermas, and the *Apocalypse of Peter*. In fact, according to Eusebius (*Hist. eccl.* VI. xiv. 1), Clement's *Hypotyposes* contained concise comments on all the canonical Scriptures (πάσης τῆς ἐνδιαθήκου γραφῆς, literally 'all the testament-ed Scripture'), 'not omitting even the disputed books—that is, the Epistle of Jude and the other Catholic Epistles, and the *Epistle of Barnabas*,[43] and the *Apocalypse of Peter*'.

In addition to referring to the sayings of Jesus recorded in the canonical Gospels, occasionally Clement makes use of other sayings ascribed to Jesus, called agrapha (ἄγραφα, 'unwritten' sayings, i.e. not written in the canonical Gospels). Three such quotations in the first book of Clement's *Stromata* are, 'Be approved money-changers' (a saying that is generally regarded by present-day scholars as probably a genuine saying of the Lord); 'You have seen your brother; you have seen your God'; and 'Ask for the great things, and the little things will be added to you'.[44]

By way of summary, one can say that, though Clement felt free to use unwritten tradition as well as to quote from a broad spectrum of Christian and pagan literature, it was the fourfold Gospels and the fourteen Epistles of Paul (including Hebrews),

---

[42] See J. Ruwet, 'Clément d'Alexandrie—Canon des Écritures et apocryphes', *Biblica*, xxix (1948), pp. 86–91.

[43] At the same time Clement does not hesitate to criticize an interpretation given by the author of the *Epistle of Barnabas* (*Paed.* II. x. 3, and *Strom.* II. xv. 67).

[44] The three ἄγραφα are quoted in *Strom.* I. xxviii. 177.2; 94.5; and 158.2. See R. P. C. Hanson, *Tradition in the Early Church* (Philadelphia, 1962), pp. 224–34, and Joachim Jeremias, *Unknown Sayings of Jesus*, 2nd ed. (London, 1964).

along with Acts, 1 Peter, 1 John, and the Apocalypse, that were regarded as authoritative Scripture. As for the other Catholic Epistles, Clement's opinion vacillated. On the whole one can say that, so far as his understanding of Scripture was concerned, he had an 'open' canon.[45]

3. ORIGEN

Among ante-Nicene writers of the Eastern Church, the greatest by far was Origen, both as a theologian and as a prolific Biblical scholar. Born of Christian parents in Egypt, probably about A.D. 185, he spent most of his life in Alexandria as a teacher, but he also visited Antioch, Athens, Arabia, Ephesus, and Rome, and lived for a rather long period at Caesarea in Palestine.

In the year 203, though then only eighteen years of age, Origen was appointed by Demetrius, the bishop, to succeed Clement as head of the catechetical school. For a dozen years he carried on that work with marked success and with increasing numbers of pupils at the school. In 215, however, as the result of the Emperor Caracalla's furious attack upon the Alexandrians, Origen's work at the school was interrupted and he was driven from the city.

Origen took refuge at Caesarea in Palestine, where he preached in churches at the request of the bishops of Jerusalem and Caesarea. As he was only a layman, this was regarded by his bishop, Demetrius, as a breach of ecclesiastical discipline, in consequence of which he was recalled to Alexandria, where he resumed his scholarly work at the catechetical school.

In 230 Origen travelled to Greece on some church business and, stopping at Caesarea on his way, was ordained as a presbyter by the same friendly bishops who had invited him to preach on his previous visit. When Demetrius learned of this, he felt that his authority had been flouted, and, on Origen's return, deposed him from his teaching office as well as excommunicated him from the Alexandrian church on the grounds of irregularity of ordination.

Origen moved now to Caesarea, where he opened a new Biblical and theological school which soon outshone that of

---

[45] See P. Dausch, *Der neutestamentliche Schriftkanon und Clemens von Alexandrien* (Freiburg i. B., 1894), pp. 40-7.

Alexandria, and where he continued his extensive literary
work, as well as preaching and giving Biblical expositions
almost every day. In 250, during the Decian persecution,
Origen was imprisoned, cruelly tortured, and condemned to
the stake. Although he regained his liberty at the death of the
emperor, he died soon afterward, in the year 253 or 254, at
Tyre, probably in consequence of that violence.

Origen was a Biblical scholar *par excellence*. Besides his epoch-
making work of textual studies of the Old Testament (the
Hexapla), he is said to have commented upon nearly all the
books of the Bible, and this three times. He wrote short
annotations (scholia), he compiled large and learned commentaries, and he preached before congregations. Only a small
part of his works has come down to us, but this fills volumes.
His testimony concerning the books of the New Testament (see
Appendix IV. 2 below) is of no little importance. Having
travelled widely he had opportunity of observing the usage of
churches not only in Egypt and Palestine, but also in Arabia,
Asia Minor, Greece, and Rome.

We find in Origen the division of books of the New
Testament in two collections: the Gospel or the Gospels and
the Apostle or the Apostles, such as we have encountered
earlier, but he joins them under the name of 'the New
Testament', and states that they are 'divine Scriptures', written by evangelists and apostles through the same Spirit and
proceeding from the same God as the Old Testament (*De
Princip*. iv. 11 and 16).

Origen's witness is clear and forthright, declaring that one
must distinguish between the Gospels that are accepted without controversy by the entire Church and the gospels of the
heretics. In his *Commentary on Matthew*, written toward the close
of his life (after 244), he states that the Gospels written by
Matthew, Mark, Luke, and John, 'are the only indisputable
(ἀναντίρρητα) ones in the Church of God under heaven'.[46] On
the other hand, among the gospels that are to be rejected as
heretical, he names those of Thomas, Matthias, the Twelve
Apostles, and Basilides, along with that according to the

---

[46] Quoted by Eusebius, *Hist. eccl.* vi. xxv. 3 f., who says that Origen 'defends the
ecclesiastical canon' (κανὼν ἐκκλσιαστικός), that is, the established and regular usage of
the Church.

Egyptians. The authors of these gospels, he says, 'rushed hastily to write without having the grace of the Holy Spirit'. He acknowledges that he has read such gospels lest 'we should seem to be unacquainted with any point for the sake of those who think they possess some valuable knowledge if they are acquainted with them. But in all these we approve nothing else but that which the Church approves, that is, four Gospels only as proper to be received' (*Homily on Luke*, i).

Now and then, however, Origen does, in fact, quote or refer to (and sometimes with approval) one or another of the gospels beyond the four 'which the Church approves'. These include the *Gospel of Peter* and 'The Book of James' (known since the sixteenth century as *Protevangelium Jacobi*) in connection with identifying the brothers of Jesus as sons of Joseph by a former wife (*Comm. in Matt.* x. 17). More than once he refers to the *Gospel according to the Hebrews*, sometimes without further comment (*Comm. in John* ii. 12; *Comm. in Matt.* xvi. 12), sometimes with a qualifying phrase, such as 'if any one receives it' (*Hom. in Jeremiah* xv. 4; *Comm. in Matt.* xv. 14).

At the same time, it is significant that, like Clement of Alexandria, Origen not infrequently makes use of unwritten sayings of Jesus, such as the well-known and possibly genuine agraphon, 'Be approved money-changers', calling it a 'command of Jesus' (*Comm. in John* xix. 2; in *Matt. comm.* xvii. 31 he refers to it as 'according to the Scripture'), and the agraphon about 'asking for great things'—which Origen embroiders by adding another pair of clauses.[47] He also quotes the beatitude, 'Blessed is he who even fasts in order that he may feed a poor man' (*Hom. on Leviticus* x. 2), as well as a version of logion 82 of the *Gospel of Thomas*, 'Whoever is near to me is near to the fire' (*Hom. on Jeremiah* xx. 3).

Origen's testimony concerning the Book of Acts and the Epistles (both Pauline and Catholic) is pervasive in his writings. As would be expected, he attributes the Acts of the Apostles to Luke, the author of the Third Gospel. He makes

[47] According to Origen (*Selecta in Psalm.* iv. 4 and *De orat.* ii. 2; xiv. 1), 'the Saviour says, "Ask for the great things, and God will add to you the little things" [thus far Origen agrees with his predecessor Clement of Alexandria, but then he adds] "and ask for the heavenly things, and God will add to you the earthly things."' The addition, as Jeremias observes, 'has a Pauline and Johannine ring, and is definitely unsynoptic' (*Unknown Sayings of Jesus*, 2nd ed., p. 100).

frequent citations from the Pauline Epistles, including even the brief letter to Philemon. Often he uses the formula 'Paul says' or 'Paul said', and sometimes adds the name of those whom the apostle addresses. Only in the case of 2 Timothy does Origen make the remark that 'some have dared to reject this Epistle, but they were not able' (*In Matt. ser. vet. interp.* 117).[48]

In a statement quoted by Eusebius (*Hist. eccl.* vi. xxv. 8) from the fifth book of Origen's *Commentary on John* (written perhaps during a trip to the East in 230–1), Origen says that 'Peter... has left one acknowledged (ὁμολογουμένη) Epistle); possibly also a second, but this is disputed' (ἀμφιβάλλεται). In the same passage he mentions that John, who wrote the Gospel and the Apocalypse, 'left also an Epistle of very few lines, and, it may be, a second and third—but not all consider these to be genuine' (οὐ πάντες φασὶ εἶναι γνησίους ταύτας).

As for the Epistle to the Hebrews, throughout Origen's writings he quotes it more than two hundred times, and in the vast majority of his references he is content to attribute it to Paul as its author. But near the close of his life (after A.D. 245), in a passage from the series of *Homilies on Hebrews* preserved to us, where Origen is speaking as a scholar, he admits freely that the tradition of its authorship is wholly uncertain. He gives as his considered opinion that, in view of the literary and stylistic problems involved, it is best to conclude that, though the Epistle contains the thoughts (νοήματα) of Paul, it was written by someone else, perhaps Luke or Clement of Rome.[49]

Although the Epistle of James is quoted several times by Origen, in his *Commentary on John* (xix. 61) he refers to it as 'the Epistle of James that is in circulation', implying some doubt as to its authenticity. One also notes that in Origen's *Commentary on Matthew*, when he speaks at length of the brothers of Jesus (ii. 17), he mentions James but says nothing of his Epistle. As for the Epistle of Jude, in the same commentary on Matthew (x. 17) Origen says: 'And Jude, who wrote an Epistle of but a few lines, yet filled with the healthful words of heavenly grace,

---

[48] According to Clement (*Strom.* ii. 11), 'the heretics reject the Epistles to Timothy because they are convicted by the passage, "Avoid the contradictions of what is falsely called knowledge"' (γνῶσις, 1 Tim. vi. 21).

[49] For an extensive statement of Origen's views on Hebrews, see Eusebius, *Hist. eccl.* VI. XXV. 11–14.

said in the salutation: Jude, a servant of Jesus Christ, and brother of James.'

From what has been mentioned thus far we can see that Origen has no question about most of the books of the New Testament; the exceptions are the Epistles of James, 2 Peter, and 2 and 3 John. In fact, he nowhere quotes or mentions 2 Peter or the two minor Johannine Epistles in any of his writings that have come down to us in Greek.

The situation is different, however, in Origen's *Homilies on Joshua* (written about A.D. 240), which have been preserved, unfortunately, only in a Latin translation, made, as it seems, by Rufinus (*c.* A.D. 345–410). Here we find, expressed in characteristic Alexandrian oratory, an incidental enumeration of all the authors of the entire New Testament. After describing how the walls of Jericho fell down Origen continues:

> So too our Lord Jesus Christ . . . sent his apostles as priests carrying well-wrought (*ductiles*) trumpets. First Matthew sounded the priestly trumpet in his Gospel. Mark also, and Luke, and John, each gave fourth a strain on their priestly trumpets. Peter moreover sounds with the two[50] trumpets of his Epistles; James also and Jude. Still the number is incomplete, and John gives forth the trumpet sound through his Epistles [and Apocalypse];[51] and Luke while describing the deeds of the apostles. Latest of all, moreover, that one comes who said, 'I think that God has set us forth as the apostles last of all' (1 Cor. iv. 9), and thundering on the fourteen trumpets of his Epistles he threw down, even to their very foundations, the walls of Jericho, that is to say, all the instruments of idolatry and the dogmas of the philosophers (*Hom. in Jos.* vii. 1).

How should one evaluate the testimony presented in this homily, where Origen seemingly mentions all[52] the books of the New Testament? It is, of course, not impossible that Rufinus altered Origen's words so as to reflect a later, fourth-century opinion concerning the extent of the canon. But, as

[50] One manuscript reads: with the three.

[51] The words *et Apocalypsin* are lacking in most manuscripts, and are probably a scribal expansion of the text.

[52] The number of the Johannine Epistles is not, to be sure, mentioned, but one can suppose on the basis of other passages that he means three. Moreover, the variant reading in connection with Peter's two (or three) Epistles may, in fact, have stood originally with the mention of John's Epistles, and by scribal error was transferred to Peter's. As regards the Apocalypse, see the preceding footnote.

Harnack has pointed out,[53] the position of the Acts of the Apostles in the list does not favour such a supposition. It is also possible to account for the differences in terms of Origen's audience and purposes; namely, in the context of a sermon Origen enumerates writings which had not yet attained universal approval but which might be used perfectly well for the edification of the faithful, whereas in more detailed discussions he customarily differentiates between the two categories of books.

In any case, the list clearly is of interest for the history of the canon. In the first place, it contains together, without mentioning any other books and without making any distinctions, the books that in A.D. 325 Eusebius would cite as 'homolegoumena' and 'antilegomena' (see p. 203 below),[54] and Athanasius in 367 would enumerate as constituting the New Testament (see pp. 211–2 below). Secondly, the order of the books in this list is noteworthy. There are three groups: Gospels; Catholic Epistles, with the Apocalypse and the Acts; and finally the Pauline Epistles. This sequence of Revelation (if Origen included it in the list) and Acts is found likewise in (only) the Catalogue Claromontanus (see Appendix IV. 4 below), which also belongs in the East.

Throughout his scholarly career Origen consulted and cited many books that contributed something of value to the subject matter that was under consideration. He refers, for example, to several of the writings of those who have now come to be called the Apostolic Fathers. Four times he quotes from Clement of Rome's *1 Epistle*, and three times from the *Epistle of Barnabas*; in fact, on one occasion he calls the latter 'Barnabas's general epistle' (τῇ Βαρνάβα καθολικῇ ἐπιστολῇ, *Contra Celsum* i. 63). He makes numerous references to the *Shepherd* of Hermas, and on one occasion, in his later years, he describes it as 'a work which seems to me very useful, and, as I believe, divinely inspired' (*Comm. in Rom.* x. 31, written about 244–6).

He flatly rejects the authenticity of the book entitled the *Preaching of Peter* (Κήρυγμα Πέτρου), saying that 'that work is

---

[53] *Der kirchengeschichtliche Ertrag der exegetischen Arbeiten des Origens* (*Texte und Untersuchungen*, xlii, 3; Leipzig, 1918), p. 12 n. 1.

[54] See J. Ruwet, 'Les "Antilegomena" dans les oeuvres d'Origène', *Biblica*, xxiii (1942), pp. 18–42; xxiv (1943), pp. 18–58; xxv (1944), pp. 143–66, 311–34.

not included among the ecclesiastical books, for we can show that it was not composed either by Peter or by any other person inspired by the Spirit of God' (Preface to *De princip.* 8). Referring on another occasion (*Comm. in Joan.* xiii. 17) to that same work, which had been cited by Heracleon, Origen enquires whether it is authentic (γνήσιον), or spurious (νόθον), or mixed (μικτόν). Origen does not explain the exact significance that he gives to the term 'mixed', but one supposes that he would have applied it to books that have, in spite of their general apocryphal character, elements of acknowledged value.

It is difficult to summarize the views on the canon entertained over the years by a mind as fertile and as wide-ranging as Origen's. Certainly it can be said, however, that he regarded the canon of the four Gospels as closed. He accepted fourteen Epistles of Paul, as well as Acts, 1 Peter, 1 John, Jude, and Revelation, but expressed reservation concerning James, 2 Peter, and 2 and 3 John. At other times Origen, like Clement before him, accepts as Christian evidence any material he finds convincing or appealing, even designating such writings on occasion as 'divinely inspired'.[55]

Here and there a certain development can be detected in Origen's thinking, or at least in the way in which he expressed himself. There is somewhat greater readiness to make use affirmatively of non-canonical texts while he was a teacher at the catechetical school of Alexandria, as compared with a certain caution and circumspection observable later in the context of giving Biblical expositions from the pulpit at Caesarea. This is particularly true with regard to the *Shepherd* of Hermas. The process of canonization represented by Origen proceded by way of selection, moving from many candidates for inclusion to fewer.

[55] See R. P. C. Hanson, *Origen's Doctrine of Tradition* (London, 1954), pp. 127–56.

VI

Development of the Canon in the West

THE Christian religion arose in the East, but soon made its way to the West. In the Book of Acts the first person mentioned by name as having become a convert to the new faith on European soil is Lydia, a business woman from the city of Thyatira in Asia Minor and now a merchant specializing in purple goods at Philippi in Macedonia (Acts xvi. 14). Other parts of the Balkan peninsula were evangelized during the apostle Paul's second missionary journey, when Lydia was converted; later he made a journey into Illyricum (Rom. xv. 19, modern Yugoslavia). Meanwhile, other, unnamed persons had brought the gospel to Rome. It is possible that this took place when certain Jews, resident at Rome, returned from Jerusalem as Jewish-Christian believers following the preaching of Peter at the first Pentecost (Acts ii. 10). However that may be, at any rate by the time that Paul was brought as a prisoner to Rome to be tried before Caesar, a considerable number of Christian believers were there, and Acts reports that a group of them came from the city about forty miles to meet him at the Forum of Appius and at Three Taverns, two way-stations on the Appian Way (Acts xxviii. 15). By the seventh decade the number of believers in the metropolis had attracted the attention of the Emperor Nero, and Tacitus (*Annals* xv. 44) refers to them as being a 'huge multitude' (*multitudo ingens*) who had suffered persecution. By the middle of the second century the Christian Church was firmly established in Rome, and outposts had been planted still farther to the west in Gaul as well as across the Mediterranean in North Africa. We must now trace the use made of New Testament books in these three geographical areas of the West.

I. ROME

1. JUSTIN MARTYR

Of early Christian Apologists—those who stepped forward to defend Christianity when it was attacked—one of the most outstanding was Justin Martyr. He was born near the beginning of the second century in Palestine, at Shechem in Samaria, a city that had been destroyed around A.D. 70 but was subsequently rebuilt and inhabited by Greek and Roman settlers.

After sampling various philosophies, Justin was converted to the Christian faith about A.D. 130. A short time later he became a Christian teacher and taught at Ephesus, where he engaged in a disputation with a Jew named Trypho (c. 135). After a few years he moved to Rome, where he founded a Christian school. Here he met vehement opposition in the Cynic philosopher Crescens whose antagonism made Justin determined to compose an 'Apology' (ἀπολογία) or reasoned defence of the Christian faith. This was issued about A.D. 150 in the form of a petition addressed to the Emperor Antoninus Pius. Sometime afterward he published his *Dialogue with Trypho the Jew*.[1] A shorter, so-called 'Second Apology' was addressed to the Senate, apparently after the accession of Marcus Aurelius (A.D. 161).

In his *First Apology* Justin seeks to exonerate Christians from various charges laid against them; then (chaps. xiii–lxvii) he turns to a justification of the Christian religion, giving a detailed description particularly of its doctrine and worship and the basis in history and reason for adherence to it. The *Second Apology* is mainly concerned with rebutting certain specific charges against the Christians, and defending the superiority of Christian moral teaching to that of the pagans. In fact, whatever of Christian truth had been proclaimed by the philosophers is due, Justin says, to their participating in the 'seminal Logos' (λόγος σπερματικός).

Justin was the most voluminous Christian writer up to his time, and his *Dialogue with Trypho*, written about the year 160 and running to 142 chapters, was probably the longest book thus far produced by an orthodox Christian writer.[2] In it Justin stresses the transitoriness of the Old Covenant and its

---

[1] Whether the *Dialogue* was intended chiefly for a Jewish reading public, as seems to be obvious from a prima-facie reading; or was directed to a pagan readership, as E. R. Goodenough thought (*The Theology of Justin Martyr* [Jena, 1923], pp. 96–110); or was written primarily for Christians, as C. H. Cosgrove has recently argued ('Justin Martyr and the Emerging Christian Canon', *Vigiliae Christianae*, xxxvi [1982], pp. 209–32), is of relatively minor interest in the present context.

[2] The twenty-four books (now lost) of Basilides' *Exegetica* (see chap. IV. I. I above) may have been longer.

precepts, and quotes the prophets as proof that Christian truth existed even before Christ. In analysing his very numerous quotations from the Old Testament, one finds that he gives preference to passages that speak of the rejection of Israel and the election of the gentiles.

We turn now to consider Justin's knowledge of the Gospels. These he describes as 'Memoirs of the apostles', using the same word that Xenophon had coined when he wrote the 'Memoirs of Socrates' (*'Ἀπομνημονεύματα Σωκράτους*).[3] These 'Memoirs', Justin tells his non-Christian readers, were called 'Gospels' (*1 Apol.* lxvi. 3). Eight times he calls them 'Memoirs of the apostles'; four times he mentions them only as 'Memoirs'. Once he calls them 'Memoirs composed by the apostles of Christ and by those who followed with them' (*Dial.* ciii. 8). In this last case he quotes Luke. And once, in quoting Mark (iii. 16–17) on the name that Jesus gave Peter and on the name Boanerges for James and John, he calls them 'his [Peter's] Memoirs' (*Dial.* cvi. 4)—doubtless alluding to the tradition reported by Papias that Mark wrote down Peter's words.

Justin also tells us something else about these Memoirs that alerts us to their importance in the early Church. In his description of the Sunday services of worship he states that 'the Memoirs of apostles or the writings of the prophets are read, for as long as time permits. Then the reader stops and the leader instructs by word of mouth, and exhorts to the imitation of these good things. Then we all stand up together and pray' (*1 Apol.* lxvii. 3–5). Here it is plain that the Memoirs were read interchangeably with the Old Testament prophets. It should be noted also that when Justin mentions the Memoirs before the Old Testament prophets, he really places them not merely on a level with them, but above them.

Several specific instances of Justin's quotations from the 'Memoirs' will be sufficient to indicate his usage. In the *Dialogue* (cvi. 4) he declares that Moses had written beforehand of the birth of Jesus in the words, 'A star shall arise from Jacob, and a leader from Israel' (Num. xxiv. 17), and accordingly, 'when a star rose in heaven at the time of his [Jesus'] birth, as is recorded in the Memoirs of his apostles, the Magi from Arabia,

---

[3] Justin is acquainted with this work, and refers to it in his *Second Apology* (xi. 3).

recognizing the sign by this, came and worshipped him' (cf. Matt. ii. 1 ff.). Again, when Justin quotes (*Dial*. ciii. 8) from the Gospel of Luke (who was not an apostle), he qualifies his introductory words: 'in the Memoirs which, as I have said, were drawn up by the apostles and their followers, [it is recorded] that sweat fell like drops of blood while he [Jesus] was praying, and saying, "If it be possible, let this cup pass"' (Luke xxii. 44, 42).

At other times Justin makes use of the customary formula of quotation, 'it is written'.

In the Gospel it is written (γέγραπται) that he said, 'All things are delivered to me by my Father' and 'No one knows the Father but the Son; nor the Son but the Father, and they to whom the Son will reveal him' (*Dial*. c. 1).

In still other instances—the great majority—Justin dispenses with such formulae that refer to written 'Memoirs' or 'the Gospel' and simply introduces the words of Christ by the phrases 'thus Christ said' or 'taught' or 'exhorted'—that is, Jesus' words are their own warrant. In such cases his quotations often show features of harmonization of Matthew and Luke, and in other cases occasionally reveal harmonization of Mark with another Synoptic Gospel.[4]

The limited evidence that Justin knew and used the Gospel of John is both general and specific. General evidence includes Justin's doctrine of the *logos*, which he presumably must have received either from John or from Philo, perhaps through Middle Platonist philosophy. Now there was a notable difference between these two forms of the *logos* doctrine, the differentiating feature being the Incarnation. Since the pre-existence of Christ is not taught anywhere in the Synoptic Gospels, it appears that it was from the Fourth Gospel that Justin obtained such an idea as this: 'That Christ is the firstborn of God, being the *logos* of which every race of people

---

[4] For examples of such harmonization, see A. J. Bellinzoni, *The Sayings of Jesus in the Writings of Justin Martyr* (Leiden, 1967), and Leslie L. Kline, 'Harmonized Sayings of Jesus in the Pseudo-Clementine Homilies and Justin Martyr', *Zeitschrift für die neutestamentlichen Wissenschaft*, lxvi (1975), pp. 223–41. But the further supposition that Justin had drawn up a harmony of the Gospels is unwarranted; see Georg Strecker, 'Eine Evangelienharmonie bei Justin und Pseudoklemens?' *New Testament Studies*, xxiv (1978), pp. 297–316.

have been partakers, we have been taught and have declared'
(*1 Apol.* xlvi. 2; cf. John i. 1 and 9).

Another distinctly Johannine idea is expressed by Justin as
follows:

> I have already shown that he was the only-begotten of the Father
> of the universe, having been begotten by him in a peculiar manner as
> his Logos and Power, and having afterward become man through the
> virgin, as we have learned from the Memoirs (*Dial.* cv. 1).

The virgin birth can be learned from the Memoirs of Matthew
and Luke, but the idea that Christ was the only-begotten Son
seems to have been derived from the Fourth Gospel.[5]

Besides such general evidence, there is also the rather clear
quotation that seems to come from the Fourth Gospel (iii. 3, 5):
'Christ also said, "Unless you are born again (ἀναγεννηθῆτε),
you will not enter into the kingdom of heaven"' (*1 Apol.* lxi. 4).

In addition to echoes and quotations from the Memoirs of the
apostles, Justin also makes use of various extraneous traditions,
probably oral, about the life of Jesus. It perhaps was noticed
above that in quoting Matt. ii. 1 ff. Justin says the Magi came
from Arabia (*Dial.* lxxxviii. 1). Likewise he states that Jesus was
born in a cave near Bethlehem (*Dial.* lxxviii. 5); that the ass colt
used in the Palm Sunday entry was found 'bound to a vine at the
entrance of the village' (*1 Apol.* xxxiii. 6);[6] and that at the
crucifixion mocking bystanders not only shook their heads and
shot out their lips (*1 Apol.* xxxviii. 8) but 'twisted their noses to
each other' (*Dial.* ci. 3) and cried, 'Let him who raised the dead
deliver himself' (*1 Apol.* xxxviii. 8).

In addition to a dozen or more glosses such as these,[7] Justin

---

[5] For a score of other minor coincidences of thought and expression between Justin
and the Fourth Gospel, see W. von Loewenich, *Das Johannes-Verständnis im zweiten
Jahrhundert* (Giessen, 1932), pp. 39–50, and E. F. Osborn, *Justin Martyr* (*Beiträge zur
historische Theologie*, xlvii; Tübingen, 1973), p. 137. On the other hand, not all scholars
are impressed by such reminiscences; see J. N. Sanders, *The Fourth Gospel in the Early
Church* (Cambridge, 1943), pp. 27–31, and M. R. Hillmer, 'The Gospel of John in the
Second Century', Ph.D. diss., Harvard University, 1966, pp. 51–73.

[6] Justin may have derived the idea from Gen. xlix. 11.

[7] For several others, see L. W. Barnard, *Justin Martyr, his Life and Thought*
(Cambridge, 1967), p. 64, who very properly comments: 'The uncanonical material
found in Justin is of small compass compared to his agreements with the Canonical
Gospels. The marvel is that so little legendary material appears in his works when we
compare them with the fanciful accounts of the second-century apocryphal Gospels
and even with traditions contained in other of the early Fathers.'

also cites two extra-canonical sayings (agrapha) of Jesus. The first, 'Our Lord Jesus Christ said: In whatever I find you, in this I will also judge you' (*Dial.* xlvii. 5), is ascribed by other Fathers to Ezekiel or to one of the prophets.[8] The other saying is: 'Christ said, "There shall be schisms and heresies"' (*Dial.* xxxv. 3), which is also found in the Syrian *Didascalia* vi. 5.

Besides the Gospels the only other book of the New Testament to which Justin alludes by name is the Book of Revelation. Even that is not quoted, but appealed to generally as proof of the existence of prophetic power in the Christian Church:

> Moreover also among us a man named John, one of the apostles of Christ, prophesied in a revelation made to him that those who have believed on our Christ will spend a thousand years in Jerusalem; and that hereafter the general and, in short, the eternal resurrection and judgement of all will likewise take place (*Dial.* lxxxi. 4).

Although Justin nowhere quotes from the Epistles of Paul, his controversy with Marcion must mean that he had knowledge of at least several of them. Furthermore, occasional Pauline forms of expression and teaching show that the Apostle to the Gentiles had helped to mould both his faith and his language.[9]

By way of summarizing Justin's thinking, if the Old Testament prophets have authority in themselves, the Gospels are of value in so far as they are authorized witnesses to Jesus' life and teaching. He makes use of the Synoptics much more frequently than the Fourth Gospel. Justin also alludes to various traditions bearing on the life of Jesus that came to be incorporated in apocryphal gospels. These items resemble the Midrashic additions that he sometimes includes in his Old Testament citations. In any case, he does not generally attribute to them an authority comparable to that of the Memoirs of the apostles; it is the latter that are read publicly on the Lord's day in services of worship. Justin does not appeal to the authority of Paul, but he considers the Apocalypse of John as both a prophetic and an apostolic work.

---

[8] See J. Jeremias, *Unknown Sayings of Jesus*, 2nd ed. (London, 1964), pp. 83 f.

[9] For examples of such echoes, see Westcott, *Canon*, 6th ed., pp. 169–71.

2. HIPPOLYTUS OF ROME

The indefatigable Hippolytus, bishop of Rome (d. 235), was a prolific author. In the variety of his interests and the number of his writings (but not in depth or independence of thought) he may be compared with his outstanding contemporary, Origen. His followers erected, probably in his burial vault, the famous marble statue to him which was recovered in 1551 just outside Rome during excavations on the Via Tiburtina.[10] While the head and the upper part of the body are gone, the marble chair proved to be of great importance, because a list of the works of Hippolytus was engraved on the back of it, including a table for calculating Easter Sundays.

Born about A.D. 170, of Hippolytus' early life very little is known. According to Photius (*Bibl. cod.* 121), Hippolytus had been a pupil of Irenaeus. During the first decades of the third century he appears to have become a figure of considerable repute in the Roman Church. When Origen visited the Christian community in Rome about the year 212, he heard Hippolytus preach in one of the churches a sermon, 'On the Praise of our Lord and Saviour'.[11]

Hippolytus subsequently came into conflict with Pope Callistus (217–22) on questions of ecclesiastical discipline, and he and some of his adherents separated from the Church. He was elected bishop of Rome by a small but influential circle and thus became the first antipope. Before the close of his life, however, Hippolytus was reconciled to the Church, died a martyr (235), and is venerated as a saint to the present day.

The literary work of Hippolytus was accomplished princi-

---

[10] Until 1959 the statue was kept in the Lateran Museum; in that year, however, Pope John had it removed to the entrance hall of the Vatican Library. For pictures of the chair, see Migne, *Patrologia Latina*, cxxvii, cols. 1295 f.

[11] So Jerome reports in *De viris ill.* 61, when listing the literary works of Hippolytus. Not only must Jerome have read Hippolytus' sermon (he calls it 'an exhortation') most carefully to recall that in it Hippolytus 'indicates that he is speaking in the church in the presence of Origen', but likewise it is significant that Hippolytus took the opportunity to recognize publicly Origen's presence in the congregation. Furthermore, the inclusion of such details and comments made during a sermon leads one to conclude that a stenographer must have been taking down what was being said. See Metzger, 'Stenography and Church History', *Twentieth Century Encyclopedia of Religious Knowledge*, ii (Grand Rapids, 1955), pp. 1060 f.

pally between A.D. 200 and 235. He was the last Christian author of Rome to employ the Greek language for his literary productions. These were more than forty in number, and included Scripture interpretation, polemic and doctrinal writing, church law, sermons, and chronology.

As concerns the canon of the New Testament, we find Hippolytus engaged in controversy with a Roman Christian named Gaius over the Johannine authorship of the Book of Revelation (see pp. 104–5 above). In rebuttal, Hippolytus wrote a treatise 'On the Gospel of John and the Apocalypse', the title of which is in the list on the statue. In this work, according to the Syrian Ebedjesu (*Cat. libr. omn. eccl.* 7), who knew the work and called it 'An Apology for the Apocalypse and the Gospel of John, Apostle and Evangelist', Hippolytus attacked, it seems, the Alogi, who denied the doctrine of the Logos.

With regard to Hippolytus' testimony to the extent of the New Testament as received at Rome in his day, though he gives no list of New Testament books (unless, as some have thought, the Muratorian Canon is a Latin translation of something from his pen), we find a fairly clear picture emerging from a close examination of his writings. He accepted the four Gospels as Scripture, and acknowledged thirteen Epistles of Paul, but not Hebrews. He also accepted Acts and three Catholic Epistles—1 Peter and 1 and 2 John. These, along with his impassioned defence of the Revelation of John, bring the total to twenty-two books. Although he did not rank the Epistle to the Hebrews as Scripture, he makes frequent quotations from it, particularly in his *Commentary on Daniel*.[12] He introduces New Testament texts with such formulas as: 'the Lord says', 'the Apostle says' (ὁ κύριος λέγει, ὁ ἀπόστολος λέγει), or sometimes by the name of the writer. He attributes the same authority to the writings of the Old and the New Testament, for in appealing to the testimony of all the Scripture (πᾶσα γραφή), he enumerates the parts, namely the prophets, the Lord, and the apostles (*Comm. on Dan.* iv. 49). The expression, 'the apostles', indicates that, for Hippolytus, the Epistles formed a collection as the Gospels.

[12] Incidentally, Hippolytus' *Commentary on Daniel*, dating from about 204, is the oldest exegetical work by an orthodox Christian on any Biblical book that has come down to us.

Hippolytus knew numerous other Christian writings from the first and second centuries, and on occasion quoted from such books as the *Shepherd* of Hermas, the *Didache*, the *Epistle of Barnabas*, the *Apocalypse of Peter*, the *Acts of Peter*, and the *Acts of Paul*. One observes, however, that all this literature does not possess in his eyes the same authority as do the Gospels or the Book of Revelation. He is the first Christian writer to reflect a knowledge of 2 Peter, but not as 'Scripture', and he must have known James and Jude at least slightly, for he once alludes to the opening verse of James with the words, 'As the saying of Jude (*sic*) in his first letter to the twelve tribes "which are scattered in the world" proves'.[13]

With Hippolytus the curtain falls upon Greek Christianity in Rome. In taking leave of him as a landmark witness to the formation of the New Testament canon in the first third of the third century, it is not without interest to observe that this Father, in his description of the end of the world, says, 'The public service of God shall be extinguished, psalmody shall cease, the reading of the Scriptures shall not be heard' (*Contra Noetum*, 9)—an unconscious testimony to the place that the public reading of the apostolic writings had come to fill in the minds of Christians.

II. GAUL

1. THE EPISTLE OF THE CHURCHES AT LYONS AND VIENNE

The missionaries who established the church at Lyons, from which the Christian faith spread little by little to other parts of Gaul, had come from Asia Minor. Many of the members of the Lyons church bore Greek names. Irenaeus (Εἰρηναῖος, 'Peaceful'), originally of Asia Minor and representing the Eastern tradition, was a living bond between Asia and Gaul. Furthermore, the church at Lyons used the Greek language, though the mother tongue of most of the population was a Celtic dialect.

During the early summer of A.D. 177, feeling among the populace of Lyons gradually seethed up against the Chris-

---

[13] Hippolytus as quoted by Dionysius bar Salibi, in Hans Achelis's edition of Hippolytus (*Griechische christliche Schriftsteller*, i, pars sec.; Leipzig, 1897), p. 231, line 10.

tians.[14] First they were banned from the baths and the market places; later they were excluded from all public places. Then, at a moment when the provincial governor was away from the city, the mob broke loose. Christians were assaulted, beaten, and stoned. After the governor had returned, a public trial of the Christians was ordered.

At the trial, to which also other Christians were brought who had been hounded out of the neighbouring city of Vienne, horrible tortures were applied in order to break their will and force them to recant. One of the victims of the brutal interrogation was the Bishop Pothinus, now over ninety years of age and physically quite infirm. Finally, the governor ordered all those who appeared to be Roman citizens to be beheaded and the rest to be exposed to the beasts in the amphitheatre.

Once popular anger had subsided following the persecution, and Christian life could resume, an epistle was sent by the survivors to their mother churches in Asia Minor in order to tell them what had taken place. Possibly Irenaeus, who presumably had been away during the crisis, had a share in drafting the missive; in any case we have Eusebius to thank for incorporating a copy in his *Ecclesiastical History* (v. i. 1–ii. 8).

The *Epistle of the Churches at Lyons and Vienne* is remarkable for the abundance and the precision of the reminiscences of New Testament texts that it contains. We find echoes of phrases that are obviously borrowed from Acts, Romans, Philippians, 1 and 2 Timothy, 1 Peter, and Hebrews. Furthermore, it presents (v. i. 15) a saying of the Lord that we know only from the Gospel according to John ('the time will come when whoever kills you will think that he is doing God service', John xvi. 2). Once there is even a direct and textual quotation, described as from Scripture (γραφή, v. i. 58); this quotation, which is loose in form, is taken from the Book of Revelation ('Let him that is unlawful be unlawful still, and he that is righteous be righteous still', Rev. xxii. 11).

Although one may not be able to draw any precise conclu-

[14] See A. Chagny, *Les Martyrs de Lyon de 177* (Lyon, 1936); Pièrre Nautin, *Lettres et écrivains des II⁰ et III⁰ siècles* (Paris, 1961), pp. 33–64; Herbert Musurillo, S. J., *The Acts of the Christian Martyrs, Introduction, Texts, and Translations* (Oxford, 1972), pp. 63–85; and *Les Martyrs de Lyon*, Lyon 20–3 Septembre 1977 (*Colloques internationaux du Centre national de la recherche scientifique*, No. 575; Paris, 1978).

sion as to the theoretical authority attributed to the New Testament, one certainly can verify the role that it played in the piety and religious thought of the Christianity current in Lyons and Vienne.[15]

2. IRENAEUS OF LYONS

Relatively little is known of the life of Irenaeus. As a boy he had, as he delighted to point out, listened to the sermons of the great bishop and martyr, Polycarp of Smyrna, who was regarded as a disciple of the apostles themselves. Here he came to know, he says, 'the genuine unadulterated gospel', to which he remained faithful throughout his life. Perhaps he also accompanied Polycarp on his journey to Rome in connection with the controversy over the date of celebrating Easter (A.D. 154). Later he went as a missionary to southern Gaul, where he became a presbyter at Lyons.

Irenaeus was absent from the city when the persecution there reached its zenith. It seems that he had been sent to Rome by the Gallican churches in order to confer with Pope Eleutherus, perhaps as a mediator in the Montanist disputes. Evidently Irenaeus stayed in Rome for just a short time, and soon after the end of the persecution we find him again in Lyons as the successor to Bishop Pothinus (A.D. 178). When and how he died is unknown to us. Jerome and others state that he died as a martyr in the persecution under the Emperor Septimus Severus (A.D. 202), but there is no certainty about this tradition.

In short, we know Irenaeus almost solely from his writings, and these have not been transmitted to us in their entirety. His chief work, *The Refutation and Overthrow of Knowledge Falsely So Called* (or, more briefly, *Against Heresies*), has been preserved in the Greek original in fragments and only in a Latin translation in its entirety. Another writing, *The Demonstration of the Apostolic Teaching*, has been made available to us only since the beginning of this century when an Armenian translation was discovered. From these two sources we can appreciate the

---

[15] Such a conclusion would remain substantially unaltered even though one supposes that an editor may have reworked the original letter sometime in the third century, giving to the earlier description of the tortures a vividness and melodrama of his own; see Musurillo, op. cit., pp. xxi et seq.

importance of Irenaeus as the first great Catholic theologian, the champion of orthodoxy against Gnostic heresy, and a mediating link between Eastern and Western Churches.

Irenaeus is the first among patristic writers who makes full use of the New Testament. The Apostolic Fathers re-echo the oral tradition; the Apologists (such as Justin and Athenagoras) are content with quoting the Old Testament prophets and the Lord's own words in the Gospels as proof of divine revelation; but Irenaeus shows the unity of the Old and New Testaments in opposition to Gnostic separation of the two. Unlike his predecessors, his citations from the New Testament are more numerous than those from the Old Testament. In his *Adversus Haereses* he quotes 1,075 passages from almost all of the books of the New Testament: 626 from the Gospels, 54 from Acts, 280 from the Pauline Epistles (but not from Philemon), 15 from the Catholic Epistles (but not 2 Peter, 3 John, or Jude), and 29 from the Book of Revelation.[16]

According to Irenaeus, the same gospel which was first orally preached and transmitted was subsequently committed to writing and faithfully preserved in all the apostolic churches through the regular succession of bishops and elders. Over against the ever-shifting and contradictory opinions of the heretics, Irenaeus places the unchanging faith of the catholic Church based on Scripture and tradition, and compacted together by the episcopal organization (*Adv. Haer.* III. i. 1).[17]

As against the multiplicity of new gospels produced by the Gnostics, the Great Church by the time of Irenaeus had ceased to recognize any but the four Gospels, or rather, as he puts it, one single gospel in four forms (τὸ εὐαγγέλιον τετράμορφον). This fixing of the number and selection is final:

> It is not possible that the Gospels can be either more or fewer in number than they are, since there are four directions of the world in which we are, and four principal winds. ... The four living creatures [of Rev. iv. 9] symbolize the four Gospels. ... and there were four

[16] For a register listing all the explicit quotations in Irenaeus, see J. Hoh, *Die Lehre des hl. Irenäus über das Neue Testament* (*Neutestamentliche Abhandlungen*, vii; Münster i. W., 1919), pp. 189–97.

[17] See W. L. Dubière, 'Le Canon néotestamentaire et les écrits chrétiens approuvés par Irénée', *La nouvelle Clio*, vi (1954), pp. 199–224.

principal covenants made with humanity, through Noah, Abraham, Moses, and Christ (*Adv. Haer.* III. xi. 8).[18]

Thus for Irenaeus the Gospel canon is closed and its text is holy. The apostolic canon, however, is not yet closed, and it does not occur to him when referring to the titles or the Pauline authorship of twelve Epistles to make similar theoretical arguments concerning their number as he had done for the Gospels.

It is significant that, during the period which followed Polycarp when writers in Asia Minor neglected the apostle Paul as compromised by the use which heretics had made of him, Irenaeus shifted tactics. In place of abandoning Paul to the heretics, he undertook to demonstrate that a sane interpretation of his Epistles confirms and justifies catholic doctrine.

The Gospels are indeed not alone in being joined to the Old Testament as holy Scripture. Once (III. xii. 12) Irenaeus plainly reckons the Pauline Epistles along with the Gospel according to Luke as 'the Scriptures' and emphatically applies (III. xii. 9) to the Acts of the Apostles the designation 'Scripture'. In view of such expressions one is not surprised that in I. iii. 6 he places 'the writings of the evangelists and the apostles' on a par with 'the law and the prophets'. Nor does the fact that he never cites Pauline passages with the formula 'it is written' come into consideration, for he prefers to use for New Testament writings the more intimate formula, 'John says...', 'Paul teaches...', so that even the evangelists are only twice introduced with 'it is written' (II. xxii. 3 and xxx. 2).

Along with this canon of Gospels and 'Apostolos' Irenaeus also includes two apocalypses, the Revelation of John and the *Shepherd* of Hermas, both of which he designates as 'Scripture'.[19]

By way of summary, in Irenaeus we have evidence that by the year 180 in southern France a three-part New Testament of about twenty-two books was known. The total number will vary depending on whether or not we include Philemon (as we probably should) and Hermas (somewhat doubtfully). Even more important than the number of books is the fact that

---

[18] Irenaeus' words about the four Gospels have passed into the literature of the Church in the closest connection with the text of the Gospels, for they are used in a very large number of manuscripts as a brief preface to the Gospels.

[19] As an example of several instances for the Book of Revelation, see *Adv. Haer.* v. v. 2; for the sole instance for the *Shepherd* of Hermas, see IV. xx. 2.

Irenaeus had a clearly defined collection of apostolic books that he regarded as equal in significance to the Old Testament. His principle of canonicity was double: apostolicity of the writings and testimony to the tradition maintained by the Churches.

III. NORTH AFRICA

I. THE ACTS OF THE SCILLITAN MARTYRS

Written very simply and with moving sobriety, the *Acts of the Scillitan Martyrs* is the oldest dated document in the history of the Latin church. A relatively brief account, the *Acts* tells how seven men and five women from the village of Scillium in Numidia (modern Tunisia) stood trial in the senate house of Carthage on 17 July 180. Boldly professing their faith, they refused to sacrifice to the gods or to swear by the 'genius' of the Roman Emperor. Accordingly they were condemned to die by the sword, and were summarily executed.

The Latin report of their martyrdom contains an interesting passage that bears on the circulation of Christian books. During the trial Saturninus the proconsul asks, among other questions, 'What things do you have there in your satchel' (*capsa*)? The answer of Speratus was, 'Books (*libri*), and Epistles of Paul, a good man' (*vir justus*).

One might well ask why these Christians were interrogated about their satchel. Had they shown a remarkable devotion to its contents, which aroused comment? Or was it simply produced as a police-court exhibit, evidence that the accused were Christians in possession of incriminating documents at the time of their arrest?

In either case, the significant fact is that the accused have in a case or satchel some Epistles of Paul along with 'books' or (since the Latin language has no definite article or distinction between lower and upper case letters) 'the Books'.[20] We have

---

[20] This is the interpretation given by the later Latin recension of the *Acts* (*libri evangeliorum*), and is generally adopted today; see Gerald Bonner, 'The Scillitan Saints and the Pauline Epistles', *Journal of Ecclesiastical History*, vii (1956), pp. 141–6, esp. 144 f., supplanting the view of Harnack that the 'books' were Old Testament scrolls; see the latter's article, 'Über das Alter der Bezeichnung "Die Bücher" ("Die Bibel") für die Heiligen Schriften in der Kirche', *Zentralblatt für Bibliothekswesen*, xlv (1928), pp. 337 ff. In any case, it is no longer thought likely that the 'books', whatever their content, were scrolls, but rather codices. For statistics as to the far greater proportion of Christian codices to rolls that have survived, see C. H. Roberts and T. C. Skeat, *The Birth of the Codex* (Oxford, 1983), pp. 38–44.

thus a reference to the Scriptures and to the Epistles of Paul, mentioned separately. These books can hardly be other than parts of the Old Testament and the Gospels, or if one considers it unlikely that the Old Testament is included, then at least the Gospels, alone. The fact that Epistles of Paul would form a natural kind of extension to the Gospels and to the Old Testament shows at the very least why they were stowed away as sacred books in a certain container.

That this is the correct understanding of Speratus' answer to the proconsul is supported by the slightly expanded account given by the nearly contemporaneous Greek translation of the Latin text. The translator was in the happy position that Greek possesses the article, and thus was able to make the meaning somewhat clearer. The Greek recension tells us that, in reply to the proconsul's question, Speretus replied, 'Our customary books, and the Epistles of Paul, the devout man, which belong with them' (αἱ καθ' ἡμᾶς βίβλοι καὶ αἱ πρὸς ἐπὶ τούτοις ἐπιστολαὶ Παύλου τοῦ ὁσίου ἀνδρός).[21] Thus the translator, instead of separating Paul's Epistles from 'the Books', binds them together.

Since it is not likely that the Scillitan Christians, so obviously plebeian and without culture, would be able to read Greek, we are driven to conclude that they possessed at least the Epistles of Paul in a Latin version. And if the Pauline Epistles were circulated in a Latin version by A.D. 180, there is little doubt that the Gospels were likewise available in Latin.

2. TERTULLIAN

Tertullian, as T. R. Glover once remarked, was 'the first man of genius of the Latin race to follow Jesus Christ, and to re-set his ideas in the language native to that race'.[22] In estimating the importance of Tertullian in the development of the New Testament canon we must not only pay attention to the scope of New Testament Scriptures that he accepted, but also take into account his part in combating the canon developed by Marcion.

[21] It is to be noted that the translation which is ordinarily given of the second phrase, 'and also besides these the Epistles of Paul', would presuppose καὶ πρὸς ἐπὶ τούτοις αἱ ἐπιστολαὶ Παύλου, whereas the position of πρός (adverb) after the definite article means that it functions as an adjective, describing the epistles as closely related to, that is, as belonging among 'our customary Books'.

[22] *The Conflict of Religions in the Early Roman Empire* (London, 1909), p. 307.

Born at Carthage of pagan parents soon after the middle of the second century, Tertullian received a sound education in literature, law, and rhetoric. He was also thoroughly familiar with Greek. He made the law his profession and, having moved to Rome, gained a reputation for himself as an advocate. After his conversion to Christianity about A.D. 195 he returned to Carthage where he energetically propagated his newly adopted faith. Some years later (about 205), 'distressed by the envy and laxity of the clergy of the Roman church', as Jerome says,[23] Tertullian joined the Montanist sect, becoming a leader of this group in Africa.

Tertullian was the most prolific of the Latin Fathers in pre-Nicene times. His writings, which treat a large range of themes, all bear the marked individuality of their author. Expressing himself in a crisp and terse style, he freely moulded Latin into quite new forms.[24] Some of these were adopted by subsequent theologians and have found a permanent place in the vocabulary of Christian dogma. One of the terms he used with evident decisiveness is 'the rule of faith' (*regula fidei*). By this he signified the common fundamental belief of the Church, orally received by the churches from the apostles and orally transmitted from generation to generation as the baptismal creed.[25] In three of his writings Tertullian formally states what this 'rule of faith' was. In one case he gives a terse form of the Apostles' Creed (*De praes. haer.* 13); in the others, he paraphrases and elaborates some of its clauses, but adds no new article (*De virg. vel.* 1; *Adv. Prax.* 2). In other words, for Tertullian the *regula fidei* is the immemorial belief of Christians, derived from the Scriptures, and most succinctly set forth in the baptismal creed, that is, what we know as the Apostles' Creed.

Tertullian's New Testament is not perceptibly different from that of the preceding period. The new element that he added is the judicial character which he gave to its authority. Of the Latin equivalents for the Greek word for the Bible ($\beta\iota\beta\lambda\iota\alpha$)

---

[23] Jerome, *De viris ill.* 53.

[24] According to H. Hoppe (*Beiträge zur Sprache und Kritik Tertullians* [Lund, 1932]), Tertullian formed 509 new nouns, 284 adjectives, 28 adverbs, and 161 verbs, that is together 982 new words. See also T. P. O'Malley, *Tertullian and the Bible: Language-Imagery-Exegesis* (Utrecht, 1967).

[25] See Bengt Hägglund, 'Die Bedeutung der "regula fidei" als Grundlage theologischer Aussagen', *Studia theologica*, xii (1958), pp. 1–44, esp. 19–29.

employed by Tertullian and other Latin writers in the West, the most important and suggestive were the words *Instrumentum* and *Testamentum*.[26] Both terms were used in Roman law, one meaning a written contract or agreement (sometimes a public document), the other a last will and testament. Tertullian, who uses both for the Scriptures, seems to prefer *Instrumentum*; he protests Marcion's attempt to set up two gods, 'one for each Instrument, or Testament, as it is more usual to call it' (*Adv. Marc.* iv. 1). The four Gospels are the *Instrumentum evangelicum*, and their authors, he insists, are either apostles or companions and disciples of apostles (ibid. iv. 2).

In the course of his denunciation of Marcion, Tertullian chides him for not accepting the Acts of the Apostles, and so depriving himself of information concerning the career of the apostle Paul (*Adv. Marc.* v. 1). He then defends, one by one, each of the Pauline Epistles (ibid. v. 2–21), expressing astonishment that Marcion has rejected the two Epistles to Timothy and the one to Titus: 'His aim was, I suppose, to carry out his interpolating process even to the number of [Paul's] Epistles' (ibid. v. 21).[27]

In another treatise Tertullian cites a passage from the Epistle to the Hebrews (vi. 4–8), which he attributes to Barnabas as the author, 'a man sufficiently accredited by God, as being one whom Paul had stationed next to himself' (*De pudic.* 20). From 1 John he quotes iv. 1–3 and launches into a long discussion of the Antichrist (*Adv. Marc.* v. 16). He quotes several passages from 1 Peter, though without explicitly identifying the epistle (*Scorp.* 12). The Epistle of Jude (verse 14) is appealed to as a testimonial to the authority of Enoch (*De cultu fem.* i. 3). Several times he refers to the Apocalypse of John in ways that prove that, for Tertullian, there is no other Apocalypse than that by the apostle John (*Adv. Marc.* iv. 5; *De fuga* 1, *De pudic.* 20).

Tertullian's opinion concerning Hermas changed over the years. In his earlier writings he speaks favourably of the *Shepherd* of Hermas (*De orat.* 16), but during his Montanist period he declares that the book has been adjudged (*judicare-*

---

[26] E.g. *Apol.* xviii. 1; xix. 1; *De praesc. haer.* 38; *Adv. Marc.* iv. 1; *Adv. Prax.* 20.

[27] Tertullian means that Marcion has not only mutilated the text of Paul's Epistles, but their number as well, by rejecting the Pastoral Epistles.

tur) by every council in early times as false and apocryphal (*De pudic.* 10).[28] As for the apocryphal *Acts of Paul*, Tertullian reports, with evident satisfaction, that the presbyter who had written the book, though claiming to be well-intentioned, was very properly brought to trial and, being convicted of composing the apocryphon, was deposed from his clerical office (*De bapt.* 17).

By way of summary, Tertullian cites all the writings of the New Testament except 2 Peter, James, and 2 and 3 John. The latter two Epistles, being rather brief and of minimal theological importance, can have been omitted by Tertullian without implying that he did not know of their existence. Tertullian regarded the Scriptures of the Old Testament as divinely given, and he attributed to the four Gospels and the apostolic Epistles an authority equal to that of the Law and the Prophets. The orally transmitted 'rule of faith' and the written Scriptures were mutually appealed to, and any writing that did not conform to the rule of faith could not be accepted as Scripture.

3. CYPRIAN OF CARTHAGE

During the seventy years from the earliest information we have about Christianity in North Africa (the incident of the Scillitan Martyrs, A.D. 180) to the death of Cyprian, bishop of Carthage (A.D. 258), the Church must have spread as if by storm. By the middle of the third century the Christian Church in North Africa had 250 bishops. Nor did the Church grow in numbers only; it also gained an inner confidence and self-assurance.

The story of Cyprian's life reflects with particular clarity how things had changed in North Africa. Thascius Caecilius Cypri-

---

[28] Although some have taken this statement about the *Shepherd* as referring to conciliar decisions made in connection with establishing the New Testament canon, von Campenhausen is altogether justified in rejecting such an interpretation: 'The word *concilium*, here as elsewhere in Tertullian, patently is not to be understood in its later technical significance, but simply means the (liturgical) congregation of the churches: the Shepherd of Hermas is rejected by every church community, by the community of all the churches, including even the catholics' (*The Formation of the Christian Bible*, p. 331 n. 14).

Another will-o'-the-wisp so far as early synods are concerned is the theory proposed by Bacon that 'Matthew received the endorsement of a synod of "men acquainted with the holy Scriptures" in Rome about A.D. 120'. The theory is based on a stray comment included in a Syriac legend entitled 'The Discourse on the Star', written about the year 400 and attributed to Eusebius of Caesarea (B. W. Bacon, 'As to the Canonization of Matthew', *Harvard Theological Review*, xxii [1929], pp. 151–73).

anus, born between A.D. 200 and 210, came from a well-to-do and evidently noble family. He received a thorough education, and began to teach rhetoric and oratory at Carthage. But he became disenchanted with pleasure in the pagan world about him, a world of luxury, vice, and moral turpitude. Having come in contact with representatives of the new faith, especially with a presbyter, Caecilian, Cyprian was converted about A.D. 246. He sold his estates for the benefit of the poor, took a vow of chastity, and received baptism, adopting, out of gratitude to his spiritual father, the name of Caecilius.

Cyprian now devoted himself zealously, in ascetic retirement, to the study of the Scriptures and earlier church teachers, especially Tertullian. Such a man, however, could not long remain concealed. Only two years after his baptism and in spite of his remonstrance, Cyprian was raised to the bishopric of Carthage by the acclamation of the people, and thus was placed at the head of the whole North African clergy.

For the space of about ten years, ending with his martyrdom in 258, Cyprian administered the episcopal office in Carthage with energy and wisdom. During these years he managed to devote a good deal of time to writing. Sixty-five of his letters, some of considerable length, have survived, along with twelve more formal literary works, treatises dealing with practical problems in the Church of that time. In all his writings Cyprian is never at a loss for apt quotations from the Scriptures. He seems to have memorized almost the whole of the sacred writings then in circulation at Carthage, and the way he uses them indicates that he had made a deep study of their meaning.

According to statistics assembled by von Soden,[29] of the 7,966 verses in the New Testament, Cyprian cites 886 verses, which represents about one-ninth of the entire New Testament. His New Testament, as reconstructed on the basis of these quotations, contained the four Gospels, the Pauline Epistles, 1 Peter, 1 John, and the Apocalypse, which he used freely. He does not cite the Epistles to Philemon, to the

---

[29] *Das lateinische Neue Testament in Afrika zur Zeit Cyprians*, ed. by Hans Freiherr von Soden (Leipzig, 1909). See especially the numerous quotations from Scripture in Cyprian's *De exhort. mart.*

Hebrews, or the Epistles of James, 2 Peter, 2 and 3 John, and Jude.[30]

It is probable that he would have known of the existence of the Epistle to the Hebrews, since Tertullian (whose writings he had studied) speaks of it, attributing it to Barnabas. But Cyprian obviously did not regard it as canonical. Of the other books from which he makes no quotation, it is altogether possible that he passed over one or another short epistle, such as Philemon, merely by accident, because it was short and offered little occasion for reference.

Cyprian scarcely ever makes a Scriptural quotation without using an introductory formula, thus separating the quotation from his own comments. The most frequent introductory formula is the expression used by New Testament writers themselves, 'It is written' (*scriptum est*). Other commonly used means of identifying a text as Biblical is the presence of the word 'Scripture' or 'Scriptures', with or without adjectives, such as 'heavenly', 'holy', 'divine', and the like.

According to statistics collected by Fahey, Cyprian cites 934 Biblical quotations (480 O.T.; 454 N.T.); these quotations are used 1,499 times (701 O.T.; 798 N.T.) in various contexts. He clearly reflects the early Church's preference for Matthew's Gospel, which he uses more frequently than any other book of the Bible (178 times). Next in importance for Cyprian among New Testament books are John (117 times); Luke (84 times); 1 Corinthians (80); Romans (53); and Revelation (53).[31]

Here and there Cyprian makes a comment on the number of the Gospels or the Epistles in the New Testament, which appear to him to have been determined beforehand by mystical correspondence. The Gospels are four in number, he declares, like the rivers of Paradise (Gen. ii. 10).[32] Paul and John wrote each to seven churches, as was prefigured by the seven sons spoken of in the song of Hannah (1 Sam. ii. 5).[33]

---

[30] If one takes into account that Cyprian does not refer to these books (amounting to 525 verses), the proportion of his 886 quotations in relation to the 7,441 verses of his New Testament will come to one-eighth of the whole.

[31] For these and other statistics relating to the books of the New Testament, see Michael A. Fahey, *Cyprian and the Bible: A Study in Third-Century Exegesis* (Tübingen, 1971), p. 43.

[32] Cyprian, *Epist.* 73.

[33] Cyprian, *De exhort. mart.* 2 and *Adv. Jud.* i. 20.

Apparently, as Irenaeus had done earlier, Cyprian derived a certain satisfaction from such correspondence.

4. 'AGAINST DICE-PLAYERS'

Under the title *Adversus aleatores* ('Against Dice-Players') there has been preserved in several manuscripts a pastoral tract against dice-playing and all games of chance as being inventions of the devil. After an introduction of four sections exhorting himself and all other bishops to be faithful shepherds of Christ's flock, in the remaining seven sections the unknown author turns to a detailed invective against gambling and its train of vices and miseries. First and foremost, it is an act of idolatry. The player begins with an act of sacrifice to the inventor (the devil), and, even when he does not himself offer sacrifice, he joins with those who do and becomes a partaker of their idolatry.

The author concludes with a really noble burst of eloquence:

> Play at least for Christian stakes (*Esto potius non aleator sed Christianus*). In Christ's presence, angels and martyrs looking on the while, cast down your money on the table of the Lord; that patrimony of yours, which in mad heat you might have lost, divide among the poor; entrust your stakes to Christ the conqueror... Play out your daily game with the poor. Divert to church purposes all your income and furniture... Give yourself to incessant almsdeeds and works of charity, that your sins may be forgiven you... Do not look back upon the dice. Amen.

Although at one time the homily was believed to be a work of Cyprian, this view has now been almost universally abandoned because of difference of style. Early in his career Harnack ascribed it to Pope Victor I (A.D. 189–99), thus making it the earliest piece of Christian Latin literature.[34] Subsequent study, however, led Harnack[35] and others[36] to explain its

---

[34] A. Harnack, *Der pseudocyprianische Tractat De Aleatoribus, die älteste lateinische Schrift, ein Werk des römischen Bischofs Victor I.* (*saec. II*) (*Texte und Untersuchungen*, v. 1; Leipzig, 1888), pp. 370–81. Harnack's views were enthusiastically adopted by H. I. D. Ryder in *Dublin Review*, Third Series, xxii (1889), pp. 82–98.

[35] In response to the adverse comments made by E. W. Benson in *Cyprian; His Life, his Times, his Work* (London, 1897), pp. 557–64, Harnack changed his opinion regarding the author of *Adv. aleatores*; see his *Zur Schrift Pseudocyprians (Sixtus II) Ad Novatianum* (*Texte und Untersuchungen*, xx, 3; Leipzig, 1900), pp. 112–16.

[36] E.g. Otto Bardenhewer, *Geschichte der altkirchlichen Literatur*, ii (Freiburg, 1914; reprinted Darmstadt, 1962), pp. 496–9, and Hugo Koch, 'Zur Schrift Adversus aleatores', *Festgabe von Fachgenossen und Freunden Karl Müller zum siebzigsten Geburtstag dargebracht* (Tübingen, 1922), pp. 58–67.

obvious relationship to Cyprian as explicable only on the supposition that the author had frequently perused the writings of the Carthaginian bishop. It is now thought that the author was a Catholic bishop writing in North Africa after Cyprian's time, perhaps about A.D. 300.

The homily is couched in awkward but powerful and spirited language, and is characterized throughout by a deep moral earnestness. Its language is the debased Latin of the Roman and African populace, in which, not infrequently, one case is substituted for another, and genders are confused and voices lost.[37]

There are seven quotations from the Old Testament, twenty-two from the New. The version used is akin to that of the Old Latin, or Itala.[38] The author makes frequent citations from the Gospel according to Matthew, and a few from John. Among the Pauline Epistles he knows and uses Roman, 1 Corinthians, Galatians, Ephesians (?), and 1 and 2 Timothy. He also shows acquaintance with 1 John and the Apocalypse. The citations are introduced by the formulas: 'The Lord says in the Gospel' (*Dominus dicit in Evangelio*), 'The apostle Paul [or, John] says' (*apostolus Paulus* [or, *Johannes*] *dicit*), and 'Scripture says' (*dicit scriptura*). But all of the texts, whether from Old or New Testament, are cited with great freedom, which one can best explain on the supposition that the tract is actually a homily and not, as Harnack once thought, a pontifical encyclical.

The unknown preacher attributes to the writings of the New Testament the same authority as that possessed by the Old Testament. He cites passages from both Testaments one after another, almost in pell-mell fashion, and in all of them it is, for him, the Lord who speaks.

Furthermore, it is noteworthy that the author quotes in chap. 2 a passage from the *Shepherd* of Hermas (Sim. IX. xxxi. 5) as 'divine Scripture' (*dicit scriptura divina*), citing it side by side with passages from the Pauline Epistles. And the same is true in chap. 4 concerning a freely quoted passage from the *Didache*, standing again amid quotations from the Pauline Epistles.

[37] See Adam Miodoński, *Anonymus Adversus aleatores* (*Gegen das Hazardspiel*) ... *kritisch verbessert, erläutert und ins Deutsche übersetzt* (Erlangen und Leipzig, 1889), and Adolf Hilgenfeld, *Libellum de aleatoribus inter Cypriani scripta conservatum* (Freiburg i. B., 1889).

[38] It is significant, however, that in two of the four manuscripts used in Hartel's edition of the tract the old Scripture quotations preserved in the other manuscripts have been conformed to the wording of Jerome's Vulgate text.

VII

Books of Temporary and Local
Canonicity:
Apocryphal Literature

IN addition to the books that eventually came to be regarded throughout the Church as canonical, there were dozens of other writings that in certain parts of the Church enjoyed temporary canonicity.[1] In the course of time, however, and for various reasons, these were judged to be unworthy of permanent inclusion in the list of authoritative books recognized by the entire Church as sacred Scripture. Some of these books were called 'apocryphal', a word of Greek derivation that means 'hidden away' ($\dot{\alpha}\pi\acute{o}\kappa\rho\nu\phi\alpha$). From the point of view of those who approved of these writings, they were 'hidden' or withdrawn from common use because they were regarded as containing mysterious or esoteric lore, too profound to be communicated to any except the initiated. From another point of view, however, it was judged that such books deserved to be 'hidden' because they were spurious or heretical.[2] Thus, the term originally had an honourable significance as well as a derogatory one, depending upon those who made use of the word.

It is obvious that the great majority of the apocryphal books are the result of attempts to produce literary forms that parallel those of the several genres of literature that came to be included in the New Testament, namely, gospels, acts, epistles, and apocalypses. Of these the epistles are the fewest in number, for clearly it was more difficult to produce an epistle that

---

[1] For English translations of New Testament apocryphal books see M. R. James, *The Apocryphal New Testament* (Oxford, 1924); Edgar Hennecke and Wilhelm Schnee-melcher, *New Testament Apocrypha*, ed. by R. McL. Wilson, 2 vols. (London and Philadelphia, 1963); and *The Nag Hammadi Library in English*, ed. by James M. Robinson (New York, 1977). See also p. 189 n. 61 below.

[2] See, for example, the discussions of Jerome (*Epist.* cvii. 12, and *Prol. gal. in Samuel et Mal.*), and Augustine (*De civit. Dei*, xv. xxiii. 4).

possessed some semblance of authenticity than it was to draw up narratives of events in which Jesus and various apostles figured as heroes.

It is, of course, not possible in the present context to give even a brief account of all Christian writings regarded at any time as authoritative by believers here and there throughout the Roman Empire. All that can be attempted here is to describe briefly a few examples that belong to each of the several categories and lingered, in some cases, on the fringes of the canon. (See also what is said concerning Nag Hammadi treatises in chap. IV. 1. 4 above.)

I. APOCRYPHAL GOSPELS

Encouragement to write gospels may have been provided by statements like the ones we find at the close of the Gospel according to John: 'Now Jesus did many other signs in the presence of the disciples, which are not written in this book' (xx. 30), and 'there are also many other things which Jesus did; were every one of them to be written, I suppose that the world itself could not contain the books that would be written' (xxi. 25). Two kinds of apocryphal gospels came to be written, those that were intended to supplement and those that were intended to supplant the four Gospels received by the Great Church.[3] Now, there were two areas of Jesus' life and ministry of which members of the early Church were most curious, but of which the canonical Gospels are virtually or totally silent, namely the infancy and childhood of Jesus (of which only Luke presents but one story, ii. 41–51), and the work that the Saviour accomplished in the unseen world between his death on the cross and his resurrection three days later. When people

---

[3] See Helmut Koester, 'Apocryphal and Canonical Gospels', *Harvard Theological Review*, lxxiii (1980), pp. 105–30, and 'Überlieferung und Geschichte der frühchristlichen Evangelienliteratur,' in *Aufstieg und Niedergang der römischen Welt*, ii, 25 (2) (Berlin, 1984), pp. 1463–542. Koester deplores what he considers to be an artificial distinction between canonical and apocryphal gospels; cf. also his comments: 'The distinctions between canonical and noncanonical, orthodox and heretical are obsolete.... There is no justification for the division between "New Testament Introduction" and "Patrology"' (J. M. Robinson and Koester, *Trajectories Through Early Christianity* [Philadelphia, 1971], pp. 270 and 273). It is certainly appropriate, from the point of view of literary analysis, that the two categories should and must be considered together, but to give the impression that, from the point of view of material content, they stand on a par is to betray a lamentable lack of sensitivity.

are curious, they usually take steps to satisfy their curiosity; so we should not be surprised that members of the early Church drew up accounts of what they supposed must have taken place.[4] Among such apocryphal gospels, produced in the second, third, and following centuries, are the *Protevangelium of James*, the *Infancy Story of Thomas*, the *Arabic Infancy Gospel*, the *Armenian Gospel of the Infancy*, the *History of Joseph the Carpenter*, the *Gospel of the Birth of Mary*, and several other similar gospels which refer to the early years of Jesus' life, while the *Gospel of Nicodemus* (otherwise known as the *Acts of Pilate*[5]) and the *Gospel of Bartholomew* refer to his visit in Hades. In general, these gospels show far less knowledge of Palestinian topography and customs than do the canonical Gospels—which is what one would expect from the circumstances and date of the composition of such books.

1. FRAGMENTS OF AN UNKNOWN GOSPEL (EGERTON PAPYRUS 2)

An important acquisition by the British Museum came to light in 1935 with the publication of several fragments of a very early and previously unknown gospel.[6] On the basis of palaeography the editors dated the fragments to the middle of the second century, and, since there is no reason to suppose that the papyrus is the autograph, the composition of the gospel has been placed at 'not later than A.D. 110–30'.[7]

Two of the fragments present parallels to narratives in the Synoptic Gospels, and a third contains Johannine echoes,

---

[4] For a discussion of the lush growth of such kinds of supplementary material, see the present writer's article, 'Names for the Nameless in the New Testament: A Study in the Growth of Christian Tradition', in *Kyriakon: Festschrift Johannes Quasten*, ed. by Patrick Granfield and J. A. Jungmann, i (Münster i. W., 1970), pp. 79–99.

[5] The work that survives today under this title is totally different from the forged Acts of Pilate which, according to Eusebius, had been fabricated to discredit the Christians. The spurious Acts, which purported to prove the justice of Christ's crucifixion, was assigned by primary teachers to school children, 'instead of lessons, for study and commital to memory' (*Hist. eccl.* IX. v. 1).

[6] *Fragments of an Unknown Gospel and Other Early Christian Papyri*, ed. by H. Idris Bell and T. C. Skeat (London, 1935). Among important studies made of the material are those of C. H. Dodd in *Bulletin of the John Rylands Library*, xx (1936), pp. 56–92, reprinted in *New Testament Studies* (New York, 1952), pp. 12–52; Goro Mayeda, *Das Leben-Jesu-Fragment Papyrus Egerton 2 und seine Stellung in der urchristlichen Literaturgeschichte* (Berne, 1946); and H. I. Bell in *Harvard Theological Review*, xlii (1949), pp. 53–63.

[7] *The New Gospel Fragments* (London, 1951), p. 17.

while the fourth describes an apocryphal miracle wrought by Jesus on the banks of the Jordan. The two Synoptic pericopes, which tell of the healing of a leper and a discourse about tribute money, are noteworthy in that they show contacts with traditions found in all three Synoptics.

As a sample, one may quote an excerpt from the verso of Fragment I, lines 5–19, with Johannine-like echoes:

> And turning to the rulers of the people, he [Jesus] spoke this word: 'Search the Scriptures in which[8] you think you have life—they testify on my behalf (John v. 39). Do not think that I have come to be your accuser before my Father; the one to accuse you is Moses, on whom you have set your hopes' (John v. 45). But then they said, 'Well, we know that God spoke to Moses, but we do not know where you come from' (John iv. 29). Jesus answered them, 'Now your unbelief accuses you . . .'

The author gives no evidence that he used any of the four Gospels in written form, but seems to reproduce his material from memory. Consequently, as Jeremias has pointed out, 'we may have before us an instance of the overlapping of written and oral tradition; although the tradition was already fixed in writing, it was still widely reproduced from memory and in this way, enriched with extra-canonical material, found new expression in writing'.[9] In other words, the Unknown Gospel reflects a situation not unlike that depicted by Papias—one in which gospel books are in circulation, but oral tradition is still valued highly, and the two kinds of sources overlap.[10] It is worth noting that the production of gospels and other apocryphal writings was not halted or even noticeably hindered by the formation of the New Testament canon. Popular piety delighted in the steady stream of romantic and fanciful

---

[8] In previous discussions of the relation of this saying (with ἐν αἷς) to John v. 39 (with ὅτι), it has been overlooked that both forms of the dominical saying may go back independently to an Aramaic original. If one postulates for the subordinate clause something like ... דְּסָבִירִין אַתּוּן בְּהוֹן, it is clear that the ambiguous דְּ could have been taken as a relative (αἷς) or as a conjunction (ὅτι). Significantly enough, the Old Latin MS *b* offers two renderings of this same clause: *scrutate scripturas quoniam putatis vos in ipsis vitam aeternam habere . . .*, and ... *in quibus putatis vos vitam habere.*

[9] J. Jeremias in Hennecke–Schneemelcher–Wilson, *New Testament Apocrypha*, i (Philadelphia, 1963), p. 95.

[10] Crossan's recent argument to show that Mark was dependent on Pap. Egerton is not convincing (John D. Crossan, *Four Other Gospels; Shadows on the Contours of Canon* [Minneapolis, 1985], pp. 83–5).

writings, the historical value of which was of slender proportions at best.[11]

2. THE GOSPEL OF THE HEBREWS

References to and quotations from several other early gospels, dating from the second and third centuries, meet us in the
writings of various Church Fathers. From such data we can
estimate the use that was made of these apocryphal books and
the authority attributed to them.

Among such books was a Jewish-Christian gospel called the
Gospel of the Hebrews, which continued to be used until at least
the fourth century. According to the stichometry of Nicephorus, it comprised 2,200 lines, which is only 300 fewer than the
length of canonical Matthew.

Jerome took a lively interest in this book, an Aramaic copy
of which he found in the famous library at Caesarea in
Palestine.[12] More than once he tells us (and with great pride)
that he made translations of it into Greek and Latin. Unfortunately these translations have been lost, and all we have today
are several quotations from the gospel made by Clement of
Alexandria, Origen, Jerome, and Cyril of Jerusalem.

The time and place of origin of the *Gospel of the Hebrews* are
disputed, but since Clement of Alexandria used it in his
Stromata (II. ix. 45) in the last quarter of the second century, it is
usually dated to about the middle of that century. The original
language of the gospel suggests that it was drawn up for
Hebrew- and Aramaic-speaking Jewish Christians in Palestine
and Syria.

In two of his commentaries (those on John ii. 6 and Jer. xv.
4) Origen preserves the following quotation from the *Gospel of
the Hebrews*: 'The Saviour himself says, "Even now my mother
the Holy Spirit has seized me by one of my hairs, and has

[11] Popular yearning for such apocryphal writings has not, in fact, subsided even
today, as is witnessed by the continuing production of still other 'new' gospels; see E. J.
Goodspeed, *Strange New Gospels* (Chicago, 1931); idem, *Modern Apocrypha* (Boston,
1956); Richard L. Anderson, 'The Fraudulent Archko Volume', *Brigham Young
University Studies*, xv (1974), pp. 43–64; and Per Beskow, *Strange Tales about Jesus; a
Survey of Unfamiliar Gospels* (Philadelphia, 1983).

[12] *De vir. ill.* 2. Apparently Jerome had also seen another copy of the gospel, for he
says, 'I have also had the opportunity (*mihi . . . facultas*) of having this volume described
to me by the Nazarenes of Beroea [*v.l.* Veria], a city of Syria, who use it' (ibid. 3).

brought me to the great mountain Tabor."'' The context of
the quotation is lost, so that we cannot tell what event is
alluded to; perhaps it was the Temptation. In any case, the
passage must have made an impression, for besides Origen
Jerome also records it in three of his commentaries (those on
Micah vii. 7; Isa. xl. 9 ff.; and Ezek. xvi. 13).

Another interesting quotation preserved by Jerome (*De viris
ill.* 2) relates to the time after Christ's resurrection:

Now the Lord, after he had given the grave clothes to the servant
of the priest, went to James and appeared to him. For James had
sworn that he would not eat bread from that hour in which he drank
the Lord's cup until he should see him risen again from among those
that sleep. And again, a little later, it says that the Lord said, 'Bring a
table and bread'. And immediately it is added: he took bread and
blessed and broke it and gave it to James the Just, and said to him:
'My brother, eat your bread, for the Son of man is risen from among
those that sleep'.

In the Coptic version of a sermon on Mary Theotokos,
ascribed to Cyril of Jerusalem.[13] the author places on the lips of
a protagonist of 'Ebionite heresy' a quotation from the *Gospel
according to the Hebrews*:

It is written in the [Gospel] according to the Hebrews that when
Christ desired to come upon the earth to men, the Good Father chose
a mighty Power in the heavens which was called Michael, and
committed Christ to his (or, its) care. And the Power came down into
the world, and it was called Mary, and [Christ] was in her womb for
seven months.

From these several quotations we can see that the *Gospel of the
Hebrews* differed considerably in substance and in character from
the gospels that were ultimately regarded as the only canonical
gospels. For this reason, as well as the fact that the *Gospel of the
Hebrews* was written in a Semitic language, we can understand
why its use was limited, chiefly among Jewish Christians (some
of whom were regarded as heretical), and was passed over by the
Great Church in the period when the canon was closed.

---

[13] The discourse on Mary is included in *Miscellaneous Coptic Texts*, ed. by E. A. W.
Budge (London, 1915), Coptic p. 60, English p. 637. See also Vacher Burch, 'The
Gospel According to the Hebrews: Some New Matter Chiefly from Coptic Sources',
Journal of Theological Studies, xxi (1920), pp. 310–15.

3. THE GOSPEL OF THE EGYPTIANS

Next in importance after the *Gospel of the Hebrews* is the *Gospel of the Egyptians*.[14] Written in Greek sometime after A.D. 150 and accepted as canonical in Egypt, its purpose was to promote doctrines held by the Encratites (such as rejection of marriage). Only a few fragments of the gospel have been preserved, chiefly by Clement of Alexandria. In a polemic with his opponent, the Gnostic Julius Passianus, Clement quoted the following portions of a dialogue from the *Gospel of the Egyptians*: 'When Salome inquired how long death should have power, the Lord (not meaning that life is evil, and the creation bad) said: "As long as you women give birth to children" ' (*Strom.* III. vi. 45). Salome's further question, whether she did well not to bear children, receives the answer: 'Eat every plant, but that which has bitterness do not eat' (ibid. III. ix. 66).

In another passage, Salome once again enquires when those things would take place about which she had asked, and the Lord replies: 'When you tread underfoot the garment of shame, and when the two become one, and the male with the female (is) neither male nor female' (ibid. III. xiii. 92). These sayings clearly demand sexual asceticism and the elimination of the sexual differences between male and female, a doctrine that is presented in other Gnostic writings from Egypt (see, e.g., Logia 37 and 114 of the *Gospel of Thomas*, p. 86 above).

4. THE GOSPEL OF PETER

Down to 1886 scholars were aware of the existence of a 'Gospel of Peter', but not so much as a single quotation from it was known. Origen casually refers to it in his *Commentary on Matthew* (x. 17) when discussing the brethren of Jesus, and Eusebius records the negative opinion expressed by Bishop Serapion after he had read a copy of this apocryphal gospel (see chap. V. 1. 3 above).

In the winter of 1886–7 a large fragment of the Greek text of the *Gospel of Peter* was discovered in a tomb of a monk at

---

[14] There is also a totally different esoteric treatise with this title among the tractates in the Nag Hammadi library, where it exists in two Coptic versions; see *The Nag Hammadi Library*, ed. J. M. Robinson, pp. 195–205.

Akhmin in Upper Egypt.[15] It is a manuscript from the eighth Christian century; a smaller but much earlier fragment was discovered later at Oxyryhynchus.[16]

The text that is preserved tells of the passion, death, and burial of Jesus, and embellishes the account of his resurrection with details concerning the miracles that followed. The responsibility for Christ's death is laid exclusively on the Jews, and Pilate is exonerated. Here and there we find traces of the Docetic heresy, and perhaps this is the reason why Jesus' cry of dereliction on the cross ('My God, my God, why have you forsaken me?') is given in the form, 'My Power, my Power, why have you forsaken me?'[17]

Written probably in Syria about the middle of the second century (or even earlier),[18] the *Gospel of Peter* shows acquaintance with all four canonical Gospels but seems, in general, to have taken only limited notice of them.[19] Vaganay's analysis of the textual relations of the *Gospel of Peter* to the families of New Testament manuscripts finds that in a significant number of cases it agrees with only the Old Syriac type of text.[20] According to the investigation made by Denker,[21] it appears that almost every sentence in the passion narrative of this gospel was composed on the basis of Scriptural references in the Old Testament, particularly in Isaiah and the Psalms. The work, Denker argues, is a product of Jewish Christianity written sometime between the two Jewish uprisings.

[15] It was published by U. Bouriant in *Memoires publiés par les membres de la mission archéologique française au Caire*, ix, 1 (Paris, 1892), pp. 93–147.

[16] *Oxyrhynchus Papyri*, ed. by G. M. Browne *et al.*, xli (London, 1972), pp. 15 f. The tiny fragment is dated to the second or third century; see also D. Lührmann in *Zeitschrift für die neutestamentliche Wissenschaft*, lxxii (1981), pp. 217–26.

[17] The word ἠλί (Matt. xxvii. 46), when pronounced ἠλί, would suggest the Hebrew word חיל ('force, power'), which is rendered in the Septuagint by δύναμις, the word employed here by the *Gospel of Peter*.

[18] Léon Vaganay, after weighing the several considerations that bear on dating the *Gospel of Peter*, finally decides that it was written about A.D. 120 (*L'Évangile de Pierre* [Paris, 1930], p. 163). Denker (see n. 21 below) dates it to A.D. 100–30.

[19] For a thorough-going critique of Crossan's attempt (*Four Other Gospels*, pp. 137–81) to isolate in the *Gospel of Peter* a Passion-Resurrection Source, and then to show that all four canonical Gospels made use of it, see Raymond E. Brown's presidential address presented at the 1986 annual meeting of SNTS, to be published in *New Testament Studies*.

[20] Cf. Vaganay, op. cit., p. 73.

[21] Jürgen Denker, *Die theologiegeschichtliche Stellung des Petrusevangeliums: Ein Beitrag zur Frühgeschichte des Doketismus* (Berne, 1975), pp. 58–77.

For a characteristic specimen of the *Gospel of Peter*[22] one may turn to a scene from the account of the resurrection of Jesus:

35. Now in the night in which the Lord's day dawned, while the soldiers, two by two in every watch, were keeping guard, there came a great sound in heaven, 36. and they saw the heavens opened and two men come down from there, shining with great brightness, and draw near to the sepulchre. 37. And that stone which had been laid at the entrance to the sepulchre rolled away by itself and went back to the side, and the sepulchre was opened, and both the young men entered in.
X. 38. When therefore those soldiers saw this, they awakened the centurion and the elders—for they also were there keeping watch. 39. And while they were telling them what they had seen, they saw again three men come out from the sepulchre, and two of them sustaining the other, and a cross following after them. 40. And the heads of the two reached to heaven, but the head of him who was led by them overpassed the heavens. 41. And they heard a voice out of the heavens crying, 'Have you preached to those that sleep?' 42. And an answer was heard from the cross, saying, 'Yes'.

By way of summary, when one compares the preceding rather widely-used apocryphal gospels (along with the more widely divergent specimens that were found at Nag Hammadi; see chap. IV. 1. 4 above), one can appreciate the difference between the character of the canonical Gospels and the near banality of most of the gospels dating from the second and third centuries. Although some of these claimed apostolic authorship, whereas of the canonical four two were in fact not apostolically titled, yet it was these four, and these alone, which ultimately established themselves. The reason, apparently, is that these four came to be recognized as authentic—authentic both in the sense that the story they told was, in its essentials, adjudged sound by a remarkably unanimous consent, and also in the sense that their interpretation of its meaning was equally widely recognized as true to the apostles' faith and teaching. Even the *Gospel of Peter* and the *Gospel of Thomas*, both of which may preserve scraps of independent tradition, are obviously inferior theologically and historically

---

[22] Two systems of dividing the text of the *Gospel of Peter* are in use; Harnack divided the text into sixty verses, and, independently of these, J. A. Robinson into fourteen chapters.

to the four accounts that eventually came to be regarded as the only canonical Gospels.[23]

II. APOCRYPHAL ACTS

Because the missionary activities of only a few of the apostles are recorded with any detail in the canonical Acts of the Apostles, authors of the second and succeeding centuries considered it useful to compose other books of 'Acts',[24] telling of the work that other apostles were reputed to have accomplished. These books include the *Acts of Andrew*, the *Acts of Thomas*, the *Acts of Philip*, the *Acts of Andrew and Matthias*, the *Acts of Bartholomew*, the *Acts of Thaddaeus*, the *Acts of Barnabas*, and others. Furthermore, even apostles whose work is mentioned in the canonical Book of Acts found admiring authors who wrote of other exploits of their heroes in such apocryphal works as, for example, the *Acts of Paul*, the *Acts of John*, and the *Acts of Peter*. These several books of 'Acts', the contents of which have only the most meagre historical basis, resemble in some respects the Graeco-Roman novels of the period, though replacing the obscenities of many of these with moralizing calculated to provide instruction in Christian piety.

1. THE ACTS OF PAUL

The *Acts of Paul* (Πράξεις Παύλου) is a romance that makes arbitrary use of the canonical Acts and the Pauline Epistles. The author, so Tertullian tells us (*de Baptismo* xvii), was a cleric who lived in the Roman province of Asia in the western part of Asia Minor, and who composed the book about A.D. 170 with

---

[23] For a nuanced evaluation of the *Gospel of Peter* in terms of 'the great fall off in quality from significant history [in the canonical Gospels] to romance [in apocryphal gospels]', see B. A. Johnson, 'The Gospel of Peter; Between Apocalypse and Romance', *Studia Patristica*, xvi, part 2, ed. E. A. Livingstone (*Texte und Untersuchungen*, cxxix; Berlin, 1985), pp. 170–7.

[24] See Rosa Söder, *Die apokryphen Apostelgeschichten und die romanhafte Literatur der Antike* (*Würzburger Studien zu Altertumswissenschaft*, Heft 3; Stuttgart, 1932, reprinted 1969); Martin Blumenthal, *Formen und Motive in den apokryphen Apostelgeschichten* (*Texte und Untersuchungen*, xlviii, 1; Leipzig, 1932); K. L. Schmidt, *Kanonische und apokryphe Evangelien und Apostelgeschichten* (Basel, 1944); Donald Guthrie, 'Acts and Epistles in Apocryphal Writings', in *Apostolic History and the Gospel: Biblical and Historical Essays Presented to F. F. Bruce*, ed. by W. Ward Gasque and R. P. Martin (Grand Rapids, 1970), pp. 328–45; *Les Actes apocryphes des Apôtres* (Geneva, 1981); and Dennis R. MacDonald, 'The Forgotten Novels of the Early Church', *Harvard Divinity Bulletin*, xvi, 4 (April–June 1986), pp. 4–6.

the avowed intent of doing honour to the apostle Paul. Although well-intentioned, the author was brought up for trial by his peers and, being convicted of falsifying the facts, was dismissed from his office. But his book, though condemned by ecclesiastical leaders, achieved considerable popularity among the laity. Certain episodes, such as the section dealing with the 'Journeys of Paul and Thecla', exist in a number of Greek manuscripts and in half a dozen ancient versions, thus testifying to their wide-spread popularity. Thecla, it may be mentioned, was a noble-born virgin from Iconium and an enthusiastic follower of the Apostle; she preached like a missionary and administered baptism.[25] In this section we find a description of the physical appearance of Paul. Literally translated, it runs thus:

A man small in size, with a bald head and crooked legs; in good health; with eyebrows that met and a rather prominent nose; full of grace, for sometimes he looked like a man and sometimes he looked like an angel.[26]

Among the episodes in this cycle of tales about Paul perhaps the most entertaining is that which concerns the Apostle and the baptized lion. Although previously known from meagre allusions to it in patristic writers, it was not until 1936 that the complete text was made available by the publication of a recently discovered Greek papyrus containing a detailed account of Paul's encounter with a lion in the amphitheatre at Ephesus.[27] Probably the imaginative author had read Paul's rhetorical question[28] in 1 Cor. xv. 32, 'What do I gain if, humanly speaking, I fought with wild beasts at Ephesus?' Wishing to supply details to supplement such a tantalizingly brief allusion, the author determined to incorporate into his religious romance a thrilling account of the intrepid apostle's experience at Ephesus. Interest is added when the reader learns that some time earlier in the wilds of the countryside Paul had

[25] It was especially Thecla's venturing, as a woman, to administer baptism that scandalized Tertullian and led him to condemn the entire book.

[26] According to R. M. Grant ('The Description of Paul in the Acts of Paul and Thecla', *Vigiliae Christianae*, xxxvi [1982], pp. 1–4), certain features in the description were apparently borrowed from the celebrated Greek poet Archilochus.

[27] Edited by Wilhelm Schubart and Carl Schmidt in *Acta Pauli* (Hamburg, 1936).

[28] That Paul was speaking figuratively is shown by his immediately preceding words, '...I die every day!' Furthermore, being a Roman citizen Paul could not be forced to fight with wild beasts in the amphitheatre.

preached to that very lion and, on its profession of faith, had baptized the beast. It is not surprising, therefore, that the outcome of the confrontation in the amphitheatre was the miraculous release of the apostle.[29]

Another section of the composite *Acts of Paul* comprises the apocryphal correspondence between the Corinthians and Paul. This consists of both a short answer of the Corinthian clergy to the apostle's Second Epistle, and a 'Third Epistle of Paul to the Corinthians'. In 1950 the latter turned up in a Greek papyrus codex, dating from the third century, which presents the apocryphal epistle separated from its context in the *Acts of Paul*.[30] The epistle treats of several important doctrinal subjects, including the status of the Old Testament prophets, creation, the Virgin Birth and the Incarnation of Christ, and the resurrection of the body. At a later date 3 Corinthians, having been translated into Syriac and Armenian, came to be regarded as canonical by these national Churches (see chap. IX. 11 below).

Although the *Acts of Paul* is almost wholly legendary, the author obviously had a very precise knowledge of the Lucan Acts and was acquainted with other New Testament books. A discourse delivered by the apostle Paul recalls the beginning of the Sermon on the Mount in the Gospel according to Matthew. The occurrence of the names Demas, Onesiphorus, and Hermogenes brings to mind 2 Timothy (i. 15–16 and iv. 10). And there are also points of contact with other Pauline Epistles. The canon list found in codex Claromontanus (see Appendix IV. 4 below) includes the *Acts of Paul*, with an indication that it contains 3,560 lines, somewhat longer than the canonical Acts of the Apostles, with 2,600 lines.

2. THE ACTS OF JOHN

The *Acts of John*[31] purports to give an eyewitness account of the missionary work of the apostle John in and around

---

[29] An English translation of Paul's encounter with the lion is given in the present writer's *Introduction to the Apocrypha* (New York, 1957), pp. 255–62.

[30] The codex was edited by M. Testuz, *Papyrus Bodmer X–XII* (Cologny–Geneva, 1959). See also A. F. J. Klijn, 'The Apocryphal Correspondence between Paul and the Corinthians', *Vigiliae Christianae*, xvii (1963), pp. 2–23.

[31] Recently edited, along with later works of the fourth to the sixth century that deal with the life of John, by Eric Junot and J.-D. Kaestli, *Acta Iohannis*, 2 vols. (*Corpus christianorum, Series apocryphorum*, 1 and 2; Turnhout, 1983).

Ephesus; it may therefore be of Ephesian provenance. Since the treatise was known to Clement of Alexandria, it cannot be later than the close of the second century or early in the third century. Although no complete text is extant, we have considerable portions of the work in Greek and in a Latin translation. The length of the original is given in the Stichometry of Nicephorus as 2,500 lines, the same number as for the Gospel of Matthew.

The author of the *Acts of John*, said to be Leucius, a real or fictitious companion of the apostle John, narrates his miracles, sermons, and death. The sermons display unmistakable Docetic tendencies, especially in the description of Jesus and the immateriality of his body, as for example in § 93:

> Sometimes when I meant to touch him [Jesus], I met with a material and solid body; but at other times when I felt him, his substance was immaterial and incorporeal, as if it did not exist at all... And I often wished, as I walked with him, to see his footprint, whether it appeared on the ground (for I saw him as it were raised up from the earth), and I never saw it.

The author relates that Jesus was constantly changing shape, appearing sometimes as a small boy, sometimes as a beautiful man; sometimes bald-headed with a long beard, sometimes as a youth with a pubescent beard (§§ 87-9).

The book includes a long hymn (§§ 94-6), which no doubt was once used as a liturgical song (with responses) in some Johannine communities.[32] Before he goes to die, Jesus gathers his apostles in a circle, and, while holding one another's hands as they circle in a dance around him, he sings a hymn to the Father. The terminology of the hymn is closely related to that of the Johannine Gospel, especially its prologue. At the same time, the author gives the whole a Docetic cast.

Besides presenting theologically-oriented teaching, the author knows how to spin strange and entertaining stories. There is, for example, the lengthy account of the devout Drusiana and her ardent lover Callimachus in a sepulchre (§§ 63-86), which was no doubt intended to provide Christians with an alternative to the widely-read libidinous story of the Ephesian

---

[32] See R. H. Miller, 'Liturgical Materials in the Acts of John', *Studia Patristica*, xiii (*Texte und Untersuchungen*, cxvii; Leipzig, 1975), pp. 375-81.

Widow and the guard at her late husband's tomb. For a lighter touch the author entertains his readers with the droll incident of the bed-bugs (§§ 60–1).

Although the *Acts of John* is without importance for the historical Jesus and the apostle John, it is nevertheless valuable for tracing the development of popular Christianity. It is, for example, the oldest source recording the celebration of the Eucharist for the dead (§ 72).

3. THE ACTS OF PETER

The earliest direct evidence for the existence of the *Acts of Peter* is the notice in Eusebius where he rejects this work as genuine (*Hist. eccl.* III. iii. 2). The question of the relation of the *Acts of Peter* to the *Acts of John* is much debated; Schmidt[33] endeavoured to prove that the author of the *Acts of Peter* used the *Acts of John*, and Koester[34] has argued for the reverse relation between the two works, while Zahn held to identity of authorship.[35] Whatever the relation, however, it is generally agreed that the *Acts of Peter* dates from the second half of the second century, and that it probably had its origin in Asia Minor.

The main part of the book, which is extant in a Latin translation, tells how Paul takes leave of the Roman Christians and sets out for Spain, how Simon Magus comes to Rome and embarrasses believers with his apparent miracles, and how Peter travels to Rome and, with the assistance of a speaking dog, overcomes the magician. The document concludes with an account of the martyrdom of Peter, recording both the 'Quo Vadis?'[36] legend and the crucifixion of Peter head downwards, at his own request. Before his death Peter delivers a long sermon concerning the cross and its symbolic meaning, which shows Gnostic influence. The same sectarian influence can be

---

[33] C. Schmidt, *Die alten Petrusakten im Zusammenhang mit der apokryphen Apostelliteratur untersucht* (*Texte und Untersuchungen*, ix, 1; Leipzig, 1903), pp. 77–9 and 97 ff.

[34] Helmut Koester, *History and Literature of Early Christianity*, ii (Philadelphia, 1982), p. 325.

[35] *Geschichte des neutestamentlichen Kanons*, ii, p. 860.

[36] According to the well-known legend, the words 'Domine, quo vadis?' ('Lord, whither are you going?') were spoken by the apostle Peter when, fleeing from Rome, he met Christ on the Appian Way. The Lord replied, 'I am coming to be crucified again', words which Peter understood to signify that the Lord was to suffer again in the death of his disciple; so he turned and went back to Rome, where he was martyred.

seen in Peter's preaching against matrimony, and his prevailing upon wives to leave their husbands.

A Coptic papyrus fragment (Berlin 8502) also survives which describes Peter's miraculous treatment of his paralytic daughter. At the behest of the crowds, Peter causes his crippled daughter to rise up and walk, but after the crowds had given praise to God for this, he commands his daughter to lie down again, saying to her, 'Return to your infirmity, for this is profitable for you and for me'. At once she becomes as she was before. The crowd laments this turn of circumstances, whereupon Peter explains that when his daughter was born a vision from God disclosed that she 'will do harm to many souls if her body remains healthy' (i.e. sexually attractive). And therefore Peter accepts as God's will his daughter's infirmity.

By the fourth century the sources that mention the *Acts of Peter* become rather plentiful.[31] Not only does the fourth-century Manichaean Psalm-Book, preserved in a Coptic translation, make use of this book along with other apocryphal Acts, but the *Acts of Peter* continued to be favourite reading among members of the Great Church for several generations.

Although the several apocryphal Acts are negligible as historical sources of information concerning the apostolic age, they still are important documents in their own way. The permanent value of this body of literature lies in reflecting the beliefs of their authors and the tastes of their early readers who found profit as well as entertainment in tales of this kind. They purport to be reliable accounts of the words and deeds of the apostles; in reality they set forth under the names of the apostles certain conceptions—both orthodox and heretical—of the Christian faith current in the second and succeeding centuries. To inculcate these ideas the authors did not hesitate to elaborate marvellous tales, and, in the credulous temper of that age, almost anything was believed.

When one compares and contrasts the several books of apocryphal Acts with the canonical Acts, in some respects certain parallels emerge. But it is obvious that 'the apocryphal

---

[37] For testimonies see L. Vouaux, *Les Actes de Pierre* (Paris, 1922).

Acts are essentially different from the Lucan Acts in genre and literary form as much as in content and theology, and despite many borrowings of details and points of connection the apocryphal Acts cannot be put on a level with the Lucan work'.[38]

III. APOCRYPHAL EPISTLES

It is not always noticed that of the four different literary genres in the New Testament (gospels, acts, epistles, and apocalypse), the epistolary genre greatly predominates. Of the twenty-seven documents in the New Testament, twenty-one, or seven-ninths of the total number, belong to the epistolary genre. On the other hand, however, among the pieces of New Testament apocryphal literature, the epistles, as was mentioned earlier, are proportionately few in number. No doubt part of the explanation for the disparity lies in the comparative difficulty in drawing up an epistle that possesses a sufficient degree of verisimilitude.

1. THE EPISTLE OF THE APOSTLES

One of the most interesting documents to come to light during the present century is the *Epistula Apostolorum*, written in the form of an encyclical addressed 'to the Churches of the East and the West, the North and the South', and sent out by the eleven apostles after the Resurrection. Nothing was known of its existence until 1895 when fifteen leaves of the text in Coptic turned up. These were edited, along with one leaf in Latin and the entire book from an Ethiopic manuscript, in 1919.[39] As to the date and character of the book, the original editor's verdict was that it was written in Asia Minor about A.D. 180 by an orthodox Catholic. Each of these items has been challenged by subsequent scholars. Bardy[40] questioned the author's ortho-

---

[38]   See the full discussion by W. Schneemelcher and K. Schäferdick in *New Testament Apocrypha*, ii (Philadelphia, 1965), pp. 169–74, of which the sentence quoted above is their conclusion.

[39]   Carl Schmidt, *Gespräche Jesu mit seinem Jüngern nach der Auferstehung* (*Texte und Untersuchungen*, xliii; Leipzig, 1919).

[40]   See Bardy's review of Schmidt in *Revue biblique*, N.S. xviii (1921), pp. 110–34. On the other hand, Quasten is generally satisfied with the author's orthodoxy (*Patrology*, i, p. 152).

doxy; Delazer[41] and Hornschuh[42] argued for a date prior to
120; and, instead of Asia Minor as its provenance, both
Egypt[43] and Syria[44] have been proposed. In any case, however, the document presents testimony to the author's acquaintance with a surprising range of Biblical books.

The book opens with a list of eleven apostles, beginning with
John, followed by Thomas and Peter and ending with Cephas,[45] who describe various miracles that Jesus performed
from infancy through his earthly ministry. After a few pages
the document changes from the form of an epistle to that of an
apocalypse, in which the risen Lord responds to questions of
the apostles as to the time of his second coming,[46] the
resurrection of the body, the last judgement, the fate of the
damned, the redemption through the pre-existent Logos,
descent into hell, missionary work of the apostles, and the
mission of Paul. The conclusion describes the ascension, which
took place accompanied by thunder, lightning, and an earth-
quake.

What is of significance for our present purpose is the
presence of very numerous echoes from all four Gospels, as well
as from other New Testament books. It is obvious that the
author was well acquainted with the Synoptic tradition.[47] It is

[41] Jacobus Delazer, 'De tempore compositionis Epistolae Apostolorum', *Antonianum*,
iv (1929), pp. 257–92, 387–430.

[42] Manfred Hornschuh, *Studien zur Epistula Apostolorum* (*Patristische Texte und Studien*,
v; Berlin, 1965), p. 118.

[43] So A. A. T. Ehrhardt, 'Judaeo-Christians in Egypt, the Epistula Apostolorum
and the Gospel to the Hebrews', *Studia Evangelica*, iii, ed. by F. L. Cross (*Texte und
Untersuchungen*, lxxxviii; Berlin, 1964), pp. 360–82, and Hornschuh, op. cit., pp.
99–115. At first Kirsopp Lake also regarded Egypt as the provenance of the *Epistola*
(*Harvard Theological Review*, xiv [1921], pp. 15–29), but later came to think that
'Schmidt's view that it comes from Ephesus probably has the most arguments in its
favour' (*The Beginning of Christianity*, Part I, *The Acts of the Apostles*, v [London, 1933],
p. 44). Still later Kirsopp Lake and Silva Lake call it, without any qualification, 'an
Ephesian document' (*An Introduction to the New Testament* [New York, 1937], p. 175).

[44] So J. de Zwaan, 'Date and Origin of the Epistle of the Eleven Disciples', *Amicitiae
Corolla; A Volume of Essays presented to James Rendel Harris*, ed. by H. G. Wood (London,
1933), pp. 344–55.

[45] On the curious differentiation of Peter and Cephas, see K. Lake, 'Simon, Cephas,
Peter', *Harvard Theological Review*, xiv (1921), pp. 95–7.

[46] According to the Coptic text, 120 years must elapse before the Parousia occurs;
according to the Ethiopic text, the interval will be 150 years.

[47] See the numerous references given throughout the text by H. Duensing in
Hennecke–Schneemelcher–Wilson, *New Testament Apocrypha*, i (Philadelphia, 1959),
pp. 192–227.

equally clear that his language and concepts have been influenced chiefly by the Gospel according to John. In addition to these sources we find in the work a number of reminiscences from the Old Testament, the Book of Acts, and other works. The citations are free and some of them cannot be identified.

The author does not hesitate to use a device which was becoming popular with the Gnostics: namely, that of imagining esoteric teachings given by Jesus in order to promote certain ideas. At the same time, though some Gnostic ways of thinking are present, the author expresses a definite anti-Gnostic emphasis on the resurrection of the flesh, and both Simon (Magus) and Cerinthus are denounced as false prophets. In short, this document represents an aggressive attack by a catholic Christian upon Gnosticism, while making use of the literary genre of 'revelations' so beloved by Gnostics.

2. THE THIRD EPISTLE OF PAUL TO THE CORINTHIANS

This apocryphal epistle, as was mentioned earlier in this chapter, is part of the composite *Acts of Paul*. It came to be highly regarded by the Armenian Church, and is included in the Appendix of Zohrab's edition of the Armenian New Testament (see chap. IX. II. 2 below).

3. THE EPISTLE TO THE LAODICEANS

At the close of the Epistle to the Colossians the request is made of its recipients: 'When this epistle has been read among you, have it read also in the church of the Laodiceans; and see that you read the epistle from Laodicea' (iv. 16). This tantalizing reference, though somewhat ambiguous as to who wrote whom,[48] offered a tempting invitation to some unknown author to provide the text of an Epistle of Paul to the Laodiceans,[49] who were neighbours of the congregation at Colossae.

---

[48] The opinion that the epistle was written by the Laodiceans to Paul was held by Theodore of Mopsuestia and other Greek commentators, and underlies the rendering of the Peshitta Syriac version. For a thorough canvassing of this and other opinions, ancient and modern, concerning the author and the recipients, see J. B. Lightfoot, *Saint Paul's Epistles to the Colossians and to Philemon*, 9th ed. (London, 1890), pp. 272–9.

[49] The Epistle to the Laodiceans that is mentioned in the Muratorian Canon is generally considered to be a different epistle, which has not come down to us.

Composed perhaps at the close of the third century,[50] by the fourth century Jerome reports that 'some read the Epistle to the Laodiceans, but it is rejected by everyone' (*De viris ill.* 5). Of all the spurious pieces produced in the early Church, this is one of the most feeble. It is mystifying how it could have commanded so much respect in the Western Church for a period of more than a thousand years. Comprising some twenty verses, the epistle is a pedestrian patchwork of phrases and sentences plagiarized from the genuine Pauline Epistles, particularly from Philippians. After the author has expressed his joy at the faith and virtue of the Laodiceans, he warns them against heretics, and exhorts them to remain faithful to Christian doctrines and the Christian pattern of life. The epistle purports to have been written from prison.

Although it is possible that the epistle was composed originally in Greek, it has come down to us chiefly in Latin manuscripts[51] of the Bible (more than one hundred in all), dating from the sixth to the fifteenth century, and representing all the great nations of the West—Italy, Spain, France, Ireland, England, Germany, and Switzerland. When the Scriptures came to be translated into the vernacular languages of modern Europe, this epistle was sometimes included (see pp. 239–40 below).

4. THE CORRESPONDENCE BETWEEN PAUL AND SENECA

The Latin apocryphal correspondence of fourteen epistles between the Stoic philosopher Seneca (eight epistles) and the apostle Paul (six epistles) has come down to us in over three hundred manuscripts.[52] The several epistles are concerned

---

[50] Although Harnack (*Sitzungsberichte der Preussischen Akademie der Wissenschaften*, phil.-hist. Kl., 1923, pp. 235–45), followed by Quispel (*Nederlands Theologisch Tijdschrift*, v [1950], pp. 43–6), regarded the epistle as a Marcionite forgery of the second half of the second century, the text presents no special features that are characteristic of the sect.

[51] The University Library at St Andrews possesses a manuscript dated A.D. 1679 that contains the Epistle to the Laodiceans in Hebrew, Greek, and Latin (cf. R. Y. Ebied, 'A Triglot Volume of the Epistle to the Laodiceans, Psalm 151 and other Biblical Materials', *Biblica*, xlvii [1966], pp. 243–54). The Epistle also exists in Arabic manuscripts; see Baron Carra de Vaux, 'L'Épître aux Laodicéens arabe', *Revue biblique*, v (1886), pp. 221–6, and Eugène Tisserant, 'La version mozarabe de l'épître aux Laodicéens', ibid., N.S. vii (1910), pp. 249–53.

[52] The standard edition with apparatus is that of C. W. Barlow, *Epistolae Senecae ad Paulum et Pauli ad Senecam quae vocantur* (*Papers and Monographs of the American Academy in Rome*, x; Rome, 1938). A critical edition is included in the *Biblia Sacra iuxta Vulgatam Versionem*, ed. R. Weber, ii (Stuttgart, 1969).

with the conversion of the apostle, the style of his letters, the persecutions of Christians under Nero, and the nomination of Seneca as preacher of the gospel at the Imperial Court! On the strength of this correspondence Jerome included Seneca in his list of illustrious Christian saints (*De viris ill.* 12),[53] but the commonplace manner and the colourless style of the epistles show that they cannot be the work either of the moralist or of the apostle Paul.

IV. APOCRYPHAL APOCALYPSES

As rivals to the canonical Apocalypse of John there circulated in the second and following centuries several apocalypses attributed to other apostles.[54]

1. THE APOCALYPSE OF PETER

The most important of the apocryphal books of revelation is the *Apocalypse of Peter*,[55] which dates from about A.D. 125–50. We first hear of this work in the Muratorian Canon, where it stands after the Apocalypse of John, with the warning that 'some of our people do not wish it to be read in church' (lines 72–3). Clement of Alexandria accepted it as the work of Peter (*Ecl. proph.* xli. 2 and xlviii. 1) and wrote comments on it (so Eusebius tells us, *Hist. eccl.* VI. xiv. 1). On the other hand, it was considered uncanonical by Eusebius (III. xxv. 4) and by Jerome (*De viris ill.* 1). Yet other Christians had a high regard for the book, for, according to the testimony of Sozomen, the fifth-century church historian (vii. 19), in his day it was customary in some of the churches of Palestine to read from the *Apocalypse of Peter* every year on Good Friday. The list of canonical books included in codex Claromontanus concludes with the *Apocalypse of Peter* (see Appendix IV. 4 below).

---

[53] On the possible historical relations between the apostle Paul and the real Seneca, see J. B. Lightfoot, 'St. Paul and Seneca', in his *Commentary on Philippians* (1868), pp. 268–331.

[54] See F. C. Burkitt, *Jewish and Christian Apocalypses* (London, 1914), and Adela Y. Collins, 'Early Christian Apocalyptic Literature', to be published in *Aufstieg und Niedergang der römischen Welt*, II. 25 (4).

[55] For a *Forschungsbericht*, see R. J. Bauckham's forthcoming contribution, 'The Apocalypse of Peter; An Account of Research', in *Aufstieg und Niedergang der römischen Welt*, II. 25 (4).

Portions of the work in Greek were found in 1886–87 in a Christian tomb at Akhmim in Upper Egypt, and the complete text in Ethiopic came to light in 1910. There is also a small parchment leaf in the Bodleian Library containing twenty-six short lines of the Greek text, and a double leaf, thought by some to be from the same codex, in the Rainer Collection in Vienna. A comparison of the Ethiopic with the Greek suggests that the latter is from a condensed and somewhat recast form of the book.

The *Apocalypse of Peter* opens with an account of how Peter and the other disciples, as they sat upon the Mount of Olives, asked Jesus about the signs that would precede his coming and the end of the world. Jesus answers their questions in language taken, for the most part, from the four Gospels. The Akhmim fragment, beginning abruptly in the midst of Jesus' discourse, describes in visions the sunny splendour of heaven and of the departed saints, then the place of punishment and the penalties of individual sinners. The Ethiopic text presents a different sequence of the descriptions, dealing first with hell and then, in connection with the story of the transfiguration of Jesus, an account of heaven. It is significant that in both forms of the book, the description of the torments of the damned is much longer than the description of the delights of heaven. The punishment of various classes of sinners is more or less suited to the nature of their crimes, as the following excerpt will show:

And I saw also another place, over against that one, very squalid; and it was a place of punishment, and they that were punished and the angels that punished them had dark raiment, according to the air of that place.

And some were hanging by their tongues; these were those who had blasphemed the way of righteousness, and under them was laid fire, blazing and tormenting them.

And there were also others, women, hanging by their hair, above that mire which boiled up—these were those who had adorned themselves for adultery.

And the men who had joined with them in the defilement of adultery were hanging by their feet, and had their heads in the mire, and cried out, 'We did not believe that we would come to this place' (§§ 21–4).

The unknown author, who is responsible for being the first to introduce pagan ideas of heaven and hell into Christian literature, derived his conception of the next life from a variety of pre-Christian traditions, such as those included in the eleventh book of Homer's *Odyssey*, the eschatological myths of Plato, the sixth book of Virgil's *Aeneid*, and various Orphic and Pythagorean traditions. From the point of view of the history of religion, the influence of these ideas, mediated through the *Apocalypse of Peter*, extended far and wide, including Dante's *Divine Comedy* as well as artistic representations in medieval sculpture and Renaissance art.

2. THE APOCALYPSE OF PAUL

More than one treatise with the title the *Apocalypse of Paul* circulated in the early Church, In addition to the Coptic tractate of this title found at Nag Hammadi, which describes Paul's ascent through the fourth to the tenth heavens, another and more widely disseminated *Apocalypse of Paul* is extant in Greek, with Syriac, Coptic, Ethiopic, Slavic, and Latin versions.[56] Written probably in Egypt about A.D. 250, the introduction to the book in a subsequent recension tells us of the marvellous discovery of the original work:

In the consulate of Theodosius Augustus the Younger and of Cynegius [i.e. A.D. 388], a certain respected man was living in Tarsus in the house that had once belonged to Saint Paul. During the night an angel appeared to him and gave him a revelation telling him to break up the foundations of the house and to make public what he found. But he thought this was a delusion.

However, the angel came the third (?) time and scourged him and compelled him to break up the foundations. And when he had dug, he discovered a marble box which was inscribed on the sides; in it was the revelation of Saint Paul and the shoes in which he would walk when teaching the word of God.

Sozomen, who repeats this account in his *Church History* (vii. 19), tells us that the work, 'Although unrecognized by the ancients, is still esteemed by most of the monks'. At the same

---

[56] For a magisterial analysis of these sources, see R. P. Casey, 'The Apocalypse of Paul', *Journal of Theological Studies*, xxxiv (1933), pp. 1–32.

time he doubts the truth of the story of its discovery and wonders 'if the heretics did not invent the story'. Augustine laughs at the folly of those who had forged an *Apocalypse of Paul*, full of fables and pretending to contain the unutterable things which, according to 2 Cor. xii. 4, the apostle had heard (*In Joh. tract.* xcviii. 8). The *Apocalypse of Paul* is mentioned in the *Decretum Gelasianum* among the apocryphal books which were not accepted.

The work is closely related to the *Apocalypse of Peter*, which it expands at considerable length. One of the angels who at sunrise and at sunset report to God on the deeds of every person (§§ 7–10) leads the apostle Paul to Paradise, the gates of which have golden tablets inscribed with the names of the righteous. From heaven he sees the ocean surrounding the earth and Lake Acherusia, whiter than milk, in which the archangel Michael baptizes repentant sinners so that they can enter the city of Christ. He reaches this city by a voyage in a golden ship, over Lake Acherusia. In the city he sees four rivers, one of honey, one of milk, one of wine, one of oil (§§ 19–30).

After this blissful journey the angel shows Paul the sufferings of the damned in hell. At the request of Michael and other angels and for the sake of Paul, Christ gives to the damned freedom from torture on Sundays (§§ 31–44).[57]

V. MISCELLANEOUS WRITINGS

Several of the writings of the Apostolic Fathers were for a time regarded in some localities as authoritative. The *Didache* was used both by Clement of Alexandria and by Origen as Scripture, and there is evidence that during the following century it continued to be so regarded in Egypt.

The text of the (First) *Epistle of Clement* is contained, along with a portion of the so-called *Second Epistle of Clement*, at the end of the fifth-century codex Alexandrinus of the Greek Bible

---

[57] The notion that souls in hell are granted respite appears occasionally in Christian writers of the fourth century and later (the most important of these is Prudentius, *Cathemerinon*, 125 ff.). It is a modification of a Rabbinic view, perhaps as early as the third century, that souls in hell are allowed to rest on the Sabbath (Israel Lévi, *Revue des études juives*, xxv [1892], pp. 1–13).

(the manuscript is defective at the end). Irenaeus, Clement of Alexandria, and Origen all made use of the epistle. We know that about A.D. 170 it was customary to read *1 Clement* in public services of worship at Corinth (see p. 124 above).

The *Epistle of Barnabas* was for a time on the fringe of the canon. Clement of Alexandria regarded it as of sufficient importance to write a commentary on it in his *Hypotyposes*, now lost. Origen calls it 'catholic', a term that he elsewhere applies to 1 Peter and 1 John. It stands after the New Testament in the fourth-century codex Sinaiticus of the Greek Bible.

The *Shepherd* of Hermas was used as Scripture by Irenaeus, Tertullian (before his conversion to Montanism), Clement of Alexandria, and Origen, though according to Origen it was not generally read in church. The Muratorian Canon reflects the esteem in which the work was held at the time that list was compiled, but according to the unknown compiler, it might be read but not proclaimed as Scripture in church (lines 73–80).

Eventually lists of apocryphal writings were drawn up, warning the faithful that they were not to be received as authoritative Scripture. One such list is included in an early Latin document, the so-called *Decretum Gelasianum*, which the manuscripts attribute indiscriminately to Popes Damasus, Hormisdas, and Gelasius. The document is in five parts, one of which gives a list of books included in the Old Testament and the New Testament (the latter is without the Book of Revelation), and another gives a lengthy list of apocryphal works (sixty-two titles) and heretical authors (thirty-five names). According to von Dobschütz[58] it is not a Papal work at all, but a private compilation that was drawn up in Italy (but not at Rome) in the early sixth century.

Still later canon lists are the Stichometry of Nicephorus;[59] the Catalogue of Sixty Canonical Books; and a hitherto unknown enumeration of thirty-five 'false gospels' that is included in the section on the Roman era in the Samaritan

---

[58] Ernst von Dobschütz, *Das Decretum Gelasianum*, De libris recipiendis et non recipiendis, *in kritischen Text* (*Texte und Untersuchungen*, xxxviii, 4; Leipzig, 1912).

[59] Nicephorus (*c.* 758–829), patriarch of Constantinople, drew up a *Chronography* reaching from Adam to the year of his death, to which he appended a canon catalogue, the origin of which has not yet been clearly settled.

Hebrew Chronicle II (*Sepher ha-Yamim*).⁶⁰ Certainly the existence of such a lush growth of apocryphal literature is testimony to the powers of imagination possessed by Christian
believers, orthodox and heretical alike.⁶¹

⁶⁰ The first two lists are given in Hennecke–Schneemelcher–Wilson, *New Testament
Apocrypha*, i, pp. 49–52; the third was published by John MacDonald and A. J. B.
Higgins in *New Testament Studies*, xviii (1971), pp. 66–9.
  Another document concerning the Samaritans is a hagiographical Syriac manuscript of A.D. 875, now in the British Museum (Wright, *Catalogue*, p. 1105); it contains
the statement that 'in one of the villages of the Samaritans... those of the heresy of the
Herodians... receive only Mark the Evangelist, three letters of Paul, and four books of
Moses....' (see F. Nau, 'Le canon biblique samaritano-chrétien des Hérodiens', *Revue
biblique*, xxxix [1931], pp. 396–400).
  ⁶¹ The continuing appetite for apocryphal literature can be gauged by the
popularity over the years of William Hone's misleading and second-rate book entitled,
*The Apocryphal New Testament, being all the Gospels, Epistles, and other pieces now extant ...
and not included in the New Testament by its Compilers* (London, 1820), which has been
reprinted again and again in Britain and America. For a severe but just criticism of the
volume, and of the popular fallacy that the New Testament was collected at a given
moment by a definite act of the authorities of the Church, see M. R. James, op. cit., pp.
xiv-xvii.

VIII

Two Early Lists of the Books of the New Testament

BY the close of the second century lists begin to be drawn up of books that had come to be regarded as authoritative Christian Scriptures. Sometimes the lists comprise only the writings that belong to one section of the New Testament. For example, as was mentioned earlier, in the first book of Origen's *Commentary on Matthew*[1] he enumerates Matthew, Mark, Luke, and John as being 'the only indisputable Gospels', and in the fifth book of his *Commentary on John*[2] he speaks of the several Epistles of Paul, Peter, and John.

Among the more comprehensive lists of New Testament books, the earliest is the so-called Muratorian Canon, a document that, on the basis of internal evidence, has been generally dated to the close of the second century.[3] This anonymous catalogue was followed more than a century later by a still more comprehensive list of New Testament books, prepared by Eusebius of Caesarea after devoting a considerable amount of research to the project. Both these lists deserve detailed analysis for what they can disclose concerning the development of the canon of the New Testament.

I. THE MURATORIAN CANON

One of the most important documents for the early history of the canon of the New Testament is the Muratorian Canon, comprising eighty-five lines written in barbarous Latin and with erratic orthography. Named after its discoverer, the distinguished Italian historian and theological scholar,

---

[1] As quoted by Eusebius, *Hist. eccl.* VI. xxv. 3.
[2] As quoted by Eusebius, *Hist. eccl.* VI. xxv. 7–9.
[3] Sundberg has argued for a fourth-century date, but his arguments are inconclusive at best; see Ferguson's critique, mentioned below.

Ludovico Antonio Muratori,[4] it was published by him in 1740 as a specimen of the very careless way in which scribes of the Middle Ages copied manuscripts.[5] The codex that preserves the list is an eighth-century manuscript, formerly from the ancient monastery at Bobbio and now in the Ambrosian Library in Milan (MS J. 101 sup.), and contains seventy-six leaves (measuring 27 by 17 cm.) on rather coarse parchment. It contains a collection of several theological treatises of three Church Fathers of the fourth and fifth centuries (Eucherius, Ambrose, and Chrysostom), concluding with five early Christian creeds. Obviously the manuscript is a commonplace book of some monk, who copied a miscellaneous assortment of texts from various sources.

The canon list begins in the middle of a sentence at the top of folio 10, and ends abruptly at the twenty-third line of the recto of folio 11, while the rest of folio 11 and the recto of folio 12 contain an extract from St Ambrose, thirty lines of which the scribe inadvertently copied twice. This repetition, along with the quite frequent variations between the two copies of the same material, vividly discloses the carelessness of the scribe,[6] and shows that the frequent orthographical mistakes are his and not those of the original author. This was shown even more clearly by the subsequent discovery at Monte Cassino of small portions of the same text[7] included in four manuscripts of

---

[4] With indefatigable scholarship and industry, Muratori, who has been called the 'Father of the history of the Middle Ages', published all told 46 volumes in folio, 34 in quarto, 13 in octavo, and many more in 12mo.

[5] It is included in Muratori's *Antiquitates Italicae Medii Aevi*, iii (Milan, 1740), pp. 851–4. A revised text is given by E. S. Buchanan in *Journal of Theological Studies*, viii (1906–7), pp. 537–45. One of the best editions of the Muratorian Canon is still that of S. P. Tregelles, *Canon Muratorianus; The Earliest Catalogue of the Books of the New Testament* (Oxford, 1867), with a facsimile. For discussion regarding Tregelles's work, see *Life and Letters of Fenton John Anthony Hort*, by A. F. Hort, i (London, 1896), p. 397, and Earle Hilgert, 'Two Unpublished Letters Regarding Tregelles' *Canon Muratorianus*', *Andrews University Seminary Studies*, v (1967), pp. 122–30. For further bibliography, see H. Leclerq in *Dictionnaire d'Archéologie Chrétienne et de Liturgie*, xii (1935), cols. 543–60 (with a good photographic reproduction), and G. Bardy in *Supplément au Dictionnaire de la Bible*, v (1957), cols. 1339–408.

[6] The lack of care on the part of the scribe can be measured by the presence of thirty blunders in the thirty lines that have been written twice. Several are omissions or additions that destroy the sense, and a few changes appear to be intentional alterations. Besides those that pertain to substance there are many instances of misspelling.

[7] Published in *Miscellanea Cassinese* (Montecassino, 1897), pp. 1–5, they comprise lines 42–50, 54–7, 63–8, and 81–5; cf. A. Harnack, *Theologische Literaturzeitung*, xxiii (1898), cols. 131–4.

Paul's Epistles belonging to the eleventh and twelfth centuries and not derived from the Milan manuscript. But even after a collation of the text of the extracts, there remain many questions which can be solved only by conjecture. Various features of the Latin text have led many scholars (but not all[8]) to believe that it is a more or less faithful translation of a Greek original.[9] The phonetic and morphological features of the Latin, and the reminiscence of Jerome's Latin Vulgate of 1 John i. 1–4 in lines 33–4, suggest that the Latin rendering was made sometime after the beginning of the fifth century.[10]

Questions of place, date, and authorship of the list have been widely debated. The arguments used recently by Sundberg[11] to prove the list to be of eastern provenance (Syria–Palestine) and from the mid-fourth century have been sufficiently refuted (not to say demolished!) by Ferguson[12] and need not be rehearsed here. The designation of Rome not only as *urbs Roma* in line 76 but as *urbs* alone in line 38 indicates a western origin, and so too (assuming the substantial completeness of the text) does the fact that James and Hebrews are not even mentioned. The remark, made with circumstantial solemnity, that the *Shepherd* of Hermas was written 'very recently, in our own times

---

[8] Among advocates for an original Latin composition are Adolf Harnack, 'Über den Verfasser und den literarischen Character des Muratorischen Fragmentes', *Zeitschrift für die neutestamentlichen Wissenschaft,* xxiv (1925), pp. 1–16, and Arnold Ehrhardt, 'The Gospels in the Muratorian Fragment', in *The Framework of the New Testament Stories* (Cambridge, Mass., 1964), pp. 11–36.

[9] Retroversions into Greek have been made by A. Hilgenfeld, *Der Kanon und die Kritik des Neuen Testaments*... (Halle, 1863), pp. 40 f., and *Zeitschrift für wissenschaftliche Theologie,* xv (1872), pp. 560–82; by P. A. Bötticher (= P. A. de Lagarde) in *Zeitschrift für die gesammte lutherische Theologie und Kirche,* x (1854), pp. 127–9; by M. Hertz for C. C. J. Bunsen's *Hippolytus* (= *Christianity and Mankind,* vol. v, or *Analecta ante-Nicaena,* vol. i; London, 1854), pp. 137 f.; by J. B. Lightfoot (in Greek verse), *Academy,* xxxvi (21 Sept. 1889), pp. 186–8, and *The Apostolic Fathers,* Part I, *Clement of Rome,* ii (1890), pp. 405–13; and by T. Zahn, *Geschichte des neutestamentlichen Kanons,* ii (Erlangen and Leipzig), pp. 140–3.

[10] So Julio Campos, 'Época del Fragmento Muratoriano', *Helmantica,* xi (1960), pp. 485–96, on the basis of phonetic, graphic, morphological, and lexical features of the Latinity of the fragment.

[11] A. C. Sundberg, Jr., 'Canon Muratori: A Fourth-Century List', *Harvard Theological Review,* lxvi (1973), pp. 1–41.

[12] Everett Ferguson, 'Canon Muratori; Date and Provenance', *Studia Patristica,* xviii (1982), pp. 677–83. Brevard Childs thinks that Sundberg's dating the Muratorian Canon to the fourth century is 'tendentious and unproven' (*The New Testament as Canon,* p. 238). See also the negative comments on Sundberg's theory by A. B. du Toit, op. cit., pp. 237 and 244.

(*nuperrime temporibus nostris*), in the city of Rome, while his brother, Pius, was occupying the bishop's chair of the church of the city of Rome' (lines 73 ff.) points to a date in the latter part of the second century and certainly not later than the year 200.[13]

Many different suggestions have been made as to the identity of the author of the list. The candidate most frequently proposed is Hippolytus (*c.* 170–235), a learned and prolific author of the Roman Church who wrote in Greek.[14] Against this suggestion, however, are (*a*) the author's total silence as to the Epistle to the Hebrews, in which Hippolytus was much interested, and (*b*) the opinion that the Book of Revelation was written before the Pauline Epistles, while Hippolytus apparently held, as did Irenaeus, that it was written under the Emperor Domitian. Perhaps the most that can be said is that a member of the Roman Church, or of some congregation not far from Rome, drew up in Greek toward the close of the second century a synopsis of the writings recognized as belonging to the New Testament in his part of the Church.

1. CONTENTS OF THE MURATORIAN CANON

The Muratorian Canon (see Appendix IV. 1) is not a canon in the narrow sense of the word, that is, a bare list of titles, but is a kind of introduction to the New Testament. Instead of merely cataloguing the books accepted by the Church as authoritative, the author discusses them and appends historical information and theological reflections as well. These comments allow us to draw conclusions as to the author's under-

---

[13] The dates of the episcopate of Pius are variously reckoned as 140–55 (Harnack), 141–55 (Lagrange), 142–55 (Quasten; Altaner), and 142–57 (Tregelles).

[14] The view of J. B. Lightfoot (see note 9 above) that the author of the Fragment was Hippolytus, was supported, with additional arguments, by T. H. Robinson (*Expositor*, Seventh Series, ii [1906], pp. 481–95), T. Zahn (*Neu kirchliche Zeitschrift*, xxxiii [1922], pp. 417–36), and M.-J. Lagrange (*Revue biblique*, xxxv [1926], pp. 83–8), and xlii [1933], pp. 161–86). On the other hand, V. Bartlet thought Melito was its author (*Expositor*, Seventh Series, ii [1906], pp. 210–24); C. Erbes attributed it to Rhodon, who drew it up about A.D. 220 (*Zeitschrift für Kirchengeschichte*, xxxv [1914], pp. 331–62); and J. Chapman argued that it was part of Clement of Alexandria's *Hypotyposes* (*Revue bénédictine*, xxi [1904], pp. 240–64; see also 369–74 and xxii [1905], pp. 62–4). Harnack maintained that it was an official list intended for the whole Church, very probably of Roman origin with the authority of either Pope Victor or Pope Zephyrinus behind it (*Zeitschrift für die neutestamentliche Wissenschaft*, xxiv [1925], pp. 1–16; see also H. Koch, ibid., xxv [1926], pp. 154–60).

standing of the motives and norms lying behind the formation of the New Testament canon.[15]

(a) The Gospels (lines 1–33)

Although the beginning of the list is fragmentary, one can be virtually certain that the Gospel according to Matthew was named first, and that the first line preserved in the Fragment refers to Mark. The mutilated sentence may have said originally that Mark was not an eyewitness of all to which he testifies, but wrote his Gospel on the testimony of one or more who were eyewitnesses.

Of Luke it is said without qualification that he was not an eyewitness but that some time after the Ascension, under the authority and as a kind of assistant of the apostle Paul,[16] he wrote the Third Gospel, commencing with an account of the birth of John the Baptist. Apart from being designated as a physician (as in Col. iv. 14), most of what is said of him seems to be taken from the introduction to his Gospel (Luke i. 1–4).

A brief but graphic description of the origin of the Fourth Gospel is given in lines 9–16: 'When John's fellow disciples and bishops urged him to write, he said, "Fast with me from today for three days, and let us tell one another whatever will be revealed to each of us." In the same night it was revealed to Andrew, one of his apostles, that John should write down everything in his own name, while all of them should review it.'[17] Obviously the idea of the author was to endow the Gospel of John with the combined authority of the twelve apostles.

The list bears testimony that the collection of Gospels was closed by the Gospel according to John, which formed an explicit conclusion to it. What is more, it had a very special significance in that it synthesized the teaching of the Twelve,

---

[15] Cf. Johannes Beumer, 'Das Fragmentum Muratori und seine Rätsel', *Theologie und Philosophie*, xlviii (1973), pp. 534–50, and Helmut Burkhardt, 'Motive und Masstäbe der Kanonbildung nach dem Canon Muratori', *Theologische Zeitschrift*, xxx (1974), pp. 207–11.

[16] For a discussion of the text of the Fragment at this place, see p. 305 n. 2 below.

[17] The Fragment says of Luke and John that each wrote 'in his own name' (lines 6, 15). This means that though they were the authors, they were not the only authorities for their works. In the case of Luke, presumably Paul or the sources referred to in the preface to the Third Gospel are understood to be his authorities. In the case of John, the sole authorization of his Gospel, divine and human, is distinctly noted — divine revelation and the approval of his fellow disciples.

whereas the other Gospels (to judge by what is said of Luke) bore witness to particular traditions.

(b) *The Acts* (lines 34–9)

The Fragmentist next mentions the Book of Acts, ascribing the authorship to Luke, and asserting that 'the acts of all the apostles are written in one book'. The implication lying behind this statement may be directed against Marcion, who identified Paul as *the* apostle, or it may be directed against the growing number of apocryphal books of acts of the apostles— none of which are really needed, the author implies, if one reads Luke's account. At the same time, the author acknowledges that Luke does not report everything relating to the apostles, his choice of topics being restricted to what fell under his own notice, therefore leaving unmentioned the martyrdom of Peter and Paul's journey to Spain.

(c) *The Epistles of Paul* (lines 39–68)

Thirteen Epistles of Paul are then mentioned. They had been sent, the author asserts, to churches in the following order: Corinthians (1 and 2), Ephesians, Philippians, Colossians, Galatians, Thessalonians (1 and 2), and Romans. In a kind of parenthesis, the author observes that though Paul, for their correction, wrote twice to the Corinthians and to the Thessalonians, he addressed only *seven* churches by name—and in this respect Paul followed the example of 'his predecessor'[18] John, who, in writing to seven churches in the Apocalypse, showed that he was addressing the one, universal Church 'spread throughout all the world'. Besides these, the Fragmentist continues, Paul also wrote four Epistles to individuals: Philemon, Titus, and two to Timothy. These were written from 'personal affection', but later were 'held sacred in the esteem of the Church catholic for the regulation of ecclesiastical discipline'.

Having thus specified thirteen genuine Epistles, the author

---

[18] Did the author imagine that John wrote the Book of Revelation before Paul had written his Epistles? Tregelles explained *prodecessoris* to mean 'the aforementioned John'; Westcott took it to mean that John was an apostle before Paul became an apostle; and Stendahl (see p. 201 n. 28 below) suggested that for the Fragmentist prophetic inspiration was the primary criterion of canonicity—even apostolic authorship took second place to it.

notices two writings that promote the heresy of Marcion and which, he says, have been falsely attributed to Paul. These, however, should not be received by the catholic Church because 'it is not fitting that gall be mixed with honey'.[19] These two are an epistle to the Laodiceans and another to the Alexandrians. It is known that Marcion entitled his version of Ephesians 'To the Laodiceans', and there is also a well-known (later) pseudo-Pauline epistle having the same title; but there is nothing to throw light on what is meant by the Epistle to the Alexandrians. That it is another name for the Epistle to the Hebrews has frequently been conjectured; yet Hebrews is nowhere else described as to the Alexandrians, has no Marcionite heresy, and is not 'forged under the name of Paul'. No more satisfactory solution of this problem has been offered than that the author is referring to a writing that has not come down to us.

(d) Other Epistles (lines 68–71)

The Muratorian Fragment next mentions the Epistle of Jude and two Epistles of John. There has been much discussion whether the latter statement means the First and the Second, or the Second and the Third Epistles. It is possible that, since the author had already alluded to the First Epistle in connection with the Fourth Gospel, he felt able here to confine himself to the two smaller Epistles. Or, according to an ingenious conjecture, the original Greek read 'two in addition to the catholic [Epistle]'.[20]

Next follows an unexpected reference to the book of

---

[19] The presence of paranomasia in the reference to gall and honey (*fel* and *mel*) is often taken to be proof that Latin is the original language of the Fragment. On the other hand, however, the author may be making a quotation or, at least, an allusion to the Greek text of the *Shepherd* of Hermas (*Mand.* v. i, 2) 'honey and wormwood mixed together').

[20] The conjecture, made originally by Peter Katz ('The Johannine Epistles in the Muratorian Canon', *Journal of Theological Studies*, N.S. viii [1957], pp. 273 f.), proposed instead of *duas in catholica* to read *dua(e) sin catholica*, corresponding to an original δύο σὺν καθολικῇ. C. F. D. Moule (*The Birth of the New Testament*, 3rd ed. [1982], p. 266 n. 2) accepts the conjecture in principle but proposes δύο πρὸς καθολικήν as the original. On the other hand, it may be significant that, according to Harnack, the Latin version of 3 John is not the work of the translator of 1 and 2 John. If, therefore, as T. W. Manson pointed out, 1 and 2 John were separately translated into Latin, 'the presumption is that there was a time in the Western church when only 1 and 2 John were in use, and this makes it probable that the reference in the Muratorianum is to these two epistles' (*Journal of Theological Studies*, xlviii [1947], p. 33).

'Wisdom, written by friends[21] of Solomon in his honour' as a kind of Festschrift. Why this intertestamental book should be included in a list of Christian gospels and epistles is a puzzle that has never been satisfactorily solved.

(e) Apocalypses (lines 71–80)

The list concludes with the mention of two apocalypses, that of John and that of Peter—'though some of us are not willing that the latter should be read in church'. This, of course, means that the text must have been read publically to congregations. Along with these two apocalypses the Fragmentist refers to the *Shepherd* of Hermas, mentioned here in connection with apocalyptic literature probably because it too contains a series of visions. This book, the writer says, was composed 'very recently, in our own times', and therefore it should not be read in divine service on a footing with the prophets and apostles. At the same time, however, the book is important and 'ought indeed to be read'—presumably in private or in small informal gatherings.

One detects an interesting development involving three stages. At the first stage there are three apocalypses (those of John, Peter, and Hermas); at the second, there are only two (John and Peter); finally, only John is apostolic. The first position has already been passed; despite the author's sympathy that he feels for Hermas, he accepts the solution of only two apocalypses. One sees a hint of the third stage when the author mentions those who accept only John's apocalypse. Although he does not share this point of view, he does not discuss the grounds for rejecting it. In fact, he seems to have lacked any precise criterion for solving the problem.

(f) Excluded Books (lines 81–5)

The text of the last lines of the document is so corrupt as to be virtually unintelligible, but we can make out that it names several books that are rejected altogether. Among these are the

---

[21] An ingenious conjecture, made independently by Bishop Fitzgerald and Tregelles, attempts to account for 'the friends' by suggesting that the Latin translator of the Muratorian Fragment had before him a Greek phrase that attributed the book of Wisdom to Philo as its author (an opinion that was fairly widespread in Western tradition; cf. Jerome, *Praef. in Libros Salomonis*; Migne, *Patrologia Latina*, xxviii, col. 1308), but misread ὑπὸ Φιλῶνος ('by Philo') as ὑπὸ φίλων ('by his friends'); see *Journal of Classical and Sacred Philology*, ii (1855), pp. 37–43, and Tregelles' edition, pp. 50–4 and note 22.

writings of Arsinous and Miltiades[22] (two otherwise obscure heretics) and those of Valentinus. Mention is also made of those who have written 'a new book of psalms for Marcion'. The concluding words, which do not constitute a sentence, refer to Basilides and the Cataphrygians (i.e. the Montanists) of Asia Minor.

2. SIGNIFICANCE OF THE MURATORIAN CANON

By way of summarizing the evidence supplied by the Muratorian Fragment, one observes that the list classifies books under four categories. First, there are those books accepted universally, namely the four Gospels, Acts, thirteen Epistles of Paul, Jude, two (perhaps three) Epistles of John, the Wisdom of Solomon, and the Johannine Apocalypse. Secondly, there is one disputed book, the *Apocalypse of Peter*, which some refuse to have read in church. Thirdly, there is one book, the *Shepherd* of Hermas, which, though rejected, still ought to be read privately.[23] Fourthly, several heretical books are mentioned as totally rejected.

The terminology usually employed in referring to those books that are regarded as canonical is *recipere* ('to recognize, or receive', lines 66, 72, 82); other verbs that are also used are *habere* ('to accept', line 69) and *sanctificatae sunt* ('are held sacred', line 63). Two other norms that indicate approval of a book as authoritative for the Church are (*a*) the public reading in a service of worship (*legere in ecclesia* or *publicare in ecclesia populo*), and (*b*) authorship by those who were eye- and ear-witnesses,[24] i.e. apostles. The criteria for refusing Hermas canonical standing is twofold: he is not numbered among the prophets, because their number has been closed, neither does he belong among the apostles. Here one could speak of the criteria of 'propheticity' and 'apostolicity'.[25]

[22] The manuscript reads Mitiades, which is ordinarily emended to Miltiades. A Montanist with the name Miltiades is mentioned by Eusebius (*Hist. eccl.* v. xvi. 3), but the reading is not free from doubt; see Harnack, *Texte und Untersuchungen*, i. i, p. 216 n.

[23] That individual Christians could read these books and yet they could not be received by the Church may imply that the Church is somehow distinct from its members.

[24] For an illuminating study of this expression, see W. C. van Unnik, *Oog en oor; Criteria voor de eerste samenstelling van Nieuwe Testament* (Rede ter gelegenheid van de 337ᵉ dies natalis der Rijksuniversiteit te Utrecht op 30 Maart 1973).

[25] For the formula 'Prophets and Apostles' in relation to the canon prior to Irenaeus, see D. M. Farkasfalvy in *Texts and Testaments: Critical Essays on the Bible and Early Church Fathers*, ed. by W. Eugene March (San Antonio, 1980), pp. 109–34.

Books that are not mentioned in the list include 1 and 2 Peter, James, and the Epistle to the Hebrews.[26] Of these the most surprising omission is that of 1 Peter. In view of the rather extensive use made of 1 Peter by several early writers, both Western and Eastern, it may be, as Zahn and others have supposed, that the list originally mentioned 1 Peter, but through scribal carelessness reference to it was accidentally omitted.

It should be observed that the tone of the whole treatise is not so much that of legislation but of explanatory statement concerning a more or less established condition of things, with only a single instance of difference of opinion among members of the Church catholic (namely, the use to be made of the *Apocalypse of Peter*). The exclusive validity of the four Gospels, with not so much as a passing reference to apocryphal gospels even by way of rejecting them, is perfectly apparent. At the same time, however, one perceives an apologetic interest in the way in which the author speaks of agreement of these four in all essentials.[27] This agreement has come about, he implies, because the several authors submitted themselves to the guidance of the Spirit (*cum uno ac principale Spiritu*, line 19).

Perhaps one may also detect in his account concerning the production of the Fourth Gospel a reply (*a*) to the Alogi, a group of heretics in Asia Minor who ascribed the Gospel and Revelation of John to a certain Gnostic named Cerinthus, and (*b*) to Gaius of Rome, who made much of the differences between the beginning of John's Gospel as compared with the beginning of the Synoptic Gospels. Furthermore, the Fragmentist's explicit rejection of various writings as heretical points to a polemical situation.

Here and there the document lays repeated emphasis upon

[26] The silence concerning the Epistle to the Hebrews, an epistle accepted in the East but not in the West at first, stands against Sundberg's theory that the Fragment is of eastern provenance, dating from the fourth century. The later in date the list, the more problematic is its silence concerning Hebrews.

[27] On the embarrassment felt by some of the Fathers at the presence of discrepancies among the canonical Gospels, see Helmut Merkel, *Die Widersprüche zwischen den Evangelien; Ihre polemische und apologetische Behandlung in der alten Kirche bis zu Augustin* (Tübingen, 1971). In the latter part of the second century Celsus' sharp eyes detected a considerable number of real and imagined contradictions in the Gospels, which later antagonists of the Church, such as Porphyry, Hierocles, the Emperor Julian, and certain Manichees, adopted and amplified.

the motif of ecumenicity. Twice the author refers to the universal or catholic Church, and once (line 69) the word *catholica* is used alone, presumably of the Church. This universal Church is one and is 'spread throughout the whole world'. The Epistles that Paul sent to specific, local congregations are, nevertheless, intended for the Church universal, he argues, inasmuch as Paul wrote to seven such churches. Here the hidden presupposition rests upon the mystical meaning conveyed by the numeral seven, implying completeness and totality.[28]

Finally, one should not overlook a comment the author makes in connection with the Epistle to the Romans: 'Christ is the principle (*principium*) of the Scriptures.' Even if Christ is characterized as the only measure of interpretation of the Scriptures of the Old Testament, we have at least indirectly something like the measure of canonicity, bearing on the material content of the document—an idea that can be compared with Martin Luther's criterion, namely 'what promotes Christ' (see pp. 242–3 below).

II. EUSEBIUS' CLASSIFICATION OF NEW TESTAMENT BOOKS

The name of Eusebius of Caesarea has been mentioned quite frequently in these pages. His *Ecclesiastical History* gives us access to a host of sources and traditions otherwise long since lost. The 'Father of church history' had at his disposal the library at Caesarea which Origen built up after he had been forced to leave Alexandria and take up residence in Palestine. Pamphilus, an enthusiastic adherent of Origen, had sought out and added many volumes to the library, and Eusebius, the pupil, co-worker, and friend of Pamphilus, became his successor when Pamphilus died as a martyr in the Diocletian persecution.

Although Eusebius leaves much to be desired as an exegete or an apologist for Christianity, he had, on the other hand, one quality that was lacking in all his predecessors as well as in all his contemporaries—the instinct for historical research. In the congenial setting offered by a well-stocked library in Caesarea,

---

[28] See Krister Stendahl, 'The Apocalypse of John and the Epistles of Paul in the Muratorian Fragment', in *Current Issues in New Testament Interpretation, Essays in honour of Otto Piper*, ed. by W. Klassen and G. F. Snyder (New York, 1962), pp. 239–45.

as well by visiting the Christian library at Jerusalem, founded in the previous century by Bishop Alexander (*Hist. eccl.* VI. xx. 1), Eusebius indulged his appetite for Christian antiquities, and began the task of collecting and organizing material covering the history of the Church, chiefly in the East, during the preceding three centuries.

Born about A.D. 260, Eusebius became bishop of Caesarea before 315, and died about 340. He wrote his *Ecclesiastical History* in sections, and issued it, with revisions and additions, several times during the first quarter of the fourth century.[29] What renders Eusebius' work most valuable to us is the marked attention that he directed towards all that concerns the history of the Christian Bible. He had read a prodigious number of authors, and in the extracts that he gives from their writings he never fails to note the use they made of Scripture, the lists of books they quote in passing or fully discuss, the judgements they pronounce on them.[30] If one asks what was the reason for this concern in registering numerous individual testimonies concerning the Scriptures, the answer certainly must point to Eusebius' search for certainty as well as to the absence of any official declaration having an absolute value, such as a canon issued by a synod, or the collective agreement among churches or bishops. Of these there is not a trace in the long series of literary notices, so conscientiously amassed by the historian. But, when all is done, the most that Eusebius can register is uncertainty so great that he seems to get confused when making a statement about it. This may be seen from an analysis of the summary he gives in *Hist. eccl.* III. xxv. 1–7,[31] to which we now turn.

---

[29] For information as to expansions and revisions that Eusebius introduced between 305 and 325, see R. Laqueur, *Eusebius als Historiker seiner Zeit* (Berlin–Leipzig, 1929), R. M. Grant, 'Eusebius and his Lives of Origen', in *Forma futuri; Studi in onore del Cardinale Michele Pellegrino* (Turin, 1975), pp. 635–49, and especially Grant's *Eusebius as Church Historian* (Oxford, 1980), pp. 10–21. According to T. D. Barnes, Eusebius' research extended over a still longer period of time: 'At least five editions of the Ecclesiastical History must be postulated, to which I would assign the following dates: first edition before 296, second 313/4, third c 315, fourth 325, and fifth after 326'; see the colloquy, *Les Martyrs de Lyons (177)* (Paris, 1978), p. 137 n.

[30] See C. Sant, 'Eusebius of Caesarea's Views on the Canon of the Holy Scriptures and the Texts he used in his Works', *Melita theologica*, xxiii (1971), pp. 23–37.

[31] Eusebius gives other, shorter comments in II. xxii. 23; III. iii. 24; v. viii. 1–9; and VI xiv. 25.

In the absence of any official list of the canonical writings of the New Testament, Eusebius finds it simplest to count the votes of his witnesses, and by this means to classify all the apostolic or pretended apostolic writings into three categories: (1) Those on whose authority and authenticity all the churches and all the authors he had consulted were agreed; (2) those which the witnesses were equally agreed in rejecting; and (3) an intermediate class regarding which the votes were divided (see Appendix IV. 3).

The books of the first category he calls 'homologoumena', that is, books that were universally acknowledged (ὁμολογού-μενα). They are twenty-two in number: the 'holy quaternion' of the Gospels, the Acts of the Apostles, the Pauline Epistles,[32] 1 Peter, and 1 John. 'In addition to these', he continues, 'should be put, if it really seems proper (εἴ γε φαινείη), the Apocalypse of John, concerning which we shall give the different opinions at the proper time'. Despite the last sentence, Eusebius concludes this list with the statement, 'These belong among the acknowledged books'.

The books that fall into the third category (the intermediary class) Eusebius designates as 'antilegomena', that is, 'disputed books, yet familiar to most people of the church' (ἀντιλεγόμενα, γνώριμα δ᾽ οὖν ὅμως τοῖς πολλοῖς). In this category he mentions the Epistles of James, Jude, 2 Peter, and 2 and 3 John.[33]

The books that fall into the category of the rejected books, which Eusebius calls 'illegitimate' or 'spurious' (νόθα),[34]

---

[32] In *Hist. eccl.* III. iii. 4 Eusebius declares that 'the Epistles of Paul are obvious and plain', but adds at once, 'yet it is not right to ignore the fact that some have rejected the Epistle to the Hebrews, saying that it is disputed (ἀντιλέγεσθαι) by the church of Rome, on the ground that it was not written by Paul'. Eusebius, in agreement with the Alexandrians (who, with the exception of Origen, unanimously accepted the Pauline authorship), looked upon it as a work of Paul but accepted Clement of Alexandria's theory that it was written in Hebrew and translated by the evangelist Luke or Clement of Rome (*Hist. eccl.* III. xxxviii. 2).

[33] It is surprising, in view of what Eusebius has said earlier about the Apocalypse of John, that this book is not described as disputed. Eusebius, however, being intolerant of apocalyptic prophecy if he could not point to its fulfilment in Constantine, will shortly classify John's Apocalypse as 'spurious'. As for his views concerning the Epistle to the Hebrews, see p. 205 below.

[34] The term νόθα in this passage, in fact, appears to have not only its common meaning 'bastard, inauthentic', that is, fictitious writings, pseudepigrapha, works bearing falsely an author's name, but also to imply works which do not carry, so to speak, the stamp of canonical legitimacy.

include the *Acts of Paul*, the *Shepherd* of Hermas, the *Apocalypse of
Peter*, the *Epistle of Barnabas*, the so-called *Teachings of the
Apostles*, and the *Gospel according to the Hebrews*. To these he adds,
inconsistently, the Apocalypse of John, 'if it seem proper
(ϵi $\phi\alpha\nu\epsilon i\eta$),[35] which some, as I said,[36] reject ($\dot{\alpha}\theta\epsilon\tau o\hat{\upsilon}\sigma\iota\nu$), while
others reckon it among the acknowledged books'. Likewise
among the spurious books, Eusebius continues, 'some have
counted the Gospel according to the Hebrews'. At this point
Eusebius further confuses the picture by grouping together the
disputed and the spurious books, and calling all of them
'disputed'.

Finally, Eusebius lists books 'put forward by heretics under
the name of the apostles'; these, he says, are worse than
spurious and must be 'set aside as altogether worthless and
impious'. Among these he mentions the gospels of Peter, of
Thomas, of Matthias, as well as the Acts of Andrew, and John,
and the other apostles.

Despite Eusebius' good intentions, he has been unable to
present a tidy listing. Although the correlative terms ('acknowledged' and 'disputed') are perfectly clear, he mixes with
them other categories that belong to a different order of ideas.
What seems at first reading to be a straightforward account, on
closer analysis leaves one perplexed.

The difficulty of analysing Eusebius' summary account
arises, as von Dobschütz saw,[37] from the tension in his thinking
between Eusebius the historian and Eusebius the churchman.
Eusebius classifies the books first in relation to canonicity,
dividing them into the canonical and the uncanonical; and
secondly, in relation to their character, dividing them into the
orthodox and the heterodox. The orthodox books embrace the
homologoumena and the *antilegomena*, which are canonical, and
the *notha*, which are uncanonical. The heterodox books,

---

[35] Does this curious expression, used both times that Eusebius speaks of the
Apocalypse, mean that he does not really know his mind on the subject, or (more
likely) that he disliked stating too bluntly an opinion which he knew that many would
not like?

[36] Eusebius here refers to the statement made in an earlier chapter regarding
disputes concerning the Apocalypse, about which 'the opinions of most people are still
divided' (III. xxiv. 18).

[37] Ernst von Dobschütz, 'The Abandonment of the Canonical Idea', *American
Journal of Theology*, xix (1915), pp. 416–29.

Eusebius says, are not and never have been accepted as of use or authority. Arranged in a chart Eusebius's categories are as follows:

A. Orthodox books:
   1. The canonical books
      a. Recognized books
         (*homologoumena*)
      b. Disputed books
         (*antilegomena*)
   2. The uncanonical books
      a. Spurious books (*notha*)

B. Unorthodox books:
      b. Fictions of heretics

Thus, the *notha* occupy a peculiar position, being orthodox but uncanonical.

Such an interpretation helps us understand how Eusebius can place the Book of Revelation conditionally into two different classes. As a historian Eusebius recognizes that it is widely received, but as a churchman he has become annoyed by the extravagant use made of this book by Montanists and other millenarians, and so is glad to report elsewhere in his history that others consider it to be not genuine.[38]

Why Eusebius does not mention in his list the Epistle to the Hebrews has been widely discussed; the simplest explanation is that he included it as canonical among the Epistles of Paul, which he does not identify one by one. True enough, the Pauline authorship of the Epistle had been disputed, and elsewhere Eusebius reports various theories that had been proposed to account for its difference in literary style from the Pauline Epistles.[39] Since, however, at this place Eusebius is simply stating, in a more or less systematic way, which books fall into which class, and is not discussing the nature and origin of those works, he could, in perfect fairness, include it among Paul's Epistles, where he himself believed it belonged.

By way of summary, one must acknowledge that, though Eusebius may not have achieved a standard acceptable to

---

[38] In VII. xxv. 18–27 Eusebius adopts the view of Dionysius of Alexandria, based on a critical analysis of style and vocabulary, and concludes that the author of the Apocalypse was not the apostle John but 'the second John', otherwise called the 'Presbyter John'. This change in Eusebius' view of the Apocalypse is reflected in some of the alterations and revisions that he made over the years in his *Church History*.

[39] See p. 203 n. 32 above.

modern historiography, his method of listing is, considering the measure of complexity that prevailed in the early Church, eminently fair and practical. He is endeavouring to give an accurate statement of the general opinion of the orthodox Church of his date in regard to the number and names of its sacred Scriptures. The lack of consistency in his account helps us recognize the honesty of Eusebius, and that he has not imposed on the data an overly neat classification. In fact, his work inspires us with greater confidence than a more rigid and dogmatic listing would have done.

Before we leave Eusebius, however, there is another piece of evidence that bears on the subject of the canon—even though we may not know exactly how to interpret it. About the year 332 the Emperor Constantine, wishing to promote and organize Christian worship in the growing number of churches in his capital city, directed Eusebius to have fifty copies of the sacred Scriptures made by practised scribes (καλλιγράφοι) and written legibly on prepared parchment. At the same time the emperor informed him, in a letter still preserved to us,[40] that everything necessary for doing this was placed at his command, among other things two public carriages for conveying the completed manuscripts to the emperor for his personal inspection. 'Such were the emperor's commands', says Eusebius, 'which were followed by the immediate execution of the work itself, which we sent him in magnificent and elaborately bound volumes of a threefold and fourfold form' (τρισσὰ καὶ τετρασσὰ διαπεμψάντων ἡμῶν).

Although the exact meaning of the concluding words has been taken in widely different senses,[41] of still more interest is the question (for which the text provides no answer), which books, and in what sequence, should be included in these

---

[40] Eusebius, *Vita Const.* IV. xxxvi. 37.

[41] Of the half dozen interpretations of the meaning of the Greek text of this clause (see Metzger, *The Text of the New Testament*, p. 7 n. 2), perhaps the most widely adopted is that the pages had three or four columns of script; see Kirsopp Lake, 'The Sinaitic and Vatican Manuscripts and the Copies sent by Eusebius to Constantinople', *Harvard Theological Review*, xi (1918), pp. 32–5, and Carl Wendel, 'Der Bibel-Auftrag Kaisar Konstantins', *Zentralblatt für Bibliotheswesen*, lxi (1939), pp. 165–75. On the other hand, T. C. Skeat ('The Use of Dictation in Ancient Book-Production', *Proceedings of the British Academy*, xlii [1956], pp. 179–208, esp. 195–7) makes an attractive case for understanding the phrase to mean that as the copies were completed they were sent off for the emperor's inspection 'three or four at a time'.

volumes? The astonishing thing is that this same Eusebius, who took care to tell us at some length about the fluctuations of opinion in regard to certain books, apostolic or supposed to be so, has not one word to say regarding the choice he made on this important occasion. Of course, fifty magnificent copies, all uniform, could not but exercise a great influence on future copies, at least within the bounds of the patriarchate of Constantinople, and would help forward the process of arriving at a commonly accepted New Testament in the East.[42]

We have today parts of two Greek manuscripts of the Old and New Testaments that some have thought may perhaps have been among the fifty commissioned by Constantine. However that may be (and their possessing an Alexandrian type of text makes this supposition unlikely), they were probably written at about that time and therefore are of special interest in this connection. One of them is codex Sinaiticus, of which the entire New Testament and part of the Old are preserved in the British Library. The New Testament portion contains the four Gospels, fourteen Epistles of Paul (with Hebrews between 2 Thessalonians and 1 Timothy), the Book of Acts, the seven Catholic Epistles, Revelation, the *Epistle of Barnabas*, and a fragment of the *Shepherd* of Hermas (as far as Mandate iv. iii. 6). The other manuscript is the Vatican codex at Rome. It contains in the New Testament section the four Gospels, the Book of Acts, the seven Catholic Epistles, the Pauline Epistles as far as Thessalonians, and Hebrews to ix. 14, where unfortunately the original manuscript breaks off.[43] It is natural to assume that it originally had the Pastoral Epistles and Philemon after Hebrews, and that it doubtless contained the Book of Revelation as well.

---

[42] See K. L. Carroll, 'Toward a Commonly Received New Testament', *Bulletin of the John Ryland Library*, xliv (1962), pp. 341 ff., and W. R. Farmer, *Jesus and the Gospel* (Philadelphia, 1981), pp. 193 f.

[43] The text of the rest of Hebrews and of the Book of Revelation was supplied by a fifteenth-century scribe. On the manner in which the restoration was accomplished, see T. C. Skeat, 'The Codex Vaticanus in the Fifteenth Century', *Journal of Theological Studies*, N.S. xxxv (1984), pp. 454–65.

IX

Attempts at Closing the Canon in the East

I. FROM CYRIL OF JERUSALEM TO THE TRULLAN SYNOD

As we have seen in the previous chapter, the Eastern Church, as reported by Eusebius about A.D. 325, was in considerable doubt concerning the authority of most of the Catholic Epistles as well as the Apocalypse. Steps to overcome this unsatisfactory condition were taken later that century, as can be seen from several lists of sacred books drawn up by such diverse churchmen as Cyril of Jerusalem, Athanasius of Alexandria, Gregory of Nazianzus, Amphilochius of Iconium, Didymus the Blind, and Epiphanius of Salamis. These lists, unlike the testimonies of preceding generations, most of which were occasional allusions or casual statements, are judgements purposely delivered in order to delineate the limits of the canon.

The chief surviving work of Cyril of Jerusalem (c. 315–86), his *Catechetical Lectures* (see Appendix IV. 5), were instructions for catechumens as Lenten preparation prior to undergoing baptism on Holy Saturday. Dating from about A.D. 350 they were delivered mostly in the Church of the Holy Sepulchre, built by Constantine, and were published from shorthand notes taken down by a member of the congregation. It is not surprising that this series of lectures, devoted, as they are, to presenting a full summary of Christian doctrine and practice, contains a list of the Scriptures of the Old and New Testaments.[1] After enumerating the books of the Old Testament, Cyril declares that the New Testament contains only four Gospels, and warns his hearers against other gospels that are forged and hurtful. Following the four Gospels are the Acts of the Twelve Apostles, the seven Catholic Epistles of James, Peter, John, and Jude, and, Cyril concludes, 'as a seal upon them all, the fourteen Epistles of Paul. But let all the rest be put aside in a secondary

[1] *Catacheses* iv. 33–36.

rank. And whatever books are not read in the churches, do not read these even by yourself' (iv. 36).

It is noteworthy that the Book of Revelation is not included as one of the books of the New Testament. Such is the state of things at Jerusalem by the middle of the fourth century.

At this point in chronology mention must be made of a synod that discussed the canon, even though it is difficult to be certain what action was taken. That a synod held about 363 at Laodicea, a city in Phrygia Pacatania of Asia Minor, took some action regarding the canon is certain, but its precise decision is unknown to us. At the close of the decrees (or 'canons' as such decrees were commonly called) issued by the thirty or so clerics in attendance[2] we read: 'Let no private psalms nor any uncanonical books (ἀκανόνιστα βιβλία) be read in the church, but only the canonical ones (τὰ κανονικά) of the New and Old Testament.' Thus far the decree is found in all accounts of the synod with but trifling variations. In the later manuscripts, however, this is followed by a list, first of Old Testament books, then of the New—the latter corresponding to our present canon, with the omission of the Book of Revelation (see Appendix IV. 7). Since the lists are also omitted in most of the Latin and Syriac versions of the decrees, most scholars consider them to have been added to the report of the Synod of Laodicea sometime after 363. Probably some later editor of the report felt that the books which might be read should be named. In any case, it is clear that the Synod of Laodicea attempted no new legislation. The decree adopted at this gathering merely recognizes the fact that there are already in existence certain books, generally recognized as suitable to be read in the public worship of the churches, which are known as the 'canonical' books. If the catalogues are genuine, they simply give the names of these books, already received as authoritative in the churches that were represented at the synod.

The most celebrated theologian of the fourth century, Athanasius of Alexandria (*c.* 296–373), had been educated probably at the catechetical school of his native city. He assisted at the Council of Nicea (325) as a deacon and as secretary of his bishop Alexander, and there gained fame by his disputes with the Arians.

---

[2] One account states that there were thirty-two members in attendance, while another mentions only twenty-four.

He succeeded Alexander as early as 328. From what we know, Athanasius appears to be the first prelate who took advantage of his position at the head of an extensive and important diocese to deal with the question of the Biblical canon.

It was an ancient custom for the bishop of Alexandria to write, if possible, every year soon after Epiphany a so-called Festal Epistle (᾿Επιστολὴ ἑορταστική) to the Egyptian churches and monasteries under his authority, in which he informed them of the date of Easter and the beginning of the Lenten fast. By fixing the date of Easter this yearly epistle fixed also the dates of all Christian festivals of the year.

In view of the reputation of Alexandrian scholars who were devoted to astronomical calculations,[3] it is not surprising that other parts of Christendom should eventually come to rely on the Egyptian Church for information concerning the date of Easter, made available to the Western Church through the bishop of Rome, and to the Syrian Church through the bishop of Antioch.

Naturally such an annual pastoral communication would provide opportunity to discuss other matters in addition to the date of Easter. Of the forty-five such festal epistles that Athanasius wrote from A.D. 329 onwards,[4] the Thirty-Ninth Festal Epistle of 367 is particularly valuable, for it contains a list of the canonical books of the Old and New Testaments.[5] In the case of the Old Testament, Athanasius excludes the deuterocanonical books,[6] permitting them only as devotional reading. The twenty-seven books of the present New Testament are stated to

---

[3] Among the succession of brilliant heads of the famed Alexandrian Library was Eratosthenes of Cyrene (c. 275–194 B.C.), who calculated with a high degree of accuracy the circumference of the earth. His Χρονογραφίαι represented the first scientific attempt to fix the dates of political and literary history.

[4] For an English translation of the fragments of Athanasius' Festal Epistles that have survived, see *A Select Library of the Nicene and Post-Nicene Fathers of the Christian Church*, Second Series, iv (New York, 1892), pp. 550–5.

[5] It has been reconstructed almost completely from Greek, Syriac, and Coptic fragmentary texts; see Theodor Zahn, 'Athanasius und der Bibelkanon', in *Festschrift seiner königlichen Hoheit dem Prinzregenten Luitpold von Bayern zum achzigsten Geburtstage dargebracht von der Universität Erlangen*, i (Erlangen, 1901), pp. 1–36.

[6] At the same time it should be observed that earlier, at least about the year A.D. 350, Athanasius distinguished between inspired books and canonical books. More than once he cited as being inspired certain books that would later be excluded from his Festal Epistle of 367; these included 3 Esdras (= our 1 Esdras) and the *Shepherd* of Hermas. See Jean Ruwet, 'Le canon alexandrin des écritures; Saint Athanase', *Biblica*, xxxiii (1952), pp. 1–29.

be the only canonical ones (see Appendix IV. 8); they stand in sequence of Gospels, Acts, the seven Catholic Epistles, the Pauline Epistles (with Hebrews inserted between 2 Thessalonians and 1 Timothy), concluding with the Apocalypse of John. 'These', he declares, 'are fountains of salvation, that they who thirst may be satisfied with the living words they contain. In these alone the teaching of godliness is proclaimed. Let no one add to these; let nothing be taken away from them.'

The year 367 marks, thus, the first time that the scope of the New Testament canon is declared to be exactly the twenty-seven books accepted today as canonical. But not every one in the Church was ready to follow the opinion of the bishop of Alexandria. For example, the distinguished theologian and contemporary of Athanasius, Gregory of Nazianzus (d. 389), toward the end of his life drew up in verse (perhaps as an aid to the memory of his readers) a catalogue of the Biblical books (see Appendix IV. 10). So far as concerns the Old Testament, he agrees with Athanasius, but when it comes to the New Testament he differs in placing the Catholic Epistles after the Pauline Epistles and, more significantly, in omitting Revelation. He then declares, '[In these] you have all. And if there is anything outside of these, it is not among the genuine [books].' Although Gregory thus excludes the Apocalypse from the canon, he knows of its existence, and on rare occasions in his other works quotes from it.

Another list of Biblical books, also in verse, dates from about the same time. It is included in a poem that is generally attributed to Amphilochius (d. after 394), a Cappadocian by birth, a lawyer, and then bishop of Iconium in Lycaonia. The poem, entitled *Iambics for Seleucus*, sometimes found among the poems of Gregory of Nazianzus, instructs Seleucus how to follow a life of study and virtue. The author urges him to apply himself to the Scriptures more than to any other writing. Apropos of this advice Amphilochius adds a complete list of the books of the Bible.

In the list of the New Testament books (see Appendix IV. 11), Amphilochius reports some of the earlier debate concerning Hebrews, the Catholic Epistles, and the Apocalypse. In fact, not only does he report the doubts of others concerning these books, but he himself appears to reject 2 Peter, 2 and 3 John, and Jude, and almost certainly rejects Revelation. The most curious feature is that, having thus stated doubts as to the right of several books to be included in the sacred collection, the author ends with the incredible phrase: 'This is perhaps the most reliable [literally, the most unfalsified] canon of the divinely inspired Scriptures' (οὗτος ἀψευδέστατος κανὼν ἂν εἴη τῶν θεοπνευστῶν γραφῶν)! The presence of the word κανών, meaning a catalogue or list, is scarcely more noteworthy than the hypothetical form of the sentence as a whole. In other words, here we have a bishop in Asia Minor, a colleague of the Gregories and of Basil, and yet he seems to be uncertain as to the exact extent of the canon!

Another celebrated teacher and head of the Alexandrian catechetical school for more than half a century was Didymus the Blind (d. *c.* 398). Although he was a layman and had become blind at the age of four, he memorized great sections of the Scriptures and, by means of secretaries, dictated numerous exegetical works. The accidental discovery in 1941 at Toura, south of Cairo, of a group of papyrus codices, dating from the sixth or seventh century and comprising nearly two thousand pages, has brought to light the text of half a dozen additional commentaries of this prolific author. Although these commentaries are on Old Testament books, Didymus includes in his exposition hundreds of citations from the New Testament. These come from all the books of the New Testament except Philemon and 2 and 3 John. While the absence of reference to Philemon can perhaps be explained in terms of its brevity, the fact that when quoting 1 John Didymus refers to it as *the* Epistle of John and not the First Epistle of John must mean that he did not accept the canonical status of 2 and 3 John.

It is noteworthy that more than once Didymus quotes from 2 Peter as altogether authentic and authoritative. This circumstance requires reassessment of a statement made in a commentary on the seven Catholic Epistles heretofore commonly attributed to Didymus, a work now extant only in a Latin translation. In connection with a discussion of 2 Peter iii. 5–8, a passage which does not suit the author, he says flatly: 'It is therefore not to be overlooked that the present Epistle is forged, which, though it is read publicly [in the churches], is nevertheless not in the canon.'[7]

[7] *Non est ignorandum praesentem epistolam esse falsatam quae licet publicetur non tamen in canone est* (Migne, *Patrologia Latina*, xxxix, col. 1742).

That there was still fluidity of the New Testament canon at Alexandria in the second half of the fourth century is disclosed not only by the absence of reference to 2 and 3 John, but also by Didymus' occasional citation of several of the Apostolic Fathers as authoritative. According to a recent study by B. D. Ehrman,[8] in the newly discovered commentaries Didymus refers to the *Shepherd* of Hermas five times, to the *Epistle of Barnabas* four times, Ignatius three times, the *Didache* twice, and *1 Clement* once.

We come now to Epiphanius, bishop of Salamis in Cyprus (d. 403), renowned as a watchdog sniffing out heresies. In his works he several times mentions the number of the sacred books, particularly those of the Old Testament. As for the New Testament, in his voluminous *Panarion*, or 'Medicine Chest' offering an antidote for all heresies (written 374–7), we find a somewhat carelessly drawn up enumeration of the books of Scripture (chap. 76). Unlike some of the other Eastern Fathers already mentioned, Epiphanius concludes his list by naming the Apocalypse as a component part of the holy Scriptures, in this respect agreeing with Athanasius. At the same time, however, his list presents a rather strange anomaly by including among the divine Scriptures, following the Book of Revelation, the Wisdom of Solomon and the Wisdom of the son of Sirach (i.e. Ecclesiasticus).

One of the most remarkable exegetes produced by the School of Antioch was John Chrysostom (*c.* 347–407), who, against his wish, was made patriarch of Constantinople in 398. Often called the Christian Demosthenes (his oratorical powers earned him the sobriquet 'Golden-mouthed', Χρυσόστομος), Chrysostom's homilies and treatises were frequently used during subsequent generations in interpreting the Bible. According to Suicer he is the first writer who gave the Bible its present name τὰ βιβλία, *The Books*.[9] Of approximately 11,000 quotations that Chrysostom makes from the New Testament, according to Baur there are none from 2 Peter, 2 and 3 John, Jude, or

---

[8] 'The New Testament Canon of Didymus the Blind', *Vigiliae Christianae*, xxxvii (1983), pp. 1–21.

[9] J. C. Suicer, *Thesaurus ecclesiasticus*, 2nd ed., i (Amsterdam, 1728), col. 6. There were, however, anticipations of this usage; see Adolf von Harnack, 'Über das Alter der Bezeichnung "die Bücher" ("Die Bibel") für die h. Schriften in der Kirchen', *Zentralblatt für Bibliothekswesen*, xlv (1928), pp. 337–42.

Revelation.[10] In other words, his canon of the New Testament appears to be the same as that of the Peshitta, the Syriac version current at Antioch in his time (see below, p. 219). With this agrees the *Synopsis of sacred Scriptures*, often attributed to Chrysostom, which gives fourteen Epistles of Paul, four Gospels, Acts, and three Catholic Epistles.[11]

Theodore, bishop of Mopsuestia in Cilicia (d. 428), was also a representative of the School of Antioch; that is, he rejected the Alexandrian use of allegorical interpretation and in his commentaries employed historical and philological methods of exegesis. Unfortunately only fragments of his extensive commentaries on John, Paul, and the Psalms have survived in Greek, Latin, and Syriac. From these it is unclear what his position was with respect to the Catholic Epistles. He is accused by Leontius of Byzantium (end of 6th century) with having rejected the Epistle of James and the other Catholic Epistles that followed it ($\kappa a i$ $\tau a s$ $\dot{\epsilon} \xi \hat{\eta} s$ $\kappa a \theta o \lambda \iota \kappa \dot{a} s$).[12] It is difficult to decide whether this means that Theodore received only 1 Peter and 1 John (as Westcott supposed) or that he clung to the Syrian canon as it was prior to the time of Rabbula and the Peshitta version, lacking all the Catholic Epistles. That the latter interpretation is correct is suggested by Isho'dad of Merv's statement that Theodore makes no reference to the three major Catholic Epistles.[13]

The last writer of the School of Antioch who needs to be mentioned here is Theodoret (*c.* A.D. 393–*c.* 466). After having been consecrated in 423 as bishop of the small town of Cyrrhus, east of Antioch on the Euphrates, he began weeding out copies of Tatian's Diatesseron and replacing them with copies of the separate Gospels. He also sought to bring a deeper knowledge of the Scriptures to his flock by writing commentaries on many

---

[10] For statistics of Chrysostom's quotations from the several books of the New Testament, see Chrysostomus Baur, 'Der Kanon des hl. Joh. Chrysostomus', *Theologische Quartalschrift*, cv (1924), pp. 258–71. In some cases scholars differ as to whether a given treatise has been correctly ascribed to Chrysostom, and this may account for the circumstance that R. A. Krupp's recently published index (*Saint John Chrysostom; A Scripture Index* [Lanham, 1984]) cites two quotations from 2 Peter, one from Jude, and nine from Revelation.

[11] Migne, *Patrologia Graeca*, lvi, cols. 313–86.

[12] *Contra Nestorianos* iii. 14 (Migne. *Patrologia Graeca*, lxxxvi, col. 1365 c).

[13] *The Commentaries of Isho'dad*, ed. by M. D. Gibson (*Horae Semiticae*, xi; Cambridge, 1913), Syriac text p. 49, English trans. p. 36.

of the books of the Old Testament (the Pentateuch, Joshua, Judges, Kings and Chronicles, Psalms, Song of Solomon, and the Major and Minor Prophets) and on the Epistles of Paul. These are among the finest specimens of the Antiochene School and are noted for their lucidity and learning. As for his New Testament canon, apparently he agreed with Chrysostom, that is, he made no use of the minor Catholic Epistles or of the Book of Revelation.

This section on 'Attempts at Closing the Canon in the East' may be brought to a close by calling attention to a most astonishing conciliar decision taken by the Trullan Synod held near the end of the seventh century. In 691 and 692 this council of Eastern bishops met in the domed room (*trullus*) of the Emperor Justinian II's palace at Constantinople in order to pass disciplinary canons by way of completing the work of the Fifth (553) and Sixth (680) General Councils (hence its other name 'Quinisext', or Fifth-Sixth, Council). By one of its first decrees[14] it determined the series of authorities which were to make law in the Church. Among these were the eighty-five so-called Apostolic Canons (see Appendix IV. 9), then the decrees of a certain number of Synods, notably those of Laodicea and Carthage; and finally a great number of Fathers, including, among others, Athanasius and Amphilochius. The Council thereby sanctioned implicitly, so far as the list of Biblical books is concerned, quite incongruous and contradictory opinions. Thus, as we have seen earlier, the Synod of Carthage and Athanasius recognized the minor Catholic Epistles and the Book of Revelation, while the Synod of Laodicea and the eighty-fifth Apostolic Canon omitted them. Furthermore, this same Canon includes as canonical the two Epistles of Clement which the other authorities did not receive. Such an extraordinary situation can be accounted for only on the supposition that the members of the Council had not even read the texts thus sanctioned.

In view of the confusion implicit in the pronouncement made on the canon at the Trullan Synod, it is not surprising that the later history of the Bible in the East continues to exhibit uncertainty and vacillation. According to a tabulation

[14] For the decree, see G. D. Mansi's *Sacrorum Conciliorum Nova et Amplissima Collectio*, xi, p. 939.

made by Westcott,[15] in the tenth century no fewer than six different lists of the Scriptures of the Old and New Testaments were received in the Greek Church.

At this point we terminate our investigation of the declarations of synods and the usage of individuals in the East, and look finally at the Greek Bibles themselves that have survived from the Byzantine period. According to statistics collected by the Institute for New Testament Text-Research at Münster,[16] as of 1980 the several parts of the New Testament were represented in Greek manuscripts as follows:

	number of surviving manuscripts
The entire Greek New Testament	59
MSS containing the Gospels, Acts, Catholic Epistles, and Pauline Epistles	149
MSS and fragments of Gospels	2120
MSS and fragments of the Acts and Catholic Epistles	447
MSS and fragments of the Pauline Epistles	571
MSS and fragments of the Book of Revelation	228

From these figures it will be seen that the testimony of the copies of the Scriptures that have survived is more eloquent, in some ways, than the Fathers and more positive than the Councils on questions relative to the canon. It is obvious that the conception of the canon of the New Testament was not essentially a dogmatic issue whereby all parts of the text were regarded as equally necessary (the Gospels exist in 2,328 copies; the Book of Revelation in 287 copies). The lower status of the Book of Revelation in the East is indicated also by the fact that it has never been included in the official lectionary of the Greek Church, whether Byzantine or modern. It is also significant, judging from the total number of surviving copies, that only a very small proportion of Christians could have ever owned, or even seen, a copy of the complete canon of the New Testament.

[15] *The Bible in the Church*, p. 227.

[16] Kurt and Barbara Aland, *Der Text des Neuen Testaments* (Stuttgart, 1982), p. 92.

II. THE CANON IN THE NATIONAL EASTERN CHURCHES

1. THE SYRIAN CHURCHES

The fact that during the first six centuries of the Christian era five or six separate versions of the Scriptures in Syriac were produced is testimony to the vitality and scholarship of Syrian churches. Indeed, as Eberhard Nestle has reminded us, 'No branch of the Early Church has done more for the translation of the Bible into their vernacular than the Syriac-speaking. In our European libraries we have Syriac Bible MSS from Lebanon, Egypt, Sinai, Mesopotamia, Armenia, India (Malabar), and even from China.'[17]   As we have seen earlier (chap. V. 1), the earliest canon in Eastern Syrian Churches consisted of 'the Gospel, the Epistles of Paul, and the Book of Acts'. That is, instead of the four separate Gospels the *Diatesseron* was used, and the Catholic Epistles and the Book of Revelation were lacking.[18]

The *Diatesseron* remained in widespread use through the following centuries, being quoted by Aphraat, Ephraem (who wrote a commentary on it), and other Syrian Fathers. Because of Tatian's reputation as a heretic, however, a reaction set in against the use of his *Diatesseron*, and Bishop Rabbula of Edessa (d. 436) instructed his priests to take care that in all the churches the four 'separated' Gospels should be available and read. In another diocese Theodoret, who, as was mentioned earlier, became bishop of Cyrrhus on the Euphrates in Upper Syria in 423, sought out and found more than two hundred copies of the *Diatesseron*, which, he says, 'I collected and put away, and introduced instead of them the Gospels of the four evangelists' (*Treatise on Heresies*, i. 20).

---

[17] 'Syriac Versions', Hastings's *Dictionary of the Bible*, iv (1902), p. 645.

[18] On the canon among the Syrians, see Theodor Zahn, 'Das Neue Testament Theodors von Mopsuestia und der ursprüngliche Kanon der Syrer', *Neue kirchliche Zeitschrift*, xi (1900), pp. 788–806; Julius A. Bewer, 'The History of the New Testament Canon in the Syrian Church', *American Journal of Theology*, iv (1900), pp. 64–98, 345–63; Walter Bauer, *Der Apostolos der Syrer in der Zeit von der Mitte des vierten Jahrhunderts bis zur Spaltung der syrischen Kirche* (Giessen, 1903); Mauricius Gordillo, *Theologia orientalium cum latinorum comparata* (*Orientalia christiana analecta*, clviii; Rome, 1960); E. B. Eising, 'Zur Geschichte des Kanons der Heiligen Schrift in der ostsyrischen Kirche im ersten Jahrtausend', Diss., Würtzburg, 1972; and Metzger, *The Early Versions of the New Testament*, pp. 4–75.

As for the Pauline corpus, in the third and fourth centuries the national Syrian Church did not receive the Epistle to Philemon. On the other hand, Ephraem knew and accepted as authentic the apocryphal 'Third Epistle of Paul to the Corinthians' (see chap. VII. III. 2 above). This correspondence, which formed part of the composite *Acts of Paul*, was written in Greek about the year 170, and was introduced into Syriac during the course of the third century. In the following century Aphraat (*c.* A.D. 340) and Ephraem (d. 373) cited 3 Corinthians as Scripture, and the latter dealt with it in his commentary on the Pauline Epistles (he omitted, however, Philemon).

By the beginning of the fifth century, if not indeed slightly earlier, the Syrian Church's version of the Bible, the so-called Peshitta, was formed. This represents for the New Testament an accommodation of the canon of the Syrians with that of the Greeks. Third Corinthians was rejected, and, in addition to the fourteen Pauline Epistles (including Hebrews, following Philemon), the three longer Catholic Epistles (James, 1 Peter, and 1 John) were included. The four shorter Catholic Epistles (2 Peter, 2 and 3 John, and Jude) and the Apocalypse are absent from the Peshitta Syriac version, and thus the Syrian canon of the New Testament contained but twenty-two writings. For a large part of the Syrian Church this constituted the closing of the canon, for after the Council of Ephesus (A.D. 431) the East Syrians separated themselves as Nestorians from the Great Church.

Among the Monophysite Syrians of the West, however, there were closer ties with their neighbouring Churches, and a further accommodation took place in the following century. In A.D. 508 Philoxenus, bishop of Mabbûg in eastern Syria, commissioned Polycarp, his chorepiscopus, to revise the Peshitta version in accordance with Greek manuscripts. This concern for a more exact translation than the current Peshitta rendering no doubt accounts for the inclusion (seemingly for the first time in Syriac) of the four smaller Catholic Epistles as well as the Book of Revelation. Since the Philoxenian version was made and sponsored by Jacobite ecclesiastics, it was accepted only by the Monophysite branch of Syriac-speaking Christendom. Yet, even so, the West Syrian Church was slow in making use of these parts of the New Testament, and the Nestorians, as was mentioned earlier, continued to accept only the twenty-two books of the Peshitta version. Thus, about the middle of the sixth century the Nestorian theologian, Paulus, a distinguished teacher of Nisibis, at that time a centre of Eastern theological education,[19] stated in a series of lectures[20] delivered at Constantinople that the books of absolute authority were the four Gospels, Acts, fourteen Epistles of Paul, 1 Peter, and 1 John. Of less authority, he declared, were James, 2 Peter, Jude, 2 and 3 John, and the Apocalypse. About A.D. 850 Isho'dad of Merv, bishop of Ḥadatha on the Tigris, wrote a commentary[21] on twenty-two books of the New Testament in which he mentions that the three larger Catholic Epistles are disputed. The last major theologian of this church was Ebedjesu, metropolitan of Nisibis and Armenia (d. 1318). Among his many writings is a list of the twenty-two books of the New Testament in the following sequence: the four Gospels, Acts, James, 1 Peter, 1 John, fourteen Epistles of Paul, concluding with Hebrews.[22]

Still today the official lectionary followed by the Syrian Orthodox Church, with headquarters at Kottayam (Kerala), and the Chaldean Syrian Church, also known as the Church of the East (Nestorian), with headquarters at Trichur (Kerala), presents lessons from only the twenty-two books of the Peshitta, the version to which appeal is made for the settlement of doctrinal questions. There are, however, some clergy who occasionally preach sermons on texts from the five non-canonical books, copies of which are, of course, available in New Testaments issued by Bible Societies in the vernacular languages of India.

Still other divergences from the Syriac canon, whether among West Syrians or among the Nestorians, are found in the following documents.

  (*a*) All seven Catholic Epistles and the Apocalypse are

---

[19] See A. Vööbus, *History of the School of Nisibis* (Louvain, 1965), and A. van Selms, *Nisibis: The Oldest University*. The Eighth T. B. Davie Memorial Lecture Delivered in the University of Cape Town on 6 Oct. 1966.

[20] A copy of the Greek text of the lectures came into the hands of Junilius Africanus, a high legal official in the court of Justinian, who made a translation into Latin, under the title *Instituta regularia divinae legis*, for the benefit of a friend of his, the African bishop Primasius; see Migne, *Patrologia Latina*, lxviii, cols. 15–42, and Heinrich Kihn, *Theodor von Mopsuestia und Junilius Africanus als Exegeten* (Freiburg im Br., 1880).

[21] Edited by M. D. Gibson (*Horae Semiticae*, vi–vii, x–xi; Cambridge, 1911–16).

[22] J. S. Assemani, *Bibliotheca Orientalis*, iii, pp. 8–12.

lacking in two similar lists, one in Syriac included in a ninth-century manuscript in the Monastery of St Catherine on Mount Sinai[23] and the other in an anonymous Arabic chronicle from the ninth or tenth century now in Berlin.[24] The Arabic list, to deal with this one first, presents the books of the Old Testament, followed by mention of 'the new books, namely, the Gospel, which is fourfold, each part going back to four of the disciples, namely Matthew, Mark, Luke, John. After the Gospel, the Book of "Action" (*fraksis*),[25] that is the Epistles of the disciples and writings of one of them to the others. And the Book of Paul, the Apostle.'

The list in the Syriac manuscript contains the books of the Old and New Testaments, with an indication of the number of stichoi for each. After the four Gospels the list continues with the 'Action' (*praksis*),[26] of the Apostles and the Pauline Epistles in the order Galatians, 1 and 2 Corinthians, Romans, Hebrews, Colossians, Ephesians, Philippians, Philippians (again!),[27] 1 and 2 Thessalonians, 2 Timothy, Titus, Philemon (this is the order in which Ephraem commented upon them). Likewise, the order of the first four is the order in which they stood in Marcion's canon. No doubt the omission of 1 Timothy is somehow connected with the mention of Philippians twice (with differing numbers of stichoi).

---

[23] Cf. *Catalogue of the Syriac MSS. in the Convent of S. Catherine on Mount Sinai*, compiled by Agnes S. Lewis (*Studia Semitica*, no. 1; London, 1894), pp. 11–14. The list is immediately preceded by a catalogue of the names of the seventy disciples, which is ascribed to Irenaeus (for similar catalogues, see Metzger, 'Names for the Nameless in the New Testament', *Kyriakon; Festschrift Johannes Quasten*, ed. by Patrick Granfield and J. A. Jungmann, i [Münster i. W., 1970], pp. 79–99).

[24] Gustav Rothstein, 'Der Kanon der biblischen Bücher bei den babylonischen Nestorianern im 9./10. Jahrhundert', *Zeitschrift der deutschen morgenländischen Gesellschaft*, lviii (1904), pp. 634–63. Another witness to Nestorian usage is 'Abd al-Mesīch al-Kindī (*c.* A.D. 821), who identifies as canonical Matthew, Mark ('son of the sister of Simon known as Peter'), Luke, John ('two are of the Twelve apostles, two are of the Seventy disciples'), Acts, and fourteen epistles of Paul (see L. Rost, 'Zur Geschichte des Kanons bei den Nestorianern', *Zeitschrift für neutestamentliche Wissenschaft*, xxvii [1927], pp. 103–6.

[25] The Assyrians regularly take πράξεις as singular (πρᾶξις).

[26] See preceding footnote.

[27] Zahn attempted to interpret the second instance of Philippians as somehow pointing to the presence originally in the list of 3 Corinthians (*Neue kirchliche Zeitschrift*, xi [1900], pp. 795, 799 f.), but the fact that the first mention of Philippians is assigned the same number of stichoi as is Ephesians, immediately preceding, seems to be proof of parablepsis resulting in dittography.

(*b*) The famous Nestorian monument erected A.D. 781 at Hsian-fu, China, preserves an extensive inscription in Chinese and a shorter one in Syriac. The former says of Christ: 'After his great works were completed, he ascended at midday to his true home. He left behind twenty-seven holy books [or, twenty-seven holy books were left behind].' It is disputed whether this refers to the books of the New Testament or to other Christian documents.[28] In a thorough study of the scattered and fragmentary data bearing on the coming of Christianity to China in the sixth century, Bugge[29] concludes that the mention of the twenty-seven holy books is not a reference to an actual collection of this number of books available in China, but rather that someone within the Syrian Church in China had indirect knowledge that the Church in other places had twenty-seven books, and so he mentions this number in the inscription both to show how many sacred books there were, and to indicate relationship with the Church in the West.[30]

(*c*) As late as A.D. 1170 the scribe Sâhdâ of the Monastery of Mâr Ṣalîbâ in Edessa wrote a copy of the Harclean Syriac New Testament (now in Cambridge University Library, Add. MS 1700) that contains 1 and 2 Clement, not at the end of the New Testament as in the fifth-century Greek codex Alexandrinus, but within the body of the manuscript, between Jude and Romans. The manuscript presents the books as follows: (1) the four Gospels, followed by a history of the Passion compiled from the four Evangelists; (2) the Acts and the seven Catholic Epistles, followed by the two Epistles of Clement to the Corinthians; and (3) the Pauline Epistles, including Hebrews, which stands last (the Book of Revelation is lacking). That the scribe must have considered 1 and 2 Clement as canonical is indicated by his dividing the text of these two epistles into pericopes numbered consecutively with those of the preceding books of the second section. It has been noted that 1 and 2

---

[28] For literature on the monument see Metzger in *Twentieth Century Encyclopedia of Religious Knowledge*, i (1955), p. 206, and *The Early Versions of the New Testament*, pp. 257 n. 1, and 275 n. 5.

[29] Sten Bugge, 'Den syriske kirkes nytestamentlige kanon i China', *Norsk teologisk tidsskrift*, xli (1940), pp. 97–118.

[30] Ibid., p. 118.

Clement were translated by a different translator from the one who produced the Harclean version.[31]

2. THE ARMENIAN CHURCH

Armenia claims the honour of being the first kingdom to accept Christianity as its official religion.[32] According to Eusebius (*Hist. eccl.* vi. xlvi. 2), the church was already established there by the middle of the third century, for he reports that Dionysius, the venerable bishop of Alexandria (d. *c.* 264), wrote an epistle on the theme of repentance 'to the brethren in Armenia, whose bishop was Meruzanes'.

At an early stage Tatian's *Diatesseron* was translated from Syriac into Armenian, and traces of its influence have been found in the writings of Agathangelos, Eznik, and other Armenian authors. According to Vööbus, however, there is no evidence that the *Diatesseron* was officially countenanced by such ecclesiastical authorities as Mesrop and Sahak. He concludes, therefore, that the Armenian text of the Gospels in official use from the beginning was based on the Old Syriac texts of the separated Gospels.[33] The Armenian Church also derived from the Syrian Bible the apocryphal Third Epistle of Paul to the Corinthians, which still stands in an appendix at the close of the New Testament in Zohrab's edition of the Armenian Bible (Venice, 1805). By the fifth century at the latest, the Armenians had a translation of the Book of Revelation, not, however, as a component of the New Testament, but as part of the apocryphal *Acts of John*. It was only at the close of the twelfth century that the celebrated Nerses of Lampron, Archbishop of Tarsus (d. 1198), had a new Armenian translation of Revelation prepared, and later arranged that a synod of the Armenian Church held at Constantinople should receive

---

[31] According to William Wright, who describes the manuscript in his *Catalogue of the Syriac Manuscripts Preserved in the Library of the University of Cambridge* (i, pp. 6–16), the translation of the two epistles of Clement 'appears to belong to the seventh century and may be assigned to the school of Athanasius of Balad and Jacob of Edessa'. For an estimate of its value, see J. B. Lightfoot, *The Apostolic Fathers*, Part I, *S. Clement of Rome*, 2nd ed., i (London, 1890; reprinted, Grand Rapids, 1973), pp. 129–36.

[32] For a brief account of the introduction of Christianity into Armenia and a discussion of the question whether the Scriptures were first translated into Armenian from Greek or from Syriac, see Metzger, *The Early Versions of the New Testament*, pp. 153–71.

[33] Arthur Vööbus, 'La première traduction arménienne des évangiles', *Recherches de science religieuse*, xxxvii (1950), pp. 581–6, and idem, *Early Versions of the New Testament* (Stockholm, 1954), pp. 152–4.

this book as holy Scripture in the New Testament.[34] During
the following century Mechitar of Aïrivank (*c.* 1290) included
in his *Chronicle* a list of apocryphal books of the Old and New
Testaments, several of which he thought ought to be included
in the canon; e.g. the *Advice of the Mother of God to the Apostles*,
the *Books of Criapos*, and the *Epistle of Barnabas*.[35]

3. THE GEORGIAN CHURCH

The country known in antiquity as Iberia appears to have
received Christianity by about the middle of the fourth
century.[36] After the invention of the Georgian alphabet the
Gospels and other parts of the New Testament were translated
before the middle of the fifth century. Whether the version was
made from the Greek directly or from the Armenian is
debated; in any case, the Book of Revelation had to wait until
the tenth century to be translated into Georgian.[37] The
translator was St Euthymius, who, in addition to translating
hagiographical and homiletic works, turned his attention to
revising and completing the Georgian New Testament. His
work on the Book of Revelation must have been completed
sometime before A.D. 987, which is the date of the earliest known
Georgian manuscript of the Apocalypse.

4. THE COPTIC CHURCH

The origins of the Church in Egypt are enveloped in deep
obscurity.[38] For the period before the beginning of the lengthy
episcopate of Bishop Demetrius of Alexandria (A.D. 188/9–231),
about whom Eusebius provides not a little information, we
look in vain for specific data concerning the spread of Christianity along the Nile. The earliest Christians, it appears, used
Greek, but soon the new faith found adherents among those
who knew only Coptic, the descendant of the ancient Egyptian
language. Among both groups alike there circulated not only

[34] See Josef Schmid, *Studien zur Geschichte des griechischen Apokalypse-Textes;* i,
Einleitung (Munich, 1956), pp. 99–113.
[35] See Theodore Zahn, 'Über einige armenische Verzeichnisse kanonischer und
apokrypher Bücher', *Forschungen zur Geschichte des neutestamentlichen Kanons*, vol. v, part i
(Erlangen and Leipzig, 1893), pp. 109–57.
[36] See Metzger, *The Early Versions of the New Testament*, pp. 190–4.
[37] According to Robert P. Blake, the Apocalypse, 'strictly speaking, never became
canonical among the Georgians' (*Harvard Theological Review*, xxi [1928], p. 287).
[38] See Metzger, *The Early Versions of the New Testament*, pp. 99–108.

copies of the New Testament books but also numerous apocryphal gospels, acts, epistles, and apocalypses.

Athanasius issued his Thirty-Ninth Festal Epistle not only in Greek but also in Coptic, in a slightly different form— though the list of twenty-seven books of the New Testament is the same in both languages. How far, however, the list remained authoritative for the Copts is problematical. The Coptic (Bohairic) translation of the collection known as the Eighty-Five Apostolic Canons[39] concludes with a different sequence of the books of the New Testament and is enlarged by the addition of two others: the four Gospels; the Acts of the Apostles; the fourteen Epistles of Paul (not mentioned individually); two Epistles of Peter, three of John, one of James, one of Jude; the Apocalypse of John; the two Epistles of Clement. The word 'Clement' is followed in the Coptic text by the clause *etetneoshou hi bol*, the significance of which has puzzled scholars. Tattam translated the words 'which you shall read out of',[40] a rendering characterized by Lightfoot as 'surely wrong'; he translates 'which ye shall read aloud'.[41] Perhaps it is better, with Guidi, to translate 'from which you are to read, outside',[42] and to understand that the two Epistles of Clement, though outside the canon, may nevertheless be read. Furthermore, manuscripts of the Arabic version (probably made in Egypt) of the Eighty-Fifth Apostolic Canon differ with respect to the list of canonical Scriptures. Three, dating from the thirteenth and fourteenth centuries, make no mention of the Epistles of Clement (omitting, of course, the puzzling clause as well). In other manuscripts, following the mention of 'the Apocalypse, vision of John', the list concludes with 'the two Epistles of Clement in one book'.[43]

5. THE ETHIOPIAN (OR ABYSSINIAN) CHURCH

The time and circumstances of the planting of the Church in Ethiopia are difficult to ascertain. Conflicting traditions assign

---

[39] Ignazio Guidi, 'Il canone biblico della chiesa copta', *Revue biblique*, x (1901), pp. 161–74.

[40] Henry Tattam, *The Apostolical Constitutions or Canons of the Apostles in Coptic* (London, 1848), p. 211. Tattam provides the text in the Bohairic version; essentially the same text is presented by the Sahidic version, edited by Paul de Lagarde in his *Aegyptica* (Göttingen, 1883), p. 236. See Appendix IV. 9 below.

[41] Lightfoot, op. cit., p. 372 n. 1.   [42] Guidi, op. cit., p. 162.

[43] Ibid., pp. 163–70.

the evangelization of the countryside to several different apostles and other evangelists.[44] In any case, when the Church in that country emerges in a more or less clear light, we find that, like the West Syrian and Coptic branches, it too was regarded as Monophysite. Since the Ethiopian Church was under the jurisdiction (until 1959) of the Abuna, or head, of the Coptic Church, it is not surprising that its canon of Scripture should parallel in some respects that of the Coptic Church.[45] At the same time, however, one encounters difficulties in attempting to draw up a list of books considered to be canonical Scripture. Although the number of canonical books of the Old and New Testaments is ordinarily reckoned to be eighty-one, this number is reached in different ways.[46] These differences are reflected among the Biblical manuscripts, none of which contains more than part of the New Testament. In addition to problems such as these, the modern investigator is confronted with a certain amount of overlapping of materials among the books that supplement the usual twenty-seven books of the New Testament, with a consequent confusion of identification.

According to the wide-ranging researches of Cowley on the Bible in classical Ethiopic (Ge'ez) and on patristic and modern commentaries in vernacular Amharic,[47] the 'broader canon' of the Ethiopic New Testament are the following thirty-five books:

---

[44] See Metzger, *The Early Versions*, pp. 215–23.

[45] See Anton Baumstark, 'Der äthiopische Bibelkanon', *Oriens Christianus*, v (1905), pp. 162–73; Marius Chaine, 'Le canon des livres saints dans l'église éthiopienne', *Recherches de science religieuse*, v (1914), pp. 22–39; J. M. Harden, *Introduction to Christian Ethiopic Literature* (London, 1926), pp. 37–50; and Kurt Wendt, 'Der Kampf um der Kanon Heiliges Schrift in der äthiopischen Kirche der Reformen des XV. Jahrhunderts', *Journal of Semitic Studies*, ix (1964), pp. 107–13.

[46] According to Cowley (see the following footnote), the 'broader canon', based on the traditional Amharic commentary on the Ge'ez text of the Canon Law (*Fetha Nagast*), comprises 46 Old Testament books and 35 New Testament books. What Cowley calls the 'narrower canon' comprises the familiar 27 New Testament books with 54 Old Testament books (including Enoch, Jubilees, etc.).

[47] Robert W. Cowley, 'The Biblical Canon of the Ethiopian Orthodox Church Today', *Ostkirchliche Studien*, xxiii (1974), pp. 318–23, and *The Traditional Interpretation of the Apocalypse of St. John in the Ethiopian Orthodox Church* (Cambridge, 1983), pp. 10–12. In the latter work Cowley identifies printed and manuscript sources of the Amharic commentaries on the several books of the Ethiopic Bible. For a thorough analysis of the relation of the present Ethiopic canon to earlier forms of the canon (chiefly Old Testament), see Roger T. Beckwith, *The Old Testament Canon of the New Testament Church*, pp. 478–505.

The four Gospels
Acts
The (seven) Catholic Epistles
The (fourteen) Epistles of Paul
The Book of Revelation
Sinodos (four sections)
Clement
The Book of the Covenant (two sections)
Didascalia

The contents of the last four titles in the list are as follows.[48] The *Sinodos* (Σύνοδος)[49] is a book of church order, comprising an extensive collection of canons, prayers, and instructions attributed to Clement of Rome.

Clement (*Qälēmenṭos*) is a book in seven parts,[50] communicated by Peter to Clement. It is not the Roman or Corinthian correspondence, nor one of the three parts of the Sinodos that are sometimes called 1, 2, and 3 Clement, nor part of the Syriac Octateuch of Clement.[51]

The Book of the Covenant (*Mäṣhafä kidan*) is counted as two parts. The first part of sixty sections comprises chiefly material on church order; section 61 is a discourse of the Lord to his disciples after his resurrection, similar to the *Testamentum Domini.*[52]

---

[48] For descriptions of the 'broader' Ethiopian canon of Scripture, see Ernst Hammerschmidt, 'Das pseudo-apostolische Schriftum in äthiopischer Überlieferung', *Journal of Semitic Studies*, ix (1964), pp. 114–21, and Sean P. Kealy, 'The Canon: An African Contribution', *Biblical Theology Bulletin*, ix (1979), pp. 13–26. A much more expanded list of holy books is given in *The Ethiopian Orthodox Church*, ed. by A. Wondmagegneliu (Addis Ababa, 1970), pp. 77 ff. (not available to me but quoted by Kealy, op. cit., p. 20).

[49] For the detailed contents of several manuscripts of the *Sinodos*, see William Wright, *Catalogue of the Ethiopic Manuscripts in the British Museum* (London, 1877), pp. 2a–4b and 266a–269a, and William Macomber, *Catalogue of Ethiopian Manuscript...*, iii (Collegeville, 1978), items #951 and #998. See also Ignazio Guidi, 'Der äthiopische "Sēnodos"', *Zeitschrift der deutschen morgenländischen Gesellschaft*, lv (1901), pp. 495–502.

[50] Translated into French by Sylvain Grébaut, 'Littérature éthiopienne pseudo-Clémentine', *Revue de l'orient chrétien*, xvi (1911), pp. 72–84, 167–75, 225–33; xvii (1912), pp. 16–31, 133–44, 244–52, 337–46; xviii (1913), pp. 69–78; xix (1914), pp. 324–30; xx (1915–17), pp. 33–7, 424–30; xxi (1918), pp. 246–52; xxii (1920), pp. 22–8, 113–17, 395–400; xxvi (1927–8), pp. 22–31.

[51] See R. W. Cowley, 'The Identification of the Ethiopian Octateuch of Clement, and its Relation to Other Christian Literature', *Ostkirchliche Studien*, xxvii (1978), pp. 37–45.

[52] Part Two (text and French translation) has been published by L. Guerrier and S. Grébaut, *Le Testament en Galilée de Notre-Seigneur Jésus-Christ (Patrologia Orientalis, ix. 3; Paris, 1913).*

The Ethiopian Didascalia (*Didesqelya*) is a book of church order in forty-three chapters, distinct from the *Didascalia Apostolorum*, but similar to books I–VII of the so-called Apostolic Constitutions.[53]

---

[53] The incomplete text and English translation were published by T. P. Platt in *The Ethiopic Didascalia; or, the Ethiopic Version of the Apostolical Constitutions, received in the Church of Abyssinia* (London, 1834). A complete English translation was made by J. M. Harden, *The Ethiopic Didascalia* (*Translations of Christian Literature*; Series IV, *Oriental Texts*; London, 1920).

X

Attempts at Closing the Canon in the West

THE Latin Church had, in general, a stronger feeling than the Greek for the necessity of making a sharp delineation with regard to the canon. It was less conscious than the Greek Church of the gradation of spiritual quality among the books that it accepted, and therefore was more often disposed to assert that the books which it rejected possessed no spiritual quality whatever. In the search for the highest authority it showed a far more lively feeling for an uncompromising Yea or Nay; a classification such as that of Origen, or still more that of Eusebius, was consequently quite unheard of.

I. FROM DIOCLETIAN TO THE END OF ANTIQUITY

At the opening of the fourth century the persecution instituted by Diocletian (303) gave a new impetus to the demarcation of sacred books. His first edict was to the effect that all church buildings should be levelled to the ground and the Scriptures destroyed by fire (Eusebius, *Hist. eccl.* VIII. ii. 4). The phrase officially used to describe the latter seems to have been 'The Writings of the Law' (*scripturae legis*), which implies a fairly definite collection. But the fact that some writings which were read here and there in Church did not possess the same status as the bulk of the collection made it possible for some Christians to surrender certain books to the Roman officials, which seemed to satisfy their demands. Other believers, however, regarded this as a traitorous subterfuge, and the violent opposition of the strict party to those whom they considered 'traditores' developed into the long-drawn-out Donatist controversy. A side-effect of persecution is seen in the circumstance that now we begin to meet more frequently with lists of sacred books.

Two lists in Latin of Old and New Testament books may be considered at this point, though their date and provenance are uncertain. In the sixth-century bilingual manuscript of the Epistles of Paul, known as codex Claromontanus (MS D), someone inserted the text of an older list of the Biblical books after the Epistle to Philemon and before the Epistle to the Hebrews (see Appendix IV. 4 below). In addition to giving the names of the Old and New Testament books, the unknown compiler supplied stichometric information—that is, he mentions the number of lines or stichoi in each of the writings, as measured by the standard stichos (containing fifteen or sixteen syllables).

This list presents several peculiarities. The order of the Gospels is Matthew, John, Mark, and Luke. These are followed by the Epistles of Paul in an unusual sequence: Romans, 1 and 2 Corinthians, Galatians, Ephesians, 1 and 2 Timothy, Titus, Colossians, and Philemon. The absence of Philippians, 1 and 2 Thessalonians, and Hebrews is probably to be accounted for by an error of the scribe (or translator?) whose eye may have jumped from Ἐφεσίους to Ἑβραίους. That the scribe was not very attentive is shown by his continuing the list with the two Epistles *to* Peter, followed then by James, 1, 2, and 3 John, and Jude. The list closes with the *Epistle of Barnabas*, the Revelation of John, the Acts of the Apostles, the *Shepherd*, the *Acts of Paul*, and the *Apocalypse of Peter*. It is significant that four of the titles in the list have a short horizontal line extending into the left-hand margin; these lines mark *Barnabas*, the *Shepherd*, the *Acts of Paul*, and the *Apocalypse of Peter*. Very likely the purpose of the lines was to distinguish these titles from those the scribe regarded as authoritative.

According to Zahn and Harnack, the original Greek form of this canon was drafted at Alexandria or in its neighbourhood about A.D. 300, for in the development of the canon it stands midway between Clement of Alexandria and Origen on the one side and Eusebius and Athanasius on the other.[1] It is testimony to the influence from the East that was then making its way into the West.[2]

---

[1] Theodor Zahn, *Geschichte des neutestamentlichen Kanons*, ii (Erlangen and Leipzig, 1890), pp. 157–72, and A. Harnack, *Chronologie der altchristlichen Literatur*, ii (Leipzig, 1904), pp. 84 ff. This opinion was adopted also by Leipoldt, *Geschichte des neutestamentlichen Kanons*, i (Leipzig, 1907; reprinted 1974), p. 77 n. 4.

[2] See H. J. Frede, *Altlateinische Paulus-Handschriften* (Freiburg, 1964), pp. 88–90, who draws attention to the Greek influence upon the Church in southern Italy.

Another Latin list of Biblical books, probably originating in North Africa soon after the middle of the fourth century (*c.* 360), is of interest in testifying to a conflict of opinion, some moving toward a wider canon than in the previous century, while more conservative minds refused (see Appendix IV. 6 below). This list, discovered by the German classical scholar Theodor Mommsen, is included in a tenth-century manuscript belonging to the Phillipps Collection at Cheltenham, England.[3] Like the previously mentioned list, this too is provided with notations giving the length of each book in terms of the number of stichoi.[4]

The order of the Gospels as well as of some of the other books is unusual. The Gospels stand in the sequence Matthew, Mark, John, and Luke,[5] and they are followed by the mention of thirteen Epistles of Paul, the Acts of the Apostles, and the Apocalypse. The list closes with the enigmatic lines:

Three Epistles of John [containing] 350 lines
one only
Two Epistles of Peter [containing] 300 lines
one only

What does 'one only'[6] mean? Harnack's suggestion,[7] adopted by Jülicher,[8] is exceedingly improbable—that the second line refers to the Epistle of James, and the fourth line to the Epistle of Jude. This would be a most unusual way in which to bring the scriptural character of James and Jude to the attention of the reader.

The words look like the expression of two opinions in the list. The writer appears to have been of reactionary opinions, for he omits Hebrews and Jude as well as James. As to the notation of

[3] Th. Mommsen, 'Zur lateinischen Stichometrie', *Hermes*, xxi (1886), pp. 142–56; cf. also W. Sanday, 'The Cheltenham List of the Canonical Books of the Old and New Testament and the Writings of Cyprian', *Studia biblica et ecclesiastica*, iii (1891), pp. 217–303.

[4] Subsequently a copy of the same canon was found inserted in a ninth-century codex in the library at St Gall (no. 133); it is published in *Miscellanea Cassinese* (Montecassino, 1897), pp. 6–7.

[5] This order is found also in the Curetonian Syriac Gospels and in the commentary of Theophilus of Antioch.

[6] The phrase 'one only' (*una sola*) occurs in only one of the two copies of the list; namely, the Cheltenham list.

[7] *Theologische Literaturzeitung*, 1886, col. 173.

[8] Adolf Jülicher, *An Introduction to the New Testament* (London, 1904), p. 538.

the Johannine and Petrine Epistles, the explanation is probably as follows. The writer copied the first and third lines from some earlier list, but he himself thought that only 1 John and 1 Peter were Scripture, and therefore added in each case 'one only'. Why did he then write 'Three Epistles of John' and 'Two Epistles of Peter'? Why did he not simply write 'One Epistle' in each instance? The reason lay in the number of stichoi lines, binding 1, 2, and 3 John together as a unit, and 1 and 2 Peter as a unit. Since he could not tell precisely how many stichoi were to be subtracted if he omitted 2 and 3 John and 2 Peter, he was, so to speak, forced to copy lines 1 and 3 each as a unit. But by adding the words 'one only' he was able to express his own opinion that the shorter Epistles were not to be reckoned as canonical.

Turning now to individual authors in the golden age of Latin Christian literature, our object will be to summarize the attitude of leading writers towards books which are absent from the canon of Cyprian, and are now in our New Testament. The books absent from the Cyprianic canon (see chap. VI. III. 3 above) are (Philemon),[9] Hebrews, James, 2 Peter, 2 and 3 John, and Jude. Perhaps it is worth mentioning that no book accepted by Cyprian was rejected by Western Fathers in subsequent ages.

Hilary, bishop of Poitiers (d. 368), often called the 'Athanasius of the West', forms a link between the East and the West. By his defence of the cause of orthodoxy in the Arian disputes at the Council of Seleucia (359), he came to be regarded as the leading and most respected Latin theologian of his age. In the prologue to his *Commentary on the Psalms* (chap. 15) Hilary gives a list of the books of the Old Testament (taken directly from Origen), but does not provide a similar list of New Testament works. He assigns the Epistle to the Hebrews to Paul, contrary to the general usage of other Latin authors, and cites it as Scripture (*de Trinit.* iv. 11). He also cites as Scripture the Epistle of James (iv. 8), being the earliest writer in the West to do so.

Lucifer of Calaris (Cagliari) in Sardinia (d. 370 or 371), a hyperorthodox and fiercely anti-Arian theologian, quotes from

---

[9] The absence of Philemon is undoubtedly accidental, arising from the brevity of the epistle and its special character.

most of the books of the New Testament, including Hebrews. In his treatise on heretics (chap. 15), he quotes nearly the whole Epistle of Jude, omitting only the passage borrowed from the Assumption of Moses (verse 9) and the citation from the Book of Enoch (verses 14–15).

Philaster (or, more correctly Filaster), bishop of Brescia (d. *c.* A.D. 397), composed between 385 and 391 a treatise of 156 chapters designed to refute 28 Jewish and 128 Christian heresies.[10] This work, entitled *Liber de haeresibus*, sweeps together an ill-digested assortment of comments compiled from Greek and Latin authors without much regard for logic or even internal consistency. As a sample of his confused and confusing compilation, in chap. 88 he names in the list of 'Scriptures' of the New Testament, authenticated by the blessed apostles and their followers, the Gospels, thirteen Epistles of Paul, and seven Catholic Epistles, passing over the Epistle to the Hebrews and even the Apocalypse in silence—but elsewhere he recognizes Hebrews as Pauline and the Apocalypse as apostolic.[11] At the same time, Philaster stands almost alone in his opinion (expressed in the same chapter) that, though apocryphal books like the Acts of Andrew, John, Peter, or Paul should not indeed be read by all believers (because heretics had added many things to the text of these books), they 'ought to be read by the "perfect" for moral edification' (*legi debent morum causa a perfectis*).

Tyrannius Rufinus was born about A.D. 345 in the small North Italian town of Concordia, at the head of the Adriatic, not far to the west of Aquileia. The son of Christian parents, he was sent as a youth to Rome to complete his education, and among his fellow students with whom he soon formed a deep friendship was another northerner of about the same age, Jerome, from Dalmatia. Later Rufinus studied for several years in Alexandria under Didymus the Blind. Though he was also an original writer, Rufinus is mainly important as a translator of Greek theological works into Latin at a time when the knowledge of Greek was declining in the West.

[10] Besides condemning such notable heretics as Simon Magus, Philaster also stigmatizes (chap. 133) those whose sole aberration was to believe that the stars occupied a fixed place in the sky instead of being set in position every evening by God!

[11] For an attempt to bring out some semblance of order in Philaster's comments on the canon, see Dionysius Portarena, *Doctrina scripturistica s. Filastrii* (Rome, 1946), pp. 14–21.

In his *Exposition of the Apostles' Creed* (chaps. 36–8) he gives a list of the canonical books of the Old and New Testaments, which reproduces nearly exactly that of Athanasius. After enumerating the books of the Old Testament, Rufinus lists those of the New: the four Gospels, the Acts of the Apostles, fourteen Epistles of Paul, two Epistles of Peter, one of James the brother of the Lord and the apostle, one of Jude, three of John, and the Apocalypse of John. Here it will be noted that the Catholic Epistles follow those of Paul (contrary to Athanasius and the usage of the Greek churches), and the Epistles of Peter stand first among the Catholic Epistles. The Johannine Epistles stand last (not Jude), so as to bring them side by side with the Apocalypse, creating a kind of *corpus Johanneum*.

Of particular interest is Rufinus' designation of a class of sacred books as 'ecclesiastical' along side of those that are 'canonical' (chap. 38). These include the *Shepherd* of Hermas, the book which is named *The Two Ways* (= the *Didache*), and *The Judgment of Peter*.[12] All these, he says, 'may be read in the churches, but appeal should not be made to them on points of faith'. Other writings designated 'apocryphal', he says, 'should not be read out in church'.[13]

Two men in the West call for special remark: one the leading Scripture scholar of the century, and the other because of his importance in the Church of his day and of the following centuries. These are Jerome and Augustine.

Born about the year 346 of Christian parents in Stridon of Dalmatia, Jerome went to Rome at the age of twelve and studied Greek, Latin, rhetoric, and philosophy under the celebrated Aelius Donatus. At the age of nineteen he was baptized. He journeyed to Gaul, and later to the East where he spent some time living as an ascetic in the desert near Chalcis. In 373, as one of the consequences of a severe illness, he determined to devote himself to the study of the Scriptures. Having been ordained a presbyter at Antioch in the year 379, he stayed for a time in Rome and later, from 386 to his death in 420, lived at Bethlehem. What concerns us most is his revision

---

[12] A work known as *The Judgment of Peter* is included among five apocryphal works ascribed to Peter by Jerome (*De viris ill.* 1). It has long since disappeared.

[13] See Meinrad Stenzel, 'Der Bibelkanon des Rufin von Aquileja', *Biblica*, xxiii (1942), pp. 43–61.

(the Vulgate) of the competing Latin translations of the New Testament, of which he delivered the Gospels to Pope Damasus in the year 384. Although it is debated how much of the rest of the New Testament he revised, and when he accomplished it,[14] Jerome's New Testament contained the books which we use, and, as it came more and more to be accepted as the chief Latin version, the books it contained became the generally accepted books of the Western Church.

In the works of Jerome there are several catalogues of the sacred books, one being complete and embracing the whole Bible. This is included in his *Epistle to Paulinus* (liii. 9), and is printed as a prologue in older editions of the Vulgate Bible. In regard to the New Testament, the dedication to Paulinus enumerates all our twenty-seven books, the Acts coming after Paul's Epistles.

Here and there in Jerome's writings we find occasional comments concerning the seven doubtful books. Speaking of James, 'who is called the brother of the Lord', he says: 'He wrote only one Epistle, which is reckoned among the seven Catholic Epistles, and even this is claimed by some to have been published by some one else under his name, and gradually, as time went on, to have gained in authority' (*De vir. ill.* 2). The Epistle of Jude, he says, is rejected by a great many because it appeals to the apocryphal *Book of Enoch*; 'Yet by age and use it has gained authority and is reckoned among the holy Scriptures' (ibid. 4).

In the case of 2 and 3 John Jerome reports that they 'are said to be the work of John the presbyter', for John the apostle was the author of the Epistle that begins, 'That which was from the beginning' (ibid. 9). As for 2 Peter, he has a special suggestion (*Epist.* 120): the difference in style between the two Epistles that are attributed to Peter arises from the apostle's having employed different amanuenses.

The remaining two disputed books, Hebrews and Revelation, are dealt with by Jerome in a letter, written in the year 414, to a patrician Claudienus Postumus Dardanus:

---

[14] For a survey of the several scholarly opinions on how much of the Latin Vulgate Bible is the result of Jerome's own work, see Metzger, *The Early Versions of the New Testament*, pp. 352–62.

The Epistle which is inscribed to the Hebrews is received not only by the Churches of the East, but also by all Church writers of the Greek language before our days, as of Paul the apostle, though many think that it is from Barnabas or Clement. And it makes no difference whose it is, since it is from a churchman, and is celebrated in the daily readings of the Churches. And if the usage of the Latins does not receive it among the canonical Scriptures, neither indeed by the same liberty do the Churches of the Greeks receive the Revelation of John. And yet we receive both, in that we follow by no means the habit of today, but the authority of ancient writers, who for the most part quote each of them, not as they are sometimes to do the apocrypha, and even also as they rarely use the examples of secular books, but as canonical and churchly (*Epist.* cxxix).

From this we can see that, contrary to his sometimes quarrel-some and irascible temperament, when it comes to the books of the New Testament, he is content to acquiesce to the list of those that were then in general use. The nearest approach to personal dissent seems to be his view of 2 and 3 John.

Oddly enough, Jerome shows a curious vacillation in regard to the *Epistle of Barnabas*. On the one hand, he acknowledges the authenticity of the Epistle as written by a companion of Paul and as being 'valuable for the edification of the Church'; yet it is reckoned among the apocryphal writings (*De vir. ill.* 6). On the other hand, Jerome shows that he considered Barnabas almost if not quite a New Testament book. In the year 388 he wrote a book *Concerning Hebrew Names* (in the Scriptures), giving their meaning, book by book. Every book of the New Testament comes into the list (except 2 John, which does not happen to contain any name); then at the end of the New Testament he gives thirteen names from the *Epistle of Barnabas*.

In a similar way Jerome shows his partiality for the *Shepherd* of Hermas, which, he says, 'is read publicly in some churches of Greece. It is in fact a useful book and many of the ancient writers quote from it as authority, but among the Latins it is almost unknown' (*De vir. ill.* 10).

With Augustine, whose influence upon the Western Church was even greater than that of Jerome, we come to a natural terminus in our survey of debate concerning the closing of the New Testament canon. Born at Tagaste in Numidia in 354 of a pagan father and a saintly mother, and following an undisciplined youth and a half-heathen early manhood, Augustine came under the influence of Bishop Ambrose of Milan, and on Easter eve, 387, was baptized. He returned to Africa an ardent Christian, and in 395 became coadjutor to Valerius, bishop of Hippo. From that time forward it may be said that Augustine's influence was pervasive in the whole African Church.

Augustine's treatise *De doctrina christiana* ('On Christian Learning' in four books) might well head his works on Biblical scholarship. The greater part of it (i. 1–iii. 24) was written in 396–7, but completed only in 426. In ii. 13 he gives our present list of New Testament books (but places James at the end of the Catholic Epistles, thus giving Peter the first place): the four Gospels, fourteen Epistles of Paul, 1 and 2 Peter, 1, 2, and 3 John, Jude, James, Acts, Apocalypse. Although he includes Hebrews in the list (following Philemon) as Paul's, in his later works when he quotes from it he assiduously avoids calling it by the Apostle's name.[15] But while he came to hesitate as to the authorship of the Epistle, he had no scruples as to its canonicity.

Before citing the list of Biblical books, Augustine exercises critical judgement, recognizing that some books are received on weightier authority than others. The Christian reader, he says,

will hold fast therefore to this measure in the canonical Scriptures, that he will prefer those that are received by all Catholic Churches to those which some of them do not receive. Among those, again, which are not received by all, let him prefer those which the more numerous and the weightier churches receive to those which fewer and less authoritative churches hold. But if, however, he finds some held by the more numerous, and some held by the churches of more authority (though this is not very likely to happen), I think that in such a case they ought to be regarded as of equal authority (*De doct. chr.* ii. 12).[16]

The great debate of so many generations was practically over. But it remained for some one to say that it was over. It

---

[15] Augustine's attitude towards Hebrews was first clearly traced by Dom Odilo Rottmanner of Munich. In his earliest writings (down to 406) Augustine cites the Epistle as Paul's; in the middle period he wavers between Pauline authorship and anonymity; in his old age (409–30) he refers to it always as anonymous. See Rottmanner's study in *Revue bénédictine*, xviii (1901), pp. 257 ff., reprinted in his *Geistesfrüchte aus der Klosterzelle* (Munich, 1908), pp. 84–90.

[16] Although Augustine's criteria seem at first sight to be clear-cut and straightforward, the practical difficulties of applying them to any given case are formidable; see C. R. Gregory, *Canon and Text of the New Testament* (New York, 1907), pp. 287–8.

was Augustine who, in three provincial synods, cast his weight for the twenty-seven books which we know as the Christian Scriptures. These synods were held, one of them in Hippo in A.D. 393, one in Carthage in 397, and the last of them again in Carthage in 419. The opening words of the statute on the canon are straightforward and forthright: 'Besides the canonical Scriptures, nothing shall be read in church under the name of the divine Scriptures'.[17] Then there follows an enumeration of the canonical Scriptures. The order of the New Testament books is Gospels, Acts, Pauline Epistles, 1 and 2 Peter, 1, 2, and 3 John, James, Jude, the Revelation of John. The only difference to be noted in the reiteration of the statute is that, in the synods of 393 and 397, the phrase runs, 'Thirteen Epistles of Paul, and the Epistle to the Hebrews, by the same', whereas the statute of 419 reads, 'Fourteen Epistles of Paul'. (See Appendix IV. 12 below.)

Twenty-seven books, no more, and no less, is henceforth the watchword throughout the Latin Church. Yet it would be a mistake to represent the question of the canon as finally settled in all Christian communities by the beginning of the fifth century. The manuscripts of the Epistles of Paul (and of entire Bibles as well) which did not include the Epistle to the Hebrews were not immediately enlarged, or rather replaced by complete copies, so as to enable the Epistle actually and everywhere to take the place that was officially recognized as its own. For example, the Greek and Latin codex Boernerianus (MS G) of the ninth century lacks Hebrews. On the other hand, manuscripts turn up containing the Epistle to the Laodiceans. Thus, despite the influence of Jerome and Augustine and the pronouncements of three provincial synods, more than once in the following centuries we come upon evidence of divergences in the canon, either by way of addition or subtraction. But an account of such variations belongs to the following section.

---

[17] This legislation, as Costello points out, did not forbid other books to be read in church; 'it simply prohibited them from being read under the title of divine Scripture. The reading of the Acts of the Martyrs on their anniversaries was expressly permitted. Moreover it was not unusual to find St. Augustine himself reading in church from the writings of Cyprian, and from ecclesiastical records, particularly in his many controversies'; see Charles J. Costello, *St. Augustine's Doctrine on the Inspiration and Canonicity of Scripture* (Washington, 1930), p. 48.

II. THE MIDDLE AGES, THE REFORMERS, AND THE COUNCIL OF TRENT

During the Middle Ages the Church in the West received the Latin New Testament in the form that Jerome had given to it, and the subject of the canon was seldom discussed. At the same time, however, we find a certain elasticity in the boundaries of the New Testament. This is shown by the presence of the Epistle of Paul to the Laodiceans in more than one hundred manuscripts of the Latin Vulgate (including the oldest, the celebrated codex Fuldensis, A.D. 546), as well as in manuscripts of early Albigensian, Bohemian, English, and Flemish versions.

Occasionally the subject emerges in discussions of the Pauline Epistles. At the close of the tenth century Aelfric, a monk in Dorset, wrote a treatise in Anglo-Saxon on the Old and New Testaments in which he states that the apostle Paul wrote fifteen Epistles.[18] In his enumeration of them he places Laodiceans after Philemon. About A.D. 1165 John of Salisbury, writing about the canon to Henry count of Champagne (*Epist.* 209), acknowledges that 'it is the common, indeed almost universal, opinion that there are only fourteen Epistles of Paul... But the fifteenth is that which is written to the church of the Laodiceans.'[19]

The Epistle to the Laodiceans is included in all eighteen German Bibles printed prior to Luther's translation, beginning with the first German Bible, issued by Johann Mental at Strassburg in 1488. In these the Pauline Epistles, with the Epistle to the Hebrews, immediately follow the Gospels, with Laodiceans standing between Galatians and Ephesians. In the first Czech (Bohemian) Bible, published at Prague in 1488 and reprinted several times in the sixteenth and seventeenth centuries, Laodiceans follows Colossians and precedes 1 Thessalonians.[20]

---

[18] *The Old English Version of the Heptateuch, Aelfric's Treatise on the Old and New Testament...*, ed. by S. J. Crawford (London, 1922), p. 57.

[19] *The Letters of John of Salisbury*; ii, *The Later Letters*, ed. by W. J. Millor and C. N. L. Brooke (Oxford, 1979), p. 323.

[20] Elias Hutter's polyglot New Testament in twelve languages (Nuremberg, 1599–1600) contains on four leaves inserted after p. 526 the Epistle to the Laodiceans in Greek, Syriac, Latin, German, and Bohemian.

Thus, as Bishop Lightfoot phrased it,[21] 'for more than nine centuries this forged epistle hovered about the doors of the sacred Canon, without either finding admission or being peremptorily excluded'. It was not until the Council of Florence (1439–43) that the See of Rome delivered for the first time a categorical opinion on the Scriptural canon. In consequence of the efforts made at this Council to bring about reunion with the Eastern Orthodox Church, which sought support from the West against the Turks, who were nearing Constantinople, Pope Eugenius IV published a bull setting forth the doctrines of the unity of the Old and New Testament, the inspiration of the Scriptures, and a statement of their extent. In the list of twenty-seven canonical books of the New Testament there are fourteen Pauline Epistles, that to the Hebrews being last, with the Book of Acts coming immediately before the Apocalypse. One observes that the Epistle to the Laodiceans is not even mentioned.

At the time of the Renaissance and the Reformation there was an awakening of earlier uncertainties concerning the authenticity of several books of the New Testament. Jacob Thomas de Vio (1469–1534), called Gaetano ('Cajetan') from his birthplace, Gaeta, produced a series of Biblical commentaries that contain much enlightened criticism of an unexpectedly 'modern' kind. In dealing with the antilegomena of the New Testament, he denied the Pauline origin of the Epistle to the Hebrews. He likewise expressed doubts concerning the apostolic authorship of the Epistles of James, of Jude, and the second and third of John. In the case of 2 Peter, however, he refused to be swayed by earlier doubts, and defended the Epistle's authenticity. We do not know what he thought of the Apocalypse, for he declined to deal with this book, confessing that he was unable to penetrate its mysteries.

Similar to the views of Cardinal Cajetan were the reservations expressed by the great humanist, Erasmus of Rotterdam (d. 1536). In the comments that he placed at the beginning of each of the New Testament books in his edition of the Greek Testament (Basle, 1516), he boldly denies that Paul wrote Hebrews and doubts that the Epistle of James was written by

---

[21] J. B. Lightfoot, *Saint Paul's Epistles to the Colossians and to Philemon*, 9th ed. (London, 1890), p. 297.

James the apostle. The traditional authorship of 2 Peter, 2 and 3 John, and Jude is freely questioned. As for the Book of Revelation, its style prevents one from attributing it to the author of the Fourth Gospel. In the course of time, however, Erasmus found that his outspokenness was unwelcome to the Church, and he became somewhat more reserved in expressing his views. Thus, in response to the censures imposed by the Theological Faculty in Paris, he declared: 'If the Church were to declare the titles they [the several New Testament books] bear to be as canonical as their contents, then I would condemn my doubts, for the opinion formulated by the Church has more value in my eyes than human reasons, whatever they may be'.[22]

Among the Reformers we find a certain openness in discussing the canon and reassessing the qualifications of the disputed books (antilegomena).[23] Andreas Bodenstein of Karlstadt (1480–1541), who is commonly known by the name of his native town, was originally a friend of Luther, but as the Reformation advanced the two were separated by theological differences. While he was still working with Luther as Archdeacon of Wittenberg, in 1520 he published a brief treatise on the question of the canon, *De canonicis libris libellus*,[24] which he followed next year with a popularization in German (*Welche Bücher heilig und biblisch seind*, Wittenberg, 1521). Repudiating conciliar pronouncements, he asserted the independent authority of holy Scripture. He divided the New Testament documents into three ranks of differing dignity, but all these are superior to any others. The first class contains the Gospels and Acts; the second, the undoubted Epistles of Paul, along with 1 Peter and 1 John; the third, the seven disputed books: James, 2 Peter, 2 and 3 John, Jude, Hebrews, and the Apocalypse. In his discussion of the disputed books Karlstadt

---

[22] Erasmus, *Declaratio ad censuram Fac. theol. Parisiensis* (*Opera* ix. 864).

[23] See Henry Howorth, 'The Origin and Authority of the Biblical Canon according to the Continental Reformers: Luther and Karlstadt', *Journal of Theological Studies*, viii (1906–7), pp. 321–65; idem, 'Luther, Zwingli, Lefevre, and Calvin', ix (1907–8), pp. 188–230; and R. A. Bohlmann, 'The Criteria of Biblical Canonicity in Sixteenth-Century Lutheran, Roman Catholic, and Reformed Theology', Ph.D. diss., Yale University, 1968.

[24] Karlstadt's volume was reprinted by K. A. Credner, *Zur Geschichte des Kanons* (Halle, 1847), pp. 316 ff.

declares that the authorship of James is not quite certain, that 2 and 3 John are not by the Evangelist, but by another John, the Presbyter; that Hebrews is not by Paul; and that there is really very little reason why the Apocalypse should be included in the canon. In the German résumé of his book, he adds the category of apocryphal writings of the New Testament, namely the ending of the Gospel according to Mark and the Epistle to the Laodiceans.[25]

Martin Luther's German translation of the New Testament was published in September of 1522, and was followed by a second edition in December in which adjustments were made in the style of the German rendering.[26] Luther's lower estimate of four books of the New Testament is disclosed in the Table of Contents, where the first twenty-three books from Matthew to 3 John are each assigned a number, whereas, after a blank space, the column of titles, without numbers, continues with Hebrews, James, Jude, and Revelation.[27] This sequence, which is without any support in manuscript evidence, is followed also in the text of the New Testament itself.

The Prefaces which Luther provided for the whole New Testament and for the individual books gave historical and theological information that would assist the reader in understanding the Scriptures. In a discussion entitled, 'Which are the true and noblest books of the New Testament', Luther distinguishes three types of New Testament books. The first type comprises those books '. . . that show you Christ and teach you all that is necessary and salvatory for you to know, even if you were never to see or hear any other book or doctrine'. Such books are John's Gospel and his First Epistle, Paul's Epistles,

[25] See Ronald J. Sider, *Andreas Bodenstein von Karlstadt; The Development of his Thought (1517–1525)* (Leiden, 1974), pp. 94–8.

[26] See R. Kuhrs, *Verhältnis der Decemberbibel zur Septemberbibel*, Kritischer Beitrag zur Geschichte der Bibelsprache M. Luthers (Greifswald, 1901).

[27] The first printed New Testament in English, translated by William Tyndale (1525), follows Luther's sequence of New Testament books and also incorporates his Prefaces. The order of books was continued in the Coverdale Bible (1535), as well as in its subsequent editions, the Nycolson Bible (1537), the Matthews or John Rogers Bible (1537), and the Tavener Bible (1539). The authorized Great Bible of 1539 reverted to the pre-Lutheran order. For information concerning the influence of Luther's New Testament on early Scandinavian and Low German Bibles, see Allen Wikgren, 'Luther and "New Testament Apocrypha"', *A Tribute to Arthur Vööbus; Studies in Early Christian Literature . . .*, ed. by Robert H. Fischer (Chicago, 1977), pp. 379–90.

especially Romans, Galatians, and Ephesians, and 1 Peter. The second group comprises the Synoptic Gospels, the other Pauline Epistles, Acts, 2 Peter, and 2 and 3 John. The third group consists of the four writings that Luther placed at the end of his translation: Hebrews, James, Jude, and Revelation.

In the Prefaces to these four writings he set forth reasons that had induced him to doubt their apostolic and canonical character. Thus, Hebrews, which comes from the second generation, teaches (contrary to Paul) that there can be no repentance for sinners after baptism; James, a 'right strawy epistle compared with the others',[28] contradicts Paul by teaching justification by works; Jude is dependent on 2 Peter and quotes apocryphal texts; and Revelation is full of visions that do not belong to the task of an apostolic writer— furthermore, this writer recommends his own book much too highly and does not show Christ clearly.[29] Somewhat inconsistently, however, in this context Luther also stresses that he does not wish to impose his opinion on others, nor does he want to remove these four writings from the New Testament.

Thus we see that, insisting on the central importance of faith as proclaimed by Paul, Luther judged that every book of the New Testament which inculcates or promotes (*treiben*, literally 'drives') Christ is apostolic, quite independent of its authorship: 'Whatever does not teach Christ is not apostolic, even though St. Peter or St. Paul does the teaching. Again, whatever preaches Christ would be apostolic, even if Judas, Annas, Pilate, and Herod were doing it.' That is to say, though here and there Luther makes historical judgements concerning the date and authorship of this or that book, relying on patristic testimony, his most basic criterion of canonicity is a theological evaluation.[30]

[28] This comment is not repeated in Luther's later editions of the New Testament.

[29] For a discussion of the validity of Luther's reasons in denying these four books the right to be included among 'the true and noblest books of the New Testament', see W. G. Kümmel, 'The Continuing Significance of Luther's Prefaces to the New Testament', *Concordia Theological Monthly*, xxxvii (1966), pp. 573–81.

[30] For modern evaluations of Luther's position, from the point of view of Reformed theology, see A. B. du Toit, op. cit., pp. 259–63, and N. B. Stonehouse; the latter comments: 'My basic criticism of his [Luther's] viewpoint is that it was narrowly Christocentric rather than God-centered, and thus involved an attenuation and impoverishment of the message of the New Testament. However significant *was Christum treibet* may be for the understanding of the New Testament, it lacks the

Following Luther's differentiation among New Testament books, several other Lutheran Reformers came to make similar estimates, and even sometimes to classify several New Testament books as 'deuterocanonical' or 'apocryphal'.[31] Johannes Oecolampadius (1482–1531), who in 1515 was appointed cathedral preacher in Basle, declared that the Reformers receive all twenty-seven books of the New Testament, but at the same time 'we do not compare (*conferamus*) the Apocalypse, along with the Epistles of James and Jude, and 2 Peter and the two later Epistles of John, with the rest [of the books]'.[32]

In the Württemberg Confession (1531) compiled by Johann Brentz, who had studied under Oecolampadius, Article XXVII declares: 'We call sacred Scripture those canonical books of the Old and New Testament of whose authority there has never been any doubt in the Church,'[33] Although Brentz does not propose to reject the antilegomena or disputed books absolutely, he asks by what right they should be put on the same level as the canonical Scriptures.[34]

A startling deviation among Lutheran editions of the Scrip-

breadth of perspective and outlook given by understanding it, for example, in terms of the coming of the kingdom of God. This essentially eschatological message, conceived in terms of realized and unrealized eschatology, prevents one from contemplating the New Testament narrowly and exclusively in terms of Christ and personal salvation' ('Luther and the New Testament Canon', *Paul Before the Areopagus, and Other New Testament Studies* [Grand Rapids, 1957], p. 196). In short, Luther was right in applying the criterion *was Christum treibet*, but wrong in not recognizing that the Epistle of James also 'promotes Christ' by its practical application of the Sermon on the Mount.

[31] Among Luther's disciples and successors who distinguished between canonical and apocryphal writings within the New Testament were Martin Chemnitz (d. 1586), Aegidius Hunnius (d. 1603), Leonhard Hutter (d. 1616), and Balthasar Mentzer (d. 1627); see Leipoldt, op. cit., ii, pp. 129–32; H. H. Howorth, 'The Canon of the Bible Among the Later Reformers', *Journal of Theological Studies*, x (1908–9), pp. 183–232; and J. A. O. Preus, 'The New Testament Canon in the Lutheran Dogmaticians', *The Springfielder*, xxv, no. 1 (Spring, 1961), pp. 8–33.

[32] *Epistolarum libri quattuor* (Basle, 1536), p. 31.

[33] *Confessio Virtembergica. Das württembergische Bekenntnis von 1551*, ed. Ernst Bizer (Stuttgart, 1952), p. 178.

[34] Brentz, *Apologia Confessionis Virtembergicae*; cf. K. Müller, *Bekenntnisschriften der reformierten Kirche* (Leipzig, 1903). That Brentz was not prepared to eject apocryphal books from the collection of canonical books is demonstrated by his edition of the Latin Bible published at Tübingen in 1564; this edition contains not only the books that are normally included in the Latin Vulgate Bible, but also has 3 Maccabees following 2 Maccabees; see Metzger, 'An Early Protestant Bible Containing the Third Book of Maccabees', *Text – Wort – Glaube, Studien zur Überlieferung, Interpretation und Autorisierung biblischer Texte; Kurt Aland gewidmet*, ed. by Martin Brecht (Berlin, 1980), pp. 123–33.

tures occurred in 1596 when Jacob Lucius published a Bible at Hamburg in which the four disputed books are given the title 'Apocrypha', followed by the explanation. 'That is, books that are not held equal to the other holy Scripture'. In the same year David Wolder, pastor of the Church of St Peter at Hamburg, published a triglot Bible in Greek, Latin (two versions), and German, the table of contents of which designates the four books as 'non canonical'. In 1614 Lucius' title and explanatory note reappear in a Bible issued at Goslar by J. Vogt. In Sweden the Gustavus Adolphus Bible (Stockholm, 1618), not only continues to separate the four dubious books at the end of the table of contents but also labels them with the caption *Apocr(yphal) New Testament.* Thus we have a threefold division of the New Testament: 'Gospels and Acts', 'Epistles and Holy Apostles', and 'Apocryphal New Testament'—an arrangement that persisted for nearly a century in half a dozen or more printings.[35]

In all the Bibles issued under the auspices of the Genevan Reformers and their followers, the New Testament books are presented in the traditional manner. It is the same with the official pronouncements of this school of Reformers.[36] According-ing to John Calvin's influential *Institutes of the Christian Religion*, the authority of the Scriptures is based, not on the pronouncement of the Church, but on the interior witness of the Holy Spirit (*testimonium Spiritus sancti internum*).[37] At the same time, however, Calvin applies philological tests as to authorship of various books, and, while recognizing the value of Hebrews, denies its Pauline authorship. The style of 2 Peter differs from that of 1 Peter and was therefore probably not written by the apostle himself, but at Peter's command by one of his disciples. Calvin says nothing specifically concerning 2 and 3 John and the Apocalypse, the only books of the New

---

[35] See Ake V. Ström's discussion of a newly-found printer's proof of the Gustavus Adolphus Bible, *Kyrkohistorisk Årsskrift*, liii (1953), pp. 142–7.

[36] For Zwingli's *ad hoc* denial of the Biblical character of the Book of Revelation, see p. 273 below.

[37] 'As to the question, how are we to know that the Scriptures come from God, if we cannot refer to the decree of the Church, we might as well ask how we are to learn to distinguish light from darkness, white from black, bitter from sweet. Scripture bears on the face of it as clear evidence of its truth, as white and black do of their colours, sweet and bitter of their taste' (*Institutes of the Christian Religion*, i. vii. 2).

Testament on which he did not write a commentary; at the same time, he occasionally makes quotations from them,[38] as he does also from several of the apocryphal books of the Old Testament.

The disrupting influences of opinions about the Scriptures expressed by such figures as Cardinal Cajetan and Erasmus, not to speak of German, Swiss, and French Reformers, prompted Pope Paul III to convene a council at Trent in order to consider what, if any, moral and administrative reforms needed to be made within the Roman Catholic Church. The Council, which held its first session on 13 December 1545, gave preliminary consideration to the subject of holy Scripture and Tradition on 12 February 1546. Considerable debate ensued on whether a distinction should be made between two classes of books (Canonical and Apocryphal) or whether three classes should be identified (Acknowledged Books; the Disputed Books of the New Testament, later generally received; and the Apocrypha of the Old Testament). Finally on 8 April 1546, by a vote of 24 to 15, with 16 abstentions, the Council issued a decree (*De Canonicis Scripturis*) in which, for the first time in the history of the Church, the question of the contents of the Bible was made an absolute article of faith and confirmed by an anathema. 'The holy ecumenical and general Council of Trent', so the decree runs, '... following the example of the orthodox Fathers receives and venerates all the books of the Old and New Testament ... and also the traditions pertaining to faith and conduct ... with an equal sense of devotion and reverence (*pari pietatis affectu ac reverentia*) ... If, however, anyone does not receive these books in their entirety, with all their parts,[39] as they are accustomed to be read in the Catholic Church and are contained in the ancient Latin Vulgate edition [i.e. Jerome's with the additions] as sacred and canonical, and

---

[38] See T. H. L. Parker, *Calvin's New Testament Commentaries* (London, 1971), pp. 69–78. For Luther's view of the Book of Revelation, see p. 243 above. In the area of hermeneutics, Luther and Calvin differed significantly. For Luther the Word is in the Bible; for Calvin the Word is the Bible. While Luther tended to view the Old Testament as law and the New Testament as gospel, Calvin stressed the similarity of Old and New Testaments (*Institutes*, II. x), regarding the differences merely as forms of presentation and not as substantial.

[39] The phrase *cum omnibus suis partibus* is intended to embrace certain doubtfully authentic deuterocanonical sections, such as Mark xvi. 9–20; Luke xxii. 19b–20, 43–4; and John vii. 53–viii. 11.

knowingly and deliberately rejects the aforesaid traditions, let him be Anathema.'[40]

Among subsequent confessions of faith drawn up by Protestants, several identify by name the twenty-seven books of the New Testament canon, including the French Confession of Faith (1559), the Belgic Confession (1561), and the Westminster Confession of Faith (1647). The Thirty-Nine Articles, issued by the Church of England in 1563, though identifying by name the books of the Old Testament separately from those of the Apocrypha, concludes the two lists with the statement, 'All the Books of the New Testament, as they are commonly received, we do receive, and account them Canonical' (Art. vi). None of the Confessional statements issued by the several Lutheran churches includes an explicit list of the canonical books.[41]

---

[40] See Albert Maichle, *Der Kanon der biblischen Bücher und das Konzil von Trent* (*Freiburger theologische Studien*, xxxiii; Freiburg im Br., 1929), and Hubert Jedin, *A History of the Council of Trent*, ii (London, 1961), pp. 52–98.

[41] This holds true for both Old Testament and New Testament canon; see A. C. Piepkorn in *Concordia Theological Monthly*, xliii (1972), pp. 449–53.

PART THREE

Historical and Theological Problems Concerning the Canon

XI

Problems Confronting the Early Church Concerning the Canon

I. CRITERIA FOR DETERMINING CANONICITY

In an earlier section (chap. IV) consideration was given to certain outside factors that must, it seems, have promoted, in one way or another, the process by which several Christian documents gradually came to occupy a unique status of sacredness and authority in the Church. Besides these external influences, however, we must also ask what criteria early Christians used in order to ascertain the worthiness of certain books to find a place in such a collection. Patristic writers would sometimes appeal in a more or less reasoned manner to specific criteria bearing on canonicity (*notae canonicitatis*). These were formulated differently at different times and places, but those to which conscious and deliberate reference was most frequently made are the following. One of them involved theological appreciation of the content of a given book, while the other two were based on historical considerations bearing on its authorship and general acceptance among the churches.

(1) A basic prerequisite for canonicity was conformity to what was called the 'rule of faith' (ὁ κανὼν τῆς πίστεως, *regula fidei*), that is, the congruity of a given document with the basic Christian tradition recognized as normative by the Church.[1] Just as under the Old Testament the message of a prophet was to be tested not merely by the success of the predictions but by the agreement of the substance of the prophecy with the fundamentals of Israel's religion, so also under the New

---

[1] On the meanings given by the Fathers to the 'rule of faith', see especially Bengt Hägglund, 'Die Bedeutung der "regula fidei" als Grundlage theologischer Aussage', *Studia theologica*, xii (1958), pp. 1–44; Richard L. Morgan, 'Regula Veritas: A Historical Investigation of the Canon of the Second Century', unpublished Th. D. diss., Union Theological Seminary (Richmond, Virginia, 1966), esp. chap. xi; and three articles on the *regula fidei* by Albert C. Outler, William R. Farmer, and Philip Schuler in *Second Century*, iv (1984), pp. 133–76.

Covenant it is clear that writings which came with any claim to be authoritative were judged by the nature of their content. The Muratorian Fragmentist will not have 'gall mixed with honey'. He vigorously rejects the literary works of heretics, just as Irenaeus and Tertullian and writers as far back as Agrippa Castor[2] in the time of Hadrian rejected them. Although modern scholars, such as Bauer[3] and Dunn,[4] have questioned whether, at the earliest stage, there was anything approaching to the idea of 'orthodoxy', it does seem to be a fact that, by the time, for instance, of 2 and 3 John, certain convictions about the Incarnation had been established in circles that were influential enough to be reflected eventually in the canon. Furthermore, the 'faithful sayings' in the Pastorals, though not representing in any sense a 'canon', betray an instinct for classification into true or false.

Besides 'the rule of faith' other terms with more or less the same meaning occur. 'The canon of truth' (δ $\kappa\alpha\nu\dot{\omega}\nu$ $\tau\hat{\eta}s$ $\dot{\alpha}\lambda\eta\theta\epsilon\dot{\iota}\alpha s$) and 'the rule of truth' (_regula veritatis_) were used apparently by Dionysius of Corinth (_c._ 160), then by Irenaeus, Clement of Alexandria, Hippolytus, Tertullian, and Novatian; they suggest that the truth itself is the standard by which teaching and practice are to be judged. It is presupposed that this truth takes for the Christian community a definite and tangible form, such as the Mosaic law was for the Jews (Rom. ii. 20). Another formulation, found only in Greek writers and versions made from them, is 'the ecclesiastical canon' or 'the canon of the church' (δ $\dot{\epsilon}\kappa\kappa\lambda\eta\sigma\iota\alpha\sigma\tau\iota\kappa\dot{\delta}s$ $\kappa\alpha\nu\dot{\omega}\nu$ or δ $\kappa\alpha\nu\dot{\omega}\nu$ $\tau\hat{\eta}s$ $\dot{\epsilon}\kappa\kappa\lambda\eta\sigma\dot{\iota}\alpha s$). Used as early as the _Martyrdom of Polycarp_ (Epilog. 2), these phrases refer to the body of church doctrine and institutions. A book that presents teachings deemed to be out of

---

[2] Agrippa Castor's work has entirely disappeared, but Eusebius says that it was 'a most powerful refutation of Basilides' (_Hist. eccl._ IV. vii. 6).

[3] Walter Bauer, _Orthodoxy and Heresy in the Earliest Christianity_ (Philadelphia, 1971). For a critique of Bauer cf. H. E. G. Turner, _The Pattern of Christian Truth_ (London, 1954), and D. J. Harrington, 'The Reception of Walter Bauer's _Orthodoxy and Heresy in Earliest Christianity_ During the Last Decade', _Harvard Theological Review_, lxxiii (1980), pp. 289–98, reprinted in Harrington's _The Light of All Nations_ (Wilmington, 1982), pp. 61–78.

[4] J. D. G. Dunn, _Unity and Diversity in the New Testament, An Inquiry into the Character of Earliest Christianity_ (Philadelphia, 1977). For a trenchant critique of Dunn, see D. A. Carson, 'Unity and Diversity within the New Testament', in _Scripture and Truth_, ed. by D. A. Carson and J. D. Woodbridge (Grand Rapids, 1983), pp. 65–95.

harmony with such tradition would exclude itself from consideration as authoritative Scripture.

(2) Another test that was applied to a given book to determine whether it deserved to belong in the New Testament was apostolicity. When the writer of the Muratorian Fragment declares against the admission of the *Shepherd* of Hermas into the canon, he does so on the ground that it is too recent, and that it cannot find a place 'among the prophets, whose number is complete, or among the apostles'. As 'the prophets' here stand for the Old Testament, so 'the apostles' are practically equivalent to the New. That is, the apostolic origin, real or putative, of a book provided a presumption of authority, for clearly an epistle attributed to the apostle Paul stood a greater likelihood of acceptance than one attributed, for example, to someone like the Montanist Themiso (see p. 103 above). In the case of Mark and Luke, the tradition of their association with the apostles Peter and Paul respectively was held to validate their writings. We observe, moreover, that in the Muratorian Canon there is still a healthy feeling that the authority of the apostles is not merely of the nature of a dogmatic assertion. In all that the writer says about the historical books of the New Testament, he insists on the personal qualification of the authors either as eyewitnesses or as careful historians.

(3) Another obvious test of authority for a book was its continuous acceptance and usage by the Church at large. This was, of course, based on the principle that a book that had enjoyed acceptance by many churches over a long period of time was in a stronger position than one accepted by only a few churches, and then only recently. Augustine's statement of this principle (see p. 237 above) was supplemented by Jerome who laid emphasis on the verdict of eminent and ancient authors. 'It does not matter', he declares in a letter written A.D. 414 to Dardanes, prefect of Gaul, 'who is the author of the Epistle to the Hebrews, for in any case it is the work of a church-writer (*ecclesiastici viri*) and is constantly read in the Churches' (*Epist.* cxxix). As the Latin Churches reject Hebrews, so the Greek Churches reject the Apocalypse, but Jerome himself accepts both on the ground that they are quoted by ancient writers as canonical.

These three[5] criteria (orthodoxy, apostolicity, and consensus among the churches) for ascertaining which books should be regarded as authoritative for the Church came to be generally adopted during the course of the second century and were never modified thereafter. At the same time, however, we find much variation in the manner in which the criteria were applied. Certainly they were not appealed to in any mechanical fashion. There were different opinions as to which criterion should be allowed chief weight. Sometimes the overriding consideration was the opinion of a much-respected bishop, or the tradition of a leading church of the area. In other words, the determination of the canon rested upon a dialectical combination of historical and theological criteria.[6] It is, therefore, not surprising that for several generations the precise status of a few books remained doubtful. What is really remarkable (as was suggested earlier) is that, though the fringes of the New Testament canon remained unsettled for centuries, a high degree of unanimity concerning the greater part of the New Testament was attained within the first two centuries among the very diverse and scattered congregations not only throughout the Mediterranean world but also over an area extending from Britain to Mesopotamia.

II. INSPIRATION AND THE CANON

It will have been noticed that in the preceding discussion concerning criteria used by early Christians in discerning the

---

[5] Among minor criteria that the ancients sometimes applied was what may be called 'number-symbolism', of which we have conspicuous examples in Irenaeus and the Muratorian Canon. According to Irenaeus, as was mentioned earlier, there must be four Gospels, as there are four quarters of the globe and four cardinal winds (*Adv. Haer.* III. xi. 8). Even Origen compares the four Gospels to the four elements (*Com. in Evang. Joan.* i. 6). And the Muratorian Fragmentist finds satisfaction in the circumstance that the apostle Paul wrote to exactly seven churches, as John had done also in the letters incorporated in the Apocalypse. It is no doubt true that this use of numbers was more often a symbolical interpretation of the facts after the settlement of the different parts of the canon than as a means of determining that settlement. One can, however, suspect that it may have had at least something to do with predisposing people's minds to accept the Epistle to the Hebrews as Paul's and so making up a total of fourteen Epistles (2×7), and also perhaps in determining the number of the Catholic Epistles.

[6] For a discussion of the interplay of historical and theological criteria, see Sigfred Pedersen, 'Die Kanonfrage als historisches und theologisches Problem', *Studia theologica*, xxxi (1977), pp. 83–136.

limits of the canon, nothing was said concerning inspiration. Though this silence may at first sight seem to be strange, the reason for it arises from the circumstance that, while the Fathers certainly agreed that the Scriptures of the Old and the New Testaments were inspired, they did not seem to have regarded inspiration as the ground of the Bible's uniqueness. That is, the inspiration they ascribe to the Scriptures was only one facet of the inspiring activity of the Holy Spirit in many aspects of the Church's life.[7] For example, while Clement of Rome speaks of the sacred Scriptures (here referring to the Old Testament) as 'true and given through the Holy Spirit' (lxiii. 2), the author of the *Epistle to Diognetus* writes for his own part to his correspondent: 'If you do not offend this grace, you will learn what the Word (λόγος) talks about through those through whom he wishes to talk, when he pleases. For whatever we have been moved painstakingly to utter by the will of the Word that commands us, it is out of love for the things revealed to us that we come to share them with you' (xi. 7–8). Among the writings of Eusebius there is a sermon attributed to the Emperor Constantine; whether or not this attribution is correct, the preacher clearly does not consider inspiration to be confined only to the Scriptures. He begins his sermon with the prayer, 'May the mighty inspiration of the Father and of his Son ... be with me in speaking these things' (*Orat. Const.* 2).

Not only do early ecclesiastical writers view themselves to be, in some degree at least, inspired, but also others affirm, in a rather broad sense, the inspiration of their predecessors, if not their contemporaries. In a letter that Augustine addressed to Jerome, the bishop of Hippo goes so far as to say (*Epist.* lxxxii. 2) not only that Jerome has been favoured with the divine grace, but also that he writes under the dictation of the Holy Spirit (*Spiritu Sancto*)—which may seem to be rather strong hyperbole

---

[7] See Gustave Bardy, 'L'Inspiration des Pères de l'Église', *Mélanges Jules Lebreton*, ii; *Recherches de science religieuse*, xl (1951–2), pp. 7–26; Everett R. Kalin, 'Argument from Inspiration in the Canonization of the New Testament', Th.D. diss., Harvard University, 1967 (summary, *Harvard Theological Review*, lx [1967], p. 491); idem, 'The Inspired Community: A Glance at Canon History', *Concordia Theological Monthly*, xlii (1971), pp. 541–9; Albert C. Sundberg, Jr., 'The Bible Canon and the Christian Doctrine of Inspiration,' *Interpretation*, xxix (1975), pp. 352–71; and Enriques Nardoni, 'Origen's Concept of Biblical Inspiration', *Second Century*, iv (1984), pp. 9–23.

applied to the often irascible Jerome. That Gregory the Great enjoyed the reputation of being inspired is easier to understand than is the case of Jerome, and Gregory's biographer, Paul the Deacon, describes how the Holy Spirit, 'under the form of a dove whiter than snow', would explain to him the mysteries of Scripture (*Vita S. Gregorii*, 28).

That the early Church saw the inspiration of the Scriptures as but one aspect of a much broader activity of inspiration is clear from the use made of the word θεόπνευστος ('divinely inspired'). This word, which is used in the affirmation that 'all Scripture is given by inspiration of God' (2 Tim. iii. 16), is chosen by Gregory of Nyssa in referring to his brother Basil's commentary on the first six days of creation as an 'exposition given by inspiration of God ... [admired] no less than the words composed by Moses himself' (*Hexaemeron*, proem.). The same word is used also in a synodical epistle from the Council of Ephesus to describe the council's condemnation of Nestorius as 'a decision given by inspiration of God'. Indeed, a still later writer even describes the epitaph on the grave of Bishop Abercius 'as a commemorative inscription inspired of God' (*Vita Abercii* 76). Thus, the Fathers do not hesitate to refer to non-Scriptural documents as 'inspired', a circumstance showing that they did not consider inspiration to be a unique characteristic of canonical writings. (See p. 211 n. 6 above.)

The same impression is conveyed when we examine patristic usage of the designation 'non-inspired'. While the Fathers again and again use the concept of inspiration in reference to the Scriptures, they seldom describe non-Scriptural writings as non-inspired. When, in fact, such a distinction is made, the designation 'non-inspired' is found to be applied to false and heretical writings, not to orthodox products of the Church's life. In other words, the concept of inspiration was not used in the early Church as a basis of designation between canonical and non-canonical orthodox Christian writings.

In short, the Scriptures, according to the early Fathers, are indeed inspired, but that is not the reason they are authoritative. They are authoritative, and hence canonical, because they are the extant literary deposit of the direct and indirect apostolic witness on which the later witness of the Church depends.

As time went on, however, theologians of the Church began to give attention to the special character of the inspiration of the Biblical writers.[8] According to modern theologians, the canonical books are one and the same as the inspired books. As du Toit puts it:

The two terms merely represent two different ways of approaching the books of the Bible. The words 'canonical' lays emphasis on the normative aspect, while 'inspired' has become the technical term to indicate that the writings in question were produced by God's special operation through the Holy Spirit. The two concepts coincide because they both refer to precisely the same books and distinguish these books from other writings.[9]

At the same time, however, there is also truth in what another Reformed theologian, Auguste Lecerf, acknowledges: 'We do not deny that God inspired other writings than those which constitute the canon.'[10] Thus, while it is true that the Biblical authors were inspired by God, this does not mean that inspiration is a criterion of canonicity. A writing is not canonical because the author was inspired, but rather an author is considered to be inspired because what he has written is recognized as canonical, that is, is recognized as authoritative in the Church.

III. WHICH PART OF THE NEW TESTAMENT WAS FIRST RECOGNIZED AS AUTHORITATIVE?

Opinions differ as to which part of the New Testament was first in attaining general recognition as authoritative in the Church. Harnack[11] held that the Gospels were the nucleus of the canon, and that the Pauline Epistles followed soon after. The Acts of the Apostles was added chiefly to prove Paul's

[8] The Church universal, however, has never defined the inspiration of the Scriptures; it can be recognized rather than defined.

[9] A. B. du Toit, 'The Canon of the New Testament', *Guide to the New Testament*, i (Pretoria, 1979), p. 88.

[10] *An Introduction to Reformed Dogmatics* (London, 1949; reprinted, Grand Rapids, 1981), p. 318.

[11] Adolf Harnack, *Das Neue Testament um das Jahr 200* (Freiburg i. Br., 1889); *History of Dogma*, ii, pp. 38–66; and *The Origin of the New Testament and the Most Important Consequences of the New Creation* (New York, 1925). For a sharp critique of the last book, see H. C. Vedder in the *Union Seminary Review* (Richmond), xxxviii (1926–7), pp. 146–58.

apostolic character and to vindicate the right of his Epistles to stand alongside the Gospels.

On the other hand, Goodspeed,[12] followed by Barnett[13] and Mitton,[14] argued that the first collection of New Testament books was made by an unknown Christian writer (later tentatively identified by Knox[15] as Onesimus) whose interest in Paul had been aroused by reading the recently published Acts of the Apostles (shortly after A.D. 90). This admirer of the apostle Paul composed a prefatory encyclical (known to us as the Epistle to the Ephesians)[16] and published at Ephesus a corpus of ten letters (i.e. all but the Pastorals), which in turn called forth the composition of other epistolary literature—namely, chapters 2 and 3 of Revelation, Hebrews, 1 Peter, and *I Clement*.

Still another theory was proposed by Windisch,[17] who, developing a suggestion made by Leipoldt,[18] held that the author of the Book of Revelation should be regarded as the founder of the canon, because this book contains the entire New Testament canon *in nuce*, namely, words of Jesus, future history of the kingdom, and seven epistles. This one book thus supplied the pattern for the canonization of documents in each of these literary genres.

Of the three theories, on chronological and geographical considerations the last mentioned seems the least probable. The Pauline Epistles as well as the Synoptic Gospels had been known and appreciated for some years before the Book of Revelation was given its present form during the last decade of

[12] E. J. Goodspeed, *New Solutions of the New Testament Problems* (Chicago, 1927), and 'The Editio Princeps of Paul', *Journal of Biblical Literature*, lxiv (1945), pp. 193–204.
[13] A. E. Barnett, *Paul Becomes a Literary Influence* (Chicago, 1941).
[14] C. Leslie Mitton, *The Formation of the Pauline Corpus of Letters* (London, 1955).
[15] John Knox, *Philemon among the Letters of Paul* (New York, 1935; 2nd ed., 1959). For a critique of Knox's view (*The Interpreter's Bible*, ix [1954], pp. 357 f.) that Paul's collected Epistles were published originally in the form of two papyrus rolls, see C. H. Buck, 'The Early Order of the Pauline Corpus', *Journal of Biblical Literature*, lxviii (1949), pp. 351–7, and Jack Finegan, 'The Original Form of the Pauline Collection', *Harvard Theological Review*, xlix (1956), pp. 85–103.
[16] E. J. Goodspeed, *The Meaning of Ephesians* (Chicago, 1933).
[17] Hans Windisch, 'Der Apokalyptiker Johannes als Begründer des neutestamentlichen Kanons', *Zeitschrift für die neutestamentliche Wissenschaft*, x (1909), pp. 148–74.
[18] Johannes Leipoldt, *Geschichte des neutestamentlichen Kanons*, i (Leipzig, 1907; reprinted, 1974), p. 33.

the first century.[19] Furthermore, as we have noticed earlier, though the Church in the West received the Apocalypse from the time of Justin Martyr onwards, in the East the book experienced much more difficulty in being accepted. While it is true that the Apocalypse embodies several kinds of literary genres, this has nothing to do with its being recognized as a model and stimulus in the canonical process.

As for the circulation of Christian documents during the first century, we know that copies of Mark,[20] written probably at Rome, must have become available through Christian travellers[21] to the authors of Matthew and of Luke, wherever it was they lived, at least as early as the seventies and eighties of the first century. That individual Epistles of Paul were circulated at an early date is clearly indicated by the warning against another epistle purporting to be Pauline (2 Thess. ii. 2) and by the request that (a copy of) the Epistle to the Colossians be sent on to Laodicea and exchanged there for another epistle (Col. iv. 16). Furthermore, Paul himself addressed the 'churches' of Galatia (Gal. i. 2), and included at the close of 1 Thessalonians an injunction that it 'be read to all the brethren' (v. 27), implying that it be made available to each of the house-churches of that community. By the time 2 Peter was sent as a general or catholic epistle to an unspecified reading public, the author could refer to the circumstance that 'our beloved brother Paul wrote to you according to the wisdom given him, speaking... in all his epistles' (iii. 15–16). This suggests that the author knew that at least three of Paul's Epistles were in circulation and had perhaps been collected.[22]

[19] The arguments of J. A. T. Robinson for an earlier date of the Apocalypse (*Redating the New Testament* [Philadelphia, 1976], pp. 221–53) have not been found generally persuasive.

[20] The two-source theory of the composition of Matthew and Luke is accepted as still valid, but the argument, *mutatis mutandis*, would still hold in terms of the so-called Griesbach hypothesis.

[21] See D. W. Riddle, 'Early Christian Hospitality: A Factor in the Gospel Transmission', *Journal of Biblical Literature*, lvii (1938), pp. 141–54.

[22] All extant manuscripts of the Pauline Epistles come from a period subsequent to their having been collected; that is, we have no copy of an individual Pauline Epistle antedating the work of the collector; we have only edited collections, or fragmentary leaves of such collections. According to Zuntz, among the Church Fathers only Clement of Rome 'is likely to have used a text prior to (or at least independent of) the production of the Pauline corpus' (Günther Zuntz, *The Text of the Epistles; A Disquisition upon the* Corpus Paulinum [London, 1953], p. 217).

The question how many epistles were included in the earliest collection of Paul's correspondence has been variously answered. Against Goodspeed's theory that ten were included, Walter Schmithals,[23] on the basis of a comparison of the sequence of Paul's Epistles in early lists and in $\mathfrak{P}^{46}$, concluded that the earliest *corpus Paulinum* contained the following seven Epistles: 1 and 2 Corinthians, Galatians, Philippians, 1 and 2 Thessalonians, and Romans.

Still another theory to account for the origin of the *corpus Paulinum* was proposed by H.-M. Schenke,[24] who suggested that the collection was the work of a 'Pauline school', that is, a group of persons who knew and admired the apostle's teaching and who, therefore, not only undertook to gather his authentic epistles, some of which they reworked, but also to compose 'new' Pauline correspondence (Colossians, Ephesians, 2 Thessalonians, 1 and 2 Timothy, Titus), finally publishing the whole corpus.

In opposition to Goodspeed, Schmithals, and Schenke, all of whom rely on historical-critical considerations, Kurt Aland analyses the question of the formation of the *corpus Paulinum* in terms of textual evidence collected by his Institute for Textual Research.[25] On the basis of collations of 634 minuscule manuscripts of Paul's Epistles in 256 selected passages, it turns out that 164 manuscripts possess an entirely diversified textual character.[26] Since this picture corresponds to the textual transmission of the uncial manuscripts,[27] and since the sequence of the Pauline Epistles varies greatly among the manuscripts, even of a late date, Aland concludes that the opinion that a uniform 'Ur-Corpus' of seven Pauline Epistles

---

[23] 'On the Composition and Earliest Collection of the Major Epistles of Paul', *Paul and the Gnostics* (New York, 1972), pp. 239–74. Schmithals, on the basis of overly subtle and unconvincing analysis, attempts to show that our 1 and 2 Corinthians are the result of an amalgamation of six letters of Paul to Corinth, that 1 and 2 Thessalonians are made up from four letters, and that Philippians comprises three letters. For an incisive critique of Schmithals, see Harry Gamble, 'The Redaction of the Pauline Letters and the Formation of the Pauline Corpus', *Journal of Biblical Literature*, xciv (1975), pp. 403–18.

[24] 'Das Weiterwirken des Paulus und die Pflege seines Erbes durch die Paulus-Schule', *New Testament Studies*, xxi (1975), pp. 505–18.

[25] 'Die Entstehung des Corpus Paulinum', *Neutestamentliche Entwürfe* (Munich, 1979), pp. 302–50.

[26] Ibid., pp. 302 and 309.   [27] Ibid., pp. 310f.

had been collected by the close of the first century, from which all later witnesses have descended, is nothing but 'a phantasy or wishful thinking'.[28] Relying on an analysis of statistical data of variant readings, Aland thinks that by about A.D. 90 several 'Ur-Corpora' of Pauline Epistles began to be made available at various places, and that these collections, of differing extent, could have included some or all of the following: 1 and 2 Corinthians, Hebrews, Romans, Galatians, Ephesians, Philippians.[29] Eventually other traditional Pauline Epistles were added to the several collections and a more or less stabilized collection finally emerged.

One avenue by which we may be able today to determine the relative degree of authority that the Gospels and Epistles[30] had in the early Church is to compare the frequency of use made of each by early ecclesiastical writers. A rough estimate can be obtained by consulting vol. i of *Biblia Patristica*,[31] which lists all the citations of individual New Testament books made by Church Fathers down to Clement of Alexandria on the one side, and down to Tertullian on the other. The following are the number of pages containing the references to citations (about 55 per page):

Matthew	about 69½ pages
Mark	about 26½ pages
Luke	about 59 pages
John	about 36¾ pages
Acts	about 12½ pages
Romans	about 16½ pages
1 Corinthians	about 30 pages
2 Corinthians	about 7¼ pages
Galatians	about 7¾ pages
Ephesians	about 10 pages

---

[28] Ibid., p. 334.   [29] Ibid., p. 335.

[30] Cf. A. Lindemann, *Paulus im ältesten Christentum. Das Bild des Apostels und die Rezeption der paulinischen Theologie in der frühchristlichen Literatur bis Marcion* (Tübingen, 1978); K. Aland, 'Methodische Bemerkungen zum Corpus Paulinum bei den Kirchenvätern des zweiten Jahrhunderts', *Kerygma und Logos... Festschift Carl Andresen* (Göttingen, 1979), pp. 29–48; and D. K. Rensberger, 'As the Apostle Teaches; The Development of the Use of Paul's Letters in Second Century Christianity', Ph.D. diss., Yale University, 1981.

[31] The subtitle is: *Index des citations et allusions bibliques dans la littérature patristique* (Paris, 1975).

Philippians	about $3\frac{1}{2}$ pages
Colossians	about $4\frac{3}{4}$ pages
1 Thessalonians	2 pages
2 Thessalonians	1 page
1 Timothy	about $4\frac{1}{2}$ pages
2 Timothy	about $2\frac{1}{4}$ pages
Philemon	about $\frac{1}{4}$ page
Hebrews	about $5\frac{1}{4}$ pages

From these statistics, and taking into account the differing lengths of the books, one sees that Matthew, followed by Luke, John, and Mark, was by far the most frequently quoted of the four Gospels. Among the Pauline Epistles, 1 Corinthians is followed by Romans, Ephesians, and Galatians in terms of popularity. These figures seem to suggest that the Gospels were recognized as authoritative before the Pauline Epistles were recognized.

IV. THE PLURALITY OF THE GOSPELS

The fact that the Church today takes the fourfold canon of the Gospels for granted makes it difficult to see how a plurality of the authoritative evangelists was ever felt to be a theological problem in the ancient Church. During the period, however, when there was still no established canon, it was, as Oscar Cullmann has shown in a perceptive study,[32] by no means universally considered to be natural that different and, to some extent, divergent[33] accounts of the life of Jesus should be regarded as equally authoritative. The offence arose from the consideration that if it is necessary to have not one but several accounts of the one life of Jesus (which, in fact, must be the foundation of all Christian belief), this is as good as admitting that none of them is perfect.

[32] 'Die Pluralität der Evangelien als theologisches Problem im Altertum', *Theologische Zeitschrift*, i (1945), pp. 23–42; English translation in Cullmann's *The Early Church* (London, 1956), pp. 37–54. The discussion above reproduces Cullmann's article *in nuce*. For patristic texts (with German translation) that bear on the subject, see Helmut Merkel, *Die Pluralität der Evangelien als theologisches und exegetisches Problem in der Alten Kirche* (*Traditio christiana*, iii; Berne, 1978).

[33] On early attempts to deal with contradictions among the four Gospels, see Helmut Merkel, *Die Widersprüche zwischen den Evangelien; Ihre polemische und apologetische Behandlung in der Alten Kirche bis zu Augustin* (*Wissenschaftliche Untersuchungen zum Neuen Testament*, xiii; Tübingen, 1971).

While the trend toward a multiplicity of Gospels existed from the very beginning (see Luke i. 1–3), it was accompanied by an opposite tendency to reduce them all to a single Gospel. Tatian's *Diatesseron*, by which the four separate Gospels were replaced by one harmonized account, was not the only attempt made in the early Church to overcome the offence of the plurality of Gospels. The best-known example of the attempt to confer exclusive authority on one of the Gospels was that of Marcion, who singled out the Gospel according to Luke as the one exclusively valid Gospel.

In order to defend the fourfold Gospel in the early Church, Irenaeus sought to show the significance of the number four in nature and in redemption. In nature there are four points of the compass corresponding to four main winds. In the scheme of salvation God instituted four covenants—with Noah, Abraham, Moses, and Christ. And, with considerable ingenuity, Irenaeus dwells on the four living creatures of Ezekiel (i. 10) and the Book of Revelation (iv. 7) in which he sees a representation of the four Gospels—an idea which later had widespread influence on Christian art.

What Irenaeus leaves out of account, however, are the purely human circumstances that prevailed before the Gospels were formed into a group. There is reason to believe that only one Gospel was in use in some churches long before the canon was finally settled. It appears that only the Gospel according to Matthew was at all widely read in Palestine, that there were churches in Asia Minor which used only the Gospel according to John from the outset, and so with Mark and Luke in their special areas. What Irenaeus fails to appreciate, as Cullmann points out in summing up his discussion, is that

The immeasurable fulness of the truth about Christ who appeared in the flesh cannot be exhausted by the evangelists, because they are only humanly imperfect instruments of the divine revelation, and [therefore] it was absolutely necessary for all the available records of the life of Jesus, deriving from apostolic times, to be collected.... Four *biographies* of the same life could not be set alongside one another as of equal value, but would have to be harmonized and reduced to a single biography in some way or other. Four Gospels, that is, four books dealing with the content of faith, cannot be harmonized, but required by their very nature to be set alongside one another. And in any case the faith cried out for manifold witness.[34]

V. THE PARTICULARITY OF THE PAULINE EPISTLES

Unlike the problem occasioned by the plurality of the Gospels in the early Church, the plurality of the Epistles caused no difficulty. In this case, however, as Dahl has pointed out in a perceptive essay,[35] it was not equally easy to see why Epistles written to particular churches on particular occasions should be regarded as universally authoritative and read in all churches. This problem was tackled on two fronts: by an attempt at theological justification through number-symbolism, and by adjustment of the text in several of the Epistles.

Number-symbolism found its earliest literary expression in the Muratorian Canon with the observation (lines 49–50) that Paul, like John in Revelation ii–iii, had written to seven churches, and thus to the whole Church. This point reappears in the writings of Cyprian, Victorinus of Pettau,[36] and later authors.

After the inclusion of the Epistle to the Hebrews in the Pauline corpus, it became difficult to maintain the idea that Paul wrote to seven churches. Then it became usual to point out that the total number of the Pauline Epistles was fourteen, or 2 times 7. Furthermore, the Muratorian Canon offers a special argument in support of the catholicity of the Epistles sent to individuals: although Paul wrote out of affection and love to Philemon, Titus, and Timothy, yet they are all 'held sacred in the esteem of the Church catholic for the regulation of ecclesiastical discipline' (lines 62–3). This argument obviously has little or no application to the problem concerning the

---

[34] Op. cit., p. 52 and 54. See also Robert Morgan, 'The Hermeneutical Significance of Four Gospels', *Interpretation*, xxxiii (1979), pp. 376–88, who concludes: 'It seems to have been a higher wisdom which resulted in a plurality of Gospels in the canon.'

[35] Nils A. Dahl, 'The Particularity of the Pauline Epistles as a Problem in the Ancient Church', *Neotestamentica et Patristica; Eine Freundesgabe, Herrn Professor Dr. Oscar Cullmann zu seinem 60 Geburtstag überreicht* (Leiden, 1962), pp. 261–71. The discussion above reproduces Dahl's essay *in nuce*.

[36] In Victorinus' commentary on Rev. i. 20 the argument is turned around and a scriptural 'proof' is adduced: the seven women who take hold of one man (Isa. iv. 1) represent the seven churches, who are the one Church, the bride of Christ, called by his name.

run-away slave Onesimus, and the Epistle to Philemon is the only known example of a Pauline letter explicitly rejected[37] because of its limited scope.

The other means by which several of the Pauline Epistles were made more universal or 'catholic' was by the adjustment of their text. The omission of the words 'in Rome' in Rom. i. 7 and 15 in certain Greek and Latin manuscripts, as well as the complicated textual problems connected with the place of the doxology (Rom. xvi. 25–7) and the ending of the Epistle, are generally taken as evidence for the existence of more than one recension of Romans, one of which was a 'catholicized' form of the Epistle.[38]

Furthermore, it is unlikely that the absence of a geographical destination in the text of Eph. i. 1, as witnessed by the oldest manuscripts, is the original text. Apart from the possibility that copies of the Epistle were sent by the writer to more than one destination, the text without any specific address is to be understood as a result, once again, of a secondary 'catholicizing'.

The same tendency is also, probably, to be observed even in the text of 1 Corinthians. The clause 'together with all...', which comes rather awkwardly in 1 Corinthians i. 2b, is often held to be an interpolation by which the Epistle was given a wider and more ecumenical address.

By way of summary, Dahl concludes:

The particularity of the Pauline Epistles was felt as a problem, from a time before the *Corpus paulinum* was published and until it had been incorporated into a complete canon of New Testament Scripture. Later on, the problem was no longer felt, but the tendency towards generalizing has remained, not only when the Epistles were used as dogmatic proof-texts, but also when they served as sources for reconstruction of a general 'biblical theology' or a system of

---

[37] Dahl comments that because it is difficult to believe that Luke, who makes no reference in Acts to Paul's Epistles, had no knowledge of their existence, it may be that he consciously ignored them, partly because they were written on particular occasions for particular destinations (op. cit., pp. 256 f.). Independently of Dahl, John Knox also argued that Luke, writing before the first 'catholicizing' of Paul's Epistles had taken place, chose to ignore them; see his 'Acts and the Pauline Letter Corpus', *Studies in Luke–Acts*, ed. by L. E. Keck and J. L. Martyn (Nashville, 1966), pp. 279–87.

[38] See Harry Gamble, Jr., *The Textual History of the Letter to the Romans, a Study in Textual and Literary History* (*Studies and Documents*, xlii; Grand Rapids, 1972).

'paulinism.' ... [Yet] to the apostle himself, letters to particular churches written on special occasions were the proper literary form for making theological statements. Of this fact both exegesis and theology, not to mention preaching, have to take account. The particularity of the Pauline epistles points to the historicalness of all theology, even that of the apostle.[39]

[39] Op. cit., p. 271.

XII

Questions Concerning the Canon Today

I. WHICH FORM OF THE TEXT IS CANONICAL?

THE textual diversity among the manuscripts of the New Testament is well known, presenting, as they do, several characteristic types of text, chief of which are the Alexandrian, the Western, and the Byzantine or Ecclesiastical text-types.[1] The question arises what attitude with respect to the canon should be taken toward these several types of text of the New Testament books. Is one type of text to be regarded as the canonical text, and if so, what authority should be accorded variant readings which differ from that text?

A century ago the Anglo-Catholic churchman, John William Burgon, challenging the principles on which Westcott and Hort had prepared their critical edition of the Greek New Testament (Cambridge, 1881), argued that the form of Greek text which had found widest approval in the Church down through the ages must be held to be the only authentic text. A similar point of view continues to be maintained today by Zane C. Hodges and Arthur L. Farstad, the editors of the recently published *Greek New Testament According to the Majority Text*,[2] who, like Burgon, follow the method (if it can be called a method) of counting New Testament manuscripts, rather than weighing them to discover in each set of variant readings which reading best accounts for the rise of the others.

The first point that needs to be made is that, instead of there being a single, monolithic text of the New Testament in the Byzantine Church, von Soden showed that several forms of the Koine or Byzantine text, differing from one another in small

---

[1] For information concerning the New Testament text-types, see Metzger, *The Test of the New Testament, its Transmission, Corruption, and Restoration*, 2nd ed. (Oxford, 1968), and Kurt and Barbara Aland, *Der Text des Neuen Testaments, Einführung in die wissenschaftlichen Ausgaben sowie in Theorie und Praxis der modernen Textkritik* (Stuttgart, 1982). [2] (Nashville, 1982).

details, circulated in Eastern Christendom. At the same time, however, all of them were regarded as authoritative.

Much more striking is the difference between the so-called Western type of New Testament text on the one hand and all other types of text on the other. In the Book of Acts, for example, the Western text is about 8½ per cent longer than what is customarily regarded as the canonical form of that book. In the eighteenth century, William Whiston[3] published what he held to be the only authentic form of the New Testament, namely an English translation resting on the two chief witnesses to the Western type of text, codex Bezae and codex Claromontanus.

In this connection one may consider the suggestion thrown out more than fifty years ago by James Hardy Ropes, to the effect that the Western text of the New Testament was created early in the second century expressly to provide a vehicle for the emerging canon of the New Testament.[4] Interesting though such a suggestion is, it is significant that Ropes presented no evidence in support of his theory. Furthermore, if one considers that philological efforts in the production of canonical texts were chiefly connected with the type of scholarship current in Alexandria, the fact that the so-called Western type of text hardly ever appears in witnesses associated with Egypt detracts from the probability of Ropes's theory.

More recently Brevard S. Childs has discussed 'The Hermeutical Problem of New Testament Text Criticism',[5] the goal of which, he says, is the recovery of the best received text rather than the author's autograph:

> The canonical mode of textual criticism proposes a continuing search in discerning the best received text which moves from the outer parameters of the common church tradition found in the *textus receptus* to the inner judgment respecting its purity.[6]

Unfortunately Childs provides no analysis of a specific textual problem, nor does he define what he understands to be

---

[3] *The Primitive New Testament Restor'd* (London, 1745); for Whiston's views concerning the canon of the New Testament, see pp. 14–15 above.

[4] *The Text of Acts*, being vol. iii of *The Beginning of Christianity*, Part I, ed. by F. J. Foakes Jackson and Kirsopp Lake (London, 1926), pp. ix, ccxlv f., and ccxci f.

[5] *The New Testament as Canon; An Introduction* (London, 1984; Philadelphia, 1985), pp. 518–30.   [6] Ibid., p. 529.

'the best received text'. One is also at a loss to understand what is involved in a continuing search for such a text. Does this imply that we have no canonical text but must continue to search for it? And how does 'the canonical mode of textual criticism' differ from ordinary textual criticism (is there also, for example, a canonical mode of doing New Testament lexicography and grammar)?

Leaving such unanswered questions aside, we may find it instructive to consider the attitude of Church Fathers toward variant readings in the text of the New Testament. On the one hand, as far as certain readings involve sensitive points of doctrine, the Fathers customarily alleged that heretics had tampered with the accuracy of the text. On the other hand, however, the question of the canonicity of a document apparently did not arise in connection with discussion of such variant readings, even though they might involve quite considerable sections of text. Today we know that the last twelve verses of the Gospel according to Mark (xvi. 9–20) are absent from the oldest Greek, Latin, Syriac, Coptic, and Armenian manuscripts, and that in other manuscripts asterisks or obeli mark the verses as doubtful or spurious. Eusebius and Jerome, well aware of such variation in the witnesses, discussed which form of text was to be preferred. It is noteworthy, however, that neither Father suggested that one form was canonical and the other was not. Furthermore, the perception that the canon was basically closed did not lead to a slavish fixing of the text of the canonical books.

Thus, the category of 'canonical' appears to have been broad enough to include all variant readings (as well as variant renderings in early versions) that emerged during the course of the transmission of the New Testament documents while apostolic tradition was still a living entity,[7] with an intermingling of written and oral forms of that tradition. Already in the second century, for example, the so-called long ending of Mark

---

[7] Parvis, who would include any and all variant readings (except obvious scribal errors), 'whether they originated in the twelfth century or in the first', blurs the qualitative difference between apostolic tradition and subsequent Church tradition (see M. M. Parvis, 'The Nature and Tasks of New Testament Textual Criticism; An Appraisal', *Journal of Religion*, xxxii [1952], pp. 165–74, and 'The Goals of New Testament Textual Studies', *Studia Evangelica*, vi [*Texte und Untersuchungen*, cxii; Berlin, 1973], pp. 393–407, esp. 402–7).

was known to Justin Martyr and to Tatian, who incorporated it into his *Diatesseron*. There seems to be good reason, therefore, to conclude that, though external and internal evidence is conclusive against the authenticity of the last twelve verses as coming from the same pen as the rest of the Gospel, the passage ought to be accepted as part of the canonical text of Mark.

It is less easy to be confident in determining the status that should be accorded to an intermediate ending of Mark that was current in certain later Greek and versional manuscripts: 'But they reported briefly to Peter and those with him all that they had been told. And after this Jesus himself sent out by means of them, from East to West, the sacred and imperishable proclamation of eternal salvation.' In the oldest Latin manuscript (*k*) these words replace verses 9–20; in other witnesses (L Ψ 099 0112 274^{mg} 579 *l*1602 sy^{hmg} sa^{mss} bo^{mss} eth^{mss}) they stand between verses 8 and 9. While there is no evidence that Christians who had copies of Mark with this ending thought any differently about the authority of the Gospel as a book than those who had copies with the usual ending, the rather grandiloquent language at the close of the addition (which is so unlike Mark's vocabulary and plain style) gives the impression of an apocryphal origin, subsequent to the apostolic age. At the same time, however, copies of the Gospel according to Mark in Greek, Latin, Syriac, Coptic, Armenian, and Ethiopic, which contain these words, have functioned as canonical Scripture in the several national Churches among which they circulated.

In short, it appears that the question of canonicity pertains to the document *qua* document, and not to one particular form or version of that document. Translated into modern terms, Churches today accept a wide variety of contemporary versions as the canonical New Testament, though the versions differ not only as to rendering but also with respect to the presence or absence of certain verses in several of the books (besides the ending of Mark's Gospel, other significant variations include Luke xxii. 43–4, John vii. 53–viii. 11,[8] and Acts viii. 37).

---

[8] For a recent discussion of the canonical status of this passage, see Gary M. Burge, 'A Specific Problem in the New Testament Text and Canon: The Woman Caught in Adultery', *Journal of the Evangelical Theological Society*, xxvii (1984), pp. 141–8.

II. IS THE CANON OPEN OR CLOSED?

To say that the canon is open implies that it is possible for the Church today either to add one or more books to the canon, or to remove one or more books that have hitherto been regarded as canonical. What, we may ask, are the theoretical and practical implications of each of these possibilities?[9]

(1) First, how far is it possible to consider adding a book to the New Testament canon? Suggestions that the canon might be enlarged by the inclusion of other 'inspirational' literature, ancient or modern, arise from a failure to recognize what the New Testament actually is. It is not an anthology of inspirational literature; it is a collection of writings that bear witness to what God has wrought through the life and work, the death and resurrection of Jesus Christ, and through the founding of his Church by his Spirit. Shortly after the assassination of Martin Luther King, Jr., in 1968, a group of ministers seriously proposed that King's 'Letter from a Birmingham Jail'[10] be added to the New Testament. All will appreciate that this letter, written in April 1964 after he had been jailed in Birmingham, Alabama, for participating in a civil-rights protest, conveys a strong prophetic witness, and interprets God's will in the spirit of Christ. At the same time, however, most will recognize that the differences as to age and character between it and the books of the New Testament are far too great to warrant its being added to the canon, and today few if any take the proposal seriously.

What, on the other hand, should be said about the possibility of adding an ancient document to the canon? The discovery some years ago at Nag Hammadi of several dozen texts from the early Church, such as the *Gospel of Thomas*, the *Gospel of Philip*, the *Epistle of Peter to Philip*, and the *Apocryphon of John*,

---

[9] For theological considerations bearing on the question of closed vs. open canon, see Karl Barth, *Church Dogmatics*, 1, 2, pp. 476–81 ('An absolute guarantee that the Canon is closed, and therefore that what we know as the Canon is also closed, cannot be given either by the Church or by individuals in the Church according to the best and most satisfactory answers to this question', p. 476).

[10] The letter, written in response to a published statement by eight fellow clergymen from Alabama, who had called King's civil-rights protest 'unwise and untimely', was published as chap. 5 in King's book entitled *Why We Can't Wait* (New York, 1964), pp. 77–100.

has greatly increased the number of candidates for possible inclusion in a revised form of the canon. Each deserves to be assessed as to its external and internal credentials. How far, for example, does the *Gospel of Thomas* (which, of all the tractates in the Nag Hammadi library, seems to be closest to the New Testament) meet the criteria of apostolicity and orthodoxy, however narrowly or broadly one defines these elusive standards? The presence within such a document of possibly genuine agrapha[11] (that is, sayings attributed to Jesus that are not preserved in the canonical Gospels) must be weighed over against the presence also of Gnostic and semi-pantheistic elements (see p. 86 above). In this case the evaluation of modern readers will no doubt corroborate that of the early Church, namely, that in the *Gospel of Thomas* the voice of the Good Shepherd is heard in only a muffled way, and that it is, in fact, often distorted beyond recognition by the presence of supplementary and even antagonistic voices.

One may also speculate what the Church should do if a hitherto unknown document were to turn up that, on unimpeachable external and internal grounds, could be proved to have been written, let us say, by the apostle Paul.[12] In such a case, the nature of its contents would surely have to be taken into account. Obviously a treatise on tent-making would lie outside the limits of apostolic testimony concerning the Christian faith! But, even if the newly discovered document could be proved by philological arguments to be a genuine epistle of Paul to (let us say) the Christians at Athens, the Church would still need to consider whether its contents added anything essentially new to what is available in Pauline Epistles already generally received.

[11] Some years ago a proposal was made by Dr Ed. Platzhoff-Lejeune of Territet/ Montreux ('Zur Problematik des biblischen Kanons', *Schweizerische theologische Umschau*, xix [1949], pp. 108–16) that the canon be enriched by the addition of agrapha, whose authenticity he considered to be on a par with that of the Biblical text.

[12] That not all of Paul's correspondence has been preserved seems to be implied by 1 Cor. v. 9–11, 2 Cor. ii. 3–11 and vii. 8–12, Phil. iii. 1, and Col. iv. 16. Bishop Lightfoot was of the opinion that 'in the epistles of our Canon we have only a part—perhaps not a very large part—of the whole correspondence of the Apostle [Paul], either with Churches or with individuals' (see the discussion, 'Lost Epistles to the Philippians?' in J. B. Lightfoot's *St. Paul's Epistle to the Philippians*, 6th ed. [London, 1896], pp. 138–42. Paul refers to 'epistles of recommendation' (2 Cor. iii. 1), i.e. personal letters of introduction, as passing frequently among the Churches. Undoubtedly, then, many private letters written by authors represented in the New Testament have been lost. See also p. 284 n. 34.

In the light of these considerations it appears that, though from a theoretical point of view the way is open for the possible addition of another book or epistle to the New Testament canon, it is problematic that any would, so to say, meet the standards, whether ancient or modern, of accreditation.

(2) On the other hand, the question may be raised as to the possibility and desirability of removing one or more of the twenty-seven books from the New Testament canon. Is the Church today bound by the decisions of the early Church as to the number and identity of the books of the New Testament?

It must be admitted that attempts at the time of the Reformation to set aside certain books that proved to be awkward or embarrassing in ecclesiastical controversy should make us exceedingly wary in assessing our own motives and standards in evaluating the canonical status of the several books in the New Testament. How easily an individual can err in these matters is shown by the untenable judgements of Luther on the Epistles of James, of Jude, to the Hebrews, and the Apocalypse—judgements that originated in his inability to appreciate the Christian message conveyed by these books and in his one-sided preference for others. Likewise, Zwingli's denial of the Biblical character of the Book of Revelation was the result of contemporary controversies growing out of what to his eyes was an eruption of pagan superstitions at Einsiedeln. When he condemned the invocation of angels, he was shown the angel in the Apocalypse causing the prayers of the faithful to ascend to heaven with the smoke of incense (Rev. viii. 3–4). Subsequently at the Berne Disputation (1528), Zwingli declared that this book is not a Biblical book. Thus, as was the case also when Eusebius denigrated the Apocalypse because of the excesses of the early chiliasts who favoured this book, Zwingli allowed a purely *ad hoc* consideration to sway his judgement concerning the character of a book otherwise widely regarded throughout the West as canonical.

Apart from the heat of theological controversy, however, and in more calm and dispassionate times, the question has been raised whether, in fact, the deletion of several books of the New Testament canon would not be advantageous in promoting the unity of the Church. In a lecture given at the Second International Congress on New Testament Studies which met at Oxford in 1961, Kurt Aland made the proposal that widely-ranging discussions among the Churches be undertaken looking toward a briefer and more unified canon as a means of forwarding church unity.[13]

On the surface, such a proposal may appear to have something to commend it. On more mature consideration, however, one must acknowledge that it is exceedingly doubtful whether the proposal would really be conducive to the welfare of the Church. There are denominations, as well as traditions within the several denominations, that find spiritual help and sustenance in all the varied parts of the Scriptures as currently received. To remove one or more books from the New Testament canon as hitherto defined would sever bonds that have united groups of believers, and thus would almost certainly result in still greater fragmentation of the Church.

Furthermore, at this late date in the history of the Christian Church, to delete one or more books from the canon, even if such a proposal could find general approval, would result in cutting off important historical roots of the Church. Instead of being a step in the direction of greater ecumenicity, such a deletion would result in the impoverishment of the Church universal.

What has been mentioned thus far is in the realm of the theoretical. If one considers the likelihood of an actual revision of the canon being undertaken, it must be admitted that such a possibility appears to be exceedingly remote. True enough, occasionally the suggestion is made that, for example, the Ignatian epistles should be added to the New Testament canon, and 2 Peter and/or Jude should be dropped. But, on the whole, there is no significant body of opinion within the churches that wishes to see the New Testament canon altered, either by enlargement or by reduction. One may predict

---

[13] *The Problem of the New Testament Canon* (London, 1962), pp. 28–33. Aland's suggestion was in response to Ernst Käsemann's challenging lecture, 'Begründet der neutestamentliche Kanon die Einheit der Kirche?' published first in *Evangelische Theologie*, xi (1951–2), pp. 13–31; reprinted in *Exegetische Versuche und Besinnungen*, i, 2nd ed. (Göttingen, 1960), pp. 214–23; English trans. 'Is the New Testament Canon the Foundation for Church Unity?' in his *Essays on New Testament Themes* (London, 1964), pp. 95–107.

that individual views and proposals will die a natural death.[14]

It may be concluded, therefore, that, while the New Testament canon should, from a theoretical point of view, be regarded as open in principle for either the addition or the deletion of one or more books, from a practical point of view such a modification can scarcely be contemplated as either possible or desirable. To say that the canon may be revised is not the same as saying it must be revised. The canon by which the Church has lived over the centuries emerged in history, the result of a slow and gradual process. To be sure, in this canon there are documents less firmly attested by external criteria than others. But the several parts have all been cemented together by usage and by general acceptance in the Church, which has recognized, and recognizes, that God has spoken and is speaking to her in and through this body of early Christian literature. As regards this social fact, nothing can be changed; the Church has received the canon of the New Testament as it is today, in the same way as the Synagogue has had bequeathed to it the Hebrew canon. In short, the canon cannot be remade—for the simple reason that history cannot be remade.[15]

III. IS THERE A CANON WITHIN THE CANON?

Recently there has been a revival, particularly on the Continent, of discussion of the 'canon within the canon'.[16] In

[14] After discussing the right and responsibility of the Church at any period in its history continually to re-examine the canon with the possibility of revising it, Emil Brunner concludes: 'If we compare the writings of the New Testament with those of the sub-Apostolic period, even those that are the nearest in point of time, we cannot avoid the conclusion that there is a very great difference between the two groups... One who, in principle, admits the necessity for a canon—that is, one who distinguishes the primitive witness, which is the basis for everything, from the witness of the Church, which is based upon it—will continually return to the present canon' (*Revelation and Reason; the Christian Doctrine of Faith and Knowledge* [Philadelphia, 1946], p. 132).

[15] Harald Riesenfeld's comments are apposite: 'Whereas the canon represents a datum which is the result of a historical process and which has to be explained as such, all criticism of the canon is in fact dependent upon the individual scholar's evaluations and prejudices, and these have always proved to be controversial.... The most remarkable feature in primitive Christianity is in fact not the diversity of congregations, writings and beliefs, but that homogeneity which made possible the acceptance and constant use of a diversity of writings which already at an early stage were considered authoritative' ('Reflections on the Unity of the New Testament,' *Religion*, iii [1973], pp. 36 and 41).

[16] Besides other literature to be mentioned below, see Inge Lønning, '*Kanon im Kanon*'; *Zum dogmatischen Grundlagenproblem des neutestamentlichen Kanons* (*Forschungen zur Geschichte und Lehre des Protestantismus*, xliii; Oslo and Munich, 1972).

this expression the two instances of the word 'canon' have different meanings. In the second instance 'canon' means the collection of New Testament Scriptures, whereas in the first instance it means the standard or centre within the twenty-seven books of the New Testament. To find the canon within the canon, therefore, means to find in Scripture a principle of hermeneutic that enables one to draw a line of demarcation between what is authoritative within the canon and what is not. The current discussion thus renews attempts made at the time of the Reformation to determine what is Christian within the New Testament.

Attempts to define the canon within the canon include the following proposals. For Kümmel,[17] for example, the 'canon' by which canonical books are to be judged is found in three areas: (*a*) in the message and figure of Jesus, as it meets us in the oldest form of the Synoptic tradition; (*b*) in the oldest kerygma of the primitive church which explains the significance of the life and death of Jesus and witnesses to the resurrection of Christ; and (*c*) in the first theological reflections on this kerygma in the theology of Paul. For Braun,[18] the 'canon within the canon' is located in the preaching of Jesus, in Paul, and in the Fourth Gospel.

For Marxsen,[19] the 'canon within the canon' is much more restricted. In his view none of the New Testament books can be said to be truly canonical, but 'the real canon is prior to the New Testament, and we are nearer to it in the sources the Synoptists used than in the Synoptic Gospels themselves'. It is thus only the scientifically trained scholar who is capable of going behind the present Gospels in order to ascertain the original apostolic testimony. But even when this is uncovered, one cannot declare forthwith that it is authoritative for us. No, for, according to Marxsen, 'no book in the New Testament

---

[17] W. G. Kümmel, 'Notwendigkeit und Grenze der neutestamentlichen Kanons', *Zeitschrift für Theologie und Kirche*, xlvii (1950), pp. 227–313, esp. 257 f. For the theological implications, see Kümmel's *The Theology of the New Testament, According to Its Major Witnesses: Jesus–Paul–John* (Nashville, 1973).

[18] Herbert Braun, 'Hebt die heutige neutestamentliche-exegetische Forschung den Kanon auf?', *Fuldaer Hefte*, xii (1960), pp. 9–24; reprinted in his *Gesammelte Studien zum Neuen Testament und seiner Umwelt* (Tübingen, 1962), pp. 310–24.

[19] Willi Marxsen, *Introduction to the New Testament, An Approach to its Problems* (Philadelphia, 1968), p. 282.

aims to speak directly to the present-day reader', and 'to use it
in this way would be to use it against the intentions of those
who wrote it'. It is therefore not a question, Marxsen concludes, 'whether Paul, Mark, Matthew, Luke or John have
something to say to me, but rather whether what these writers
sought to say to their readers can become something that is
addressed to me as well'.[20] In other words, the real test for
discerning what is authoritative is whether the kerygma exis-
tentially confronts me in my situation.

What shall we say of such an argument? Well, in the first
place, if Marxsen's interpretative principle is taken seriously, no
part of the New Testament can ever be authoritative today, for no
two life-situations are identical, and this is particularly true when
so many centuries separate the apostolic age from the modern
period.[21] Furthermore, Marxsen's argument that, because no
book in the New Testament aims to speak directly to the present-
day reader, therefore 'to use it in this way would be to use it
against the intentions of those who wrote it', can be turned
against his own position—for it is just as certain that those who
wrote the books of the New Testament had no intention of
compiling a handbook of situations that have the potential of
producing an existentialist type of confrontation for twentieth-
century readers. Nor did the Evangelists imagine that what they
had collected and/or edited would be by-passed in an effort to
ascertain the sources that they had incorporated with a variety of
modifications. Marxsen's argument, therefore, is self-defeating.

More serious attention deserves to be paid to the reasons
suggested, for example, by Harbsmeier,[22] Vielhauer,[23] Käsemann,[24] and others that make it necessary to seek a 'canon

---

[20] Ibid., pp. 283 f.; see also Marxsen, *The New Testament as the Church's Book*
(Philadelphia, 1972).

[21] This point is made by Nikolaas Appel in his *Kanon und Kirche. Die Kanonkrise im
heutigen Protestantismus als kontroverstheologisches Problem* (Paderborn, 1964), pp. 308–37;
see also Appel, 'The New Testament Canon: Historical Process and Spirit's Witness',
Theological Studies, xxxii (1971), pp. 627–46.

[22] G. Harbsmeier, 'Unsere Predigt im Spiegel der Apostelgeschichte,' *Evangelische
Theologie*, x (1950–1), pp. 161–70.

[23] Philipp Vielhauer, 'Zum "Paulinismus" der Apostelgeschichte', ib. x (1950–1),
pp. 1–15; English trans., 'On the "Paulinism" of Acts', *Studies in Luke–Acts*, ed. by
L. E. Keck and J. L. Martin (New York, 1966), pp. 33–50.

[24] Ernst Käsemann, 'Paulus und der Frühkatholizismus', *Zeitschrift für Theologie und
Kirche*, lx (1962), pp. 75–89; English trans. in *New Testament Questions of Today*
(Philadelphia, 1969), pp. 236–51.

within the canon'. According to these scholars the presence of contradictions between New Testament books, or even within a given book, makes it necessary to establish a critical canon within the canon. For example, the eschatology of Luke–Acts cannot, it is said, be harmonized with Paul's eschatology, and to attempt to do so results in surrendering the heart of the Christian kerygma. Again, the outlook on the Old Testament law in the Epistle to the Romans certainly appears to be different from the outlook in Matt. v. 18 ('Not one jot or tittle will pass from the law till all is accomplished'). Moreover, the Pauline rejection of the Mosaic law as a means of attaining a right standing in the sight of God is said to be compromised in the Pastoral Epistles, which preserve the Pauline formula of justification but, so to speak, 'paralyse' its effectiveness by introducing moralism and the rationalization of faith. Further-more, the Epistle of James attacks the Pauline doctrine of justification by faith alone. For these and similar reasons, it is argued, not only is there no unity within the canon, but it is vain to expect that the Church can achieve unity on the basis of the canon. It is thus necessary for both the individual Christian and the Church at large to operate with a 'canon within the canon'. In such a circumstance the canon will outwardly remain as it has been, but the effective principle of interpretation will set aside or denigrate certain portions while emphasizing certain others that are held to present the 'central core' of the canon.[25]

On the surface such a suggestion may appear to have some degree of persuasion. Certainly the differences among the traditions within the New Testament must be acknowledged, and artificial attempts at harmonization should be resisted. At the same time, however, it is legitimate to ask the question why the New Testament should have to be consistent in all its parts. Why should all the writers have to think alike on all subjects in order to be included in the canon? Furthermore, there is

---

[25] Käsemann suggests that, rather than eliminating certain books from the New Testament, they should be retained so as to provide the foil against which the teachings of other New Testament books can be more sharply focused for the sake of speaking to the contemporary situation. Diem correctly sees that Käsemann's selectivity is fraught with subjective arbitrariness and must never be allowed to harden into an a priori principle; see Hermann Diem, *Das Problem des Schriftkanons* (*Theologische Studien*, xxxii; Zollikon-Zurich, 1952), pp. 16–21, and *Dogmatics* (Edinburgh and London, 1959), pp. 229–34.

nothing objectionable in seeking a 'central core' in the New Testament. In point of fact, in all ages of the Church certain books of the Scriptures, and certain key passages within each book, have been more beloved, and therefore more influential, than others.

On the other hand, however, it can scarcely be denied that the effort to erect any one principle or any one doctrine as the only valid rule by which to estimate the authority of this or that book within the canon has been a notorious source of imbalance and one-sidedness in the Church, resulting in the impoverishment of Christian faith and life. The Pauline principle which Marcion adopted as the norm for his canon, while good in itself, would have almost certainly been unable to prevent Christianity from becoming an anti-Jewish, Gnostic sect. The rich diversity of early Christian thought, preserving insights both Jewish and Greek, is reflected in the spectrum of the twenty-seven books in our canon today. This does not mean, of course, that all New Testament books have been or are equally influential. But the needs of the Church universal over the centuries have been varied—including both doctrinal and practical aspects of the Christian life, corporate and individual—and the several portions of the canonical Scriptures have spoken to and answered those needs. In fact, the differences that exist among the books of the New Testament, and even within the several writings of the same author, are not so much the cause of divisions in the Church today as reflections of theological pluralism within the primitive Christian communities themselves.[26] The slogan 'early Catholicism',[27] which has done considerable mischief in systematic

---

[26] Krister Stendahl concludes a lively critique of the idea of a canon within the canon with an analogy: 'Any reference to the kerygma as singular, or to a center which makes the totality less important and interesting, suggests that there is a master key which opens all the locks. But this is perhaps a hermeneutical mirage. I would rather use the whole set of keys supplied by the Scriptures. And the canon is the key ring' ('One Canon is Enough', *Meanings; The Bible as Document and as Guide* [Philadelphia, 1984], pp. 55–68).

[27] The term 'early Catholicism' (*Frühkatholizismus*) was first used in 1908 by Ernst Troeltsch in a sociological setting (cf. his *Social Teaching of the Christian Churches*, English trans. i [London, 1931], pp. 89–200), but later it came to be used to describe (*a*) the growing emphasis on the development of the Church as an institution, (*b*) the stress on 'orthodoxy' and 'sound doctrine', and (*c*) the moralization of the faith and a conception of the gospel as a new law. For the history of the usage of the expression, see K. H. Neufeld, '"Frühkatholizismus"—Idee und Begriff', *Zeitschrift für katholische*

theology in recent years, is, in fact, testimony to the presence of diversity within and among the apostolic witnesses. If we accept the presence of both an early Catholicism and an early Protestantism in the New Testament, by the same right we may discover also a distinctive early Eastern Orthodox trend, especially in the Johannine Gospel and Epistles. The formation of the canon, incorporating all the three trends as equally valid and justified modes of Christian thought and existence, offers us a basic pattern and understanding of Christianity in its widest extent.

As long as the chief doctrines and patterns of Christian life and thought within the New Testament at least point in the same direction, and not away from one another, they can coexist in the same canon. The homogeneity of the canon is not jeopardized even in the face of tensions that exist within the New Testament. These tensions, however, must not be exaggerated into contradictions as a result of giving inadequate consideration to the divergent situations in the early Church to which the writers addressed themselves. To propose, therefore, to trim the dimensions of the canon in accord with an arbitrarily chosen 'canon within the canon' would result only in muting certain voices in the choir of witnesses that the Church has long found to be normative. Even the most obvious so-called 'contradiction'—that between Paul and James—finds what seems to many to be a reasonable resolution when one observes that the two authors were considering the nature of faith as it existed within each of two different polemic situations in the Church.[28] On the one hand, James was seeking to show that a merely intellectual acknowledgment of the

Theologie, xciv (1972), pp. 1–28. In Käsemann's essay (see n. 24 above) the expression 'Early Catholicism' is not so much a historical category as a theological accusation, to which Hans Küng made a vigorous response in ' "Early Catholicism" in the New Testament as a Problem in Controversial Theology', *The Living Church* (London, 1963) = *The Council in Action* (New York, 1963), pp. 159–95, declaring forthrightly: 'The bold programme of "a Canon within the Canon" amounts to a demand to be more biblical than the Bible, more New Testament-minded than the New Testament, more evangelical than the Gospel, more Pauline, even, than Paul! ... The true Paul is the entire Paul, and the true New Testament is the entire New Testament' (p. 176).

[28] Even Marxsen acknowledges that 'the contradiction disappears when we consider to whom each statement is made.... What appears at first glance as a contradiction vanishes if both ... are understood as *specific statements* to a particular group of people at a particular place in the history of the preaching of the early Church' (*The New Testament as the Church's Book*, pp. 47 f.).

existence of God—a belief, he comments, that even demons share (ii. 18), though without altering their character—is insufficient when it does not also impel wealthy Christians to provide in practical ways for the welfare of their poverty-stricken brothers and sisters. On the other hand, Paul, who emphasized that one is saved by faith alone, also acknowledged that the faith that saves does not remain alone, for it is followed by works of charity and mercy giving proof of its reality and vitality (Gal. v. 6).

But even if, as some scholars continue to insist, the Epistles of Paul and of James cannot be amalgamated theologically, it is a fact that each writer in his historical individuality has served to guard the other against the extremes of misinterpretation. Thus, both writers have proved themselves indispensable to the health of the Church universal.[29] Likewise, as Ernest Best points out, 'the Gospel of Luke and the Pastoral Epistles with their non-existentialist interpretation clearly met a need in the late first century and the beginning of the second, and it can be argued that they have met the need of many Christians since then.'[30] That is, the so-called 'early Catholic' writings of the New Testament have assisted and do assist the Church in adjusting to recurring practical demands that confront believers.[31] In short, the canon recognizes the validity of diversity of

[29] Schlatter was undoubtedly correct in observing that churches 'have done serious harm to themselves by giving James only a superficial hearing' (*Der Brief des Jakobus* [Stuttgart, 1932], p. 7); see also G. Eichholz, *Jakobus und Paulus. Ein Beitrag zum Problem des Kanons* (*Theologische Existenz Heute*, N.F. nr. 39; Munich, 1953), and J. A. Brooks, 'The Place of James in the New Testament Canon', *Southwestern Journal of Theology*, N.S. xii (1969–70), pp. 41–55, esp. 53–5. Never, even at the height of his criticism of the Epistle of James, did Luther omit it from his editions of the Bible. From his own experience he could testify that often a Christian found one or another book of the canon difficult or useless at a particular time, only to discover later that it then was just what was needed in a time of trouble or temptation (see Paul Althaus, 'Gehorsam und Freiheit in Luthers Stellung zur Bibel', *Theologische Aufsätze* [Gütersloh, 1929], pp. 140–52).

[30] 'Scripture, Tradition and the Canon of the New Testament', *Bulletin of the John Rylands University Library*, lxi (1978–9), p. 286. Best also comments (p. 275): 'It is true that the individual in his individual judgment can say, "This is the centre for me", but he cannot say quite as easily, "This (naming some other centre) cannot be the centre for you", i.e. for some other Christian'.

[31] For development of this idea, see F. V. Filson, *Which Books Belong in the Bible?* (Philadelphia, 1957), pp. 133–5; D. J. Harrington, 'The "Early Catholic" Writings of the New Testament: The Church Adjusting to World-History', *The World and the World*, ed. by R. J. Clifford and G. W. MacRae (Cambridge, Mass., 1973), pp. 97–113; and Dunn, *Unity and Diversity*, pp. 374–82.

theological expression, and marks the limits of acceptable diversity within the Church.

From what has been said thus far it can be appreciated that there exists a twofold danger in setting up a 'canon within the canon'. First, the concept is differently understood by different persons and shifts from age to age.[32] A 'canon' that alters is scarcely worthy of the name. Secondly, to operate with a 'canon within the canon' will prevent all elements within the New Testament from being heard. Instead, therefore, of concentrating their efforts to ascertain a norm within the canon, New Testament scholars have the responsibility as servants of the Church to investigate, understand, and elucidate, for the development of the Christian life of believers, the full meaning of every book within the canon and not only of those which may be most popular in certain circles and at certain times. Only in such a way will the Church be able to hear the Word of God in all of its breadth and depth.

The canon stands as a perpetual reminder to the several Churches of the need to examine critically their own interpretation and proclamation of the apostolic witness, and to listen attentively to the interpretations offered by other believers. In this way the dynamic leaven within the entire New Testament canon will work creatively in and among the Churches. Unity will be achieved, not by an initial agreement on doctrine and practice, but by the willingness to grow together in the common search for a renewed understanding of the several traditions embodied within the entire range of the New Testament canon.

IV. THE CANON: COLLECTION OF AUTHORITATIVE BOOKS OR AUTHORITATIVE COLLECTION OF BOOKS?

In most discussions of the canon of the New Testament little or no attention is paid to the basic question whether the canon should be described as a collection of authoritative books or as an authoritative collection of books. These two formulations differ fundamentally and involve totally different implications.

---

[32] Recently, for example, a canon within the canon has been sought on the basis of liberationist hermeneutic; for a critique of such 'very slim foundations', see Carolyn Osiek in *Feminist Perspectives in Biblical Scholarship*, ed. A. Y. Collins (Chico, 1985), p. 104.

(A third formulation, that the canon is an authoritative collection of authoritative books, is merely a modification of the second formulation, and may be set aside in the present discussion.)

The word 'canon', whether in Greek, Latin, or English, conveys many different meanings. In Greek, among the several major meanings which the word κανών bears (see Appendix I below), these are two uses that, for the sake of clarity, must be distinguished when considering the development of the New Testament canon. The word κανών has an active sense, referring to those books that serve to mark out the norm for Christian faith and life; it has also a passive sense, referring to the list of books that have been marked out by the Church as normative.[33] The two usages may be succinctly designated by two Latin tags, *norma normans*, that is, 'the rule that prescribes', and *norma normata*, that is, 'the rule that is prescribed', i.e. by the Church. According to these two senses of κανών the New Testament can be described either as a collection of authoritative books, or as an authoritative collection of books.

In the former case, the books within the collection are regarded as possessing an intrinsic worth prior to their having been assembled, and their authority is grounded in their nature and source. In the latter case, the collection itself is regarded as giving the books an authority they did not possess before they were designated as belonging to the collection. That is to say, the canon is invested with dogmatic significance arising from the activity of canonization. In one case the Church recognizes the inherent authority of the Scriptures; in the other she creates their authority by collecting them and placing on the collection the label of canonicity.

If the authority of the New Testament books resides not in the circumstance of their inclusion within a collection made by the Church, but in the source from which they came, then the New Testament was in principle complete when the various elements coming from this source had been written. That is to say, when once the principle of the canon has been determined, then ideally its extent is fixed and the canon is complete when the books which by principle belong to it have been written.

---

[33] For the distinction, see H. J. Holtzmann, *Lehrbuch der historisch-kritischen Einleitung in das Neue Testament*, 3rd ed. (Freiburg i. B., 1892), p. 143.

Actually, however, the making of the empirical canon required a long period of time and involved a complex historical process that progressed, not in a straight line, but in a zig-zag development. The realization which the Church finally attained concerning the limits of the canon, and her appreciation of its completeness,[34] was the result of a long process in which many forces were operative and in which many differences of opinion found expression.

Discussion of the *notae canonicitatis*, therefore, should distinguish between the ground of canonicity and the grounds for the conviction of canonicity. The former has to do with the idea of the canon and falls within the province of theology; the latter has to do with the extent of the canon and falls within the domain of the historian. The grounds were variously apprehended in different parts of the ancient Church, and the edges of the canon remained somewhat indistinct for several centuries. There were two tendencies in the Church, the maximists and the minimists. In Alexandria, for example, where for a time a large number of 'inspired' books had been circulating, the process of canonization proceeded by way of selection, moving from many books to few. In other areas, such as in Syria, the Church was content for many centuries with a canon of twenty-two books. In either case the grounds for the conviction of canonicity involved a variety of considerations—whether literary, liturgical, or doctrinal—bearing upon the authorship, content, and use of a given book. In short, the status of canonicity is not an objectively demonstrable claim, but is a statement of Christian belief. It is not affected by features that are open to adjudication, such as matters of authorship and genuineness, for a pseudepigraphon is not necessarily to be excluded from the canon.[35]

---

[34] For a discussion of 'lost' books of the Bible, see Anthony C. Cotter, 'Lost Books of the Bible?', *Theological Studies*, vi (1945), pp. 206–8. See also p. 272 n. 12 above.

[35] See Metzger, 'Literary Forgeries and Canonical Pseudepigrapha', *Journal of Biblical Literature*, xci (1972), pp. 3–24; David G. Meade, 'Pseudonymity and the Canon: An Investigation into the Relationship of Authorship and Authority in Jewish and Earliest Christian Tradition', Ph.D. diss., University of Nottingham, 1984; and Petr Pokorný, 'Das theologische Problem der neutestamentlichen Pseudepigraphie', *Evangelische Theologie*, xliv (1984), pp. 486–96. Pokorný, after raising the question whether pseudepigraphic writings should be removed from the canon, writes: 'That would be the consequence if we regarded the canon as a direct revelation from God, somewhat as Moslems regard the Koran. The Biblical canon, on the other hand, is a

At this point it is appropriate to consider another aspect of the development of the canon—its apparently fortuitous character.[36] To some scholars the seemingly haphazard manner in which the canon was delimited is an offence. It is sometimes asked how the canon can be regarded as a special gift of God to the Church when its development from a 'soft' to a 'hard' canon progressed in what appears to be such a random and, indeed, haphazard manner. According to Willi Marxsen, 'from the historical point of view the fixing of the Canon of the New Testament is accidental'.[37]

Without entering here into a discussion of the paradox of double-agency, creaturely and divine (that is, the manner in which human events are jointly caused by both God and the individual),[38] one may question whether Marxsen is justified in declaring that 'the historical point of view' proves that the fixing of the New Testament canon was accidental. Instead of being a necessary deduction from history, Marxsen's judgement rests upon a philosophical rather than an historical basis. There are, in fact, no historical data that prevent one from acquiescing in the conviction held by the Church Universal that, despite the very human factors (the *confusio hominum*) in the production, preservation, and collection of the books of the New Testament, the whole process can also be rightly characterized as the result of divine overruling in the *providentia Dei*. This is nowhere more apparent than in those instances when a book seemingly came to be regarded as canonical for the wrong

human testimony to the revelation of God. If the Church has received and canonized even pseudepigraphic writings as apostolic witness, that means for us (and we see it today more clearly than earlier) that even the Biblical canon is validated through God's grace and not through the work of any human being' (p. 496); cf. also Pokorný's discussion of canonization in his *Die Entstehung der Christologie; Voraussetzungen einer Theologie der Neuen Testaments* (Berlin, 1985), pp. 162–6. See also p. 36 above.

[36] On contingent happenings and the formation of the canon, see W. Marxsen, 'Kontingenz der Offenbarung oder (und?) Kontingenz des Kanons', *Neue Zeitschrift für systematische Theologie*, ii (1966), pp. 355–64; A. Sand, 'Die Diskrepanz zwischen historischer Zufälligkeit und normativen Charakter des neutestamentlichen Kanons als hermeneutisches Problem', *Münchener theologische Zeitschrift*, xxiv (1973), pp. 147–60; and James Barr, *The Bible in the Modern World* (New York, 1973), pp. 150–6.   [37] *Introduction to the New Testament*, p. 281.

[38] On the paradox of double-agency, which, according to Austin Farrer, is 'all-pervasive' (*Faith and Speculation; An Essay in Philosophical Theology* [New York, 1967], p. 173), see most recently Vincent Brümmer, *What are We Doing When We Pray? A Philosophical Inquiry* (London, 1984), p. 65, and Jeffrey C. Eaton, 'The Problem of Miracles and the Paradox of Double Agency', *Modern Theology*, i (1984–5), pp. 217–22.

reasons. For example, though a large section of the Church was in error in attributing authorship of the anonymous Epistle to the Hebrews to the apostle Paul, all will agree that she was intuitively right in eventually acknowledging the intrinsic worth of the document. When one considers Hebrews in comparison with, let us say, the *Epistle of Barnabas*, which also deals with a Christian interpretation of the Old Testament, and which was attributed to a companion of the Apostle, it is surely not surprising that eventually the Church became persuaded that the former was worthy of inclusion in the canon. The fact that 'reasons' were subsequently found why it should be deemed Pauline and thus to qualify in every respect for inclusion in the canon has no bearing on the question of its intrinsic right to canonical status.

Put in another way, instead of suggesting that certain books were accidentally included and others were accidentally excluded from the New Testament canon—whether the exclusion be defined in terms of the activity of individuals, or synods, or councils—it is more accurate to say that certain books excluded themselves from the canon. Among the dozen or more gospels that circulated in the early Church, the question how, and when, and why our four Gospels came to be selected for their supreme position may seem to be a mystery—but it is a clear case of the survival of the fittest. As Arthur Darby Nock used to say to his students at Harvard with reference to the canon, 'The most travelled roads in Europe are the best roads; that is why they are so heavily travelled.' William Barclay put the matter still more pointedly: 'It is the simple truth to say that the New Testament books became canonical because no one could stop them doing so.'[39]

The distinction between the New Testament writings and later ecclesiastical literature is not based upon arbitrary fiat; it has historical reasons. The generations following the apostles bore witness to the effect that certain writings had on their faith and life. The self-authenticating witness of the word testified to the divine origin of the gospel that had brought the Church into being; such is the implication of Paul's words to the Thessalonians: 'We thank God constantly for this, that

[39] *The Making of the Bible* (London and New York, 1961), p. 78.

when you received the word of God which you heard from us, you accepted it not as the word of any human being but as what it really is, the word of God which is at work in you believers' (1 Thess. ii. 13). During the second and succeeding centuries, this authoritative word was found, not in the utterances of contemporary leaders and teachers, but in the apostolic testimony contained within certain early Christian writings. From this point of view the Church did not create the canon, but came to recognize, accept, affirm, and confirm the self-authenticating quality of certain documents that imposed themselves as such upon the Church.[40] If this fact is obscured, one comes into serious conflict not with dogma but with history.

By way of conclusion, and in comparison with the dozens of gospels, acts, letters, and apocalypses that have recently come to the Church's attention in the Nag Hammadi library, one can say with even greater assurance than before that no books or collection of books from the ancient Church may be compared with the New Testament in importance for Christian history or doctrine. The knowledge that our New Testament contains the best sources for the history of Jesus is the most valuable knowledge that can be obtained from study of the early history of the canon. In fact, whatever judgement we may form of the Christianity of the earliest times, it is certain that those who discerned the limits of the canon had a clear and balanced perception of the gospel of Jesus Christ.

But such words of commendation are superfluous. Neither religious nor artistic works really gain anything by having an official stamp put on them. If, for example, all the academies of music in the world were to unite in declaring Bach and Beethoven to be great musicians, we should reply, 'Thank you for nothing; we knew that already.' And what the musical public can recognize unaided, those with spiritual discernment in the early Church were able to recognize in the case of their

---

[40] For an elaboration of such an assessment, see Karl Barth, *Church Dogmatics*, I, 2, pp. 485–92. History records many instances of the self-evidencing power of Scripture (even, in some cases, of only a few pages discovered by chance) to bring a person, hitherto antagonistic to all that is good, into the presence of God and Jesus Christ in a unique way; see, for example, A. M. Chirgwin, *The Bible in World Evangelism* (London, 1954), pp. 64–90.

sacred writings through what Calvin[41] called the interior
witness of the Holy Spirit. This *testimonium Spiritus Sancti
internum*, however, does not create the authority of Scripture
(which exists already in its own right), but is the means by
which believers come to acknowledge that authority. It is the
correlative to the self-authentication (*autopistia*) of Scripture,
and neither the Fathers nor Calvin attempted to resolve
differences over the delineation of the canon by a simple appeal
to the Holy Spirit's dictates.[42]

The manner in which God's word is contained in Scripture
must not be envisaged statically as a material content, but
dynamically as a spiritual charge. The word and the Scripture
are united in such a way that they constitute an organic unity;
they are to each other as the soul to the body. But, in fact, no
analogy drawn from the realm of our experience is adequate to
express the relation of the word of God to the Bible. That
relation is unique; its closest parallel is the relation of the divine
and human natures in the person of Jesus Christ, who is the
Word incarnate.

[41] *Institutes of the Christian Religion*, Bk. i, ch. vii, § 4. See also p. 245 n. 37 above.
[42] The idea is expressed somewhat similarly by S. J. P. K. Riekert, 'To the objective
principle of the self-evidence of Scripture corresponds the subjective principle of the
testimonium Spiritus Sancti internum. The Holy Spirit testifies to the Word in co-operation
with it. This testimony does not present the grounds for the recognition, but it explains
the way in which or the means by which the authority receives the recognition due to
it.... The recognition of the Canon is not the subjective act of every individual
believer, but of the church reaching back to the past and even stretching into the
future. This act is a confession of the worshipping and witnessing church, namely, that
in the biblical books she finds the gospel message in its fullness and richness' ('Critical
Research and the one Christian Canon comprising Two Testaments', *Neotestamentica*,
xiv [1981], pp. 25–6).

APPENDIX I

History of the Word Κανών

THE word 'canon', whether in Greek, Latin, or English, is used in a kaleidoscopic variety of senses.[1] The Oxford *New English Dictionary* presents no fewer than eleven meanings of the word, and the *Thesaurus Linguae Latinae* lists nine meanings. The development and chief meanings of the word in Greek are the following.

The Greek (ὁ) κανών (related to κάννα or κάνη, *a reed;* cf. Hebrew קָנֶה, *a reed* or *rod*) denotes primarily *a straight rod*, and from this comes numerous derivative uses of the term, in many of which the idea of *straightness* is manifest. Since a rod was employed to keep other things straight, or as a test of straightness, κανών frequently refers to a *level* or *plumbline*, the tool used by a carpenter or a mason in determining the right direction of a piece of wood or a stone that is used in a building. Besides being straight, for other uses the κανών had to be incapable of bending. Thus, the word refers to the beam of a balance as well as the scribe's ruler (translated by the Latin *regula*). It is from this literal sense of a *level* or a *ruler* that all the metaphorical senses are derived. These include the following.

Very broadly, a κανών provides one with a *criterion* or *standard* (Latin *norma*) by reference to which the rectitude of opinions or actions may be determined. Thus, the Greeks spoke of the ideal or exemplary person as the canon of the good (κανὼν τοῦ καλοῦ, Euripides, *Hecuba* 602), and Aristotle described the good person as 'a canon and measure' of the truth (κανὼν καὶ μέτρον, *Ethica Nicom.* iii. 6). Epictetus (*Diss.* i. 28) calls the man who could serve as a model to others because of the integrity of his life a κανών. With reference to literature and style, the grammarians of Alexandria gave the name κανών to the collection of classical works deemed worthy of being

---

[1] See H. Oppel, *KANΩN. Zur Bedeutungsgeschichte des Wortes und seiner lateinischen Entsprechungen (regula—norma)* (*Philologus*, Supplement Band xxx, 4; Leipzig, 1937); H. W. Beyer, 'κανών' in Kittel, *Theological Dictionary of the New Testament*, iii, pp. 596–602; Leopold Wenger, 'Canon in den römischen Rechtsquellen und in den Papyri; Eine Wortstudie', *Sitzungsberichte der Akademie der Wissenschaften in Wien*, Philos.-hist. Kl., ccxx, 2 (1942); A. Arthur Schiller, '*KANΩN* and *KANΩNIZE* in the Coptic Texts', *Coptic Studies in Honor of Walter Ewing Crum* (Boston, Mass., 1950), pp. 175–84; E. Schott, 'Kanon', *Religion in Geschichte und Gegenwart*, 3rd ed., iii, cols. 1117 ff.; and David L. Dungan, 'The Cultural Context of the Use of the Term KANŌN in Early Christianity', to be published in *Aufstieg und Niedergang der römischen Welt*.

followed as models because of the purity of their language. In the field of art, as Pliny tells us (*Hist. nat.* XXXIV. viii. 55), the statue of a spearman modelled by Polyclitus was considered the *canon*, being so nearly perfect that it was acknowledged to be the norm for the proportions of a beautiful human body. In chronology the canons (κανόνες χρονικοί) were the *chief epochs* or *eras*, which served to determine all intermediate dates (Plutarch, *Solon* 27). In music the monochord, by which all other tonal relationships are controlled, was described as the κανὼν μουσικός (Nicomachus Gerasenus, *Arithmetica* ii. 27). The schedule or ordinance fixing the amount of grain or other tribute to be paid by a province gives its name to the amount itself, and so κανών comes to mean a (yearly) *tax*.[2] Finally, in Latin during the Middle Ages the word was used for the straight metal tube directing a gunpowder projectile, and in this sense it eventually came to be spelled 'cannon'.

Turning now to the use of the word κανών by early Christian authors, we find that in the New Testament it occurs only in the Epistles of Paul, and then only rarely (four times in two passages).[3] In his declaration, 'Peace and mercy be upon all who walk according to this κανών' (Gal. vi. 16), the apostle uses the word in its customary sense of norm or standard, here referring to acknowledged Christian behaviour. Much disputed is the import of the word in the exegetically difficult passage of 2 Cor. x. 13–16, where it occurs thrice in connection with the field or sphere that God has alloted to Paul for his work as a missionary. This God-given κανών ('province') refers, it seems, not so much to the nature and orientation of the work laid on Paul, but rather to the circumscribed, geographical area in which he is to labour.[4]

As for the use of κανών by early patristic writers, we are not surprised that they often employ the word in the sense of *rule* or *norm*. Thus, Clement of Rome urges his readers to 'leave the empty and vain cares and pass on to the glorious and venerable *rule* of our tradition (... ἐπὶ τὴν εὐκλεῆ καὶ σεμνὸν τῆς παραδόσεως ἡμῶν κανόνα, vii. 2). Clement of Alexandria, enlarging upon Paul's admonitions to the Corinthian Christians not to give offence, but 'whatever you do,

---

[2] See Wenger, op. cit. pp. 26–47.

[3] In a third passage (Phil. iii. 16) scribes of later manuscripts (‭א‬, D, and the Byzantine text), being influenced by Gal. vi. 16, added κανών with the verb 'to walk' so as to read 'let us walk by the same *rule*'.

[4] The word is used in this sense in a bilingual inscription from Pisidia, in an edict dated A.D. 18/19 concerning the imposition of billeting and transport services upon local communities in Asia Minor; see G. H. P. Horsley, *New Documents Illustrating Early Christianity*, i (North Ryde, 1981), no. 9, and ii (1982), no. 55.

do all to the glory of God', sums up his exhortations by urging believers to live in accord with 'the *rule* of the faith' (ὁ κανὼν τῆς πίστεως, *Strom.* IV. xv. 98). In another passage the same writer refers to a mode of life that is lived 'according to the *rule* of the truth' (κατὰ τὸν κανόνα τῆς ἀληθείας, *Strom.* VI. xv. 124). Even Porphyry, the bitter antagonist of Christianity who wrote *Against the Christians* about A.D. 270, knows that the churches uphold a 'canon of truth', handed down from Jesus.[5] Hegesippus speaks of those who attempt 'to corrupt the sound *norm* (κανών) of the preaching of salvation' (quoted in Eusebius, *Hist. eccl.* III. xxxii. 7). Polycrates of Ephesus (A.D. 190) refers to the time-honoured practice of observing Easter following the fourteenth day of the Pascha as being in accord with 'the *rule* of faith' (κατὰ τὸν κανόνα τῆς πίστεως, quoted in Eusebius, ibid. v. xxiv. 6). All these expressions refer in different ways to the ideal norm according to which the Christian's life and teaching must be conformed.

Little by little the word 'canon' came to be used in the Church for a concrete thing, for a definite and certain decision, and even for a person. From about A.D. 300 onwards the word occurs also in the plural number. Thus, the regulations or decrees promulgated by councils and synods are designated κανόνες of Christian action. The first Council that gave the name canons to its decisions on doctrine and discipline was that held at Antioch in A.D. 341. Not far from this meaning is the use of 'canon' to designate religious or monastic rules (Athanasius, *de Virg.* 12; Basil, *Reg. fus.* xlv. 1; Gregory Naz. *Ep.* 6), as well as those who live according to a certain ecclesiastical rule.

Another development in the use of the word κανών (and one that bears closely upon its subsequent reference to the books of Scripture) was the application of the word to a list, index, or table—terms that carry the suggestion of something fixed and established, by which one can orient oneself. The astronomical tables of Claudius Ptolemaeus (c. A.D. 150), called κανόνες πρόχειροι ('hand-lists'), offered fixed reference points in the changes of the seasons. In a related usage, the ten κανόνες that Eusebius drew up for his edition of the four Gospels were not some kind of rules or principles, but were systematically arranged lists of numerals that corresponded to the numbered sections in the text of the Gospels, by which one could quickly locate parallel passages. The method by which they had been elaborated, and the directions for their use, were set forth in an accompanying letter that Eusebius addressed to his friend Carpianus.[6] Somewhat

[5] Frag. 38 of *Against the Christians*, preserved in the *Apocriticus* of Macarius Magnes.

[6] The Greek text of the letter, with the Canon Tables, may be consulted in the Nestle–Aland edition of the Greek New Testament. For an English translation of Eusebius' *Epistle to Carpianus*, see H. H. Oliver in *Novum Testamentum*, iii (1959), pp. 138–45.

similar were the *canones* drawn up in Latin by Priscillian (*c.* 375), listing the subject-matter in the Pauline Epistles, with references attached. The word κανών was also applied by the Council of Nicaea (*Can.* 16, 17, 19) to an official list or catalogue of clergy who were attached to a given church, and those members of the clergy who were thus enrolled were referred to as οἱ ἐν τῷ κανόνι (ibid. 16 and 17).

Within the broad spectrum of these many applications of the word κανών, it is not surprising that eventually the word came also to be applied to the list of books regarded as authoritative for Christians. This use of κανών was late in developing; so far as we have evidence, it was not until the second half of the fourth century that κανών and its derivatives κανονικός and κανονίζειν were applied to the Scriptures. The first instance is in Athanasius' *Decrees of the Synod of Nicaea*, written soon after 350, in which (no. 18) he describes the *Shepherd* of Hermas as not belonging to the canon (μὴ ὂν ἐκ τοῦ κανόνος). In A.D. 363 the Council of Laodicea in Phrygia declared (*Can.* 59) that only the canonical books (τὰ κανονικά), as opposed to the uncanonical books (τὰ ἀκανόνιστα), ought to be read in Church (see Appendix IV. 7 below). In 367 Athanasius identified which books are in fact the canonical books (βιβλία κανονιζόμενα) in opposition to the apocrypha (ἀπόκρυφα; *Epist. fest.* 39); this is the earliest listing of the twenty-seven books of the New Testament (see Appendix IV. 8 below). The use of the word κανών for the whole collection is still later, the clearest instance occurring in a poem (*Iambi ad Seleucum*) composed about A.D. 380 by Amphilochius, bishop of Iconium (see Appendix IV. 11 below). At the close of an enumeration of the books of the Old and New Testaments, he declares, 'This is perhaps the most reliable canon of the divinely inspired Scriptures' (κανὼν ... τῶν θεοπνεύστων γραφῶν). The expression 'canon of the New Testament' (κανὼν τῆς καινῆς διαθήκης) occurs for the first time in the *Apocriticus* (iv. 10) of Macarius Magnes, an apologia written about A.D. 400.

Other terms besides κανών are also employed by the Fathers to describe the special nature of the Scriptures. Both Origen (*Philocalia* iii) and Eusebius (*Hist. eccl.* III. iii. 1; xxv. 6; VI. xiv. 1) use the adjective ἐνδιάθηκος (formed from διαθήκη), meaning 'contained in the covenant', as opposed to 'apocryphal'. Later writers, including Basil (*Ascet. disc.* 12) and Epiphanius (*Haer.* lv. 2), use ἐνδιάθετος with similar overtones. Another description of canonical books as δεδημοσιευμέναι γραφαί ('writings that have been made public') occurs in the writings of Origen, Basil, and later writers. This expression is to be understood as referring to books which, unlike apocryphal works that are to be read only in private, may be freely and openly read in divine services.

By way of summary, ecclesiastical writers during the first three centuries used the word κανών to refer to what was for Christianity an inner law and binding norm of belief ('rule of faith' and/or 'rule of truth'). From the middle of the fourth century onward the word also came to be used in connection with the sacred writings of the Old and New Testaments. Scholars today dispute whether the meaning 'rule' (that is, 'standard' or 'norm') or the meaning 'list' was uppermost in the minds of those who first applied the word to the Scriptures. According to Westcott[7] and Beyer,[8] it was the material content of the books that prompted believers to regard them as the 'rule' of faith and life. On the other hand, according to Zahn[9] and Souter,[10] the formal meaning of κανών as 'a list' was primary, for otherwise it would be difficult to explain the use of the verb κανονίζειν ('to include in the canon'[11]) when it is applied to particular books and to the books collectively. Both the material and the formal senses eventually were seen to be appropriate, for the recognized custom of the Church in looking to a certain group of books as providing the standard for faith and life[12] would naturally cause the books that conformed to it to be written in a list. And thus the canon of Scripture became equivalent to the contents of the writings included in such a list.

---

[7] *A General Survey of the History of the Canon*, 6th ed., pp. 509–11.
[8] In Kittel's *Theological Dictionary*, iii, p. 601.   [9] *Grundriss*, 2nd ed., pp. 7–11.
[10] *Text and Canon*, 2nd ed., p. 143.   [11] See Lampe's *Patristic Greek Lexicon*, s.v.
[12] Isidore of Pelusium (d. *c.* 440), for example, brings the two together when he exhorts his readers, 'Let us examine the canon of truth, I mean the divine Scriptures' (τὸν κανόνα τῆς ἀληθείας, τὰς θείας φημὶ γραφάς, κατοπτεύσωμεν, *Epist.* iv. 114).

Variations in the Sequence of the Books of the New Testament

I. THE SEQUENCE OF THE COMPONENT SECTIONS

THE twenty-seven books of the New Testament, as we know it today, fall into five main sections or groups: Gospels, Acts, Pauline Epistles, Catholic (or General) Epistles, and Apocalypse. It is natural that the Gospels should almost invariably be placed first, owing to the nature of their contents and the honour paid to their authors. Likewise the Apocalypse, dealing, as it does, with the 'Last Things', would obviously gravitate to the close of the New Testament.[1] Prior to the invention of printing, however, there were many other sequences, not only of the five main groups of books, but also of the several books within each group.

It is easy to see why Acts almost always links Gospels with Epistles: there was a feeling that the historical books should go together. Yet, for reasons best known to the scribes of the fourth-century codex Sinaiticus and the sixth-century codex Fuldensis, in these manu-scripts the Pauline Epistles (with Hebrews) stand directly after the Gospels and before Acts. This is the sequence also in the first printed (but not the first published) Greek New Testament, vol. v of the Complutensian Polyglot Bible (1514).

Contrary to the order customary in English Bibles, virtually all Greek manuscripts of the New Testament place the Catholic Epistles

---

[1] On the other hand, occasionally the Book of Revelation, containing, as it does, the words of the heavenly Christ directed to the seven Churches, follows immediately upon the Gospels. Such is the sequence in two Syriac manuscripts, the Crawford MS (12th or 13th cent.) of the Peshitta version, edited by John Gwynn (Dublin, 1897), and a Harclean MS of the New Testament (13th cent.), edited by Arthur Vööbus (Louvain, 1978). The same sequence is followed in the commentary on the New Testament written in the twelfth century by Dionysius bar Ṣalībī. Computations of space in the lost pages of codex Bezae led John Chapman to conclude that originally this manuscript had the Apocalypse following the Gospels (*Expositor*, Sixth Series, xii [1905], pp. 51–3). In the first printed edition of the Ethiopic New Testament (Rome, 1548–9) vol. I contains the Gospels followed by the Apocalypse. For other sequences of the parts of the New Testament, see F. H. A. Scrivener, *A Plain Introduction to the Criticism of the New Testament*, 4th ed., i (London, 1894), pp. 72–4; C. R. Gregory, *Textkritik des Neuen Testamentes*, ii (Leipzig, 1902), pp. 848–58; and Kurt and Barbara Aland, *Der Text des Neuen Testaments* (Stuttgart, 1982), pp. 91–2.

immediately after Acts and before the Pauline Epistles.[2] This sequence was favoured, no doubt, partly because the Catholic Epistles were attributed to apostles who had been associated with Jesus, three of whom were known as 'pillar apostles' (Gal. ii. 9), whereas Paul was 'the least of the apostles' (1 Cor. xv. 9), and partly because they were addressed, not to individual churches, but to any and all Christians. The presence of these seven Epistles of a general character, along with the Pauline Epistles, was intended to document the consensus among the chief apostles concerning the rule of faith.[3]

II. THE SEQUENCE WITHIN EACH SECTION

I. THE GOSPELS

(*a*) It is not known when our four Gospels were first collected into one codex and arranged in the order that now is common. The Muratorian Fragment on the canon is defective at the beginning, but seems to imply the sequence Matthew, Mark, Luke, John. This order, which is found in nearly all Greek manuscripts, was made popular by Eusebius and Jerome; the former followed it in his useful Canon Tables, which were afterwards adopted by Jerome for his Latin Bible.

The Gospels are found also in the following sequences:

(*b*) Matthew, John, Luke, Mark
(*c*) Matthew, John, Mark, Luke
(*d*) Matthew, Mark, John, Luke
(*e*) Matthew, Luke, Mark, John
(*f*) John, Matthew, Mark, Luke
(*g*) John, Matthew, Luke, Mark
(*h*) Mark, Matthew, Luke, John
(*i*) Mark, Luke, Matthew, John

Sequence (*b*) is followed in two fifth-century manuscripts, codex Bezae (D) and codex Washingtoniensis (W), in the tenth-century MS X, in several of the older Greek minuscule MSS, in the Gothic version, in a few of the older MSS of the Peshitta Syriac, and in a considerable number of Old Latin MSS. This order seems to have arisen from a desire to give the two apostles a leading place. As for the

---

[2] This sequence was adopted in the editions of the Greek New Testament published by Lachmann (1842–50), Tischendorf (1869–72), Tregelles (1857–79), Westcott and Hort (1881), Baljon (1898), von Gebhardt (1901), and von Soden (1913).

[3] See Dieter Lührmann, 'Gal 2. 9 und die katholischen Briefe. Bemerkungen zum Kanon und zur regula fidei', *Zeitschrift für die neutestamentliche Wissenschaft*, lxxii (1981), pp. 65–87.

two who were held to be associated with apostles, the greater length of Luke's Gospel takes precedence over Mark's Gospel.

Sequence (c) is given in a catalogue of unknown date, bound up in the sixth-century codex Claromontanus (see Appendix IV, 4 below), and in one of the later Greek codices of the Gospels (MS 888) of the fourteenth or fifteenth century.

Sequence (d) is found in the Curetonian MS of the Old Syriac version, in the Cheltenham Catalogue (see Appendix IV, 6 below), and in the Latin translation of the Gospel commentary by Theophilus. How far the orders in (c) and (d) may have been influenced by a desire to bring the two books by Luke side by side we are not able to say.

Sequence (e) is followed by the so-called Ambrosiaster (c. A.D. 380) and is found also in a list of Biblical books included in MS 498 (14th cent.; see C. R. Gregory, *Textkritik*, i, p. 196).

Sequence (f) was known in parts of Egypt, as is seen from the order of quotations in the Sahidic vocabulary described by Woide.[4]

Sequence (g), mentioned by the *Synopsis Veteris et Novi Testamenti* (attributed to John Chrysostom; Migne, *Patrologia Graeca*, lvi, 317) as well as by the Palatine Anthology, i, 80–5 (Loeb Classical Library, i, p. 37), is followed in MS 19 (12th cent.) and in MS 90 (15th cent.).

Sequence (h) is that of the four-Gospel manuscript in West Saxon dating from the latter part of the twelfth century (British Museum MS Royal I A. xiv). The sequence may also be intended by the artist of the mosaic in the Mausoleum of the Empress Galla Placidia at Ravenna, dating from c. A.D. 440, which depicts a cabinet with two shelves on which lie four codices of the Gospels, arranged as follows:

MARCUS   LUCAS
MATTEUS   IOANNES

Sequence (i) is followed in a manuscript of the West Saxon Gospels, dating from the twelfth or thirteenth century (Bodleian MS Hatton 38).

2. THE PAULINE EPISTLES

In the traditional sequence of the Pauline Epistles, those that were written to churches are followed by those written to individuals, and within each group the order is that of decreasing length,[5] except that Galatians is (slightly) shorter than Ephesians, which follows it.

---

[4] See C. G. Woide, *Appendix ad editionem Novi Testamenti Graeci...* (Oxford, 1799), pp. 18f., and J. B. Lightfoot in F. H. A. Scrivener, *A Plain Introduction to the Criticism of the New Testament*, 2nd ed. (Cambridge, 1874), pp. 343 and 351.

[5] Other ancient religious texts were also arranged in accord with the principle of decreasing length; these include the sequence of the tractates within each of the six

The position of the Epistle to the Hebrews is altogether unsettled.[6] In the oldest known copy of the Pauline Epistles, the Chester Beatty Biblical Papyrus II ($\mathfrak{p}^{46}$),[7] Hebrews follows Romans. The Sahidic Coptic version places Hebrews after the Epistles to the Corinthians, while the order of the chapter numbers in codex Vaticanus indicates that in an ancestor of that manuscript Hebrews stood after Galatians and before Ephesians. In codex Vaticanus and codex Sinaiticus, along with seven later uncial manuscripts and about sixty minuscules, Hebrews stands between 2 Thessalonians and before 1 Timothy (that is, it follows the Epistles to the churches and precedes those to individuals). In the great majority of the Greek MSS Hebrews follows Philemon.[8]

Scribes of Biblical manuscripts would sometimes indicate the length of each Epistle in terms of number of lines, called stichoi.[9] The statistics are as follows:

To Churches		*To Individuals*	
Romans	979 stichoi	1 Timonthy	238 stichoi
1 Corinthians	908 stichoi	2 Timothy	182 stichoi
2 Corinthians	607 stichoi	Titus	100 stichoi
Galatians	311 stichoi	Philemon	44 stichoi
Ephesians	331 stichoi		
Philippians	221 stichoi		
Colossians	215 stichoi		
1 Thessalonians	207 stichoi		
2 Thessalonians	111 stichoi		
	Hebrews	243 stichoi	

Sedarim (orders) of the Mishnah except the first; the suras of the Koran (apart from the opening Fatiḥa); the 1628 hymns within each of the manifold sections comprising the Rig-Veda; and the texts included in the Suttapitaka of the second part of the Buddhist Pali canon (cf. H. L. Strack, *Introduction to the Talmud and Midrash* [Philadelphia, 1931], p. 27, and J. Brinktrine, 'Nach welchen Gesichtspunkten warden die einselnen Gruppen des neutestamentlichen Kanons geordnet?', *Biblische Zeitschrift*, xxiv, [1938–9], pp. 125–35.

[6] W. H. P. Hatch, 'The Position of Hebrews in the Canon of the New Testament', *Harvard Theological Review*, xxix (1936), pp. 133–51.

[7] See H. F. D. Sparks, 'The Order of the Epistles in $\mathfrak{p}^{46}$', *Journal of Theological Studies*, xlii (1941), pp. 180–1, and Elliott J. Mason, 'The Position of Hebrews in the Pauline Corpus in the Light of Chester Beatty Papyrus II', Ph.D. diss., University of Southern California, 1968. Mason argues that the Alexandrian scribe of $\mathfrak{p}^{46}$ opposed the view held at Rome and deliberately ranged Hebrews among the Pauline Epistles.

[8] For information about different sequences (seventeen in all!) in the order of the Pauline Epistles in manuscripts, see H. J. Frede, *Epistula ad Colossenses* (*Vetus Latina*, 24/2; Freiburg, 1969), pp. 290–303.

[9] A stichos (στίχος) comprises sixteen syllables of about thirty-six letters. For further details as to the uses made in antiquity of counting the stichoi of a document, see Metzger, *Manuscripts of the Greek Bible* (New York, 1981), pp. 38–40.

From these statistics it can be seen that the order of the Epistles in the Pauline corpus was roughly determined by their respective lengths, and that the distinction between ecclesiastical and private or personal letters was maintained.[10]

3. THE CATHOLIC EPISTLES

The Catholic, or General, Epistles are named according to their presumed authors, not as the Pauline Epistles (including Hebrews), according to their recipients.

(*a*) In antiquity, the seven Catholic Epistles commonly stood in the order of James, Peter, John, and Jude[11]—so codices Vaticanus, Sinaiticus, Alexandrinus; Synod of Laodicea (A.D. 363); Cyril of Jerusalem; Epiphanius; Athanasius; Gregory Nazianzus; Nicephorus. The sequence is again in accord with decreasing lengths,[12] except that Epistles by the same author are kept together. Thus,

James	247 stichoi	
1 Peter	237 stichoi	
2 Peter	166 stichoi	} 403 stichoi
1 John	269 stichoi	
2 John	32 stichoi	} 332 stichoi
3 John	31 stichoi	
Jude	71 stichoi	

Several other sequences of the Catholic Epistles were current at various times (but never, it seems, with Jude standing first and 2 Peter last). In the West the primacy of Peter is reflected in the first four of the following sequences:

(*b*) Peter, John, James, Jude—the Council of Carthage (A.D. 397); Apostolic Canon no. 85; a Latin canon of the sixth or seventh century.[13] In this sequence the principle of length prevails: 1 and 2 Peter together (as is indicated above) have 403 stichoi; 1, 2, and 3 John, 332; James, 247, and Jude 71.

[10] Altogether idiosyncratic is Renner's opinion that the Pauline Epistles once stood in alphabetical order; see Frumentius Renner, '*An die Hebräer*'—*ein pseudepigraphischer Brief* (Münsterschwarzach, 1970), pp. 54–61. On the limited practice of alphabetizing in antiquity, see Lloyd W. Daly, *Contributions to the History of Alphabetization in Antiquity and the Middle Ages* (*Collection Latomus*, xc; Brussels, 1967).

[11] Beginning with the Great Bible (1539), it became customary in English to give the name 'Jude' to the writer of the Epistle of Jude, though his name in Greek and Latin is identical with the name 'Judas'. The translations of William Tyndale (1535) and James Moffatt (1913) use 'Judas' throughout the New Testament.

[12] Likewise the first three are in the sequence mentioned in Gal. ii. 9 (James, Cephas, John); see also p. 296 n. 3 above.

[13] See Zahn, *Geschichte*, ii. p. 285.

(*c*) Peter, James, John, Jude—so codex Ψ; Catalogue Claromontanus (see Appendix IV. 4 below); Decretum Gelasianum.

(*d*) Peter, John, Jude, James—so Philaster (4th cent.); Augustine (*De doctr. christ.* ii. 13); Cassiodorus.

(*e*) Peter, James, Jude, John—so Rufinus.

(*f*) John, Peter, Jude, James—so Innocent I (A.D. 405); Isidore of Seville. Here the order reflects the number of the Epistles attributed to each writer: John with three, Peter with two, and Jude and James with one each.

(*g*) James, Jude, Peter, John—so MS 326 (12th cent.).

The preceding survey of the very great variety in order, both of the several parts of the New Testament as well as of books within each part, leads one to conclude that such matters were of no great significance for the ancient and medieval Church; they became an issue only with later editors and publishers.

Titles of the Books of
the New Testament

IN antiquity the title of a book[1] was not considered such an essential and unalterable part of the book as in later times, especially since the invention of printing. Our ignorance as to what title Josephus gave or meant to give to his *War of the Jews* is not due to the loss of the original title; Josephus himself quotes the work under different titles in his *Antiquities* (I. xi. 4; XIII. iii. 3, v. 9, x. 6; *Vita*, 74), as do also the ancient writers and the manuscripts of Josephus' works.[2] Plotinus began late in life to write down his thoughts, and he did so without giving titles to the individual works. Twenty-eight years later Porphyry collected them, and, interestingly enough, referred to them by different titles. Correspondence between Augustine and Jerome[3] concerning the latter's treatise *On Famous Men* (a kind of 'Who's Who among Early Christians'), incorrectly called *Epitaphs*, shows that the title was still unsettled several years after the appearance of the work. Least of all was a formal title necessary in the case of a writing that was designed and presented by the author as a private document, with no expectation that it would have wider circulation.

In the book trade of antiquity the title of a roll that contained a single work would have its title written on a strip or tag ($\sigma\iota\lambda\lambda\upsilon\beta\sigma$) of papyrus or vellum, projecting from the back of the roll. Inside the roll the title was placed also at the end of the work. Usually the title is

---

[1] Discussions concerning book-titles in antiquity include Eduard Lohan, *De Librorum titulis apud classicos scriptores Graecos nobis occurrentibus* (Marburg, 1890); Henrik Zilliacus, 'Boktiteln in antik litteratur', *Eranos*, xxxvi (1938), pp. 1–41; E. Nachmanson, *Der griechische Buchtitel, Einige Beobachtungen* (Göteborgs högskolas årsskrift, xlvii, 19; 1941); Revilo P. Oliver, 'The First Medicean MS. of Tacitus and the Titulature of Ancient Books', *Transactions and Proceedings of the American Philological Association*, lxxxii (1951), pp. 232–61; H. J. M. Milne and T. C. Skeat, *Scribes and Correctors of Codex Sinaiticus* (London, 1955), pp. 30–4 and 38; Karl-Erik Henriksson, *Griechische Büchertitel in der römischen Literatur* (Annales academiae scientiarum fennicae, Ser. B. cii, 1; Helsinki, 1956); Wilhelm Schubart, *Das Buch bei den Griechen und Römern*, 3rd ed. by E. Paul (Heidelberg, 1962), pp. 88–93; Johannes Munk, 'Evangelium Veritatis and Greek Usage as to Book Titles', *Studia theologica*, xvii (1963), pp. 133–8; Eric G. Turner, *Greek Manuscripts of the Ancient World* (Princeton, 1971), pp. 16–17; and Martin Hengel, 'The Titles of the Gospels and the Gospel of Mark', in his *Studies in the Gospel of Mark* (London and Philadelphia, 1985), pp. 64–84.

[2] B. Niese, ed. maj., vi (Berlin, 1889), p. iii.

[3] Jerome, *Epist.* lxvii. 2 and cxii. 3.

expressed in the simplest possible form: the author's name in the genitive case, then the title, followed (if applicable) by the number of the book.

In the papyrus letters that have come down to us, the address consists as a rule of nothing but the name of the person addressed, with sometimes a descriptive epithet added. Since a general postal system was not available in the Roman Empire for ordinary correspondence, private letters had to be carried by the favour of some friend or passing traveller. This means that apostolic communications could be entrusted with safety only to Christian messengers, who would supply orally any additional information (as Tychicus, for example, had been charged to do, Eph. vi. 12 f.).

The point of all this is that originally none of the documents now included in the New Testament had the titles to which we have become accustomed in the headings of the different books in traditional English versions. At first, before the necessity had arisen of distinguishing one Gospel from another, or one Epistle from another, the opening words of the document itself were sufficient to indicate its contents. Only after several Gospels or several Epistles had been collected together was there need for separate designations in order to distinguish one from another. Since the writings of the four Evangelists have one and the same title ($\epsilon \dot{v} a \gamma \gamma \dot{\epsilon} \lambda \iota o \nu$), this general title probably was added to the four by the same person.[4] Each of the four parts is identified by the phrase $K a \tau \dot{a} \ M a \theta \theta a \hat{\iota} o \nu$, $K a \tau \dot{a} \ M \hat{a} \rho \kappa o \nu$, etc.[5] The meaning of the title 'Gospel according to Matthew' is significantly different from 'Gospel of Matthew' or 'Gospel by Matthew'. As Westcott and Hort say in the volume of *Introduction* to their edition of the Greek New Testament (§ 423, p. 321):

---

[4] Other early editorial work on the text of the New Testament resulted in the creation of a system of contractions for certain words regarded as sacred (*nomina sacra*). These words, which, after a little experimenting, eventually came to include fifteen such terms, include the Greek words for God, Lord, Jesus, Christ, Son (when referring to Christ), man (when part of the expression 'Son of man'), Spirit, and others. Without attempting to resolve the much debated question of where and why they were developed (for bibliography, see Metzger, *Manuscripts of the Greek Bible*, pp. 36–7), it is enough to mention here that, along with the early adoption of the codex form for manuscripts of the New Testament, the widespread use of the special system of writing sacred names implies a high degree of organization. In fact, C. H. Roberts has ventured to suggest that 'guidelines for the treatment of the sacred names had been laid down by the Church at Jerusalem, probably before A.D. 70. . . . The system was too complex for the ordinary scribe to operate without either rules or an authoritative exemplar' (*Manuscript, Society and Belief in the Early Church* [London, 1979], p. 46).

[5] In Latin *Cata* was kept in the titles of the Gospels down to about the fourth century, suggesting that the titles were reproduced literalistically by the early translators.

Appendix III

303

In prefixing the name *EYAΓΓEΛION* in the singular to the quaternion of 'the Gospels,' we have wished to supply the antecedent which alone gives an adequate sense to the preposition *KATA* in the several titles. The idea, if not the name, of a collective 'Gospel' is implied throughout the well-known passage in the third book of Irenaeus, who doubtless received it from earlier generations. It evidently preceded and produced the commoner usage by which the term Gospel denotes a single written representation of the one fundamental Gospel.

As time went on scribes would enlarge the title, first by individualizing each Gospel by using the article, 'The Gospel according to...,' and later by emphasizing the character of the book by the addition of the adjective 'holy' (τὸ ἅγιον εὐαγγέλιον κτλ.).[6]

The Book of Acts is generally headed by the familiar title, πράξεις τῶν (ἁγίων) ἀποστόλων, but in some cases its author is directly mentioned by name, as Λουκᾶ εὐαγγελίστου πράξεις τῶν ἀποστόλων.[7]

As in the case of the Gospels, the Pauline Epistles formed a definite class, and the collection was sometimes introduced by some such general title as ἐπιστολαὶ (τοῦ ἁγίου) Παύλου (τοῦ ἀποστόλου), while the individual Epistles were known simply as πρὸς Ῥωμαίους, πρὸς Κορινθίους α΄, κτλ. Gradually, however, these individual titles are expanded to ἐπιστολὴ Παύλου πρὸς κτλ., while before 'Apostle' various epithets are frequently added, such as ἁγίου, ἁγίου καὶ πανευφήμου, or μακαριωτάτου.

Occasionally the Epistles are numbered throughout; hence such a title as Παύλου ἐπιστολὴ δευτέρα, α΄ δὲ πρὸς Κορινθίους, 'The Second Epistle of Paul, but the First to the Corinthians'.

A problem emerges with regard to the Epistle to the Colossians, where the oldest manuscript evidence (𝔭⁴⁶, A, B*, K, al.) spells the name in the title Κολασσαεῖς, whereas in Col. i. 2 almost all witnesses spell the name Κολοσσαῖς.[8] Apart from the question what a modern editor should do, the evidence proves that the title was added at a different time (and place) from the writing of the Epistle.

---

[6] For further information concerning titles in Greek manuscripts of the New Testament, see Hermann von Soden, *Die Schriften des Neuen Testaments in ihrer ältesten erreichbaren Textgestalt*, i (Berlin, 1902), pp. 294–300, from which most of the information given here is derived. The exact dates of the manuscripts are not given, but it must be kept in mind throughout that many of those referred to belong to the later Byzantine period.

[7] In Syriac the Greek word πράξεις (written πράξις) was taken as if it were singular (πρᾶξις) and transliterated *praksis*, literally 'action'.

[8] For evidence concerning the change in the pronunciation of the name Colossae, see J. B. Lightfoot's *Commentary* on Colossians (pp. 16–17), who boldly prints the name in the title with -a- and in i. 2 with -o-. It should perhaps be pointed out that in Kenyon's edition of 𝔭⁴⁶ κολασσαις stands in a lacuna at Col. i. 2 and has been supplied by the editor. See also p. 314 n. 10 below

The Catholic Epistles (which, as was mentioned earlier, in the Greek manuscripts of the New Testament almost always follow Acts and precede the Pauline Epistles) are seldom introduced by a general title, such as αἱ ἑπτὰ ἐπιστολαί. As is the case with the Pauline Epistles, in the earlier manuscripts the title of each is brief, e.g. Πέτρου ἐπιστολὴ αʹ, and only at a later date is the designation καθολική added. Still later such expansions as the following occur:

ἐπιστολὴ καθολικὴ τοῦ ἁγίου ἀποστόλου Ἰακώβου τοῦ ἀδελφοῦ θεοῦ (MS 425)

γράμμα πρὸς Ἑβραίους Ἰακώβου ἀδελφοῦ θεοῦ (MS 1405)

τοῦ ἁγίου Ἰωάννου τοῦ θεολόγου ἐπιστολὴ καθολικὴ πρώτη (MS 425)

A curious variation in the title of 1 John turns up in Augustine's commentary (written A.D. 415) on this Epistle, which he entitled *On the Epistle of John to the Parthians*. Several later writers follow Augustine in this designation, and from the ninth century onward, 1 John is entitled 'To the Parthians' in many copies of the Latin Vulgate. In a scattering of Greek witnesses we likewise find this tradition; where and how it arose is not known.[9]

The earlier copies of the Book of Revelation have the simple title ἀποκάλυψις Ἰωάννου, but over the years this is expanded in different ways, such as: ἀποκάλυψις (τοῦ ἁγίου) Ἰωάννου τοῦ θεολόγου and ἀποκάλυψις Ἰωάννου τοῦ θεολόγου ἣν ἐν Πάτμῳ τῇ νήσῳ ἐθεάσατο. The longest and most fulsome title is that found in a very recent manuscript at Mount Athos (MS 1775): Ἡ ἀποκάλυψις τοῦ πανενδόξου εὐαγγελιστοῦ, ἐπιστηθίου φίλου, παρθένου, ἠγαπημένου τῷ Χριστῷ, Ἰωάννου τοῦ θεολόγου, υἱοῦ Σαλώμης καὶ Ζεβεδαίου, θετοῦ δὲ υἱοῦ τῆς θεοτόκου Μαρίας, καὶ υἱοῦ βροντῆς ('The Revelation of the all-glorious Evangelist, bosom friend [of Jesus], virgin, beloved to Christ, John the theologian, son of Salome and Zebedee, but adopted son of Mary the Mother of God, and Son of Thunder'). The only designation that is omitted (perhaps by accident!) is 'apostle'.

---

[9] For further discussion see A. Bludau, 'Die "Epistola ad Parthos"', *Theologie und Glaube*, xi (1919), pp. 223–36, and Raymond E. Brown, *The Epistles of John* (Anchor Bible, xxx; New York, 1982), pp. 772–4.

APPENDIX IV

Early Lists of the Books of the New Testament

I. THE MURATORIAN CANON

THE following translation usually follows the amended text edited by Hans Lietzmann, *Das Muratorische Fragment und die Monarchianischen Prologue zu den Evangelien* (*Kleine Texte*, i; Bonn, 1902; 2nd ed., Berlin, 1933). Owing to the wretched state of the Latin text, it is sometimes difficult to know what the writer intended; several phrases, therefore, are provided with alternative renderings (enclosed within parentheses). Translational expansions are enclosed within square brackets. The numerals indicate the lines of the original text. For a discussion, see chap. VIII.1 above, where freer renderings are sometimes given in place of the following literalistic translation.

... at which nevertheless he was present, and so he placed [them in his narrative].[1] (2) The third book of the Gospel is that according to Luke. (3) Luke, the well-known physician, after the ascension of Christ, (4-5) when Paul had taken him with him as one zealous for the law,[2] (6) composed it in his own name, according to [the

[1] The meaning may be that Mark arranged the material of his Gospel in the order indicated by Peter, who was participant in the events narrated.

[2] The reading of the Fragment, *quasi ut iuris studiosum*, 'as, so to speak, one zealous for (or, learned in) the law', has been variously interpreted and/or emended. For example, Routh took *iuris* as translating τοῦ δικαίου, i.e. Luke was studious of righteousness; Buchanan replaced *ut iuris* with *adiutorem*, 'assistant'; Bartlet supposed that the translator read νόσου as νόμου (Luke was 'a student of disease'); Zahn replaced *ut iuris* with *itineris*, thereby referring to Luke's readiness to accompany Paul on his journeys; Lietzmann conjectured *litteris*, i.e. Luke was well versed as an author. Harnack (*Sitzungsberichte der königlich Preussischen Akademie der Wissenschaften* [1903], p. 213) and Ehrhardt (op. cit.), who retain *iuris studiosus* of the Fragment, have pointed out that in technical language of Roman law this could refer to an assessor or legal expert who served on the staff of a Roman official. Although this title was current prior to the time of Justinian's *Digest* (published in 533) and so was available to the translator of the Fragment, it is anybody's guess what Greek phrase it represented—assuming, of course, that the Canon was drawn up originally in Greek (unfortunately no help is provided in David Magie, *De Romanorum iuris publici sacrisque vocabulis sollemnibus in Graecum sermonem conversis* [Leipzig, 1905]).

It is significant that the Latin text of the Fragment appears to have been a source for Chromace of Aquileia, who in his commentary on Matthew (written between 398 and 407) refers to Luke as follows: *Dominum in carne non vidit, sed quia eruditissimus legis erat quippe qui comes Pauli apostoli....* (see Joseph Lemarié, 'Saint Chromace d'Aquilée témoin du Canon de Muratori', *Revue des études augustiniennes*, xxiv [1978], pp. 101-2).

general] belief.[3] Yet he himself had not (7) seen the Lord in the flesh; and therefore, as he was able to ascertain events, (8) so indeed he begins to tell the story from the birth of John. (9) The fourth of the Gospels is that of John, [one] of the disciples. (10) To his fellow disciples and bishops, who had been urging him [to write], (11) he said, 'Fast with me from today for three days, and what (12) will be revealed to each one (13) let us tell it to one another.' In the same night it was revealed (14) to Andrew, [one] of the apostles, (15–16) that John should write down all things in his own name while all of them should review it. And so, though various (17) elements may be taught in the individual books of the Gospels, (18) nevertheless this makes no difference to the faith of believers, since by the one sovereign Spirit all things (20) have been declared in all [the Gospels]: concerning the (21) nativity, concerning the passion, concerning the resurrection, (22) concerning life with his disciples, (23) and concerning his twofold coming; (24) the first in lowliness when he was despised, which has taken place, (25) the second glorious in royal power, (26) which is still in the future. What (27) marvel is it, then, if John so consistently (28) mentions these particular points also in his Epistles, (29) saying about himself: 'What we have seen with our eyes (30) and heard with our ears and our hands (31) have handled, these things we have written to you'?[4] (32) For in this way he professes [himself] to be not only an eye-witness and hearer, (33) but also a writer of all the marvelous deeds of the Lord, in their order. (34) Moreover, the acts of all the apostles (35) were written in one book. For 'most excellent Theophilus'[5] Luke compiled (36) the individual events that took place in his presence—(37) as he plainly shows by omitting the martyrdom of Peter (38) as well as the departure of Paul from the city [of Rome] (39) when he journeyed to Spain. As for the Epistles of (40–1) Paul, they themselves make clear to those desiring to understand, which ones [they are], from what place, or for what reason they were sent. (42) First of all, to the Corinthians, prohibiting their heretical schisms; (43) next,[6] to the Galatians, against circumcision; (44–6) then to the Romans he wrote at length, explaining the order (or, plan) of the Scriptures, and also that Christ is their principle (or, main theme). It is necessary (47) for us to discuss these one by one, since the blessed (48) apostle Paul himself, following the example of his predecessor (49–50) John, writes by name to only seven churches in the following

---

[3] Here *ex opinione* is taken as the equivalent of ἐξ ἀκοῆς. Others conjecture *ex ordine*, representing καθεξῆς ('orderly sequence', Luke i. 3).

[4] 1 John i. 1–3.   [5] Luke i. 3.

[6] The letter 'b' in the Latin text before 'Galatians' may belong to 'Corinthians' (πρὸς Κορινθίους β').

sequence: to the Corinthians (51) first, to the Ephesians second, to the Philippians third, (52) to the Colossians fourth, to the Galatians fifth, (53) to the Thessalonians sixth, to the Romans (54-5) seventh. It is true that he writes once more to the Corinthians and to the Thessalonians for the sake of admonition, (56-7), yet it is clearly recognizable that there is one Church spread throughout the whole extent of the earth. For John also in the (58) Apocalypse, though he writes to seven churches, (59-60) nevertheless speaks to all. [Paul also wrote] out of affection and love one to Philemon, one to Titus, and two to Timothy; and these are held sacred (62-3) in the esteem of the Church catholic for the regulation of ecclesiastical discipline. There is current also [an epistle] to (64) the Laodiceans, [and] another to the Alexandrians, [both] forged in Paul's (65) name to [further] the heresy of Marcion, and several others (66) which cannot be received into the catholic church (67)—for it is not fitting that gall be mixed with honey. (68) Moreover, the Epistle of Jude and two of the above-mentioned (or, bearing the name of) John are counted (or, used) in the catholic [Church];[7] and [the book of] Wisdom, (70) written by the friends of Solomon in his honour. (71) We receive only the apocalypses of John and Peter, (72) though some of us are not willing that the latter be read in church. (73) But Hermas wrote the *Shepherd* (74) very recently, in our times, in the city of Rome, (75) while bishop Pius, his brother, was occupying the [episcopal] chair (76) of the church of the city of Rome. (77) And therefore it ought indeed to be read; but (78) it cannot be read publicly to the people in church either among (79) the prophets, whose number is complete,[8] or among (80) the apostles, for it is after [their] time. (81) But we accept nothing whatever of Arsinous or Valentinus or Miltiades, (82) who also composed (83) a new book of psalms for Marcion, (84-5) together with Basilides, the Asian founder of the Cataphrygians....

2. THE CANON OF ORIGEN (A.D. *c*. 185-254)

From the composite account put together by Eusebius in his *Ecclesiastical History*, VI. xxv. 3-14. For a discussion, see chap. V. IV. 3 above.

In the first book of his [Origen's] *Commentary on the Gospel according to Matthew*, defending the canon of the Church, he testifies that he knows only four Gospels, writing somewhat as follows:

(4) 'Among the four Gospels, which are the only indisputable ones in the Church of God under heaven, I have learned by tradition that

---

[7] It may be, as Zahn (*Geschichte*, ii, 66) and others have supposed, that a negative has fallen out of the text here.

[8] Perhaps the Fragmentist means that there are three major Prophets and twelve minor Prophets.

first was written that according to Matthew, who was once a tax collector but afterwards an apostle of Jesus Christ, who published it for those who from Judaism came to believe, composed as it was in the Hebrew language. (5) Secondly, that according to Mark, who composed it in accordance with the instructions of Peter, who in the catholic Epistle acknowledges him as a son, saying, "She that is in Babylon, elect together with you, salutes you, and so does Mark, my son" (1 Pet. v. 13). (6) And thirdly, that according to Luke, the Gospel commended by Paul (cf. 2 Cor. viii. 18) and composed for those who from the Gentiles [came to believe]. After them all, that according to John.'

(7) And in the fifth book of his *Expositions on the Gospel according to John*, the same person says this with reference to the Epistles of the apostles:

'But he who was made sufficient to become a minister of the new covenant, not of the letter but of the Spirit (cf. 2 Cor. iii. 6), that is, Paul, who "fully preached the gospel from Jerusalem and round about even unto Illyricum" (Rom. xv. 19), did not write to all the churches which he had instructed; and even to those to which he wrote he sent but a few lines. (8) And Peter, on whom the Church of Christ is built, "against which the gates of hell shall not prevail" (Matt. xvi. 18), has left one acknowledged Epistle; possibly also a second, but this is disputed. (9) Why need I speak of him who leaned back on Jesus' breast (John xiii. 25), John, who has left behind one Gospel, though he confessed that he could write so many that even the world itself could not contain them (John xxi. 25)? And he wrote also the Apocalypse, being ordered to keep silence and not to write the voices of the seven thunders (Rev. x. 4). (10) He has left also an Epistle of a very few lines; and, it may be, a second and a third; for not all say that these are genuine—but the two of them are not a hundred lines long'.

(11) In addition he makes the following statements concerning the Epistle to the Hebrews, in his *Homilies* upon it: 'That the character of the diction of the Epistle entitled "To the Hebrews" has not the apostle's rudeness in speech, who acknowledged himself to be rude in speech (2 Cor. xi. 6), that is, in style, but that the Epistle is better Greek in the framing of its diction, will be admitted by everyone who is able to discern differences of style. (12) But again, on the other hand, that the thoughts of the Epistle are admirable, and not inferior to the acknowledged writings of the apostle, this also everyone who carefully examines the apostolic text will admit'.

(13) Further on he adds: 'If I gave my opinion, I should say that the thoughts are those of the apostle, but the style and composition belong to some one who remembered the apostle's teachings and wrote down

at his leisure what had been said by his teacher. Therefore, if any church holds that this Epistle is by Paul, let it be commended for this also. For it is not without reason that the men of old time have handed it down as Paul's. (14) But who wrote the Epistle, in truth, God knows. Yet the account that has reached us [is twofold], some saying that Clement, bishop of the Romans, wrote the Epistle, and others, that it was Luke, the one who wrote the Gospel and the Acts'.

3. THE CANON OF EUSEBIUS OF CAESAREA (A.D. 265–340)

From Eusebius' *Ecclesiastical History*, III. xxv. 1–7. For a discussion, see chap. VIII. II above.

At this point it seems appropriate to summarize the writings of the New Testament which have already been mentioned. In the first place must be put the holy quaternion of the Gospels, which are followed by the book of the Acts of the Apostles. (2) After this must be reckoned the Epistles of Paul; next in order the extant former Epistle of John, and likewise the Epistle of Peter must be recognized. After these must be put, if it really seems right, the Apocalypse of John, concerning which we shall give the different opinions at the proper time. (3) These, then, [are to be placed] among the recognized books. Of the disputed books, which are nevertheless familiar to the majority, there are extant the Epistle of James, as it is called; and that of Jude; and the second Epistle of Peter; and those that are called the Second and Third of John, whether they belong to the evangelist or to another person of the same name.

(4) Among the spurious books must be reckoned also the Acts of Paul, and the Shepherd, as it is called, and the Apocalypse of Peter; and, in addition to these, the extant Epistle of Barnabas, and the Teachings of the Apostles, as it is called. And, in addition, as I said, the Apocalypse of John, if it seem right. (This last, as I said, is rejected by some, but others count it among the recognized books.) (5) And among these some have counted also the Gospel of the Hebrews, with which those of the Hebrews who have accepted Christ take a special pleasure.

(6) Now all these would be among the disputed books; but nevertheless we have felt compelled to make this catalogue of them, distinguishing between those writings which, according to the tradition of the Church, are true and genuine and recognized, from the others which differ from them in that they are not canonical [lit., en-testamented], but disputed, yet nevertheless are known to most churchmen. [And this we have done] in order that we might be able to know both these same writings and also those which the heretics put forward under the name of the apostles; including, for instance,

such books as the Gospels of Peter, of Thomas, of Matthias, or even of some others besides these, and the Acts of Andrew and John and the other apostles. To none of these has any who belonged to the succession of ecclesiastical writers ever thought it right to refer in his writings. (7) Moreover, the character of the style also is far removed from apostolic usage, and the thought and purport of their contents are completely out of harmony with true orthodoxy and clearly show themselves that they are the forgeries of heretics. For this reason they ought not even to be reckoned among the spurious books, but are to be cast aside as altogether absurd and impious.

4. A CANON OF UNCERTAIN DATE AND PROVENANCE INSERTED IN CODEX CLAROMONTANUS

In the sixth-century codex Claromontanus (D), a Greek and Latin manuscript of the Epistles of Paul, someone placed between Philemon and Hebrews a Latin list of the books of the Bible. Zahn (*Geschichte*, ii, pp. 157–72) and Harnack (*Chronologie*, ii, pp. 84–8) were of the opinion that this list had been drawn up originally in Greek at Alexandria or its neighbourhood about A.D. 300. J. Weiss suggested a North-African origin (*Zeitschrift für wissenschaftliche Theologie*, xxx [1887], pp. 169 f.). For a discussion, see p. 230 above.

[An Old Testament list is followed by:]

Four Gospels:
   Matthew, 2600 lines
   John, 2000 lines
   Mark, 1600 lines
   Luke, 2900 lines
Epistles of Paul:
   To the Romans, 1040 lines
   The First to the Corinthians, 1060 lines
   The Second to the Corinthians, 70 (*sic*) lines
   To the Galatians, 350 lines
   To the Ephesians, 365 lines
   The First to Timothy, 209 lines
   The Second to Timothy, 289 lines
   To Titus, 140 lines
   To the Colossians, 251 lines
   To Philemon, 50 lines
—The First to (*sic*) Peter,[9] 200 lines

---

[9] The dash before 1 Peter may be only a 'paragraphus', or Greek paragraph mark, to suggest that 1 Peter and the items that follow are not part of the 'Epistles of Paul'. The other four dashes lower in the list identify works of doubtful or disputed canonicity.

The Second to (*sic*) Peter, 140 lines
Of James, 220 lines
The First Epistle of John, 220
The Second Epistle of John, 20
The Third Epistle of John, 20
The Epistle of Jude, 60 lines
—Epistle of Barnabas, 850 lines
The Revelation of John, 1200
The Acts of the Apostles, 2600
—The Shepherd, 4000 lines
—The Acts of Paul, 3560 lines
—The Apocalypse of Peter, 270

5. THE CANON OF CYRIL OF JERUSALEM (*c.* A.D. 350)

From Cyril's *Catechetical Lectures*, iv. 36. For a discussion, see pp. 209–10 above.

Then of the New Testament there are four Gospels only, for the rest have false titles and are harmful. The Manichaeans also wrote a Gospel according to Thomas, which being smeared with the fragrance of the name 'Gospel' destroys the souls of those who are rather simple-minded. Receive also the Acts of the Twelve Apostles; and in addition to these the seven Catholic Epistles of James, Peter, John, and Jude; and as a seal upon them all, and the latest work of disciples, the fourteen Epistles of Paul.

But let all the rest be put aside in a secondary rank. And whatever books are not read in the churches, do not read these even by yourself, as you have already heard [me say concerning the Old Testament apocrypha].

6. THE CHELTENHAM CANON (*c.* A.D. 360)

From a list contained in a tenth-century Latin manuscript of miscellaneous content (chiefly patristic) that once belonged to the library of Thomas Phillipps at Cheltenham, England; it was identified in 1886 by Theodor Mommsen. For a discussion, see pp. 231–2 above.

[An Old Testament list is followed by:]

Likewise the catalogue of the New Testament:
 Four Gospels: Matthew, 2700 lines
        Mark, 1700 lines
        John, 1800 lines
        Luke, 3300 lines
 All the lines make 10,000 lines
 Epistles of Paul, 13 in number
 The Acts of the Apostles, 3600 lines

The Apocalypse, 1800 lines
Three Epistles of John, 350 lines
One only
Two Epistles of Peter, 300 lines
One only

Since the index of lines [= stichometry] in the city of Rome is not
clearly given, and elsewhere too through avarice for gain they do not
preserve it in full, I have gone through the books singly, counting
sixteen syllables to the line, and have appended to every book the
number of Virgilian hexameters.

7. THE CANON APPROVED BY THE SYNOD OF LAODICEA (*c.* A.D. 363)

The absence of Canon 60 in a variety of Greek, Latin, and Syriac
manuscripts makes it probable that it was a somewhat later appendage,
clarifying Canon 59. For a discussion, see p. 210 above.

Can. 59. Let no private psalms nor any uncanonical books be read in
church, but only the canonical ones of the New and Old Testament.

Can. 60. [After listing the books of the Old Testament, the canon
continues:] And these are the books of the New Testament: four
Gospels, according to Matthew, Mark, Luke, and John; the Acts of
the Apostles; seven Catholic Epistles, namely, one of James, two of
Peter, three of John, one of Jude; fourteen Epistles of Paul, one to the
Romans, two to the Corinthians, one to the Galatians, one to the
Ephesians, one to the Philippians, one to the Colossians, two to
the Thessalonians, one to the Hebrews, two to Timothy, one to
Titus, and one to Philemon.

8. THE CANON OF ATHANASIUS (A.D. 367)

From Athanasius' Thirty-Ninth Festal Epistle (A.D. 367). For a discussion,
see pp. 210–12 above.

...Again [after a list of the Old Testament books] it is not tedious
to speak of the [books] of the New Testament. These are, the four
Gospels, according to Matthew, Mark, Luke, and John. After these,
the Acts of the Apostles and Epistles called Catholic, of the seven
apostles: of James, one; of Peter, two; of John, three; after these, one
of Jude. In addition, there are fourteen Epistles of Paul the apostle,
written in this order: the first, to the Romans; then, two to the
Corinthians; after these, to the Galatians; next, to the Ephesians;
then, to the Philippians; then, to the Colossians; after these, two of the
Thessalonians; and that to the Hebrews; and again, two to Timothy;
one to Titus; and lastly, that to Philemon. And besides, the Revelation of John.

These are fountains of salvation, that he who thirsts may be satisfied with the living words they contain. In these alone the teaching of godliness is proclaimed. Let no one add to these; let nothing be taken away from them...

9. THE CANON APPROVED BY THE 'APOSTOLIC CANONS' (*c.* A.D. 380)

A series of eighty-five Canons attributed to the apostles was compiled in the late fourth century by the redactor of the *Apostolic Constitutions*, of which it forms the concluding chapter; see pp. 216 and 225 above.

Can. 85. Let the following books be esteemed venerable and holy by all of you, both clergy and laity. [A list of books of the Old Testament...] And our sacred books, that is, of the New Testament, are the four Gospels, of Matthew, Mark, Luke, John; the fourteen Epistles of Paul; two Epistles of Peter; three of John; one of James; one of Jude; two Epistles of Clement; and the Constitutions dedicated to you, the bishops, by me, Clement, in eight books, which it is not appropriate to make public before all, because of the mysteries contained in them; and the Acts of us, the Apostles.

10. THE CANON OF GREGORY OF NAZIANZUS (A.D. 329–89)

This canon, included among Gregory's poems (1. xii. 5 ff.), was ratified by the Trullan Synod in 692. It is in iambic verse, the lineation of which (but not the rhythm) is preserved, so far as possible, in the translation. Only the New Testament part is given here. For a discussion, see p. 212 above.

[List of books of the Old Testament....]
But now count also [the books] of the New Mystery;
Matthew indeed wrote for the Hebrews the wonderful works of Christ,
And Mark for Italy, Luke for Greece,
John, the great preacher, for all, walking in heaven.
Then the Acts of the wise apostles,
And fourteen Epistles of Paul,
And seven Catholic [Epistles], of which James is one,
Two of Peter, three of John again.
And Jude's is the seventh. You have all.
If there is any besides these, it is not among the genuine [books].

11. THE CANON OF AMPHILOCHIUS OF ICONIUM (D. AFTER 394)

This canon, like the preceding, is in iambic verse; it was written for Seleucus, a friend of Amphilochius. Only the New Testament part (lines 289–319) is given here. For a discussion, see pp. 212–3 above.

[List of books of the Old Testament....]
It is time for me to speak of the books of the New Testament.
Receive only four evangelists:
Matthew, then Mark, to whom, having added Luke
As third, count John as fourth in time,
But first in height of teachings,
For I call this one rightly a son of thunder,
Sounding out most greatly with the word of God.
And receive also the second book of Luke,
That of the catholic Acts of the Apostles.
Add next the chosen vessel,
The herald of the Gentiles, the apostle
Paul, having written wisely to the churches
Twice seven Epistles: to the Romans one,
To which one must add two to the Corinthians,
That to the Galatians, and that to the Ephesians, after which
That in Philippi, then the one written
To the Colassians,[10] two to the Thessalonians,
Two to Timothy, and to Titus and the Philemon,
One each, and one to the Hebrews.
But some say the one to the Hebrews is spurious,
not saying well, for the grace is genuine.
Well, what remains? Of the Catholic Epistles
Some say we must receive seven, but others say
Only three should be received—that of James, one,
And one of Peter, and those of John, one.
And some receive three [of John], and besides these, two
of Peter, and that of Jude a seventh.
And again the Revelation of John,
Some approve, but the most
Say it is spurious, This is
Perhaps the most reliable (lit., most unfalsified)
canon of the divinely inspired Scriptures.

12. THE CANON APPROVED BY THE THIRD SYNOD OF CARTHAGE (A.D. 397)

The first council that accepted the present canon of the books of the New
Testament was the Synod of Hippo Regius in North Africa (A.D. 393); the
acts of this council, however, are lost. A brief summary of the acts was read at
and accepted by the Synod of Carthage, A.D. 397.[11]

---

[10] Most of the manuscripts spell the word Κολασσ- (so Eberhard Oberg, *Amphilochii
Iconiensis, Iambi ad Seleucum* [Berlin, 1969], p. 75); see also p. 303 n. 8 above.

[11] See C. J. Hefele, *A History of the Councils of the Church, from the original Documents*, ii
(Edinburgh, 1876), pp. 394–8.

Can. 24. Besides the canonical Scriptures, nothing shall be read in church under the name of divine Scriptures. Moreover, the canonical Scriptures are these: [then follows a list of Old Testament books]. The [books of the] New Testament: the Gospels, four books; the Acts of the Apostles, one book; the Epistles of Paul, thirteen; of the same to the Hebrews, one Epistle; of Peter, two; of John, apostle, three; of James, one; of Jude, one; the Revelation of John. Concerning the confirmation of this canon, the transmarine Church shall be consulted. On the anniversaries of martyrs, their acts shall also be read.

According to Zahn,[12] in 419 another Synod held at Carthage gave the concluding words in the following form:

... the Revelation of John, one book. Let this be sent to our brother and fellow-bishop, Boniface [of Rome], and to the other bishops of those parts, that they may confirm this canon, for these are the things that we have received from our fathers to be read in church.

[12] *Geschichte*, ii, pp. 252–3.

Index

'Abd al-Mesīch al-Kindī, 221 n. 24
Abercius, 256
Abyssinian Church, *see* Ethiopian Church
Achtemeier, P. J., 132 n. 39
Acts of Barnabas, *see* Barnabas, Acts of
Acts of Bartholomew, *see* Bartholomew, Acts of
Acts of John, *see* John, Acts of
Acts of Paul, *see* Paul, Acts of
Acts of Peter, *see* Peter, Acts of
Acts of Philip, *see* Philip, Acts of
Acts of Pilate, *see* Pilate, Acts of
Acts of Thaddeus, *see* Thaddeus, Acts of
Acts of Thomas, *see* Thomas, Acts of
Addai, Doctrine of, 114
Adversus Aleatores, 163 f.
Aegidius Hunnius, 244 n. 31
Aelfric, 239
Agathangelos, 223
agrapha, 134, 137, 148, 272 n. 11
Agrippa Castor, 252
Aland, B., 91 n. 30, 217 n. 16, 267 n. 1, 295 n. 1
Aland, K., 33, 217 n. 16, 260 f., 274, 295n. 1
Aletti, J.-N., 32
Alexander, A., 18
Alexander, J. A., 19
Alexandria, canon of, 284
Alexandrian Catechetical School, 129
Alexandrian Library and Museum, 111
Alexandrian text of the New Testament, 267
Alexandrians, Epistle to the, 197
Alogi, 105, 150, 200
Altaner, B., 194 n. 13
Althaus, P., 281 n. 29
Ambrosiaster, 297
Amphilochius of Iconium, 209, 212 f., 216, 292, 313 f.
amulets, 112
anagnosis, 23
Andrew, Acts of, 174, 204, 233
Andrew and Matthias, Acts of, 174
anti-Marcionite prologues, 94 n. 34
Antioch, Council of, 291
Antioch, School of, 214 f.

Aphraat, 218 f.
Apocalypse of Paul, *see* Paul, Apocalypse of
Apocalypse of Peter, *see* Peter, Apocalypse of
apocalypses, Christian, 25
Apocrypha of the New Testament, 165–189
Apocryphon of James, *see* James, Apocryphon of
Apocryphon of John, *see* John, Apocryphon of
Apollinaris of Laodicea, 53 n. 23
Apollonius of Ephesus, 103
Apologists, 33
Apostles, Epistle of the, 180 ff.
Apostolic Canons, 216, 225, 313
Apostolic Constitutions, 14, 228
Apostolic Fathers, 7, 33, 39 f., 72 f., 75, 214
apostolicity, criterion of canonicity, 253
Appel, N., 31, 32, 277 n. 21
Arabic Infancy Gospel, 167
Arai, S., 31
Aristarchus of Samothrace, 111
Aristides, 127 f.
Aristophanes of Byzantium, 111
Aristotle, 289
Armenian Church, canon of, 223 f.
Armenian Gospel of the Infancy, 167
Armstrong, W. P., 19 n. 25
Arnold, M., 23 n. 43
Arntzen, M. J., 29
Assemani, J. S., 220 n. 22
Athanasius, 7 f., 65, 140, 209, 210 ff., 216, 225, 291 f., 299, 312 f.
Athenagoras, 125 ff., 154
Audet, J.-P., 49 n. 16
Augustine, 107 n. 76, 165 n. 2, 187, 236 ff., 253, 255
authority of the canon, *see* canon, authority of
authority of canonical books, *see* canonical books, authority of

Baarda, Tj., 70 n. 45
Bacon, B. W. 160 n. 28
Balás, D. L., 99 n. 50